VIMY RIDGE AND ARRAS

THE SPRING 1917 OFFENSIVE IN PANORAMAS

Peter Barton

VIMY RIDGE AND ARRAS

THE SPRING 1917 OFFENSIVE IN PANORAMAS

Peter Barton

In association with the Imperial War Museum

With research by Jeremy Banning

DUNDURN PRESS

TORONTO

For the two Bernards Heptonstall

First published in North America in 2010 by Dundurn Press, Ltd.
First published in the UK in 2010 by Constable, an imprint of Constable & Robinson Ltd

Library and Archives Canada Cataloguing in Publication

Barton, Peter
      Vimy Ridge and Arras : the spring 1917 offensive in panoramas / by Peter Barton.

Includes bibliographical references and index.

ISBN 978-1-55488-744-6

      1. Vimy Ridge, Battle of, France, 1917--Pictorial works. 2. Arras, Battle of, Arras, France, 1917--Pictorial works.
3. World War, 1914-1918--Battlefields--France--Pictorial works. I. Title.

D639.P39B38 2009   940.4'31   C2009-906583-5

Designed by Les Dominey
Cartography by William Smuts
Printed and bound in Singapore

www.dundurn.com

Dundurn Press
3 Church Street, Suite 500, Toronto, Ontario, Canada
M5E 1M2

Dundurn Press
2250 Military Road, Tonawanda, NY, U.S.A.
14150

Title page British Military band playing in the *Grand Place*, Arras, on 29 April 1917.
IWM Q6444

CONTENTS

Introduction

I shall never forget Sir Edward Grey's [British Foreign Secretary] telling me of the ultimatum – while he wept; nor the poor German Ambassador who has lost in his high game – almost a demented man; nor the King as he declaimed at me for half an hour and threw up his hands and said, "My God, Mr. Page, what else could we do?" Nor the Austrian Ambassador's wringing his hands and weeping and crying out, "My dear Colleague, my dear Colleague."

WALTER H. PAGE, UNITED STATES AMBASSADOR, LONDON, ON THE DECLARATION OF WAR, AUGUST 1914.

By Christmas 1916 much of Europe was in a state of martial, political and social chaos. The first two years of war had seen ever-increasing slaughter, but 1917 would be a year characterized by suffering and misery on an unimaginable scale. At its bitterly cold January debut an end to the conflict was still nowhere in sight, and neither politician nor soldier was agreed on how to bring it about. The armies of the British Empire were by now largely composed of civilians, the majority of field commanders included. It was not the case with their superiors, and a gulf existed between the old and the new, the staff officer and the 'trench' officer. As Basil Liddell Hart wrote in 1936:

The decisions which an army commander had to take in the last war, though great in responsibility, were simple in their technical elements compared with those of a battalion commander. If a layman had attended a conference of army commanders he would have been able to follow the discussion with far more understanding than if he had been present at a conference of company or battery commanders.
LIDDELL HART, *THE WAR IN OUTLINE*

Within this short paragraph lies the root of many of the troubles that would be revealed so starkly at Arras.

For the belligerent nations, the War dominated all of life. Peacetime practices had been quickly subsumed by the appetite of enmity, to the extent that the most 'advanced' peoples of the world no longer appeared to consist of individuals but colossal factional groups. Whether in uniform or in the factories and fields, the workforces of entire countries were engaged solely in conflict-associated activity, living within a miasma of propaganda, secrecy and censorship, all contrived to stiffen the sinews of odium and maintain the struggle. Throughout Britain and her dominions the Battle of the Somme had been trumpeted as a victory, and a neutral observer basing his conclusions solely upon newspaper reports would probably have wondered why the war had not long ago been concluded to the benefit of the united nations of the Empire.

Principles – religious included – had been discarded, effortlessly in many cases. It was as if the rules by which ostensibly civilised peoples had once lived, and by all accounts been inordinately proud of, had vanished in a surge of patriotism so extreme as to dispel all hope of peace by discourse and political agreement. Better the spectre of bankruptcy than the bruising of pride that entering into a dialogue would produce.

In early 1917 America was still neutral and Russia falling towards the treacherous limbo of revolution. Not only was the Allied territorial share of the Western Front largely the same as it had been after the first winter of the war, but the Central Powers were still in the ascendancy. Serbia was theirs, large areas of Russia and parts of Italy occupied, and Russian Poland overwhelmed; the Allies had been forced to scuttle ignominiously from the Dardanelles, Romania had collapsed and Greece was teetering towards military union with the Kaiser. Never had Britain and her Empire been in such peril. To prevail *and to win*, the Allies needed to maintain enmity and unity. It was as essential as the supply of bread.

Meanwhile, Germany was standing firmly on the defensive, content to let the *Entente* break their heads and spirits against the protective wall of fieldworks that now traversed Europe. For every French or British battalion that took the field in attack, the Germans were able to defend with two-thirds the number, often suffering half the casualties in the process. Since Day One there had not been the smallest sign of change in this grim status. By 1917, five out of every nine front-line soldiers could expect to become casualties, but the victory hunger was unassuaged. How it may be achieved and at what cost overwhelmed humanitarian principles, and nations struggled on within a mindset of mass sacrifice encouraged by a carefully engineered war hysteria. Military high command had become inured to criticism by a century of empire building that had bred soaring pride and arrogance: treacherous attributes in a global conflict against a numerically equivalent and supremely professional adversary.

Since New Year 1915, David Lloyd George and others had been arguing ever more vehemently for a shift of offensive emphasis from French and Belgian battlegrounds to fronts where at least an element of surprise might be utilized, and for the forces of the whole *Entente* to fight as one, i.e. plan and execute offensives as a cohesive unit rather than taking bites out of the enemy 'by nationality'. The war was being fought between two alliances, not, as had historically so often been the case, between two nations. With her sprawling empire, Britain held strong cards, but she was playing with a partner – France. Not unnaturally the French still wished to win the war on their own turf by vanquishing the invader in front of Paris, whilst Field Marshal Sir Douglas Haig had come to the conclusion that it would best be done by British forces in Belgium, a domain almost exclusively theirs since early 1915 and symbolically 'anglicized' by uninterrupted loss of life. Neither France nor Britain were strong enough to achieve the miracle alone, but with many more fighting men in the field and holding a considerably greater stretch of line, the French were indisputably the 'senior partners'; it was also, of course, their land that was being occupied and ravaged. So how, when and where could this catastrophic business be concluded? At Easter 1917 the British would lay out their hand in Artois, whilst the French played the trumps in Champagne.

The British official history of the First World War records the narratives of three battles of Arras. The latter two, rather curiously known as the First and Second, both took place in 1918, but it is the action east of the city and against Vimy Ridge beginning on Easter Monday, 9 April 1917 that is the subject of this volume. In truth it incorporated the three Battles of the Scarpe, the Battle of Vimy Ridge, two Battles of Bullecourt, the Battle of Lagnicourt, and the Battle of Arleux.

This book is again predominantly based upon the words of eyewitnesses of those actions, the most accurate chronicles we possess. The era deserves a volume considerably more comprehensive than this offering, but I hope the result of these labours has some value, not least to the memory of those who served in The Battle of Arras, the ultimate *bataille d'usure*.

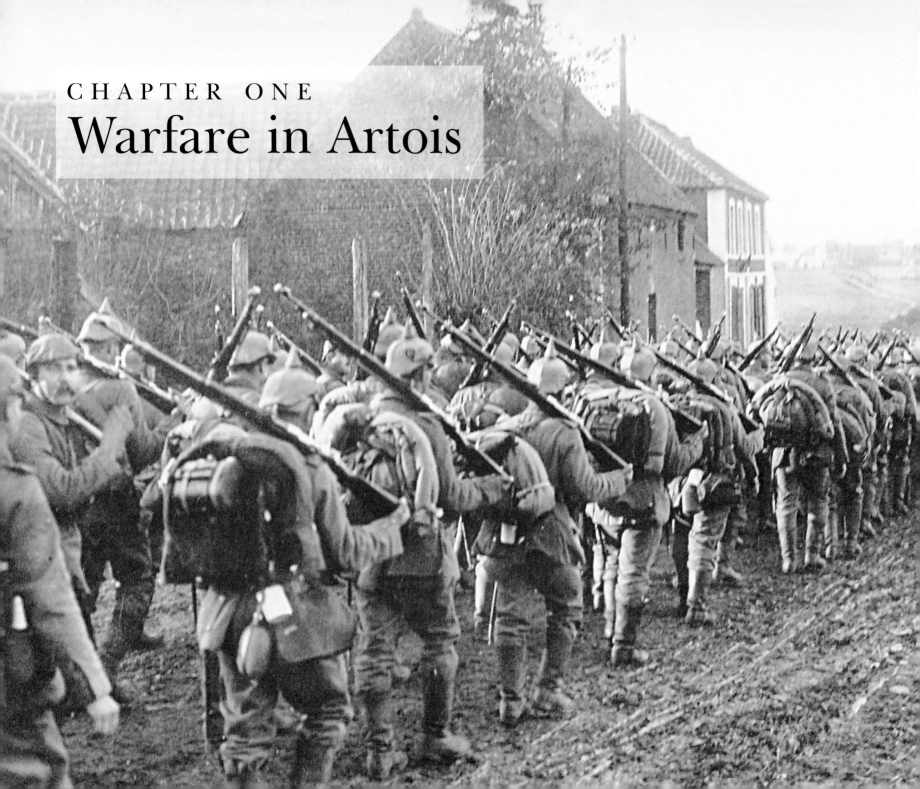

Warfare in Artois

In 1904 France and Britain signed the *Entente Cordiale,* a set of formal agreements created as a shield against the growing risk of German and Austrian military power. Critically, further alliances also included Russia. As a result, Germany, pincered as she was between the horns of Russia and France, not unnaturally became anxious about the threat to her own security. Count Alfred von Schlieffen, the German Army's Chief of Staff, was requested to devise a strategy of protection through aggression. In December 1905, he produced what became known as the Schlieffen Plan. It argued that if military action became necessary, it was vital that Germany struck first, fast and with resolve, for if the scheme was to succeed France must be swiftly crushed. By simply occupying Paris, it was believed, the nation would be subjugated. Belgium was not seen as a serious obstacle. The simultaneous annexation of French, Belgian and Dutch Channel ports would deny Britain practical access to the European mainland. Given the fragile history of Anglo-French relations it was felt that Britain – especially with the complication of certain significant German blood ties (until mid-1917 the British Royal family would still carry the name Saxe-Coburg-Gotha) – would accept the revised territorial situation, and despite the *Entente* agreement remain neutral even if France fell: it was an interesting theory never put to the test. As for Russia, she would almost certainly be unwilling to wage a lone conflict against Germany. With the outbreak of war in August 1914, the *Entente Cordiale,* the Anglo-Russian *Entente,* and the Franco-Russian Alliance coalesced into the Triple *Entente.* They faced the might of the 'Central Powers': Germany, Austria-Hungary, the Ottoman (Turkish) Empire, and later, Bulgaria.

From a modern perspective Schlieffen's plan appears monstrously ambitious, but at the time it was seen as not only necessary but eminently workable. The key to success lay in the timing. It was calculated that Russia would require six weeks to mobilize, and therefore essential that France was paralysed in a matter of a fortnight or so. Schlieffen petitioned for fully 91 per cent of the German military establishment to sweep across the French frontier, the grand assault wheeling anti-clockwise through northern France avoiding a string of newly-refurbished border forts astride Verdun, and at the same time incorporating Holland, Belgium and Luxembourg. To deter the Russians, the remaining 9 per cent of the Army would be despatched to pre-prepared defensive positions in the east.

Helmuth von Moltke succeeded Alfred von Schlieffen as German Army Chief of Staff in 1906. As the years passed an ever-growing fear of Russia compelled him to make diluting changes. First he proposed that Holland should not be invaded; the main route would now be through the flat plains of Flanders, von Moltke still agreeing that Belgium's small army would be unable to baulk the assault. The critical mitigation, however, was to earmark more troops for East Prussia to defend the Russo-German border. In the space of six years Schlieffen's invasion force of 2.1 million men was eroded to 1.5. The remodelling did not end there.

On 4 August 1914, Europe tumbled into a four-year abyss of conflict and within a matter of weeks the invader was already walking in the streets of Arras. During the frantic retreat of French troops following clashes near Charleroi on 23 and 25 August 1914, a passage into northern France was opened. The Germans swarmed into the Pas de Calais and Nord *départements*. Here, though, von Moltke's Russian fears once more resurfaced, stoked by the fact that the 'bear' was mobilizing fast and indeed already engaging German troops. Another six German army corps were despatched eastwards. He also feared the British response, especially a sea-borne landing to assist Belgium, and yet more men were held back from the central thrust, further diminishing its potency.

By 30 August 1914, German troops had pushed into Artois. To the south, Paris was almost in clear view, and French and British defences worn out from perpetual retirement. Although behind schedule the viability of the original invasion plan was now actually academic: the conflict had reached a point where there was no choice but to persevere. On 3 September, Joseph Joffre, Commander-in-Chief of French forces, was forced to order withdrawal to a line along the River Seine. With the rumble and flashes of gunfire now discernible from the French capital, Sir John French, commanding the British Expeditionary Force, sent every unit he could spare to help repulse attacks north and east of the city. Then on the morning of 6 September, the French Sixth Army attacked the German First Army on the Marne. General Alexander von Kluck, choosing to wheel *en masse* to meet the assaults, opened a 45-kilometre gap between his men and those of the neighbouring Second Army. British and French troops surged into the breach, dispersed the meagre garrison of cavalry left as a guard, and decisively split the two armies. The sheer surprise of the action brought the German surge to a standstill. On this same day squadrons of Uhlan horsemen reached and entered Arras.

Because of von Moltke's nervous troop shuffling earlier in the month, for the next three days the Germans were fighting with almost exactly half the number of divisions originally earmarked for the Franco-Belgian venture. What had begun on the Marne as an Allied incursion then turned into a pursuit and the Germans withdrew.

On 9 September, rumours of a large Anglo-Russian landing on the Belgian coast filtered into a shaky German HQ, the story inflated by a sly dose of British misinformation. If true, however, it threatened both the German right flank and their rear. The report was nonsense, but given von Moltke's heightened state of anxiety, it was all too believable. The German High Command acted, sending more troops northward and temporarily suspending the assault on Paris to consolidate in pre-prepared positions on the heights above the river valleys to the north-east, ground the Germans knew well as a result of the invasion of 1870-1.

From 14 September 1914, the French made further gains, holding off a sequence of fresh enemy surges before movement stalled and stilled. Then the action shifted north to Picardy where the Battle of Albert raged for four days, again ending in stalemate. By the end of the month the battlefronts that had most threatened the French capital had fallen almost silent.

THE RACE NORTHWARDS

The halting of attacks on Paris left several German-held French towns exposed to Allied counter-attack. The list included Arras. The three strategically most important cities of the northern region, Lille, Lens and Douai, were destined to remain under foreign rule for most of the war, but like Ypres, Arras was to escape –

Above The tide of invasion sweeps into the Meuse-Argonne region. IWM Q96060

Below German troops man a barricade in early street fighting in a village near Arras. AJ

just. Upon the approach of French mounted patrols the German garrison departed the town, pulling back to more propitious positions in the surrounding eastern hills. Action then shifted again. Seeking a weak Allied flank to exploit, towards the end of September the Germans began streaming towards the Belgian border. British and French troops, including General De Maud'huy's Tenth Army, rushing north from the Vosges, mirrored the relocation. The German Sixth Army under Crown Prince Rupprecht of Bavaria, also serving in the Vosges, was issued with the same movement orders at almost exactly the same time. They too hastened northwards, but into Artois, the Prince's determination being to rekindle lost momentum by driving through the Arras/ Vimy/Lens sectors towards the Channel coast before veering south to trace a route between Abbeville and Amiens across the Somme, for a new thrust upon Paris. Buoyed with success on the Aisne and Marne, but starved of accurate intelligence, De Maud'huy was contemplating an advance of his own, not only towards Douai but – if German fortunes were appropriately reversed – a triumphal march upon Berlin itself! But whilst De Maud'huy commanded two army corps – a considerable body of troops – Prince Rupprecht was able to deploy three, plus another of cavalry. Many German field guns too were on their way. De Maud'huy's counter-offensive and Rupprecht's offensive began on 1 October 1914, the first day of the First Battle of Artois. Arras was the nucleus.

The axis of the German attack was exactly that used by Rommel's 7th Panzer Division in May 1940. Then, the mechanized tide of invasion was to sweep through and beyond the town, but in 1914 and without tanks the results were a little different, for at the same time De

Maud'huy was planning to advance eastwards along the very same axis – the Cambrai road. On the first evening the Germans managed to reach Arras's outlying eastern villages before the French. They barricaded the streets and installed machine guns. Throughout that night there was a mess of close-quarter fighting, and by morning – a foggy one – the situation was simply confused. Eventually it transpired that Monchy-le-Preux was shared, Wancourt lost, and Neuville under severe pressure. By 9.00 a.m. the following day Monchy had been abandoned and the invader was now trying his luck north and south. Fighting – and shelling – became frantic, and soon it appeared as if the game was up for the French, for large numbers of disoriented troops were becoming isolated behind the hostile surge.

Suffering from further erroneous intelligence reports, De Maud'huy chose to give up counter-attacks on Marlière, Neuville-Vitasse, Guémappe, Wancourt and Monchy-le-Preux. On 4 October, with the Kaiser himself in the region, the crucial strategic target of Lens, along with its great mines and stockpiles of coal, fell to the Germans. The next day Bavarian troops began a push towards Arras from the north, taking Vimy village and the Point du Jour. Then Vimy Ridge fell, the invaders surging into the Souchez valley and climbing the slopes beyond towards the heights of Notre Dame de Lorette, where they were held. On 6 October, French support to repel sustained assault was dwindling.

By 8 October, Lens, Lille, Douai, Vimy and parts of the Lorette Ridge heights were under firm German occupation. The battering continued and many of Arras's small satellite villages fell, including Beaurains, Tilloy and Feuchy. A German encirclement plan came to nothing,

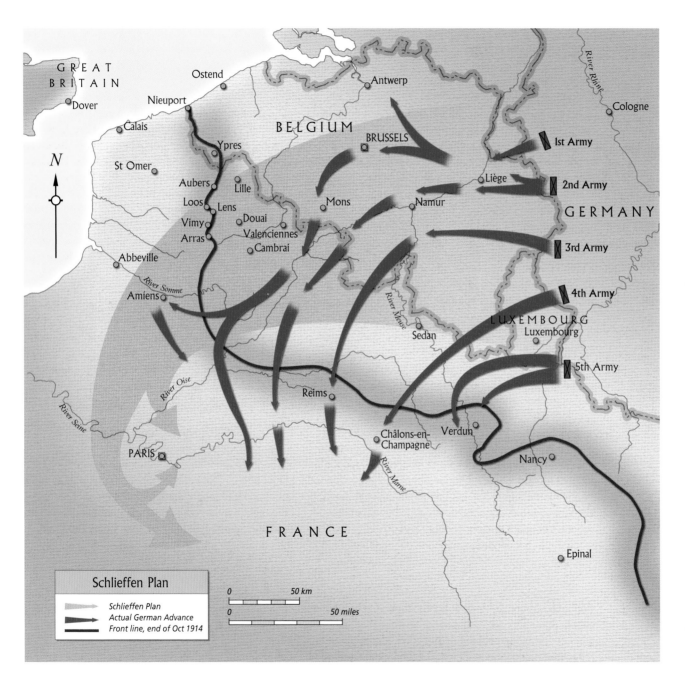

N

GREAT
BRITAIN
Dover
Calais
Nieuport
Ostend
St Omer
Ypres
Aubers
Loos
Lille
Lens
Vimy
Douai
Arras
Valenciennes
Cambrai
Abbeville
River Somme
Amiens
River Oise
River Seine
PARIS
Reims
River Marne
Châlons-en-Champagne
FRANCE
BELGIUM
Mons
BRUSSELS
Antwerp
Namur
Liège
River Meuse
Sedan
LUXEMBOURG
Luxembourg
Verdun
Nancy
Epinal
River Rhine
Cologne
GERMANY
1st Army
2nd Army
3rd Army
4th Army
5th Army

Schlieffen Plan

Schlieffen Plan
Actual German Advance
Front line, end of Oct 1914

0   50 km

0   50 miles

Above The Kaiser halts for refreshments on the Arras–Cambrai road on 4 October 1914. AJ

Right The Crown Prince Rupprecht of Bavaria. PC

and at 10.45 a.m. on 21 October, the celebrated and ancient Arras Belfry, commenced in 1463 and completed in 1554, providentially collapsed; on this same day skirmishing finally waned. The reason lay not only in the fact that the troops of both sides were exhausted, but because of turmoil yet further north at Ypres in Belgium, where the earliest of four colossal clashes to blight the region was getting underway: the First Battle of Ypres.

It was now in Belgian Flanders that the Germans had to be held – or if possible turned. In a brilliant, daring and indeed ancient manoeuvre Belgian Army engineers assisted by two civilian specialists began the flooding of a vast area of inland plain by the controlled opening of sea locks and sluices in and around the town of Nieuport. As the tides rose, so valves were thrown open, to be closed again on the ebb. For several nights the sea rushed into the Yser estuary, through the open sluices and onto the billiard-table-flat Polders. Closing the sluices held it there. The result – forever known as the inundations – left only a thin ribbon of sand dunes for military manoeuvre. Here, however, the wide tidal river formed a hurdle too difficult to vault. Inland, the waters continued to seethe across the fields, daily claiming more and more potential battlefield. Just thigh-deep but impenetrable to man, machine and animal, the inundations neutralized the German thrust. As more and more farms and fields were swamped, the invader was forced back inland. Dixmuide, some 20 kilometres from the coast, received the next bludgeoning, but the exhausted remnants of the Belgian Army again held on. Critically, whilst battle raged here, the engineers further extended the inundations almost to the western ramparts of Ypres. Now, with the coastal route closed, and stalemate in

Arras and French Flanders, the only sector left at German offensive 'disposal' was that lying between Armentières and Boesinghe – the Ypres and Messines sectors.

In an effort to secure victory as a Christmas gift for the Kaiser (he had moved north into Belgium to overlook this endeavour), every spare German soldier was pushed into the cauldron of Ypres, including the Guards Division from Arras. The combination of a Flemish winter and crippling mutual losses during the actions of 19 October to 22 November was to crush all hope of breakthrough and victory before Christmas 1914. The battle also erased a hefty percentage of Britain's small professional army, the British Expeditionary Force (BEF). Sir Douglas Haig, then a corps commander, served during the battle. He knew how close to disaster the British and French had come, and came to believe that German failure could be put down simply to lack of perseverance – they had not delivered the final kick. It is thought by many that Haig's later tactical approach as Commander-in-Chief was strongly influenced by this belief.

As a result of actions on the Yser and around Ypres, German units in Artois found themselves with insufficient reserves to pursue even small endeavours, and so the pressure upon Arras was relieved. The town now faced almost four years of molestation. This was German Sixth Army territory and its commander Crown Prince Rupprecht had long been looking forward to facing the British.

We are now lucky enough to have the English on our front too; the troops of a nation whose ambition it has been, all these years, to surround us with a ring of enemies to suffocate us. It is thanks to them that we are engaged in this terrible war. Therefore when you attack

this enemy, take your revenge for their deceitful enmity and for so many heavy sacrifices. Show him that the Germans are not so easily blotted out of the World's History; show him this with the very best of German bows. Here is the enemy who stands most in the way of peace … Up and at him!

19 OCTOBER 1914. MESSAGE FROM CROWN PRINCE RUPPRECHT OF BAVARIA TO SOLDIERS OF THE SIXTH ARMY

Rupprecht's time was still some twenty-nine months away.

Left Theatres of war in Europe, the Balkans and the Middle East.

Right A German officer scans the horizon from an early trench near the Point du Jour. ING G3547b-148

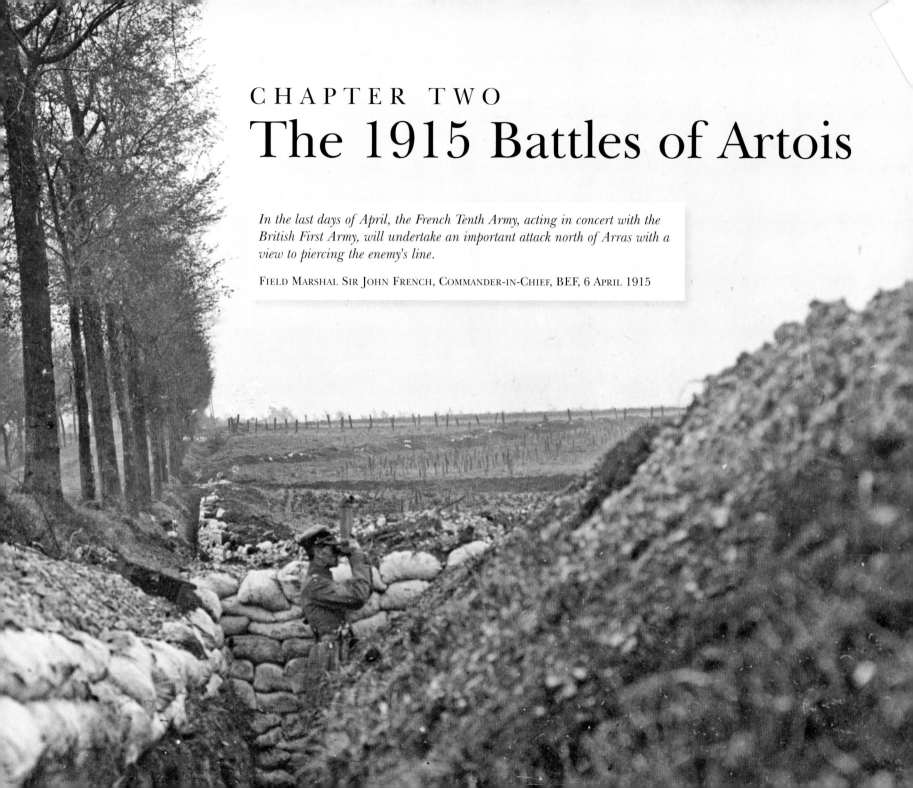

CHAPTER TWO
The 1915 Battles of Artois

In the last days of April, the French Tenth Army, acting in concert with the British First Army, will undertake an important attack north of Arras with a view to piercing the enemy's line.

FIELD MARSHAL SIR JOHN FRENCH, COMMANDER-IN-CHIEF, BEF, 6 APRIL 1915

During the early months of 1915 it became clear that the Germans were concentrating much effort on waging war in the East against Russia. This, it was believed, presented the British and French with not just an opportunity but an obligation to attack in the West. Three schemes, all French-led, were drawn up for the spring. They could not all be pressed simultaneously and action in Artois was given precedence. It would be, said Joseph Joffre, the beginning of the end: in three months the war would be over.

The BEF took over parts of the Aubers sector north of the La Bassée Canal, at the same time making plans for a diversionary action there to assist the grand attack that was to be pressed on a front extending from north of the Lorette Spur to the Point du Jour directly east of Arras. The purpose was to precipitate an advance upon Lens, and possibly even Douai.

THE SECOND BATTLE OF ARTOIS

The question facing the French was how could enemy garrisons be sufficiently weakened to allow the attacks to prosper? Whilst more than a thousand small- and medium-calibre guns were obtainable, Joffre and his commanders, Foch and D'Urbal, were conscious that the 293 heavies were unlikely to be sufficient to force a breach by firepower alone.

After a bombardment exceeding two million shells and lasting six days, at 10.00 a.m. on 9 May 1915, French infantry clambered from their trenches. Initially, surprise gave them some outstanding early gains in the centre of the battleground, the 77th and Moroccan Divisions advancing almost 4 kilometres, the latter onto the heights of Vimy Ridge itself. It so shook German poise that preparations were instigated to evacuate Lille. But French tenure of contour 145, the crest, was to be brief, for reserves had been stationed too far away to exploit success, a weakness that on many a future occasion was also to dog the BEF. The advance came to a standstill. Every moment of delay offered time for German recovery, a skill at which they excelled, and of course for counter-attack. The reinforcements arrived fast – by lorry – and the French were forced to withdraw. Action then dissipated into localized assaults. Fought amongst the maze of partly overrun German trenches across the entire sector throughout the rest of the month and well into June, none achieved any worthwhile gains. True, the Germans had been forced back, but their support and reserve positions were so carefully sited that the lines now occupied were significantly more dominant than before. In the face of more than 100,000 casualties by 15 June, it was hard to identify any meaningful French benefit.

The two British diversionary attacks at Aubers and Givenchy were equally costly and strategically barren. Afterwards, Lord Kitchener, British Secretary of State for War, recommended the cessation of all offensive schemes, advocating a purely defensive policy until the BEF was strong enough to launch a fatal blow. Kitchener's standing was low in the eyes of the French military, however: they dismissed the notion as 'heresy', adding that such words could only have been uttered by someone whose native lands were not under the German boot.

THE THIRD BATTLE OF ARTOIS

During the Second Battle of Ypres French, British and Belgian troops performed their

Above French trenches on the Notre Dame de Lorette ridge overlooking Lens. IWM Q49240

Below French dead awaiting burial after an abortive attack upon the Vimy Ridge. AJ

own defensive miracle by holding off the massive German thrust. By now Turkey had entered the war on the German side and in the same week that Second Ypres began, the Allied campaign in the Dardanelles was set in motion. On 25 April it made a ghastly start, failing to gain any objectives except that of a tenuous foothold on the shores and cliffs of the Gallipoli peninsular. In June 1915, when the next Anglo-French strike in the West was being considered, prospects had not improved. If eventually the offensive was to fail, Russia could relinquish all hope of receiving Allied material assistance via the Black Sea ports.

Attention was maintained upon the Western Front. Joffre drew up another scheme. He would attack in Champagne and Artois, whilst once more the British would attract attention elsewhere, this time in the Loos sector, north of Arras and Vimy. The attacks would be on a much grander scale, employing a weapon that had only recently become available – poison gas. Douai and its railhead was again the French goal – via Vimy Ridge. To several commanders Joffre's plans appeared disturbingly similar to those of the failed spring attacks, the only difference being that with additional medium-calibre artillery arriving from Verdun, there were now more guns available – 420 as opposed to 290 in May.

Between 25 September, the day the Third Battle of Artois began, and 11 October, when Joffre was once more forced to draw a bloody line under proceedings – another 47,000 Frenchmen were killed, wounded or missing for relatively insignificant gains. At no point was the crest of ridge threatened. It was at this time that a situation arose that would rear its head on a far greater and more serious scale later in the war. In November 1915, a battalion

of the 63rd Infantry Regiment, a unit that had been thrust into action three times but granted no rest between, refused to attack. The entire battalion was court-martialled and six men selected for execution – by the drawing of lots. Despite the commanding officer's strenuous resistance, five were shot.

At Loos, the British First Army, using chlorine gas for the first time, enjoyed a certain initial success, the first waves occupying several key positions including Loos itself. Once more, though, support troops were late in arriving and the offensive slowed, stopped and eventually crumbled in the face of well co-ordinated German counter-attacks. For losses of around 50,000 men, the BEF had gained a few acres of worthless ground. This battle, the third British failure of the year, forced Commander-in-Chief, Sir John French, into resignation. His place was soon to be given to Sir Douglas Haig.

As 1915 closed, the nature of war on the Western Front was about to change. Along the entire line siege mentality was now deeply rooted. Thanks to the defensive systems adopted by the Germans in the West, an early form of attritional warfare had also been forced into being. It was clear that in order to be successful an opposing garrison must be made to suffer not less than but as many – or preferably more – casualties than one's own attacking force. On no occasion in 1915 had this been the Allied experience, indeed the opposite had been the case, with the Germans all too often sustaining half as many losses. There now appeared only one answer to the conundrum of breaking the deadlock: deploy sufficient artillery firepower to utterly destroy both the target and its garrison prior to assault. 1916, therefore, was to be the year of the artillery prize fight.

(Givenchy-en-Gohelle out of sight behind hill)

Northern part of the Vimy Ridge as seen from the Lorette Ridge. (Left half *above*, right half *below*.) IWM First Army panorama P136

Souchez village in valley (Valley of Death)   Bois de La Folie

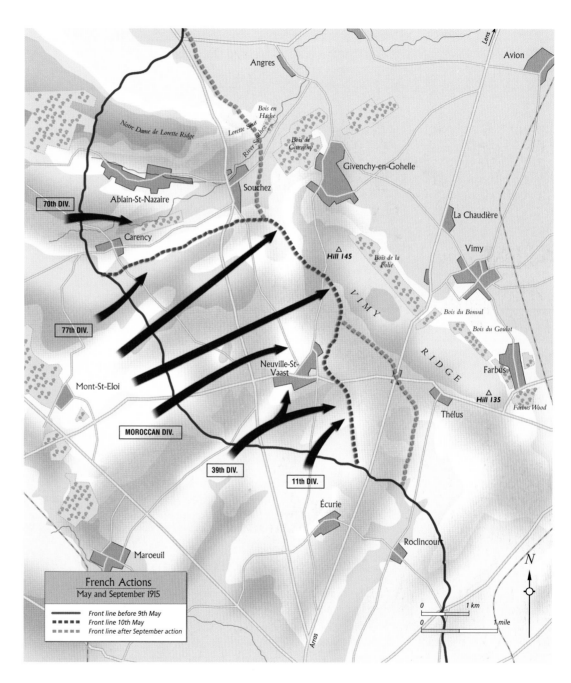

French Actions
May and September 1915

——————— Front line before 9th May
- - - - - - - Front line 10th May
- - - - - - - Front line after September action

CHAPTER THREE
The British Arrival

From 20 December 1915, the Allies began to secretly extricate themselves from the Gallipoli Peninsula, the final parties leaving the shores of Lancashire Landing at Cape Helles on 9 January 1916, self-firing rifles persuading the Turks their enemy was still in occupation. Crafty and successful though the evacuation was, the campaign itself was a humiliating defeat: 141,000 casualties and no strategic benefit. Turkey was of course jubilant, the victory swelling an ambition to expand Ottoman influence during the coming year. Her Austrian and German allies were less satisfied: the Dardanelles campaign had engaged large numbers of enemy troops whilst drawing only minimally on their own resources; in contrast, by pulling out the *Entente* gained 90,000 extra British, French, Australian, Indian, Newfoundland and New Zealand troops for deployment in other theatres. For Russia, the result was disastrous for her Black Sea ports were now terminally unreachable without risky action elsewhere.

On 24 February, a rumour emerged that the French Tenth Army was to leave Artois and move south to the Verdun sector, at this time under the German hammer for just three days. Rumour was soon confirmed as fact and on 1 March the British Third Army began to take over the 30-odd kilometres that made up the Arras and Vimy sectors.

The relief took place without crises, and by the end of the month the mission was completed, the Tommies now becoming guardians of an unbroken line from Ypres to the Somme River. There were two downsides to their arrival in Arras. The first was that they were quickly perceived – and all too often proven – to be inveterate drinkers. The *Arrageois*, who still numbered between 1,000 and 1,500 in the town, had also endured over a year of looting problems with their own troops, but the newcomers took the skill a step further, and many a dugout (as far away as the Lens sector) was embellished with stoves, furniture, even pictures and bedding liberated from the town's broken and sagging houses.

The military authorities did their best to eliminate the problem, but with so many goods 'on show' in the faceless streets, temptation was frequently too strong. Very often it was mundane items which disappeared: cutlery, a towel, blankets, soap. But the inhabitants were by no means unsympathetic to 'visiting' foreign troops who were after all their guardians and potential salvation. The French acknowledged the problem the nation faced in ejecting the invader single-handed and could see the dishevelled and fatigued condition of British troops coming out of the line, the walking wounded shuffling through the streets after dark, and the ever-expanding

Right The vanguard of British troops marches through Anzin towards Arras. IWM

Below British officers of 15th Royal Warwicks in the Arras trenches in summer 1916. IWM HU87160

military cemeteries. Yet it was imperative that the local people must at least be allowed the dream of returning to find some personal possessions still *in situ* – if indeed the property housing them still existed. Arras was a pretty comfortable billet. The first British garrisons on the ridge, however, were in sore need of shelter and warmth.

31ST MARCH 1916

Dear Mother,

We have had a rotten time in the trenches. The weather has been awful. When it wasn't raining, it was snowing and freezing. And to make matters worse we had no dugouts or shelters of any kind. The snow and rain came in very handy in one way. We were very short of water so we melted the snow and collected all the water in the numerous shell holes that were to be found. If it hadn't been for that then we should have had no tea and that would have been rotten. We have had a very peaceful time with the Germans. They used to walk about on top with our chaps, exchanging cigarettes, tobacco and shaking hands with us. It was a curious sight to see them strolling about in "No Man's Land" as though war was the last thing they thought about. It has been a unique experience which I shan't forget for a long time to come.

RIFLEMAN RICHARD HARVEY, 1/6TH LONDON REGIMENT

In this Vimy sector many an arriving Tommy remarked that there appeared to be more dead than live Frenchmen – the 1915 battlefields had still not been cleared, and in places lay mantled with corpses, the Souchez 'valley of death' being an especially gloomy spot.

It would remain thus for at least another two years. And yet at the same time the British were entering an unfamiliar world of peace, for after the bloodbaths of 1915 an unwritten live-and-let-live arrangement had informally been established.

We marched in Batteries independently, so were able to pass many troops and got to our billet at 1p.m. It was a lovely chateau which had been occupied by the French. Spring beds and sheets, horses under cover, and Persian carpets. Monsieur le Comte was there also. We stayed there one day, then came up here into action. It is a lovely town. We were invited to dine with the officers of the French Battery and had a gorgeous spread in a tunnel under a railway embankment – eight course dinner with a variety of wines and we toasted each other in champagne.

The next morning we took over from the French Battery. At the O.P. there was only one peep hole. Monsieur le Capitaine looked through first, trying to describe the salient points, saying, 'You see that so and so', and the Captain would reply in French that he could not see it. Then the Captain examined the sector through the peep hole, and he, without thinking, would say, 'You see that so and so'. Monsieur le Capitaine would reply, 'Excuse, I do not see'. They then both burst out laughing and shook hands … Then, in the afternoon, I joined the signallers in the cellar of the O.P. where they were having drinks of wine offered by the French signallers and were toasting everything they could think of. One of ours, a Cockney, jokingly said, 'Vive le Bosch'. The French were just about to drink, when the forms of their visages suddenly changed. I quickly tapped my head and pointed to the Cockney with a laugh. He laughed and they all laughed, and started slapping each other on the back in great camaraderie.

We fight in peace here and live in a most wonderful chateau with porcelain bath and hot and cold water laid on. How quiet compared with Tom's Dog [pet-name for Ypres]. Hardly a shot fired. We will be having to get mess dress soon! I hope it will liven up a bit as the war will never end at this rate.

The dugouts are twenty feet deep. Everything is most luxurious. Even the sergeants have separate rooms with spring beds. Of course, all the men have beds and sofas and pianos, etc. On the way to the O.P. there are many shops where we can buy fresh fish, watches, groceries, etc., and even a photographer! It is odd to hear

the Battery suddenly open up while lying in one's bath in the morning and I wonder what the chap at the O.P. has spotted. With private stables and the garden of fruit and vegetables being looked after for our comfort by a French gardener left by the owner of the place, we feel as if we have arrived in a sort of wonderland. We had an elderly Captain staying with us here for a few days (the War Office sends out officers from Home Divisions on Cook's Tours to get some idea of what active service is like). He wrote us such a nice letter thanking us for our hospitality, and said the only thing he had to complain of was that his sleep was occasionally disturbed by the songs of the nightingales! Since he left, however, a stray whizz-bang actually did hit our chateau, just above the upstairs bathroom, showering the place with plaster and brick dust. I was shaving at the time and was so startled that I nearly cut myself!

We are having perfectly glorious weather now. The violets in the garden are lovely and the goldfish in the pond come to the top to sun themselves. You can picture us war-wracked fellows now undergoing our daily hardships of awakening to the songs of nightingales and coming down to breakfast of porridge, bacon and eggs and coffee at a great mahogany table with the scent of the pines wafting through the open windows.

LIEUTENANT C.J. TYNDALE-BISCOE MC, 48TH BRIGADE, ROYAL FIELD ARTILLERY

Tyndale-Biscoe's cosseted existence behind the lines was a far cry from living conditions in the forward zones, but nevertheless on regular visits to the trenches he encountered a certain 'understanding' between the opposing troops.

The Captain and I went down to the remains of a village [Blangy] through which both ours and the enemy trenches run.

It is a most extraordinary mix-up, since, in places, the trenches are so close that they run through the remains of the same houses. In consequence, nobody

Right German front line in Blangy. Their enemy lie just a few metres away. ING 1071-83-64

Below British front line trench with observer in a mine crater field near Arras. IWM HU87168

thinks of throwing grenades about – a case of 'those who live in glass houses … ' Wanting to find vantage points where we could see the lie of the land on the enemy side, we went up into the roof of a part of a house that was still standing and which we thought was about 100 yards from the enemy's lines. Most of the tiles were missing, and as we were looking through the rafters the Captain touched me and pointed to our left. There we were, looking down on German trenches a few yards away and saw some Germans standing there. I gasped and whispered: 'Why don't they shoot us?'

'I can't think,' said he with a grin, but we crept softly away.

LIEUTENANT C.J. TYNDALE-BISCOE MC, 48TH BRIGADE, ROYAL FIELD ARTILLERY

The general situation followed the same pattern, continuing when Canadian troops marched into the Vimy sector. There was a pattern to trench life that was redolent of domesticity.

Below French *paysannes* and German troops continue to work the fields close behind the lines. AJ

Then there is the trench cat. A strict neutral, we call him "Wilson" [after Woodrow Wilson, President of the United States, at this time an affirmed neutral] because we found him asleep on a haversack with a rat rifling the contents! "Too proud to fight". He walks across no man's land at will and knows the meal hours on both sides. The loveliest sight I ever saw was one night of full moon. We were on top of the ridge just behind Duffield Crater; looking back to our side one saw the chalk ruins of Neuville and La Targette and then a sea of mist to the towers of Mont St Eloi. A curious picture of a dead world, in the immediate foreground trenches and mine craters. It was an uncanny moment as the war seemed to have ceased – no flares – they were not needed, and it was too bright for men to expose themselves. We were behind the lip of the crater and partly concealed. The mist slowly rose in the still air and finally became a layer of cloud which by some chance broke into the form of a cross, the arms being formed by lanes through the cloud so that it looked like a huge purple cross. (This cross caused much comment later and was quoted as supernatural, but was really a simple meteorological effect caused by currents of air higher up and the final result was a mackerel sky).

For the time being everyone was looking at this curious cloud and the war was forgotten for some half an hour. Then our battery in Neuville fired their midnight salvo and went back to sleep. A German machine gun fired a burst of fire over our head and war was resumed.

CORPORAL G.W. DURHAM, 7TH CANADIAN INFANTRY BRIGADE

Wherever it was possible to retain a semblance of normality, efforts were made to do so, especially by the local population who, as on the opposite side of no man's land, continued to live and work close up behind the battlefront.

I remember one gallant and very tough old lady who lived in a tiny cottage in a little depression about half a

mile behind our Front Line, half way up the Vimy Ridge. She used to waddle up and down the long communicating trench that wound its way back almost to Mont St Eloi to buy her food. The speciality of this old lady was bee-keeping and the sale of honey.

"You see," she explained to me, "No-Man's-Land is a mass of wild flowers and it is really beautiful. It's so wonderful for my bees, and I am so near no-mans-land that they don't have to fly very far. That is why I have so much honey to sell." So we all used to buy her honey. Then one day when I went up to buy some more she was gone and so was her cottage which had been hit by a crump (German 5.9-inch shell). But the bees were still there and as busy as ever. I tried to find out what happened to her and whether she was still alive, but nobody knew.
LIEUTENANT HAROLD, HEMMING, 84TH BRIGADE, ROYAL FIELD ARTILLERY

A local Arras chronicler, one of a surprising number of civilians who contrived to stay behind to see if a living could be made from the 'friendly invaders', noted that the British were 'not easily irritated, and constantly whistle'. Like Ypres, from 1916 to the end of the war the town became almost entirely anglicized. Many shops remained open and the Tommies were able to purchase newspapers, fancy goods, gifts, postcards, and foodstuffs. There were even restaurants.

War scarred and desolate as the town was there were, at that time, two old ladies, residents of Arras whose house had tumbled down about them but who continued to live in the cellars, part of which they had converted into a restaurant. This diversion was known to us as 'Aunties' and on many an evening when duty allowed we gathered there for a most excellent meal, cooked in the truly French style, and a bottle or so of wine. What gallant and cheerful ladies these were and how well they served us.
LIEUTENANT ARTHUR WORMAN, 6TH QUEEN'S (ROYAL WEST SURREY REGIMENT)

Men could get a haircut, dental treatment and have photographs taken, usually captioned 'Somewhere in France'. Prostitution was rife. Estaminets offered a glass of wine or beer, plus the ubiquitous egg and chips. Even the latest 'moving pictures' were available.

In the evening we decide to visit the local "cinema" which occupies a deserted factory on the Anzin road, and which has the disadvantages of being under observation from the German lines. Caution is therefore necessary and we have to queue up behind a wall at the far side of the road, and make a hurried crossing, two or three at a time to the pay-box. The audience is composed of men from the surrounding districts, but we, and a few of the Headquarters Staff, are the only Royal Scots present. We sit on spars with the bare earth for a floor and enjoy ourselves immensely although the pictures are pretty antiquated and the titles all in French, but the varied and loud-voiced interpretation by the troops are really the best part of the show. One fellow sitting next to me says he has been to the performance four times in the last three weeks and the pictures are still the same.
PRIVATE A. ANDERSON, 1/9TH ROYAL SCOTS

Although the British had come to Arras in order to display obligatory belligerence, the ambience was a pleasant one compared to many other sectors, and for some time the live-and-let-live attitude enjoyed by the French continued to pervade much of the front line. The town may have been persistently shelled, but hostile activity in no man's land was sporadic. Patrols were the key feature.

Snow persisted into mid-March. It was far from welcome now that we had relieved the French 83rd Regiment and were manning a strange front line. I well recall, for instance, that two of us, Sherwood, an amateur artist, and myself found ourselves in a listening

Above A lady restaurateur who chose to stay behind in Arras. IWM Q11301

Below Mediaeval statues from Arras in safe keeping behind the battlefront. IWM CO1506

post, out in no man's land, completely isolated in a blanket of drifting snow in an eerie silence that was alive with the threat of creeping enemy patrols. The battered bodies on the wire in front were only just identifiable and even swinging tin cans were muffled. It was the time for "night gown raids" so we spent the dark hours standing, cold and snow covered, with constant tense alertness. The women's white nightwear, for which the countryside behind the opposing forces had been scoured, were wonderful camouflage for patrols and raiders. There were grim jokes if the muffled yell of a surprised raid victim was heard.

PRIVATE F.J. FIELD, 15TH ROYAL WARWICKSHIRE REGIMENT (2ND BIRMINGHAM PALS)

On Vimy Ridge the situation soon became somewhat different to Arras – because of tunnelling. When one looks at sectors noted in countless narratives to be the foulest spots on the Western Front, one finds that all are directly associated with underground warfare: Hill 60, the Hohenzollern Redoubt, La Boisselle, Hooge, the Bluff, Cuinchy Brickstacks etc. Vimy would become one of the most comprehensively undermined sectors of all, and join the ranks of the most dangerous. Upon arrival British tunnelling companies had encountered fieldworks with which they were unaccustomed. There were no linear trench systems, but isolated posts protecting a 'sketchy' front line. From these posts, the French *Genie* had driven shallow tunnels, largely for protective purposes – i.e. to detect and halt by underground explosion, hostile underground activity. Elsewhere, the British dominated the subterranean battlefield; here, it was the Germans who were in the ascendancy, for they had discovered a series of ancient civilian mine workings. The new arrivals required instruction.

Above A German cinema in Roeux. BHK Abt. IV BS-N 63/4 17 48

We were received by a French Engineer subaltern who was most friendly and anxious to show us the underground work then in progress. He occupied a comfortable dugout short of the Vimy Ridge on the east side of the valley leading up to it. Looking back from his dugout to the west side toward the deep communication trench through which we had just come, I was astounded to see a line of Zouave troops, in their brilliant red pantaloons, lying where they had fallen in the attack the previous September. Later I learned the French had named the valley Zouave Valley after this famous regiment. There was much to be done in arranging the sectors to be taken over: dugout accommodation, rations, transportation to the forward area of troops and equipment, the supply of explosive, liaison with the French etc. etc. Numerous trips to and from the front line were necessary, and as I passed nearby their positions I was struck by the tremendous activity of the French gunners. It is probable that they were giving the Hun a final strafing before pulling out. Be that as it may, the effect of the bombardment was to make us feel that this was no soft spot to which we had come. The men realised they were being placed on their mettle and they rose gallantly to the occasion. The morale of the company, which had been improving with marked rapidity, was given a further impetus and all ranks were quick to appreciate that they had been paid the high tribute of being ordered to a really sticky and important area.

The Hun was very considerate and gave us almost a month to become established and organised before active underground warfare broke out. The men, whose experience had been in clay, were given an opportunity of becoming familiar with the different methods of mining in chalk. It was possible for their ears to become tuned to the markedly different underground noises. Our officers and listeners had a welcome period of training in the location of enemy operations. All in all we were most fortunate that we were not pitchforked into situations where our lack of experience might well have led to serious consequences.

MAJOR F. J. MULQUEEN, 182 TUNNELLING COMPANY, RE

As time passed, tunnelling activity beneath the ridge became more widespread and more lethal, but the British soon reached subterranean parity with the enemy. The German answer was simple and devastating. From 21 to 24 May 1916, Operation Schleswig-Holstein was enacted, the biggest action since the French attacks of the previous year. Protected by finely tuned barrages, four German regiments (163rd Regiment, 86th Reserve, 9th Reserve, 5th Foot Guards) surprised the British and overran 2 kilometres of front and support line in the Berthonval and Carency sectors. In a matter of hours the entire British mining effort of shafts, dugouts, inclines, galleries and mine chambers was overrun – permanently. The Germans immediately installed a new front line some 300 metres ahead of their old positions. Counter-attacks were fruitless. Further tunnelling schemes were immediately put forward, but it was the Somme that was now dominating thought. For the time being, Vimy had to wait, but Sir Douglas Haig instigated the design of an assault that would conclusively appropriate the entire ridge. Thus, tunnelling companies were forced to begin their work anew. As they delved gingerly beneath no man's land, another potent German weapon was employed.

Not long after their successful attack the Germans introduced an instrument in the use of which they had become most adept – sabotage of the French war effort by false propaganda. It was directed at the French Poilu, who at that time was putting up such a courageous defence at Verdun. The British were reported to have lost the Vimy Ridge which the French had captured at such terrific cost. The effect of the propaganda became so serious that two French troops were brought from Verdun and shown our

new positions. I was one of the group which accompanied them over part of the front. They went away reassured.
MAJOR F.J. MULQUEEN, 182 TUNNELLING COMPANY, RE

Gradually, parity was once more regained and the intensity of tunnel warfare receded, but not before the entire ridge had been comprehensively undermined to a depth of almost 50 metres. It was now difficult for either side to operate without the other responding, so security in the trenches was slowly enhanced. Engineer minds turned to the future, and Haig's request. First, a plan was hatched to put an end to the long and dangerous trek along overlooked communication trenches. By the use of subways, troops could be taken safely to their destinations. With 20 feet of chalk overhead they were safe from all but the heaviest shells, and because they were dug in a straight line unlike the meandering or fire-bayed trace of surface works, walking distances were cut by almost a third. The scheme did not end there.

Each contained a Medical Dressing Station so situated that stretchers could be moved quite easily in and out; Battalion and Company headquarters (Tottenham Road contained Brigade Headquarters as well); several large dugouts and a cookhouse. The smoke from the cook's fire was carried in an eight-inch chimney bored through the chalk to the surface at a point remote from any trenches. We obtained a great deal of amusement when we observed the Hun regularly shelled the spot where the smoke from Cavalier cookhouse was discharged. An engine room was built into each, designed to hold a petrol-driven electric power plant. One of the Company's officers located a number of Decauville [light railway] dump trucks in an abandoned quarry, and all were promptly corralled. The trucks were too wide for the galleries, but fortunately the rails fitted them and it was a relatively simple matter for the Company's blacksmith to

Left German tunnellers in a chalk gallery beneath Vimy Ridge. ING G3551-9

Below left and right An electricity generating station and cookhouse in the Arras caves. IWM Q10400 and Q10713

cut down the trucks. Instead of going through the slow performance of filling the chalk into sandbags, it was shovelled directly into the trucks and hauled up an incline whose entrance was built in the open far from any trenches. Camouflage screens were built on either side of the opening and tracks were laid behind them. The side-dumping trucks were then hauled up the incline with a winch and the chalk quickly dumped in the open.
MAJOR F.J. MULQUEEN, 182 TUNNELLING COMPANY, RE

When it came to the projected offensive, the benefit of the subway complex soon became clear: men could not only be brought safely but *secretly* to their jumping-off positions.

Further south on the Arras front, mining of the offensive and defensive variety had started in 1915. A year later several sectors were still active, but like Vimy, fighting was dwindling as a similar stalemate ensued, and the Sappers were also able to turn their attention to underground communication and protection. Their achievements were extraordinary – and established upon the work of ancient French predecessors. In 1916 and early 1917, a city beneath the city was created. The first workings were simply based upon the *caves* (cellars) that existed beneath every house, often on two and even three levels. By simply tunnelling from one to the other a splendid network of safe, dry and warm shelters was created. The next step was to connect the cellars with the city's Crinchon sewer. This extended the underground system eastwards in the direction of the railway station. The front lines lay beyond; they too were to be incorporated.

The visitor to Arras today will notice that the older buildings in the city are constructed from limestone blocks; they may also note than such stone is not visible on the surface of the Artois region. Like every ancient town and vil-

lage in the area, for centuries building material had been sourced *underground*; to a British quarryman the resulting caverns would be known as 'closeheads', to the French they were *Boves*. Here, some 10-20 metres beneath the surface, stone was quarried, shaped and dressed, then lifted by ropes through an aperture in the 'roof', resembling a well. It will be appreciated that in order to produce sufficient stone to build a city like Arras (and indeed, all of its satellite villages), the scale of extraction was substantial. The result was a vast system of 'pillar and stall' workings. Fortuitously discovered during 1916, these were not only connected to each other, but also to the Arras sewer system, the city's cellars, and the public buildings.

The caves are very old and originated in what manner I know not: it is said they used to form a subterranean connection of five miles with Arras. The great dynamo, the electric lighting plant presumably remain and will so remain until Time dissolves them – or some contractor more enterprising than Time. But what visions those dark entrances conjured up! Something implicit to the war, something of its grotesqueness and insanity. You came from the upper ground, from its bleakness, greyness: you found yourself in these grottoes and galleries, lit mysteriously by electric lights, incurably reminiscent at times of Earl's Court: where everything echoed. Here eternal night reigned. Here the clangour of machinery never ceased or the driving of the great dynamo. Water dripped. All day long and all night men tramped back and forth, Dostoyevskeian figures in rough garb – and slept there, rested and ate there, held services even.
CAPTAIN WILFRID EWART, 2ND SCOTS GUARDS

This scheme extended underground communication to the front lines themselves. On the other side of no man's land the Germans had also taken advantage of *Katakomben*. Although

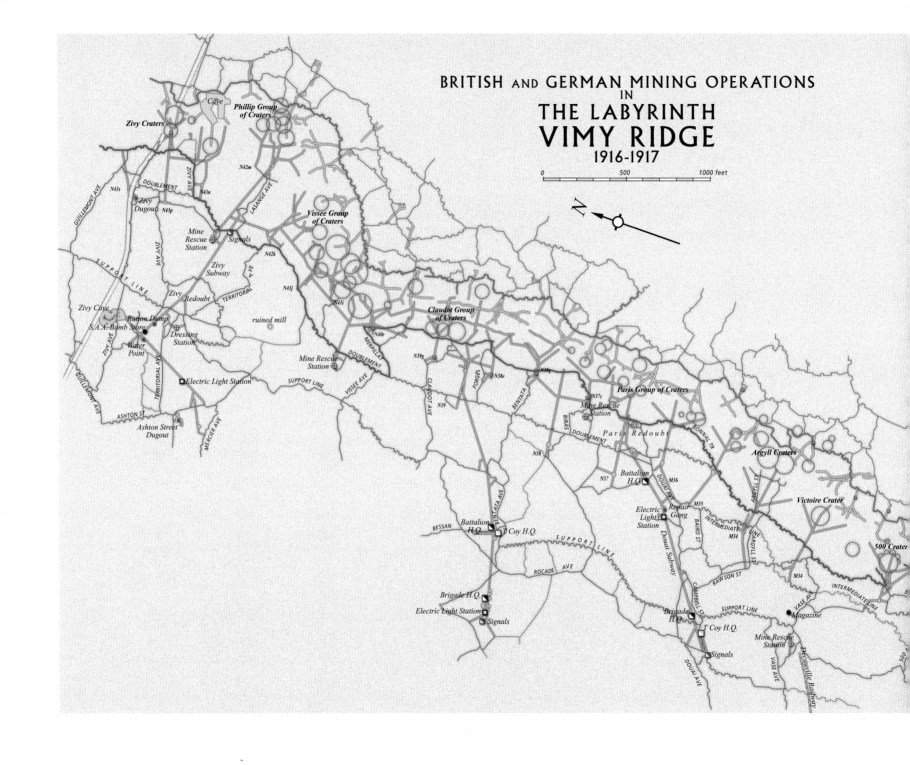

BRITISH AND GERMAN MINING OPERATIONS
IN
THE LABYRINTH
VIMY RIDGE
1916-1917

0   500   1000 feet

N

Cave

Phillip Group of Craters

Zivy Craters

GUILLEMONT AVE

N43s

DOUBLEMENT

ZIVY AVE

N43n

N42m

LASANGE AVE

Zivy Dugout

N43p

Vissée Group of Craters

Mine Rescue Station

Signals

ZIVY AVE

SUPPORT LINE

Zivy Subway

N42k

N41j

A VE

TERRITORIAL

Zivy Redoubt

Zivy

N41i

Claudot Group of Craters

Zivy Cave

Ration Dump

S.A.A. Bomb Store

Dressing Station

Water Point

ZIVY AVE

ruined mill

N40r

MERPILLAT

N39g

Mine Rescue Station

DOUBLEMENT

VISSEE AVE

SUPPORT LINE

FORGE5

N38e

N38g

N37c

Paris Group of Craters

Mine Rescue Station

Electric Light Station

TERRITORIAL AVE

GUILLEMONT AVE

ASHTON ST

Ashton Street Dugout

MERCER AVE

CLAUDOT AVE

N39

BENTATA

BIRAS

DOUBLEMENT

Paris Redoubt

BONNAL TR

Argyll Craters

ARGYLL ST

N38

N37

Battalion H.Q.

DOUAI AVE

M36

M35

Electric Light Station

Repair Gang

BAIRD ST

INTERMEDIATE

LINE

M34

Victoire Crater

ARGYLL ST

BESSAN

Battalion H.Q.

T Coy H.Q.

BENTATA AVE

SUPPORT LINE

ROCADE AVE

RAWSON ST

Douai Subway

CAMPBELL ST

500 Crater

INTERMEDIATE LINE

VASE AVE

Brigade H.Q.

Electric Light Station

Signals

SUPPORT LINE

Brigade H.Q.

T Coy H.Q.

Signals

DOUAI AVE

Mine Rescue Station

Magazine

VASE AVE

Decauville Railway

500 A

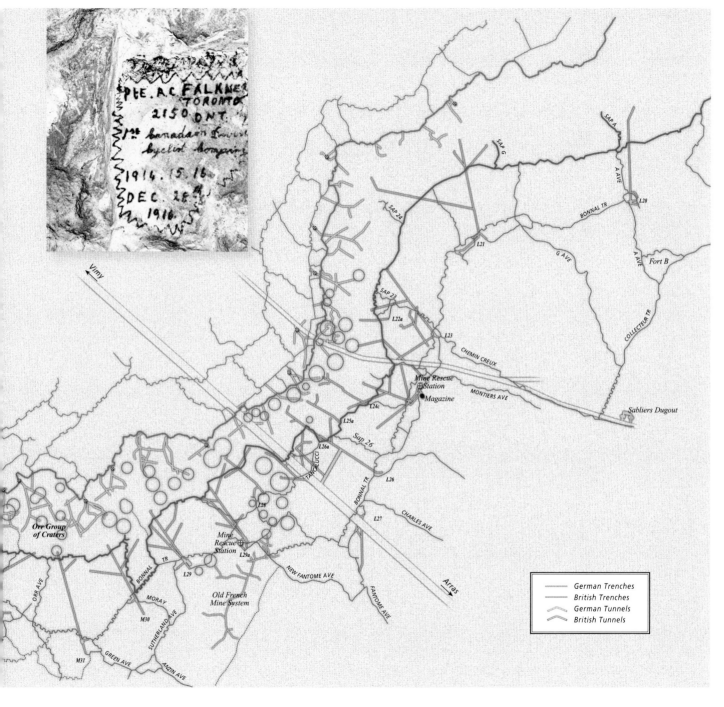

Left Part of the mining system beneath the Vimy Ridge. The circles represent surface craters (blown by both sides), mainly in no man's land. Note the several subways serving the British/ Canadian lines plus their associated dugouts, and the main Arras-Vimy road passing perpendicularly through the lines.

Inset One of thousands of names inscribed upon subway and dugout walls beneath the Vimy Ridge. This one, written on 28 December 1916, records the presence of 2150 Private A C Falkner of Toronto, serving with 1st Canadian Division Cyclist Company. AC

German Trenches
British Trenches
German Tunnels
British Tunnels

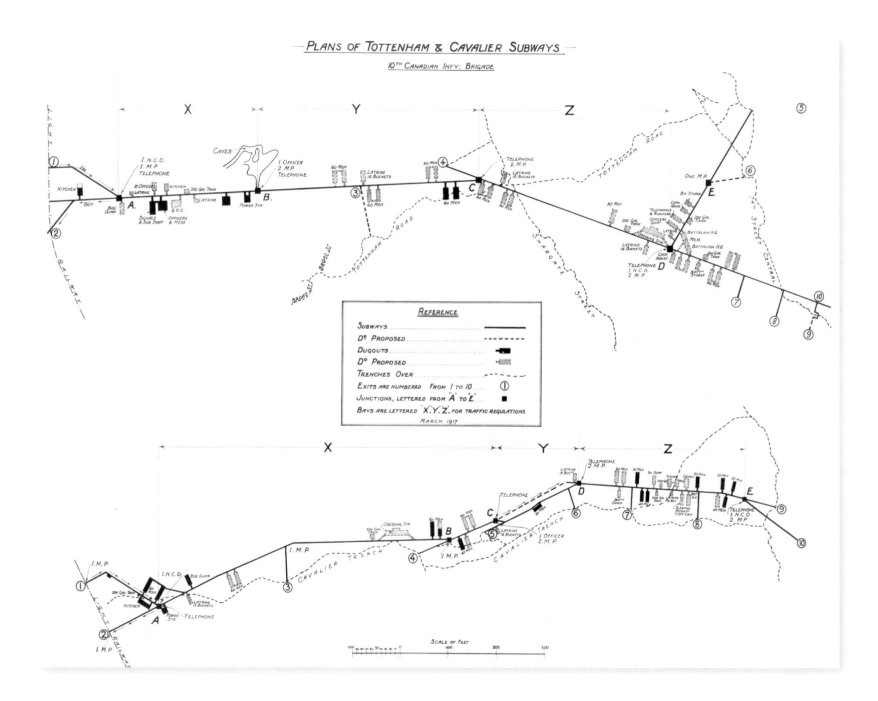

PLANS OF TOTTENHAM & CAVALIER SUBWAYS

10TH CANADIAN INFY: BRIGADE

REFERENCE

SUBWAYS ....
D° PROPOSED ....
DUGOUTS ....
D° PROPOSED ....
TRENCHES OVER ....
EXITS ARE NUMBERED FROM 1 TO 10 ①
JUNCTIONS, LETTERED FROM "A" TO "E"
BAYS ARE LETTERED X.Y.Z. FOR TRAFFIC REGULATIONS.

MARCH 1917

SCALE OF FEET

nowhere as extensive as the Arras *Boves*, the cover they afforded when battle was joined would in places serve to create serious problems for the British.

The work of connecting and developing the *Boves* not unnaturally fell to military miners, originally the New Zealand Tunnelling Company, hence the nationalized nomenclature of the caverns and galleries of the Ronville system, the first to be found. Later they were joined by British Sappers, whose influence can be seen in the St Sauveur complex, with names such as Crewe, Chatham, Carlisle, etc. For months before battle, the caves and tunnels saved countless lives, dramatically contributing to the lowering of 'wastage', and in consequence they played a key role in the maintenance of high morale: when underground the troops *knew* they were safe. Come April 1917 the *Boves* would be packed with troops impatient for action.

Left Detailed plan of two subways serving the Vimy trenches. Note the integral accomodation, telephonic communication and number of exits.

Right How the subways east of Arras connected with the caves and the city sewer and cellars.

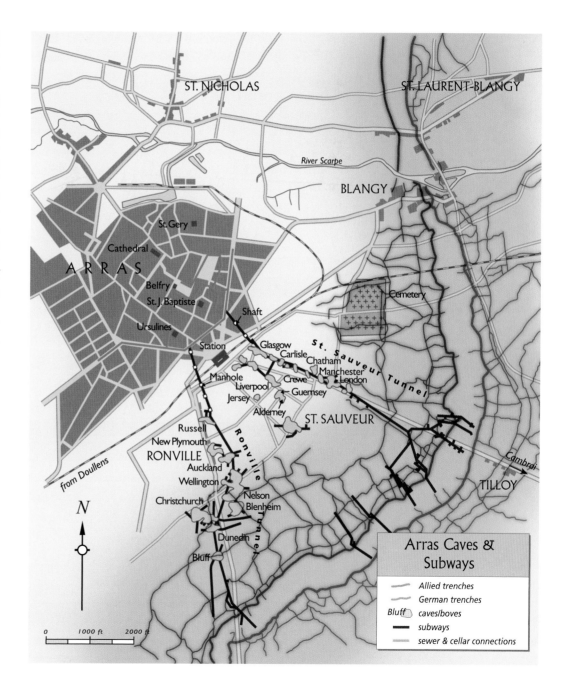

CHAPTER FOUR
Backcloth to Battle

WAR OFFICE
4 DECEMBER 1916

We are in a great political muddle here, and goodness knows what will happen. The Prime Minister [Herbert Asquith] has not kept his team in hand. They have now revolted. He has never 'commanded' them, and has sadly been lacking in decision and firmness. The trouble has arisen because certain members of the Cabinet objected to the industrial compulsion scheme we got through the War Committee on Thursday last, and the Prime Minister at once began to wobble, and once again the whole thing was thrown back into the talking pot. It is impossible to do business so long as each of 23 [War Committee members] claim the right to 'object' or 'consent' in regard to War Committee decisions. I sincerely hope they will get rid of their grievances soon and settle down or the result may be very serious.

GENERAL SIR WILLIAM ROBERTSON
TO SIR DOUGLAS HAIG

Above British Prime Minister Herbert Asquith

Left German officers in a summer shelter enjoy the British newspapers. AC

On 15 November 1916, a few days before the Somme reached its desolate close, French Commander-in-Chief, General Joseph Joffre, convened a meeting at the Hotel du Grand Condé in Chantilly. Present were his British counterpart, General Sir Douglas Haig, and high-ranking military and political representatives from other Allied countries. It had already been agreed that hostilities must continue to keep the enemy weak in body and spirit. These were left to the discretion of corps and divisional commanders; there was no need to bother Downing Street with small enterprises. Great offensives, however, demanded close integration between politician and soldier.

The Anglo-French offensive of 1916, although attaining the most meagre of Allied territorial hopes, had severely depleted the military strength of Germany. According to Ludendorff, his men were 'fought to a standstill and utterly worn out'. Between January and October 1916 Western Front losses totalled some 1,400,000 men killed, wounded and missing; just under half were Somme-related. The attacks at Verdun, designed to terminally cripple the French, also played their brutal part. The Allies were now in a numerically advantageous position, the 'balance' being almost 1.5 million men in their favour. In imperative addition, guns of all calibres were speeding from Anglo-French production lines, and a colossal stockpile of munitions was appearing, the British contribution being largely as a result of David Lloyd George's period of tenure as Minister of Munitions. For a host of reasons the superiority had to be exercised. But where?

It is important to understand the relationship between the British government and the Army during the era preceding the spring offensives of 1917, for it has direct relevance to the outcome of the entire year. David Lloyd George was all for decisive military resolution – but attrition was not his chosen route. Five months of fighting on the Somme had cost 614,105 Allied casualties for a gain of 7 miles of territory over a front of 30 miles – no part of which was of any strategic benefit. Sir Douglas Haig's statement (in a dispatch) that the battle had 'placed beyond doubt the ability of the Allies to achieve their aim', i.e. so weakened the enemy that ultimate victory was assured, angered Lloyd George. But in Haig, Joffre and Robertson he was dealing with men who looked upon attrition as the answer. During a personally successful period in government before becoming Prime Minister, Lloyd George had come to believe that the military were responsible for a 'harvest of wrong policies', and that at the end of 1916 it was Britain and her Empire, not Germany, that had been brought to the brink of catastrophe.

The tenure of his predecessor, Herbert Asquith, was enjoyed by the military simply because 'Squiff's' interference had been minimal. By comparison, Asquith was a political featherweight. After the Labour Party had been persuaded to join the coalition (by a margin of one vote), political factions were unified, and Lloyd George could select his War Cabinet and thus enjoy the powerful influence on military policy that he desired.

The Chantilly conference had laid solid foundations for an offensive in 1917, to be launched as early in the year as was possible. In his diary Sir Douglas Haig lists the (four main) conclusions of the meeting. The first was that, 'all are unanimously of the opinion that the Western Theatre is the main one, and that resources employed in other theatres should be reduced to the smallest possible.'

Given that plans were already in place when Lloyd George became Prime Minister a month later, obtaining 'adjustments' would need to be carefully made through argument, persuasion and universal agreement; without the latter any change of plan at this late stage would make the military leaders look indecisive and foolish. The task was both difficult and delicate. The truth is that Lloyd George would have dearly liked to simply dispose of Sir Douglas Haig. As Prime Minister he could indeed have done so, but it would have demanded tremendous courage. First, the British press had reported months of miserable yields on the Somme as a succession of victories: the battle was proclaimed a triumph; by extension, Haig must therefore be the hero. Second, who would or could replace Haig? No one else possessed the required attributes. Third, the C-in-C had the support of his entire Staff, men who were so deeply entrenched in their ways that they might be even more difficult to deal with if the leader was evicted. So no changes in Army Command were immediately proposed. If it was not possible to sack Haig, he must be persuaded to leave by other means.

IN GERMANY

In stark contrast to the British model, military authority in Germany was totally eclipsing the influence of the politicians. When in the autumn of 1916 the French snatched back almost all the blood-soaked ground lost at Verdun, it had left deeply wounded German prides and egos, and generated profound public concern. There were deficiencies every-

where: transport delays on the railways, lack of coal for war industries and a shortage of miners (10,000 were later recalled from the Army). As a result the most senior commanders, Field Marshal Paul von Hindenburg and General Erich Ludendorff, demanded absolute control of both policy and purse strings, and got it. Neither man carried a pacific bone in their body; their intention was to wage an 'absolute' war, a war that would cripple enemy morale as well as supply, a war aimed at civilian targets as well as military, an unbridled war on land, in the air, and on, *but especially beneath*, the waves. The decision was taken against the advice of most German politicians who, looking favourably upon the international flux and power-shifts of late-1916, were not only advocating but actively suing for peace. Things simply could not continue like this, they appealed.

The risk in waging a 'total war' was indeed immense for the Central Powers, for the book of humanitarian rules was effectively in danger of being torn up by Hindenburg and Ludendorff. To take the most prominent example, heretofore on the high seas it had been a case of 'visit and search'; in total war a vessel could be sunk without warning; without, indeed, the attacker – principally the U-Boat – being glimpsed at all.

Given the effect such a move might have upon the United States, many high-ranking German politicians predicted disaster. Foreign Minister Gottlieb von Jagow held that his country would be 'treated like a mad dog against which everybody combines', whilst Minister of Finance Karl Helfferich saw 'nothing but catastrophe' ensuing. Their warnings fell upon predominantly deaf ears. Whilst unable to fully support total war, German politicians were all

Above Body language. Haig (left) and Joffre putting their view to Lloyd George

Right Generalquartiermeister Erich Ludendorff

Above Chief of General Staff Paul von Hindenburg

Right U-Boat Captain Hans Rose

too aware that their country was being asphyxiated by the Allied blockade.

The seas alone offered the solution. Despite her exalted position in the world of commerce, if Britain could be made to collapse financially, she could no longer expect to receive credit, especially from the United States. Her peoples would experience privation, and the war effort suffer to the point of breakdown. France too would lose a great tranche of her own cross-Channel hardware needs, and of course be entirely unable herself to provision an ailing ally. So German Supreme Command decided to target *all* forms of UK-bound shipping, neutral or otherwise, and regardless of whether or not they carried civilians. The logic may have been brutal, but it was sound. German political resistance was made to wither and diplomacy was cast aside. Total war was now a reality.

BENEATH THE WAVES

In September 1916 more than thirty merchant ships were sunk by no more than three U-Boats in the *English Channel itself*, a waterway ostensibly guarded by well over 500 Allied craft. Unless the threat could be countered, the risks were colossal for the endless stream of uniformed human life traversing the waves between Britain and France.

In early October, with the United States still guarding her neutrality, the latest German submarine cruiser was anchored off Newport, Rhode Island. Captain Hans Rose happily allowed visitors to view his boat, the U-53. On the 8th he cruised into international waters off Nantucket Island, and whilst the crews of sixteen American destroyers looked on, torpedoed and sank seven foreign merchant ships. Rose is

said to have requested one US destroyer to move so he could target a Dutch merchantman. It was also liberally broadcast that he had travelled 7,550 miles without refueling. To Admiralty and Merchant Navy ears such reports were chilling. At conference, the convoy protection system had regularly been on the agenda, Lloyd George himself being an advocate. Each time, however, it received a frigid response from the Navy: hundreds of merchant vessels crossed and recrossed the Atlantic every week; how could they all possibly be protected? Sir Henry Jackson, the First Sea Lord, and Admiral Sir Alexander Duff, Director of the Anti-Submarine Division were deeply resistant, enough to make the Admiralty, who were unwilling even to experiment, stoop to massaging the facts to suggest protection was impossible: they advised that more than 2,500 merchant crossings per week would have to be cosseted by their precious ships. The number raised eyebrows at the

Shipping Control Committee, who knowing the precise situation reduced the figure to around 150. The Senior Service had 'accidentally' included lighters, coasters and other short-haul vessels that plied their trades around UK shores, voyages that were at best peripheral to the computations. The advent of total war would change Admiralty attitudes, but not before hundreds of thousands of tons of ships, valuable cargoes and their far more precious merchant crews were lying on the seabed.

Such, therefore, was the grim predicament facing and about to face the *Entente* when Lloyd George stepped across the threshold of 10 Downing Street in early December 1916. But there was a 'brighter side'. Like munitions, the supply of manpower was now under closer control and better managed, and the British Military Service Act of 27 January 1916 had inaugurated the era of conscription. Camps throughout Britain were swollen with troops in training; thanks largely to Lloyd George they were also well equipped.

With the submarine predicament fixed in their consciousness, at Chantilly Joffre and Haig discussed designs for a sequence of 'final conquest' offensives, utilizing the influx of fresh troops. For the spring of 1917, Joffre favoured renewal of joint offensive action centred upon the Somme, but with a hugely widened battle front, the British taking the sectors north of the river and the French the ground southwards to the River Oise (see pages 40–41). The attacks were to be largely British led, which pleased Haig, who agreed to further assist Joffre by taking over a portion of French line south of the Somme. After the British had made initial progress, a secondary but smaller French assault would then take place in the Champagne region.

Lloyd George and Haig had already met during the Somme offensive when the new Prime Minister had still been responsible for munitions. Given the miraculous transformation in supply of British armaments during the twelve months prior to the battle, Lloyd George had not taken kindly to Haig's criticisms about a lack of heavy guns and the variable quality of shells: British industry had performed miracles for the military and Lloyd George let his feelings be known. An indication of Haig's estimation at this time can be found in a letter to his wife:

Above General Sir William Robertson

SEPTEMBER 13 1916.

Lloyd George has been with me during the past two days; so I have been able to notice the difference in the two men [Asquith and Lloyd George].

L.G.'s visit [to the Somme battle-fields] has been a huge "joy-ride"! Breakfasts with newspaper men, and posings for the Cinema Shows, pleased him more than anything else. No doubt with the ulterior motive of catching votes. From what I have written, you will gather that I have no great opinion of L.G. as a man or a leader.

On 15 December 1916, Haig, accompanied by the Chief of the Imperial General Staff (CIGS), Sir William Robertson, attended a meeting at 11 Downing Street. Earlier in the day Robertson had assured his C-in-C that Lloyd George was 'in real earnest to leave nothing undone to win the war'. This, they would come

to believe, signified no more than a willingness to 'meddle' in strategy, matters that the military hierarchy considered outside the Prime Minister's sphere of direct responsibility. Lloyd George laid the foundations for further 'discussion' by expressing his disbelief that the Germans could be beaten on the Western Front, this despite Robertson's widespread broadcast to other high-ranking officers, both British and French, that Haig had the Germans 'very tame'. The Prime Minister was as keen as anyone to see the enemy vanquished in the field, but not at the cost that had seemingly become the norm; during the two days the Allies had sat around the Chantilly conference table exactly a month before, British divisions fighting on the Ancre had suffered between seven and eight thousand losses. Lloyd George felt that if Haig was to continue in post the casualty lists would continue to scandalize, simply because broken offensives were allowed to drag on in exactly that unnecessary fashion. If a venture failed in its critical initial stages, he believed, it should be stopped. He was ferociously determined to avoid more of what he called the 'barren and bloody tragedies of 1915 and 1916', and it was to land him in hot water in the planning for Arras.

Left An illustration from Punch showing David Lloyd George during his highly successful period as Minister of Munitions. His horses, Labour and Capital, rush the essential hardware of war – shells – to the troops

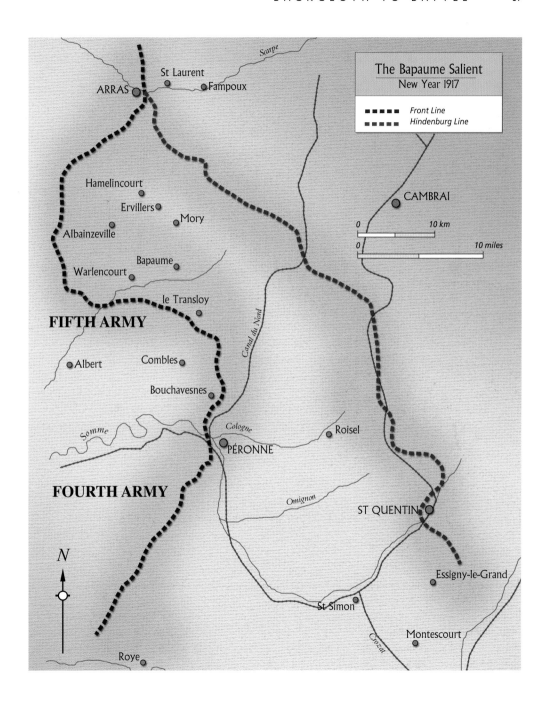

The Bapaume Salient
New Year 1917

▪▪▪▪▪ *Front Line*
▬ ▬ ▬ *Hindenburg Line*

CHAPTER FIVE
Political Prelude

Two key events were to hinder the Chantilly plans. First, General Joseph Joffre was 'moved on'. Despite several times securing a greater role for British forces, thus relieving pressure upon French troops, political briefings began in June 1916 and his influence had waned ever since. Now, the point had been reached where both the French *Parlement* and public contrived to blame Joffre for every failure from the initial setbacks at Verdun, poor results on the Somme, to the recent fall of Romania to a combined force of Germans, Austro-Hungarians, Bulgarians and Ottoman Turks. This latter was indeed a disaster, but one that could not be laid solely at Joffre's door. Through their combined disinterest in theatres beyond the Western Front, the Allies only had themselves to blame. Relinquishing his role on 26 December 1916, Joffre assumed the exalted title of *Marechal de France* becoming a powerless 'technical adviser' and no longer enjoying control over Army matters. His successor would be under no obligation to report to the *Marechal*. That successor was France's man of the moment, General Robert Nivelle.

The nature of Nivelle's elevation was almost as unusual as Joffre's 'promotion'. He too was not given complete military control, but received orders from the French government. Nivelle had been selected largely in response to the part he had played at Verdun on 24 October 1916, snatching back in a few hours that which

the Germans had taken eight months to capture. For this feat he was flamboyantly feted. Despite his age, experience and a reputation for prudence and patience, the heady combination of extravagant plaudits, both civil and military, and the elevation to command the northern and north-eastern armies (above the heads of men whom many others felt more deserving), appears to have engendered a sense of infallibility and overconfidence.

Sir Douglas Haig had grave doubts about the expulsion of Joffre, and these he openly expressed to the French political elite. Having somewhat surprisingly only met Nivelle ('a most straightforward and soldierly man') for the first time on Wednesday, 20 December 1916, Haig wrote:

Nivelle stated that he is unable to accept the plans which had been worked out for the French Armies under Joffre's directions. He is confident of breaking the Enemy's front now that the Enemy's morale is weakened, but the blow must be struck by surprise and go through in 24 hours. This necessity for surprise after all is our own conclusion. Our objective on the Somme was the relief of Verdun, and to wear out the Enemy's Forces with a view to striking the decisive blow later, when the Enemy's reserves are used up. Altogether I was pleased with my first meeting with Nivelle. He is in his 61st year. Is alert in mind, and has had much practical experience in this war as a gunner, then in turn a Divisional, Corps, and lastly, Army Commander. He is to write to me his views. Nivelle also mentioned that Lloyd George had said to him at Verdun that 'the British are not a military people'. I said, LG had never studied our military history.

General Sir William Robertson's disdainful estimation of Nivelle (and his troops) is revealed in a letter of 31 January 1917 to General Sir Charles Monro, British C-in-C in India:

The French have got a new Commander-in-Chief who seems to know what he wants but unfortunately has a good deal to learn in regard to the management of large armies. He is cocksure of success which is all to the good but is rather French, as you well know. We have got the Germans pretty cold on our front [Western] at the present time and are entering their trenches whenever we wish. Desertions are very frequent and 150 men came in during the first three weeks of this month. This as you are aware is a new feature. Along the French front little or nothing is being done as usual.

Again, Robertson can be found assuring that the Germans are fully under the British thumb. What neither he nor Sir Douglas Haig knew was that Lloyd George was soon to have meetings with the French with the goal of engineering Haig's resignation – meetings that included Nivelle.

Ironically, on the same day that the diary entry above was written, a catalytic event took place across the Atlantic. President Woodrow Wilson, encouraged by the delivery of an earnest German 'Peace Note', said that America was now being 'seriously affected' by the war. He suggested a conference to be attended by all the belligerents where each could outline their views and state conditions. The Anglo-French response was plain: the note could not be genuine for it contained no terms; the Austrians

may have a desire for peace, but Germany could only have been driven to such a suggestion by a sense of impending defeat, so neither the note nor the President's offer were therefore remotely satisfactory. Russia too would only make peace after victory. The Italians suspected that the Germans were *hoping* for its rejection, and suggested throwing down the gauntlet by demanding to see the 'missing' peace terms; Belgium was of the same mind. The British said that Germany had broken her word on more than one occasion, concluding that, 'The putting forward by the Imperial Government of a sham proposal, lacking all substance and precision, would appear to be less an offer of peace than a war manoeuvre.'

The stance of the United States thus became more and more precarious. Germany had pledged that American neutrality would be honoured. For Wilson this had been enough to keep his country out of the maelstrom (and in the process win him re-election), but there had been another reason for steering clear of conflict: the US military was entirely unready for war on the Western Front – which is almost certainly where it would be required to play a part.

THE NIVELLE PLAN

Nivelle promised to write to Haig outlining his offensive concepts. The document, which was delivered on 21 December, proposed a set of colossal but finely coordinated surprise attacks that would break the front in three places and thus end the war – a bold design that might have been much in line with Haig's natural inclinations some eighteen months earlier. Undeterred by the fact that the proposed new front was at least ten times broader than the Verdun battleground, and involved three

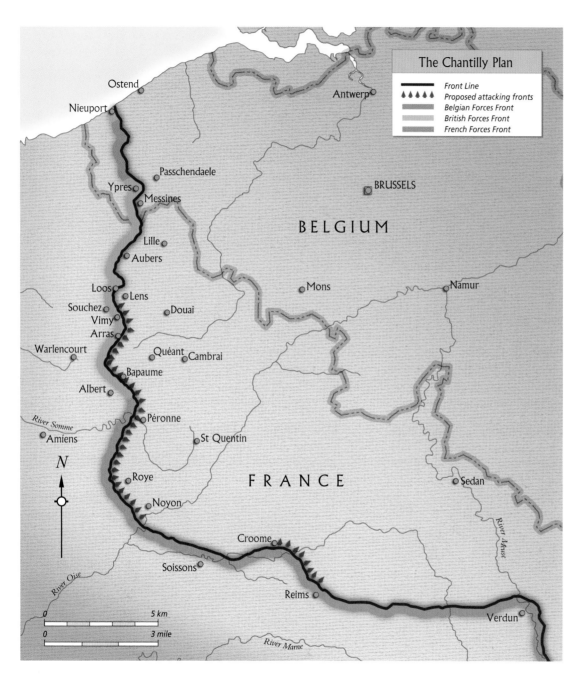

The Chantilly Plan

▬▬▬	Front Line
♣♣♣♣♣	Proposed attacking fronts
▬▬▬	Belgian Forces Front
▬▬▬	British Forces Front
▬▬▬	French Forces Front

widely separated attacks, he approached the nature of the terrain and the German defences in the same bullish way as had the British on the Somme: the artillery, indisputably now stronger than ever (which it was for every successive offensive of the war), would destroy everything in its path, leaving the infantry with the simple task of swarming through and mopping up.

As for the British, they were again to occupy German attentions *and* take on more French line – that between Bouchavesnes and Roye, a section of some 32 kilometres. Sir Douglas Haig was furious. Nivelle had only been in command a fortnight and was already demanding diminution of the original British offensive role to one of simple absorption, with a chance of following up any success that the French might deliver. It was radically different to the scheme he had agreed with Joffre.

In order to comply, Haig shrewdly demanded the return of British divisions from Salonika, fully aware that this was an impossibility because a) an enemy attack was anticipated, b) the troops would not reach the Western Front in time to be fully trained for the offensive, c) the Navy was so busy there were no ships to transport them, and d) General Sir William Robertson was in the process of coordinating the despatch of reinforcements to that very front – at the request of the French! There was a brief hiatus whilst both men pondered further.

On New Year's Day 1917, Sir Douglas Haig was promoted to Field

Marshal, a position that outranked Nivelle. Between 4 and 7 January, at a conference in Rome, Lloyd George sought definitive answers as to how the Allies were going to work as a team instead of disparate bodies.

Are we to look on as anxious but impotent spectators whilst Germany destroys our friends one after another? This is our present position in reference to Roumania. Now what, I ask, are the plans of the Allies for meeting any of these contingencies? No doubt General Gourko [Russia], General Sarrail [France, Salonika Force] and General Cadorna [Italy] has each an admirable plan of his own for meeting the contingency. But what is the plan of the Allies as a whole? The combined offensive against Bulgaria, as planned at Chantilly, is no longer practicable and so far as we know the Allies have absolutely no plan except for each General to continue 'punching' on his own front.

The questions were very fair and very necessary. Once more Lloyd George stressed that the Germans were simply too well dug in on the Western Front – even the Allies' 'triumphant' 1916 attacks had not forced them into drawing reserves from the East. If proof were required, he said, look at the ghastly cost paid for the capture of even the smallest Somme hamlet or wood. The enemy could give up a hundred such positions on a depth of 20 kilometres without the Allies gaining any strategic advantage whatsoever. And remember too, he added, that losses were made up by *government*, not military action. Were they going to allow this kind of

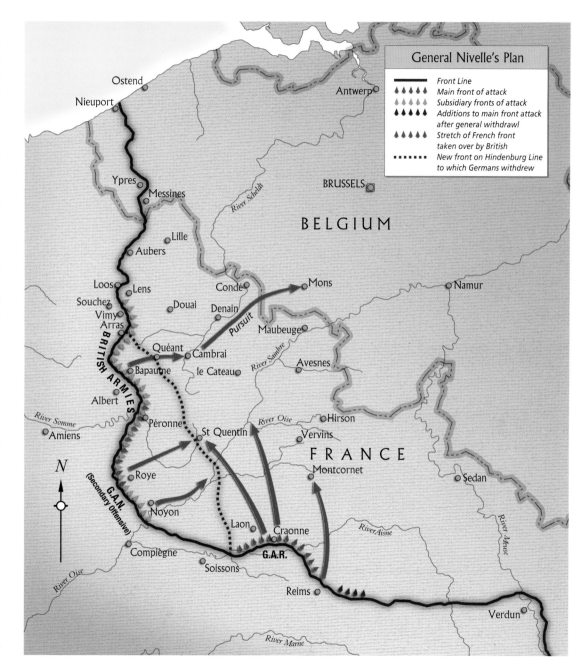

General Nivelle's Plan

▬▬▬	Front Line
▲▲▲▲▲	Main front of attack
▲▲▲▲▲	Subsidiary fronts of attack
▲▲▲▲▲	Additions to main front attack after general withdrawl
▲▲▲▲▲	Stretch of French front taken over by British
▪▪▪▪▪	New front on Hindenburg Line to which Germans withdrew

victorious catastrophe to occur again in 1917?

Action on the Salonika Front, he said, was no longer realistic; Italy was the spot to strike. Surely this was a key worth turning, for an advance of 50 kilometres here would 'reach the enemy's vitals' – Germany itself – through a weakened Austria. Italian forces were clearly capable, determined and numerous; all they lacked was support. Lloyd George offered almost 700 heavy guns.

The ideas appeared to meet with some approval, but it soon transpired that France would not support an Italian venture, and Italy had become indifferent. The British military delegation said little, falling back upon the declaration that offensive strategy had already been agreed at Chantilly and to change plans now would be too disruptive.

In October 1916 Lloyd George had requested Sir William Robertson to supply a memorandum stating how and when he felt the war might be brought to an end. The resulting document was now extremely useful. Although the British had increased their mechanical strength and troop numbers on the Western Front, wrote Robertson, the *Entente* Powers – apart from France and England – were

suffering from bad communications and defective co-operation. The value of the Entente *troops of Roumania, Belgium, Serbia, Portugal and Russia is low – in the case of Russia through lack of equipment. The enemy troops are more mobile and have a moral superiority. The duration of the War depends on the staying power of Germany's allies. Austria and Turkey are growing exhausted, and Bulgaria is weakened by its previous wars. Germany is, however, fighting with undiminished vigour, and can continue the War for as yet an indefinite period … The end of the War could not yet be predicted.*

The tenor was somewhat different to the buoyant reports Sir William was wont to liberally broadcast. Lloyd George also noted other phrases: 'The attitude of the British Empire up to the present time has been lamentable', and, 'At the present time we are practically committing suicide'. It was of course Robertson's 'undiminished' German forces that Britain and France faced on the Western Front, and were proposing to face again in 1917. Small wonder then that Lloyd George should propose offensive action against Austria, an enemy that was 'growing exhausted'.

Despite these sentiments, the plan appeared dead in the water, and the Prime Minister was tumbling into a thorny personal position.

Rather than upsetting the entire Rome apple-cart by rejecting everything out of hand, Sir Douglas Haig neatly avoided several issues by expressing the need to employ all British resources to help assure a conclusive victory *with and for the French, and by natural extension the British*, in the upcoming offensive on the Western Front – on French soil. He need have said little more. On his way home from Rome, however, Lloyd George spoke with Robert Nivelle on the platform of the Gare du Nord in Paris. For the '*Entente* team' agenda to succeed, it must have a leader – why not Nivelle? If this could be engineered, Haig need not be sacked but simply sidelined.

Ultimately, the Cabinet requested Haig to conform to the French requests. On Tuesday 16 January, he signed up to all the modifications except the projected start date, which was adjusted to 'not later than 1 April'. Both Haig and Robertson strongly sensed a hostile alliance that required careful handling. In Haig's diary entry for 7 February, one can see foundations for future political defence being laid:

I reminded Maurice [Major General Frederick Barton Maurice, Director of Military Operations] of what I told the PM before the Nivelle Conference in London, that by employing British Divisions to extend the line to the Roye road, we deprived the British Army of its chance of attacking in force and reaping a decisive success. We willingly play a secondary role to the French, that is, we are to make a holding attack to draw in the Enemy's reserves so as to make the task of the French easier. We shall at any rate have heavy losses, with the possibility of no showy successes, whereas the French are to make the decisive attack with every prospect of gaining the fruits of victory. I think it is for the general good that we play this role in support of the French, but let the future critics know that we have adopted it with our eyes open as to the probable consequences. I also pointed out to Maurice that in urging to commence offensive operations before things were fully prepared and troops adequately trained, the War Committee were incurring a grave responsibility for failure … I also told Maurice that I am going to write a note on the subject to the War Office, so that my views may be on record.

Haig's plans for Flanders appeared to be coming under ever-greater threat. Nivelle, convinced of success, stated that British hopes for a northern campaign would fall far better into place when his own schemes came to fruition, simply because the Germans would be forced to withdraw so many men and guns from Belgian Flanders, especially on the coast which bristled with 'unemployed' artillery pointing out to sea: the entire Belgian battle front would be severely weakened. If Haig agreed to wait, therefore, he could do what he wanted in Flanders with greater ease and almost certainly at a substantially lower cost in lives, and thus share in the 'fruits of victory'. But the British C-in-C was all too aware of the ticking clock – if Nivelle's attacks dragged on

but ultimately disappointed, he would be left with precious little time to take the Messines Ridge (a prerequisite for any action in Flanders), punch through the awesome German fortifications in front of Ypres, and at the same time overcome defences on the North Sea coast. To deliver an 'assured' Allied spring victory, Haig judged that to bring in fresh drafts, reorganize and supply the line, and fully train the required troops, the offensive – whose British boundaries were still to be properly agreed – could not possibly begin before 1 May. No date was actually agreed. As a final flourish, he insisted upon Nivelle's consent to a stringent pledge:

It must be distinctly understood between us that if I am not satisfied that this larger plan, as events develop, promises the degree of success necessary to clear the Belgian coast, then I not only cannot continue the battle but I will look to you to fulfil the undertaking you have given me verbally to relieve on the defensive front the troops I require for my northern offensive.

PENULTIMATE CONFERENCE

On 26 February, there was another conference, this time in Calais. Ostensibly the key topic on the agenda was how the French railways could be better organized to serve the offensive needs of both nations – a critical question. If the weekly delivery of 250,000 tons of material was not assured, Sir Douglas Haig let it be known that he entertained serious doubts as to whether offensive obligations could be fulfilled. Nivelle had already approved the suggestion that the British would not attack until transport problems were solved and boundaries and objectives fully agreed. The railways, staffed by a mixture of French civilians and British military, were permanently congested and could not possibly deal with the colossal amount of traffic demanded by two huge offensives. There were those (Lloyd George included) who believed that British GHQ was deliberately demanding more rolling stock to slow the scurry towards action, and it is true that eyebrows were raised by the British deploying half as many troops as the French, but requesting twice as many wagons and locomotives. Tellingly, it later transpired that much materiel carried by the additional capacity was destined not for Arras, but Flanders. As discussions delved into technical detail Lloyd George interrupted, saying that the meeting must now turn to strategy, and the respective commanders-in-chief needed to be totally frank. Nivelle explained his plans once more, whilst Haig again clarified the reasons for wishing to include Vimy Ridge in his tactical equation – a continual sticking point in negotiations: leave the ridge unconquered and the British left flank would be vulnerable. Nivelle conceded and the conversation moved on until at 6.45 p.m. Lloyd George requested clarification of the system of command.

In the two key accounts of the evening's proceedings, Lloyd George's war memoirs and Sir Douglas Haig's diary, certain things are included in one that do not appear in the other. Lloyd George says nothing of a French proposal that Haig's duties be restricted to the administration of discipline, deployment of reinforcements, and the establishment of a British Mission at French GHQ, but this indeed was the case.

On receiving the document after the meeting, the C-in-C was incandescent, and went with Robertson directly to confront the Prime Minister. Lloyd George explained that (according to Haig's diary) 'the War Cabinet had decided last week that since this was likely to be the last effort of the French, and they had the larger numbers involved, "in fact, it was their battle", the British Army should work under the French C-in-C's orders.'

Haig said, 'it would be madness to place the British under the French, and that I did not believe that our troops would fight under French leadership.' Apparently, Lloyd George 'agreed that the French demands were absurd ['excessive' in an another version of Haig's diary, for there is more than one], but insisted upon Robertson and myself considering a scheme for giving effect to the War Cabinet's decision'.

The following day the group assembled again, but before this took place Robertson summoned Haig to his room to show him Lloyd George's 'solution', a note which had just arrived. The Prime Minister had been induced to change his mind. The C-in-C largely accepted the fresh proposal, and required only minimal change to the wording. Shortly before midnight the final agreement was signed (opposite).

Haig, a more skilful diplomat than many believe, had engineered a settlement whereby he consented to abide by Nivelle's orders during the coming offensive, but only if a route of appeal to the British government was left open should he disagree with what was demanded of his troops. He knew that what might look to all the world like a compromise, even a climbdown, was in fact practically meaningless, for in the heat of battle no government was likely to gainsay the judgment of their own Commander-in-Chief, when ignoring such a judgment might result in the impairment of national prospects. In this way Haig effectively

AGREEMENT SIGNED AT ANGLO-FRENCH CONFERENCE HELD IN CALAIS 26th AND 27th FEBRUARY, 1917.

1. The French War Committee and the British War Cabinet approve of the plan of operations on the Western Front as explained to them by General Nivelle and Field Marshal Sir Douglas Haig on 26th February 1917.

2. With the object of ensuring complete unity of command, during the forthcoming military operations referred to above, the French War Committee and the British War Cabinet have agreed to the following arrangements:

(1) Whereas the primary object of the forthcoming military operations referred to in paragraph 1 is to drive the enemy from French soil, and whereas the French Army disposes of larger effectives than the British, the British War Cabinet recognises that the general direction of the campaign should be in the hands of the French Commander-in-Chief.

(2) With this object in view, the British War Cabinet engages itself to direct the Field Marshal Commanding the British Expeditionary Force to conform his plans of operation to the plan of the Commander-in-Chief of the French Army.

(3) The British War Cabinet further engages itself to direct that during the period intervening between the date of the signature of this agreement and the date of the commencement of the operations referred to in paragraph 1, the Field Marshal Commanding the British Expeditionary Force shall conform his preparations to the views of the Commander-in-Chief of the French Army, except in so far as he considers that this would prejudice its success, and, in any case where Field Marshal Sir Douglas Haig may feel bound on these grounds to depart from General Nivelle's instructions, he shall report the action taken together with the reasons for such action, to the Chief of the Imperial General Staff, for the information of the British War Cabinet.

(4) The British War Cabinet further engages itself to instruct the Field Marshal Commanding the British Expeditionary Force that, after the date of the commencement of the forthcoming operations referred to in paragraph 1, and up to the termination of these operations, he shall conform to the orders of the Commander-in-Chief of the French Army in all matters relating to the conduct of operations, it being understood that the British Commander will be left free to choose the means he will employ, and the methods of utilising his troops in that sector of operations allotted to him by the French Commander-in-Chief in the original plan.

(5) The British War Cabinet and Government and the French Government, each so far as concerns its own Army, will be the judge of the date at which the operations referred to in paragraph 1 are to be considered as at an end. When so ended, the arrangement in force before the commencement of the operations will be established.

(SIGNED)
M. BRIAND, D. LLOYD GEORGE, LYAUTEY, W.R. ROBERTSON, C.I.G.S., R. NIVELLE, D. HAIG, FM.

retained full command and control of the BEF, whilst – to a select few – he *temporarily appeared* to occupy a secondary station. Lloyd George was delighted: Nivelle had overall military control, at least for the time being, and Haig had agreed to report to the War Cabinet. It was a partial emasculation. Within days the entire situation blew up once more when Haig received a letter outlining French requirements. Although signed by Nivelle, it was not composed by him, but by an aide who was clearly unaware of protocol. Lloyd George agreed that it was 'brusque and impertinent' and 'couched in the tones of a peremptory order from a chief to a subordinate'. Regardless of whether he wrote it or not, Nivelle *must* have seen it before despatch. It was a stupid mistake that necessitated yet another meeting, on 12 March at 10 Downing Street. At this conference Lloyd George stood staunchly by Haig, calming the waters in both camps for this time business *had* to be conclusive. Trust was evaporating and the British were simply wasting precious time, said Nivelle. The prospect for further delay and even terminal mistrust looked gloomy. However, the atmosphere was uniquely charged by the inception of the German withdrawal (described in full in the next chapter) – Operation *Alberich*. Should it spread it might rob both Allies of their proposed battlegrounds. Later, simply by talking face to face in private, Haig and Nivelle mediated, and serious dispute was again avoided. If Nivelle's offensive plans were to go awry, after such an obvious display of intriguing and antagonism by Lloyd George it would be very difficult for the War Cabinet to object to any of Haig's future offensive desires. With this last meeting, the Arras offensive was set in stone.

CHAPTER SIX
Flies in the Ointment: the East, *Alberich* and the Leaks

I do not know whether to be gratified or not by the enemy's withdrawal from Grandcourt. I fear we may have missed some prisoners, and our carrying troubles are rather increased, but there are great compensations. We are busy trying to find out where he has gone and what he is doing.

LETTER FROM NEILL MALCOLM TO GENERAL KIGGELL, 15 FEBRUARY 1917

Left Liberated French children pose beneath a sign written by the Germans in a village vacated during Operation *Alberich*. IWM Q1904

Below Third Army message indicating the first sign of German retirement. 24 February 1917. REL

The *Entente*'s great ally in the East, Russia, was suffering. Whereas the nation's manpower appeared virtually inexhaustible, industry was struggling to provide for the 14 million men now in uniform. Food supplies dwindled and in the trenches soldiers were short of rations, lacking replacement kit, and in places even munitions and weapons. At the same time the demands of war were bringing civilian life to its knees. Famine threatened many a larger city, and for the Russian people – the working classes who bore the brunt of production to perpetuate the conflict – the phrase 'war weariness' was an understatement. Conditions were grim and outlooks leaden. By February 1917, the country was not only on the brink of economic collapse, but revolution.

On 11 March, troops were called out in Petrograd to suppress unrest. Shots were fired and a number of demonstrators killed, but it did not keep the people off the streets. Soldiers refused further orders to shoot. The people, without whom war could not be waged, industry maintained, nor governments operated, prevailed, and were soon joined by 150,000 troops. Tsar Nicholas II was compelled to dissolve parliament, and by the evening of 15 March had abdicated the throne.

The potential repercussions for the rest of the *Entente* were severe. Part of the reason for French and British actions in 1915 and 1916 had been to relieve pressure on Russia; should she crumble it would release the entire German eastern garrison to fight elsewhere, throwing every offensive scheme into confusion. Whilst the Russian drama was being played out, however, another more unexpected event was occupying *Entente* minds.

THE GREAT DEPARTURE: *ALBERICH*

Thanks to the corrosive effects of the Somme and Verdun, Germany was too weak to cling to all her late-1916 positions on the Western Front. A strategic withdrawal would reduce the line by over 40 kilometres. General Erich Ludendorff, now Quartermaster-General and effectively second in overall command, saw his plan achieving two important aims: first, shortening the battle front not only diminished the numbers required for defence, but it facilitated the establishment of a substantial 'strategic reserve' that could be swiftly despatched to counter threats wherever they appeared; second, the artillery was better concentrated. It was primarily a question of fall back, wait and if necessary defend, and observe exactly what effect the new submarine policy might have on the war, and what was likely to transpire in Russia, i.e. buy time. This could only be done from a position of maximum security, and that position was the formidable *Siegfried Stellung* – the Hindenburg Line.

Unusual German behaviour had first been noted on 22 February 1917 when a patrol of Royal West Kents reported unmanned enemy outposts in front of Miraumont on the Somme battlefield. Others noted similar occurrences and three days later the first stage of the chase began when men of the 2nd Australian Division climbed from their sodden trenches in front of the Butte de Warlencourt to move gingerly towards Bapaume. The opposing trenches were indeed empty, but from the ridges ahead a fusillade of long-range hostile machine-gun fire greeted the advancing troops. Only then was it realized that this was no retreat but a potentially very dangerous retirement. On the

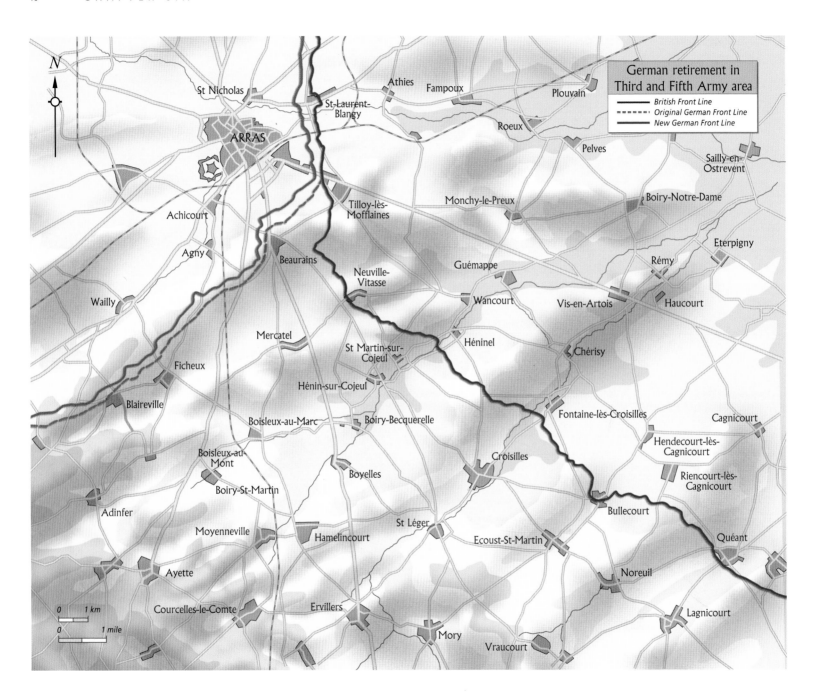

N

German retirement in
Third and Fifth Army area
——— British Front Line
- - - - Original German Front Line
——— New German Front Line

St Nicholas

St-Laurent-
Blangy

Athies   Fampoux

Plouvain

ARRAS

Roeux

Pelves

Sailly-en-
Ostrevent

Tilloy-lès-
Mofflaines

Monchy-le-Preux

Boiry-Notre-Dame

Achicourt

Éterpigny

Agny

Beaurains

Neuville-
Vitasse

Guémappe

Rémy

Haucourt

Wailly

Wancourt

Vis-en-Artois

Mercatel

Héninel

Chérisy

Ficheux

St Martin-sur-
Cojeul

Hénin-sur-Cojeul

Fontaine-lès-Croisilles

Cagnicourt

Blaireville

Boisleux-au-Marc

Boiry-Becquerelle

Hendecourt-lès-
Cagnicourt

Boisleux-au-
Mont

Croisilles

Riencourt-lès-
Cagnicourt

Boyelles

Boiry-St-Martin

Bullecourt

Adinfer

Quéant

Moyenneville

St Léger

Ecoust-St-Martin

Hamelincourt

Noreuil

Ayette

0   1 km

0   1 mile

Courcelles-le-Comte

Ervillers

Lagnicourt

Mory

Vraucourt

Left The extent of German withdrawal in the sector south-east of Arras. Most of the villages vacated between the old and new line were destroyed

*Paul Maze (1887-1979) enjoyed a most unusual military career. A French citizen, the sight of BEF cavalry disembarking at Le Havre in August 1914 was so stirring that he decided to try to join the unit. The 2nd Dragoons (Royal Scots Greys) quickly engaged him as interpreter. Maze remained with them during the advance to Mons and the subsequent retreat, at one point almost being shot as a spy. His talents were then solicited by General Sir Hubert Gough, with whom he travelled from Division through Corps to the command of the Fifth Army. Upon Gough's relief in 1918, Maze transferred to General Sir Henry Rawlinson. Throughout the war he enjoyed the utmost confidence of GHQ Staff, serving the British in a curiously mixed role of interpreter, scout and liaison officer. Very often the reliable first-hand intelligence he sought could only be found in the melée of battle itself. Four times wounded, Paul Maze was awarded the DCM, MM and Bar, and the Croix de Guerre.

same day, a patrol of Sopwith Pups of 54 Squadron returned with evidence of widespread German withdrawal.

The exodus involved the evacuation of the salient (see opposite), formed by Anglo-French territorial gains made during the summer and autumn of 1916, plus a huge tract of territory southwards past Péronne and St Quentin. To the north, it encompassed the entire line to a point directly east of Arras. It had no precedent.

Frenchman Paul Maze,* attached to British Fifth Army Command, was one of the first to know for certain that the Germans had left their trenches:

To hide their design from us the enemy increased their activity, especially at night, when they lit the line continuously with their flares and kept up a constant machine-gun and rifle fire. One night one of our patrols succeeded in getting through the German front line and boldly wandered about beyond it for a considerable time without finding a trace of occupation. This confirmed all our conjectures.

The Army Commander [General Sir Hubert Gough], who had decided on a general forward movement to probe the situation, allotted me to a battalion that was to take part in the attack. We were, if possible, to continue to advance, occupy the high ground beyond, take the village of Serre in our stride, and if no serious opposition were encountered push on to Puisieux, a village on the way to Bapaume.

The attack had to be directed by compass; each company took its bearings on definite objectives, which only with God's help could they hope ever to find. The second-in-command having returned to say that everything was ready, I went forward with him to await the five minutes' bombardment that was to precede a barrage which no human being in that mud could have followed up.

It was now exactly 5.30 a.m. We were very tired.

As the barrage crept up the rising ground in front, a slow movement from the forward men launched the rest into the fog. Picking our way in the dark, we stumbled on, and eventually slid down a steep, greasy bank, landing, to our great relief and surprise, in Ten-Tree Alley itself, the object of our attack. The trench was battered. Amongst dirty straw like a midden, British ground-sheets and used rockets, sprawled the corpses of a few Germans. Everything showed signs of recent occupation, but, strangely enough, we had made no prisoners and the front waves had gone on …

The fog grew thicker; the cold and damp increased. We were now directed entirely by compass, the visibility being about fifteen or twenty yards, sometimes less. The men kept very quiet; the ground rose gently and was strewn everywhere with German equipment; there was no sound of shooting. Now and again I got a glimpse of men in the first wave, apprehensively clustered together; the voice of the second-in-command was constantly heard bawling at them to spread out – they separated reluctantly as though their safety depended on physical contact with each other.

Nothing stirred before us as we went on. Not a shot had been fired. Suddenly we came on the first wave halted in an abandoned trench. Which was it? No one could locate it. There was an acute divergence of opinion between company commanders as to our direction. We stared at the indicator pointing north, but whichever way we looked we saw no landmark …

Some German shrapnel had so far only torn the fog above our heads, and we had taken little notice until some of the soldiers lay groaning in the mud and shouts for stretcher-bearers went up. By then our barrage was rolling away well beyond us, probably where we were expected to have been at the time. Again we came on a newly deserted German trench. As no one was in it, we began to wonder if the first waves had missed it. No word had come from them.

We passed an old German gun position completely smashed up by our guns, where nearby three

Strafsenkreuz im Plan Qu. 7607/21%c Bo

Above Segment of German panorama taken from the Hindenburg Line near Croisilles on 4 March 1917. Note the burning villages. BHK Rundbild VII 19

1. Str. Goisilles – Henin.
2. " Goisilles – St. Martin.

Boiry – Bécquerelle.

dead Germans lay facing their line, probably hit as they were running back.

We walked on a while and approached some gaunt, shapeless trees rising above dismal ruins. We were on the outskirts of Serre. We went on carefully and came to a dug-out. I looked down through its gaping entrance and saw clods of mud freshly dropped from boots on every step. A smell of mildew rose from the bottom. All was still. Farther on we came to a shattered house, where I peeped through a broken window. Roof, bricks and furniture were as one. There was not a sound except the dripping of water from a beam punctuating the oppressive silence with a melancholy regularity. I had to pull myself together to advance a short way inside the village. I hated the look of it, and so did my guide. Something was urging me to get out of the place, and quickly. Every yard I took forward marked a moment. Was I walking into a trap? I felt the enemy must be watching us all the time. As a matter of fact, nobody at that time was in Serre.

The French military and political hierarchy were struck dumb by the retirement. What did it mean? Was the invader no longer bent on defeating their nation? How would it affect Nivelle's plans? The answer to the latter took French Headquarters Staff some time to come to terms with. Because all the lines they had planned to attack were now devoid of enemy troops, would not the commander's stratagem require complete revision? Nivelle was brutally obstinate that it should not, holding to his original scheme as if nothing untoward was taking place. When the news was broken to the French nation it required careful handling.

Like a train of powder, the news spread. "The Germans are going back". Without a doubt, the enemy, unwilling to withstand the shock of the coming offensive, had preferred to retreat. How far would they go? To the Meuse?

Throughout the G.Q.G. [General Headquarters] the satisfaction was profound. But almost immediately experienced officers realized that this withdrawal had nullified the preparations for the offensive. For that morning this view worried nobody; the joy of seeing the Boche retire drowned everything. "We can still attack them at once and surprise them in full retreat", was the comment, "and so inflict a disaster upon them. That is evidently what the General will do immediately."

But the Third Bureau [Information Department – press releases] remained silent and sphinx-like. If the retreat was mentioned to them, they replied only with ironical smiles. In reality, the Third Bureau did not believe in the German retreat. An army which had given so many proofs of tenacity was not going to give so much ground without fighting for it. Was not the territory occupied by them the basis on which they reckoned to bargain for peace? Besides, they were soldiers before everything, and a soldier never abandons hope of victory. Now this retreat, if it should be genuine, would be an avowal that they had lost all hopes of beating us. Never would a true soldier, so long as he possessed men and material, consent to recognize such a thing. Such were the arguments of the Third Bureau. They forget that a retreat under certain circumstances may be a strategic move. Since we had struggled desperately for tiny patches of ground, torn strip by strip from the enemy, it had seemed that the whole of military science consisted in disputing ground foot by foot. Although I had heard it mentioned at the time of the battle of Verdun that ground had no importance, now it was declared to be everything.

Future events showed us, at all events, that the Commander-in-Chief had refused to believe, in spite of everything, in the German withdrawal. On March 15th, when it was impossible any longer to doubt the German retreat, the account from the Army stated that the enemy's trenches were everywhere empty. A few machine-gun posts had opened fire on our troops, but this had been a feint. Besides, these posts had retired hastily. The order to follow up was therefore issued to all the units of the G.A.N.

Consternation reigned among the General's entourage, and only gloomy faces were to be seen. The offensive prepared with so much care had become void. I was told to convey the impression in the communiqué that the enemy had retired under constant pressure from us, and that we were energetically pursuing him, engaging his rearguard and harassing his troops. They endeavoured to persuade me of the truth of this, in order to make my task easier, and I did not fail to believe them willingly.

JEAN DE PIERREFEU, DRAFTSMAN OF DAILY PRESS COMMUNIQUÉS AT FRENCH HEADQUARTERS

Believing that victory must surely now be at hand, the *poilus* in the French trenches were generally delighted. But consternation was still rife at Nivelle's headquarters for news had also arrived of a robust new German line under construction in Champagne – a line out of range of French guns. The great offensive – so advanced in preparation – was falling apart.

Whilst plans for the main southern assault at the Chemin des Dames were unaffected, the Oise-Avre battleground had been rendered completely obsolete. Reserve Army Group commander General Joseph Micheler, suggested (not directly to Nivelle) that an Italian venture was now the safer option, but official French communiqués entirely concealed any manifestation of surprise, giving the impression that the Germans had buckled beneath relentless Anglo-French pressure and were now fleeing with the Allies snapping at their heels. It was also this propaganda that the troops were fed. Nivelle's comments at this time still not only exuded a lack of concern, they were positively dismissive. No mention was made about plans being ruined, indeed during the coming offensive his troops would crush the enemy with negligible loss, for it was clear that all the Germans wanted to do was go home. Micheler re-expressed his

concerns, and despite disapproving warnings from a host of other generals and advisers, including the newly appointed French Minister of War, Paul Painlevé, the garrulous Nivelle simply threatened resignation and spouted extravagantly in public, thus advertising his purpose to a grateful enemy, an enemy who was managing to calmly withdraw thirty-five divisions from beneath the noses of the Allies.

INTO THE VOID

Code-named *Alberich*, the scheme was meticulously planned. To the disgust of several commanders, not least Crown Prince Rupprecht of Bavaria who threatened resignation, in their wake and over an average depth of 16 kilometres the Germans left utter desolation. Buildings were gutted, communications severed, observation positions blown up, roads mined, churches demolished, orchards hacked down, cables ripped up and wells polluted. There were booby traps everywhere. No useful resource of any kind was left intact or unsullied for British and French troops to exploit; everything needed major repair or complete renewal. It brought about a situation that made labourers and beasts of burden of thousands who would otherwise have been hunting the enemy down. For almost everyone, this was a new form of warfare that few had any experience of.

MONDAY, 19 MARCH 1917

The Boche is burning villages all over the place and it seems possible that where he burns, there he will retire, otherwise why burn? If he retires behind the burning line, he will go back beyond the Hindenburg Line (Arras-Cambrai-St Quentin-La Fère-Vailly sur Aisne). There seems to be no very good reason to think this. I think he will go back as far as the Hindenburg Line and

K'-St. Marc.

Hénin sur Cojeul.

Left to right

1. Hindenburg line wire. IWM CO3392
2 and 3. Systematic destruction: the church of St Martin is demolished, and a village burns. AJ
4. Trees cut down. IWM Q2093
5. British troops advance past a ruined orchard. IWM Q1880

1

2

will either assume the offensive, or be ready to make peace on very reasonable terms. The weather has turned out wet and there is a howling gale blowing. A nice start for our 4th and 5th Divisions and it will do the horses no good either.
BRIGADIER GENERAL SIR ARCHIBALD HOME DSO, BGGS, CAVALRY CORPS

Every night the horizon flickered with the fires of burning villages and hamlets. In these shattered places only women, children and the aged were to be found; every able-bodied man who might have assisted in the clear-up being taken eastwards – to work for the Germans on their new lines of defence. News of developments needed to be transmitted to HQs and beyond, but this proved more than problematic. Trees were felled to rob signallers of anywhere to hang essential telephone cables; almost every German pole had been felled so close to the ground that not even a stump was left to bolt a temporary 'comic' airline to; as for enemy cables, they had been dragged into impenetrable and useless masses. Whereas for years British signallers had been called upon to maintain and repair fixed stretches of line in the forward areas, now they were presented with a blank canvas, the empty landscape requiring the installation of up to 10 kilometres of wire per day. The retirement/advance often outran their capabilities, so old-fashioned flags and heliographs – visual signalling – and the newly-introduced wireless were pressed into service. Excitement was everywhere tangible, but as the wantonness and scale of the German destruction became evident, shock set in.

MARCH 19, 1917. CAMP 56, CAPPY.

Here we are still. We have not yet started in pursuit, as there is such a lot to do in the way of road-making and bridging. But we shall be off very soon now. It will be

The inhabitants of Croisilles are evacuated by the Germans: the village now lies close to the new front line. HS 06/6/28

strange to do open warfare for a bit, and rather exciting … The Huns did certainly put arsenic in the wells at Basleux, and they have left all sorts of little booby-traps behind them. I quite forgot to look for them the other night when I got into their trenches, until the C.O. sent me up two Sappers the next morning to examine the captured dug-outs. They have left stoves in the dug-outs all ready for lighting which also blew up – in fact, they have done this retreat as thoroughly as they do everything else, and in spite of all that the papers say they have had very few casualties and have lost an extraordinarily small number of guns.

MARCH 21, 1917. CARTIGNY.

At last we are really busy – open warfare is in full swing … We are already ten or fifteen miles from our old positions … We got orders to move up directly new bridges had been made, and we spent our first night in Bocheland proper at Peronne. It is a pretty large town, as you know, and its evacuation was hailed with joy. But the whole place is irretrievably destroyed, though not by shell-fire, mark you, because the Allies had purposely spared it. The fronts of the houses had been carefully dynamited on to the streets; fires were still burning, the whole place looted – even the chairs had their legs broken off. In the main "Place" a large notice was stuck up in German, "Don't be angry – only wonder at us!".

In the next village, only a small place, we saw that the work had again been systematically carried out. Not a house was standing and it is the same for miles round. The Germans must have used tons of high explosive, as nothing has been left except the bare walls. Even the apple trees have been cut down. This morning the rest of the Battalion moved up and I have been on my legs since 9 a.m. hunting for cellar accommodation for Oxfords, Gloucesters, R.E. and Gunners, until I was off my head and told them all to go to the devil.

From the two villages in front of us, to which I sent out small patrols this morning, it is reported that about five hundred civilians have been left with a day or two's

rations. Meanwhile we are waiting to push on, but the Boche has got the start of us, as we can't advance without proper roads for the guns and for supplies.

Captain Graham Greenwell MC, 1/4th Oxfordshire and Buckinghamshire Light Infantry

The aspect that caused most anger was the felling of fruit trees; rebuilding a house was not especially time-consuming, for war and destruction had passed this way before, but establishing new and productive orchards was the work of a decade.

Bridging suddenly became of paramount importance. Until now, two and a half years into the conflict, the skill had been mainly restricted to the maintenance and upgrade of existing civilian structures and the installation of supplementary but fairly mundane timber crossings. There had been little requirement for heavy bridging since Christmas 1914; now, in order to follow the enemy, medium crossings were required for 'first-line transport': troops, horses, mules, and light artillery and supply vehicles such as wagons and lorries. At the same time six bridges capable of taking serious motorized traffic such as tanks, heavy guns and caterpillars tractors were immediately required to negotiate the Somme River and Canal. Despite lack of familiarity and practice (and the trucks carrying all the requisite bolts being delayed) within a week the Royal Engineers had requisitioned, delivered and constructed five steel-girder bridges, two of which were of 60-foot span. A number of others followed soon afterwards. Those erected first were makeshift and received a hammering from traffic.

We are having great difficulties with the commissariat, as transport is difficult and there are only about two bridges over the Somme. Two or three R.E.s stand by

them night and day with hammers and tin-tacks, and every time a wagon passes over they rush forward, put in a few extra nails and let the next one go over. I hear that a whole gunner limber – six mules – careered over the side the other day and went right in. It contained all the officers' mess stuff, and for days afterwards their servants were to be seen angling for lost tins of salmon and bottles of whisky, to the joy of the spectators.
CAPTAIN GRAHAM GREENWELL MC, 1/4TH OXFORDSHIRE AND BUCKINGHAMSHIRE LIGHT INFANTRY

One bridge had been left only partly demolished by the Germans, although it was still useable as a solid base. The RE duly erected a new crossing in double-quick time, but the entire structure blew up two days after completion.

Civilians had deliberately been left with just a few days' supply of food, forcing the British and French to share rations, and thus further slow the chase. The aforementioned booby traps were a serious problem. Designed with macabre cunning and laid in thousands both above and below ground, no item however innocent looking was safe to tamper with.

Wherever possible roads and tracks were flooded by destroying culverts and drains, and diverting streams and ditches. Water supplies were ruined by the introduction of creosote, whilst occasionally explosive charges were found to have been detonated in 4- to 6-metre-deep holes bored parallel to a well, permanently but invisibly ruining this most precious of resources.

Understanding and spotting potential traps was essential. Tunnelling Company personnel – unemployed and indeed unemployable in their habitual role during mobile warfare, were detailed to deal with the threat with their intimate knowledge of explosives and the calm approach of the military miner. They found that

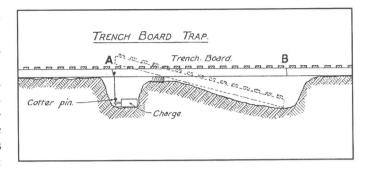

the material generally utilized was Donarit, Westphalite and Perdit. As all were hygroscopic, i.e. absorbed moisture, once a threat had been identified it could often be neutralized simply by dousing the charge with water. Others were more troublesome: obstructions in dugouts or trenches were found, each of which would have to be moved to gain access. Slight structural alterations, if they could be recognized as such, might mean traps: false steps, a loose handrail, or fuzes set in a chimney. In houses and dugouts the charges were usually set to explode behind unwary troops, blocking an exit (usually an only one) or bringing the roof down. Soon, with a grisly form of cunning, a partial answer to the problem was found.

Some of our patrols adopted an expedient which was effective if not pretty. A German prisoner became a valuable possession instead of a nuisance: since duck-boards and dugouts blew up at the first footstep, let the German tread the first. If he knew of traps, assuredly he would reveal them: if not – well, it was better for him to die than us. Several hundred booby-traps and delay-action mines were located by the Tunnellers, often moving forward in advance of the infantry. The Inspector of Mines rendered very valuable assistance by collecting information, and circulating sketches and full descriptions of any new devices discovered, so that all companies were well posted with up-to-date information. The Tunnellers soon developed almost an instinct for locating and dealing with these ruses, so that, in spite of the extremely hazardous nature of the work, casualties were surprisingly few.
GRANT GRIEVE & NEWMAN, *TUNNELLERS*

Right Bapaume Town Hall. AC

Below Makeshift British bridge crossing the Somme marshes. IWM Q1872

Prisoners confirmed that sites had been evaluated as to their likely use, and a suitable 'surprise' devised for each. Delayed-action mines were placed. The mine that destroyed Bapaume Town Hall over a week after it had been evacuated was blown by clockwork. It had been seen as a potential Divisional HQ, which of course would take some little time to be fully prepared, and therefore fully occupied. The longest delay was a bomb set beneath a railway that exploded twenty-eight days later, thus causing maximum disruption. Altogether, during the period of withdrawal, British tunnellers removed some 22,000lb (9,979kg) of booby-trap explosive. The many and varied devices invented by the Germans required careful study in order to be properly dealt with.

The employment of traps was left to the discretion of German divisional commanders, and it is true that in certain areas where officers spurned such behaviour none at all were encountered.

Direct hostile action by German infantry and artillery during the withdrawal was by no means especially great, but quite sufficient to sow seeds of doubt as to hazards that might lie ahead. Neither the Allied artillery nor truck-loads of supplies could maintain the pace of the infantry advance. Until repaired, the shattered roads would baulk all wheeled traffic, leaving only mules, packhorses and men to lug forward the essential materiel to press the few opportunities presented. It was not long before GHQ realized the infantry were in danger of pushing on too fast, and susceptible to counter-attack, so orders were issued to slow the pursuit until lines of communication had been adequately repaired: another German aim satisfied. The situation was simply weird. Counter-attacks *had* to be expected.

One night in a half-dug trench with no wire out, we heard a sentry shouting – they are coming over with white waistcoats on! Everybody stood to arms. S.O.S. rockets went up. Heavy fire was opened up and when the alarm was over it was found that some white goats *had strayed on to our wire. The man who gave the alarm was an old soldier, formerly of the Lancashire Fusiliers who was war shocked. He used to go out in no-mans-land looking for watches etc. He was sent home (war-worn!!)*
PRIVATE PADDY KENNEDY, 18TH MANCHESTER REGIMENT

It was on 20 March 1917 that the chasing Allies came to a standstill in front of the Hindenburg Line. The use of the words 'in front of' is deliberate, as ahead of the great forests of barbed wire seething across the ridges lay a deep belt of isolated strongpoints, including villages and hamlets – the 'outpost zone' that would bring Allied progress to a scornful halt. In conjunction with other British and Australian infantry units, General Gough's Lucknow Cavalry had been sent forward to oust the enemy from several villages about Bullecourt. Several days of attacks all failed, some encounters causing serious loss; it was both a warning and a rehearsal of what was to happen in the same sectors in April and May.

Throughout the withdrawal there was not an *Entente* politician or soldier that knew what the Germans were truly up to. Fresh rumours appeared each day, many of which were exaggerated or blatantly untrue, being simply designed to make everyone feel better.

SATURDAY, 24 MARCH 1917

Had an interesting conference this morning. The situation in Austria is bad as regards food. The reserves for Vienna have been finished. It has been said that Austria may be forced to ask for a separate peace. This is also said so often that I don't believe it. In Germany there seems to be a good deal of discontent. Riots have occurred in Berlin, Hamburg and Hanover. Agents say that parts of Hamburg are in flames and that the soldiers refused to fire on the rioters – that martial law has been proclaimed. This may be an exaggeration, but there is certainly something behind it.

Continual rumours are being circulated that the Germans are preparing an offensive against the Ypres salient. It is very curious as the indications as we see there, i.e. guns, work and so on, lead one to believe that there is no offensive completed. The main interest at present is: will the Boche hold on opposite Arras and on the Vimy Ridge or does he intend to retire? As far as our information goes at present, it appears to be an even money chance. If he holds on, he is once more forming a salient, the southern line being a single line of trenches and very little behind them. He is laying himself open to a rather big smack there.

Opinion is gaining ground that he does not intend to hold the Hindenburg Line. If this is the case, he intends retiring to the Meuse, fighting all the way. Once out of France he will offer her such terms of peace that she will not be able to refuse and that will end the war. Will such an end be a drawn war? I should like to see a

fight in the open with large effectives and then a Boche retreat, there would be no question about it then. I believe the Cavalry will have a chance this year. If they don't, it will be a sad thing after two years of waiting.

BRIGADIER GENERAL SIR ARCHIBALD HOME DSO, BGGS, CAVALRY CORPS

The terrible irony that infuses Operation *Alberich* is that had Joffre and Haig's original Chantilly plans been allowed to stand, and had the attack on the Bapaume salient actually been able to take place in mid-February instead of April, the Germans may well have been caught in the very act of retirement.

LEAKS

The biggest bluebottle to land in the ointment was a sequence of disastrous French security lapses.

In the middle of February, 1917, in order to improve its position, the [German] Third Army had undertaken a local operation [trench raid] on the Champagne

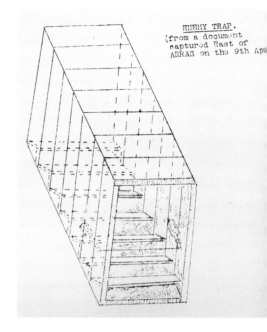

Above Booby-trap grenades secreted in a dugout entrance. AC

battlefields of September, 1915. This operation was successful. Amongst the captured material was found an order of the 2nd French Infantry Division, dated 29 January, clearly pointing to a great French offensive on the Aisne for April. This gave us an extremely important clue. Little attention was now paid to rumours of attack in Lorraine and the Sundgau.

LUDENDORFF, *WAR MEMOIRS*

At first glance it may seem unlikely that such a document would have been carried into the front line, and there is no French evidence to support the claim, but the fact remains that from that moment the Germans began to reinforce the Aisne trenches. The order did not warn the Germans exactly where or how they would be assaulted, just the general sector and the likely start date. But it was enough: by the time the attacks went in, instead of facing eight German divisions, the French would confront forty-five.

On 3 March, Crown Prince Rupprecht's diary also noted the appearance of additional intelligence. Another trench raid 'brought us into possession of the French regulation document known as Instructions Concerning the Aim and Conditions of a General Offensive. This had been implemented by Nivelle on 16 December 1916. It contained invaluable information, making it clear that this time it would not be a limited attack, but a sweeping offensive designed to break through.'

Later that same month a French lieutenant carrying documents and maps was reported missing, but the final lapse was far more serious and far more controversial, and later the subject of a commission of enquiry by the French War Cabinet. On 4 April 1917, a French NCO was captured. He was carrying the order of battle, plus the timings and details of each corps' objectives. This was ruinous, for now the Germans were aware of the entire scheme: the initial Anglo-French diversionary attacks, and the later main strike in the south.

There is no indication that the French were aware of the first lapse, but the others were immediately made known to the French General Staff. There is, however, no record of

Below The right-hand section of the gatefold panorama between pages 51 and 52 showing the open fields of fire before the Hindenburg Line wire entanglements near Croisilles. 4 March 1917. BHK Rundbild VII 19

the information having been passed on to gov-
ernmental colleagues, nor their British military
or political allies. Had these sombre facts been
presented at the time it is quite possible that the
offensive might never have taken place, for
Haig would certainly have seen it as an opportune moment to concentrate on Flanders. And
he may well have been supported by a prime
minister seeking minimalization of casualties.

The Germans, meanwhile, were augment-
ing field defences, reinforcing front-line
garrisons, and multiplying the number of gun
batteries from fifty-three at the beginning of
March to 392 by 15 April. More than twelve
divisions of support troops were made ready
for immediate deployment in the case of
French breakthrough. The combination of the
intelligence leaks and the tactical master stroke
of *Alberich* was catastrophic: it spoiled wholesale
Nivelle's plans for his *Groupe des Armées du Nord*
(GAN) for both the enemy and the projected
northern battleground evaporated.

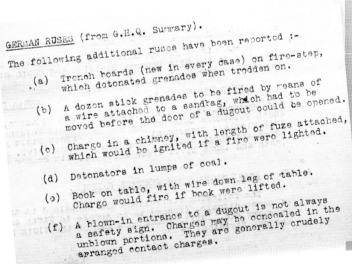

GERMAN RUSES (from G.H.Q. Summary).
The following additional ruses have been reported :-

.(a) Trench boards (new in every case) on fire-step,
      which detonated grenades when trodden on.

(b) A dozen stick grenades to be fired by means of
     a wire attached to a sandbag, which had to be
     moved before the door of a dugout could be opened.

(c) Charge in a chimney, with length of fuze attached,
     which would be ignited if a fire were lighted.

(d) Detonators in lumps of coal.

(e) Book on table, with wire down leg of table.
     Charge would fire if book were lifted.

(f) A blown-in entrance to a dugout is not always
     a safety sign. Charges may be concealed in the
     unblown portions. They are generally crudely
     arranged contact charges.

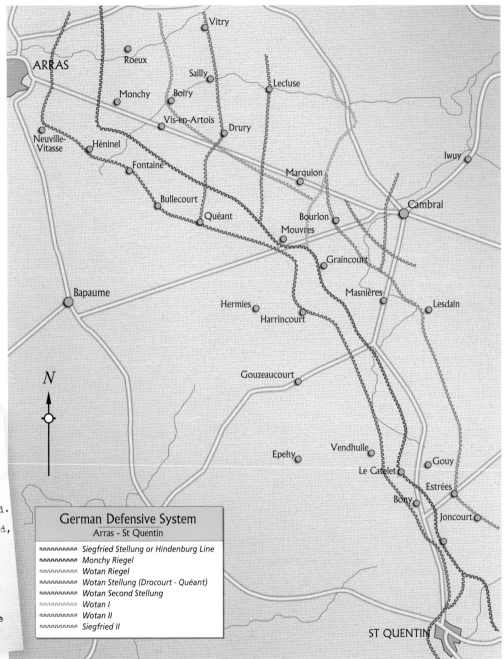

German Defensive System
Arras - St Quentin

〰〰〰	*Siegfried Stellung or Hindenburg Line*
〰〰〰	*Monchy Riegel*
〰〰〰	*Wotan Riegel*
〰〰〰	*Wotan Stellung (Drocourt - Quéant)*
〰〰〰	*Wotan Second Stellung*
〰〰〰	*Wotan I*
〰〰〰	*Wotan II*
〰〰〰	*Siegfried II*

CHAPTER SEVEN

Command and Control

From the point of view of battlefield tactics, the period embracing Vimy and Arras forms one of the most interesting eras of the war, for after more than two years of positional conflict featuring numerous actions large and small, offensive and defensive, the British and French High Command now believed they had accrued ample knowledge and firepower to break the deadlock. The Somme, with all its tactical novelties, variations – and especially mistakes – was still a raw memory to many, but reams had been written on 'lessons learned'. The Germans, too, had carried out extensive post-mortems on what had and had not worked for them in Picardy. So how would the British masters of war approach the fresh challenge? Who were they? And how would the habitually erudite and imaginative enemy choose to defend this fresh onslaught?

The Germans had drawn up a list of potential locations for Allied attack in 1917. Arras and Vimy were included, the latter especially so as it was receiving almost constant attention from British guns and the lion's share of trench raids, but at no point was it considered likely that a comprehensive assault could begin before March. By the end of February sectors such as Messines, the Ypres Salient, the flatlands of French Flanders, and the industrial Loos/Lens battlegrounds had been discounted as candidates by German intelligence. It was also thought unlikely that attacks would take place where the *Alberich* withdrawal had been at its deepest, for here it would take too long to install infrastructure. Regarding potential British action there remained two prime contenders: the Arras and Vimy sectors.

Both fell under the auspices of the German Sixth Army commanded by Crown Prince Rupprecht of Bavaria. In the opinion of Rupprecht's superiors at OHL (*Oberste Heeresleitung* – Supreme Command), Vimy Ridge was 'ripe for assault'. In early March the Germans envisaged as 'possible' a hostile thrust centred upon Arras; by the middle of the month it was considered likely, not least because prisoners captured during recent raids were offering more than just hints. Half a dozen men said they had taken part in practice attacks, others revealed that models of German trench systems were to be found in several places in the rear areas, and some mentioned the arrival of new divisions and concentrations of guns. Augmentation of British batteries was also being nervously reported by artillery observers and soon there would be notes of a 'massing of enemy forces astride Arras', including the arrival of cavalry west of the town. By the third week in March the intelligence picture was sufficiently clear to announce a general alert across all sectors between Souchez and Ecoust St Mein. Emergency procedures were set in motion: Arras and its surroundings were drenched in gas and reserves moved forward in readiness for counter-stroke.

ELASTICITY

Not the least important of these measures were the changes we introduced into our previous system of defence. They were based upon our experience in the earlier battles. In future our defensive positions were no longer to consist of single lines and strongpoints, but of a network of lines and groups of strongpoints. In the deep zones thus formed we did not intend to dispose our troops on a rigid and continuous front, but in a complex system of nuclei, and distributed in breadth and depth. The defender had to keep his forces mobile to avoid the destructive effects of the enemy fire during the period of artillery preparation, as well as voluntarily to abandon

Above General Fritz von Lossberg. PC

Right Simplified schematic of von Lossberg's defence-in-depth scheme

any parts of the line which could no longer be held, and then to recover by a counter-attack all the points which were essential to the maintenance of the whole position.
HINDENBURG, *OUT OF MY LIFE*

The German defence for most of the battle, but importantly not for the preamble and the first few days, was to be coordinated by the newly appointed Chief of Staff of Prince Rupprecht's Sixth Army, General Fritz von Lossberg. One of the most respected officers in the entire German military, he provided OHL with fresh approaches based upon recent combat experience. A calm and speedy response to crises, and the ability to restore stability and reverse disadvantage were von Lossberg's trademarks; his nickname, 'the firefighter', was both appropri-ate and well earned. Whilst with the Third Army he had reorganized defences to defy the French in Champagne, and in July 1916 when the British attacked on the Somme performed similar marvels on behalf of the Second Army. By the end of that year he had assumed the reputation of having 'iron nerves' and enjoyed the confidence of all, including the Kaiser himself; indeed, there was no shortage of admirers amongst Allied command.

But like Lloyd George and his followers, the acute losses of the Somme campaign sounded alarms bells at OHL: unless tactics were modified, the ever-growing and seemingly limitless firepower of the Allied artillery might ultimately sweep all German resistance before it. Against resolute attrition, the long-observed doctrine of

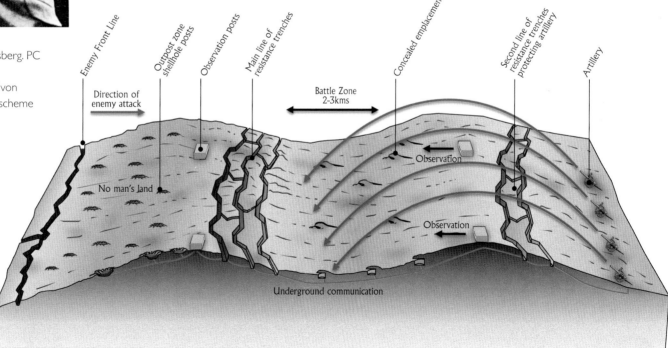

Halten, was zu halten ist – hold what there is to hold – could no longer be countenanced. Preservation of an effective fighting strength was the key and this could not be achieved without a general revision of policy. *Alberich* played its part (von Lossberg was intimately involved in the planning of the Hindenburg Line), but much more was required.

Whilst the Somme was still in full flow Ludendorff applied himself personally to imposing change. On 8 September 1916, at a meeting in Cambrai, he began the process of designing new defensive principles. Those employed at Arras were founded upon the proceeds of his enquiries and a document by Colonel Bauer and Captain Geyer published on 1 December 1916 entitled 'The Principles of Command in the Defensive Battle in Position Warfare'. Based upon French models (developed by Joseph Joffre) it rejected the principle of holding the forward line at all costs, and advocated an entirely reorganized defence that did not regard the protection of terrain as the prime objective. It was a question of operating an *offensive defence* that never surrendered initiative, that counter-attacked locally and persistently, that was to a large degree mobile, that relied upon premeditated firepower rather than large garrisons and massed small arms, and that was carefully emplaced in the landscape of battle across a broad band of territory. To this was added von Lossberg's most recent reappraisal: 'Experiences of the First Army in the Somme Battles'. The amalgamation was to form the basis for German defensive training for the rest of the war.

Machine-guns, light and heavy, were still the decisive weapon and the new system was based largely upon its efficient employment. It was in the sphere of training, field fortifications and troop deployment that the greatest alterations were made. Heavily manned forward trenches were to be dispensed with in favour of a *Vorpostenfeld*, an outpost zone of separate small but mutually supporting posts armed with light machine guns that provided warning of attacks, raids and patrols. This was situated *ahead* of the front-line trench. Thus any attack would first be slowed by unexpected fire – fire that was multi-angled, not simply frontal. Behind the screen of posts lay the heavily wired-in first line of resistance. Wherever possible it was situated on reverse slopes of hills, partly to impair enemy observation, and partly to create surprise, for experience had shown that a single protected and concealed machine gun opening fire unexpectedly from short range had a far greater effect than anticipated massed fire fired from medium or long range. To the rear of this system lay the main battle zone, a belt of open territory up to 3 kilometres deep. It was here that the Germans believed the battle could be fought and won, for the lack of cover unlocked not only the killing potential of machine guns in protected posts and fortified and camouflaged shell holes, but the potential of the artillery too, especially field guns firing shrapnel situated behind further folds in the landscape, and out of range of most of their enemy counterparts. Where topographic conditions were suitable, the battle zone should always be in full view of ground-based German observers, but entirely hidden to those of their enemy except through the use of balloons or aircraft. Front-to-rear communication was clearly critical, so stitching the entire system together was a web of telephone cables, deeply buried for protection.

The overall objective was simple: to better preserve the lives of defenders so that they

Right General Sir Edmund Allenby. PC

Below German troops training with light machine-guns. The weapon on the left is a Lewis Gun, the model favoured by the British. PC

could better defend. Another keystone was decentralized command. It may be thought that those in the forward posts were placed in an almost suicidal position, one which might encourage flight rather than fight, but careful training and selection of personnel allowed for flexibility: if hostile artillery fire grew too hot, or to assist against a heavier adjacent attack, men were encouraged to move – sideways, backwards, even forwards – and to gauge for themselves the moment when a tactical retirement deeper into the defensive zone was required. Instead of being trapped and overwhelmed in a trench, they were encouraged to fall back to pre-prepared posts and continue the defence from there. In addition, each group was acutely aware that although ostensibly 'disconnected' they were part of a wider team; to fail in their own duty, therefore, was to fail all, an attitude fiercely indoctrinated during training. Likewise, the garrisons of the first line of resistance were equally at liberty to move out of harm's way behind their trench – and of course move back in again if required. To achieve this end an enlightened and aggressive spirit was nurtured amongst troops whose stance for much of the war had been strictly linear and immobile.

Once the first line of resistance (trench line) had been overcome a hostile force was presented with a form of open warfare in the 'battle zone', ideally under complete observation, in an exposed and unfamiliar landscape dotted with hidden machine guns, under hostile shellfire, unsupported by their own unsighted artillery, without trenches for cover – and therefore supremely vulnerable. As an assault slowed, thinned and was picked off, losing shape and confidence, so counter-attacks by specially trained *Sturmbataillone* units would

throw back, envelop, or destroy it; this was the essence of 'elastic defence-in-depth': let the enemy gain ground at cost, then fling him out or annihilate him.

Although only the section of German line southwards from Tilloy-lès-Mofflaines had been rearranged to link with the new Hindenburg system, subsequent German positions on all the parallel undulating ridges north, east and south of Arras lent themselves to the application of the principles above. Much of the Vimy battleground, however, was of the 'old style' – a narrow, linear, trench-based fortress – but it was not the Allies' specific intent to push far forward here. The topography from Thélus southwards to the River Scarpe was suitable for a mixture of old and new tactics. In the meagre five months since the Somme, and despite severe economic and manpower deficiencies, the Germans had been trained, equipped and were now led according to this new belligerent doctrine.

BREAKOUT ZONE

The principal British battleground in the two compass quadrants east of Arras was the sole responsibility of General Sir Edmund Allenby's Third Army. By extending the attacking front northwards to include Vimy Ridge, Sir Douglas Haig also necessitated the employment of First Army troops to secure the northern flank. To the south of the city lay the ground from which the Germans had recently withdrawn, now lying razed and brutalized. By comparison to other sectors, however, the retirement in the projected zone of attack had been minimal, making it still possible to incorporate 9 kilometres of *Alberich*-affected' front into the plan. Action on the southernmost flank around Bullecourt was allotted to seven divisions of the Fifth Army under General Sir Hubert Gough; four of these, part of 1 Anzac Corps, were Australian.

Third Army was able to deploy sixteen divisions distributed within three attacking corps – VI, VII, and XVII – plus a reserve, Sir Ivor Maxse's XVIII Corps. Theirs was the breakthrough and breakout zone, so to exploit potential success two divisions of the Cavalry Corps were also attached (one also went to Fifth Army).

Sir Edmund Allenby had been a professional soldier since 1881. He had seen nine years of service in South Africa in the 1880s before returning to the Staff College, Camberley, where in 1896 he met Douglas Haig for the first time. It is said that here were sown the first seeds of competition between the two cavalrymen. Both served with some distinction during the Second Boer War, each emerging as colonels and continuing to scale the military ladder throughout the first decade of the century. At the outbreak of war in 1914 Allenby commanded a cavalry division, whilst Haig controlled a corps. In 1915, both were given an Army, then Douglas Haig stepped up to Commander-in-Chief, achieving the rank of Field Marshal as 1916 closed. At no time was there anything more than a professional courtesy between the two; neither admired the other, and they were never friends.

Like so many on the Western Front, Sir Edmund Allenby realized no especially distinguishing successes to separate him from other colleagues; prominence sprung mainly from his ebullience. Like fellow cavalryman General Sir Hubert Gough, Edmund Allenby acquired a reputation for an apparent disregard for loss of life. As long as objectives were being achieved, it was said by some, he cared little for the casualty count. Friends refute the accusation, citing in his defence a profound military professionalism; indeed the evidence supports this case for he was constantly seeking ways to improve his troops' conditions and chances of success, and often unwilling to commit them if the situation was not to his liking. There is little doubt amongst historians that Allenby was more hands-on than other generals; as a matter of course, he paid regular visits to the front line, and personally made certain his casualties were both secure from enemy harassment and properly cared for. Lloyd George was known to be an admirer. Allenby was regarded as a supremely competent commander and a man with an especially powerful sense of duty, a trait that was always likely to stand a soldier in good stead with his peers. It was said that once a plan had been discussed and agreed, for him it was anathema to gainsay an order. Open minded when it came to new technology, he was more convinced than most that modern weaponry, including tanks and aircraft, were likely to play key roles in future campaigns. Indeed, in 1910 he had strongly espoused the general employment of machine guns by and with the infantry, a suggestion that failed to attract the universal sympathy of the military hierarchy of the time. Above all, the impression Allenby gave on first meeting was almost unanimously positive: a most useful characteristic.

All in all, the troops beneath Allenby's control were confident of their commander. It has never been clear whether he was fully aware of the strength of the German defence at Arras, but there were clearly discrepancies in perceptions because when it came to planning the all-important pre-attack bombardment, Sir Douglas Haig was unimpressed with Third Army's fire plan. Given weeks of intense

General Sir Hubert Gough. PC

General Sir Henry Horne.
PC

preparatory activity, it was accepted that the Germans would be aware of an imminent British assault. In an effort to achieve surprise, Allenby chose to depart from the stereotype and employ a super-intense two-day 'hurricane bombardment', followed by a rapid infantry advance protected by creeping barrages. The surprise would lie in the brevity of the bombardment, for the 'normal' duration was at least a week. The enemy, therefore, would not be expecting the infantry attack at the time it was launched. Third Army thoroughly analysed the idea, taking advice from commanders of batteries of all calibres, and felt that their gunners and guns were up to the task if they were used in carefully regulated shifts.

Haig, however, thought the plan nonsensical and forced change, despite Allenby's vehement disagreement. Here, Haig showed one of his own character traits. To avoid detraction and difficult discussion he effected a strategic promotion, an act that removed Major General Arthur Holland, Third Army's artillery adviser, who had helped fashion and test the scheme, from the equation; he was offered a corps command. Haig had taken advice from his own consultant at GHQ, Major General Noel Birch RA, who said that regulated shifts or not, neither crews nor guns could sustain such a schedule, and besides, forty-eight hours was wholly insufficient for effective wire-cutting. Allenby was furious and fought on. The trench mortars were to attend to wire-cutting, and if we do achieve surprise, he argued, the troops could cut the wire by hand. But if the bombardment was to be non-stop, questioned Haig and Birch, how could observation of its efficacy be ascertained by either aerial or surface reconnaissance – would not the battlefield be permanently swathed in smoke and dust? And

what of the weather? It was to be April, a decidedly untrustworthy month: one could not depend upon good visibility. Here, Allenby had to concede a point, for he and Major General Holland had planned to carry out their bombardment 'from the map' – firing by mathematical calculation rather than observed fall of shot; it was a risky endeavour.

Haig also asserted that trying to achieve surprise was almost pointless: the Germans would be ignorant of only two things: – the exact moment of the infantry attack and the exact boundaries of the chosen battleground. But Allenby still stood fast: it was precisely that exact moment that he wished to conceal. The C-in-C was in potential danger of alienating an army commander who would be difficult to replace, and recognised that compromise was required. What about a five-day bombardment by no fewer than 1,773 artillery pieces – one weapon for every 11 metres of Third Army front? Allenby saw the way the wind was blowing and reluctantly agreed. The Germans were later to note that the duration was still unexpectedly brief.

THE NORTHERN FLANK

Having consistently worked beneath him since August 1914, First Army commander Lieutenant General Sir Henry Horne knew Sir Douglas Haig well. Partly perhaps because of a fighting rearguard action after the Battle of Mons in 1914 that permitted Haig's I Corps to escape relatively unscathed from potential catastrophe, the two men had long enjoyed a personal and professional rapport.

A respected soldier who by October 1916 had also risen from division through corps to command an army, Henry Horne was the sole Gunner of the entire war to attain such high rank; Haig's patronage may well have assisted this unusually rapid elevation. Horne too was keen on new technology and original ideas, encouraging those beneath him to think beyond accepted military conventions – men such as Sir William Congreve and Sir Ivor Maxse. The artillery being his natural habitat, he devoted much thought to devising schemes that might break the wretched deadlock of positional warfare, and during his period commanding XV Corps on the Somme won acclaim for the development of the 'creeping barrage', a protective curtain of shellfire that infantry were trained to follow across the battlefield.

In the vanguard of his attack upon Vimy Ridge, Horne elected to deploy all four divisions of the Canadian Corps alongside a smaller British contingent (24th Division), the latter occupying the far left flank, the northern hinge of the offensive front. Curiously, for almost a year before the battle, the Canadian Corps had been commanded by an Englishman, Lieutenant General the Hon. Sir Julian Byng; indeed, Byng's entire staff were British. 'Bungo' too was a listener, always willing to discuss options and suggestions, no matter what their provenance. He entered the planning stage for Vimy in just such an open frame of mind. Having served at Ypres early in the war, then as a corps commander in Gallipoli, and from early 1916 on the Western Front, he had come to be widely recognized as devoted to his men. Canadian accomplishments at Courcelette and Regina Trench on the Somme in September and October 1916 had cemented a profound attachment. It was after these actions that Byng's Canadians transferred to the Vimy sector.

Sir Julian Byng held one of his subordinates in very high esteem. Major General Arthur Currie, commander of 1st (Canadian) Division, *was* a Canadian, and although suffering from a reputation for being pretentious, haughty and even linguistically crude, he also displayed a tactical sure-footedness. The 41-year old Currie drew many a sideways look from the British 'old and bold', for he was not a career soldier but a territorial, a lieutenant colonel commanding a battalion of the Gordon Highlanders of Canada. But he was universally admired by those he came into contact with and served under, and by mid-1915 had already been earmarked as a leader.

Before Christmas 1916 General Sir Julian Byng instructed Currie to help produce the battle plan for Vimy, despatching him southwards to examine the tactics employed by French and German commanders at Verdun. Currie returned with the advice that success could only be founded upon overwhelming artillery superiority: in the creeping barrage, destruction of entrenchments, wire-cutting, targetting of strongpoints, key points and communications, and effective counter-battery fire. In his opinion, the keys were speed and momentum of attack, and persistence by the artillery, who must not only perform efficiently before and throughout the assault, but afterwards, continuing to destroy, harass and *protect* without respite until all objectives had been thoroughly consolidated. First Army was thus allocated 1,106 guns – a colossal concentration of firepower on a battlefront of less than six kilometres. With Allenby's 1,773, and the 519 with Fifth Army in the south, the total was a staggering 3,398 artillery pieces, the majority being of heavier calibre. A stockpile of 43,000 tons of shells was allotted to First Army alone, plus a further daily allocation of 2,500. Preliminary bombardments were to begin on 20 March.

Above The German Albatross scout. AC

General Sir Julian Byng. PC

THE AERIAL BATTLEGROUND

In a good photo, taken from a reasonable height, 6 to 8000 feet, and enlarged from a quarter-plate to a half-plate, it is wonderful what you can see. You can count railway trucks and engines in sidings; from their positions you can frequently tell whether they are empty or full. You can distinguish between main lines, temporary light railways, roads, cart tracks and footpaths; and if you march a dozen men across a field in single file, their tracks can be picked up with a magnifying glass. The gunners spend half their lives trying to hide their guns or camouflage their battery positions and it frequently deceives the casual glance of an observer; but if you once get a photo of a the field that they are in, you will even, in all probability, see the muzzle of their guns, to say nothing of the limber tracks along the hedges. If you make a trench and enforced it with barbed-wire, you will not only be able to see it is a deep trench by the shadows, or if it has water in it, but you will be able to see how many rows of barbed-wire entanglement it has in front of it and which way the field was ploughed.

CAPTAIN ROBIN ROWELL, 12 SQUADRON RFC

General Sir Arthur Currie

Although things were coming together agreeably on the ground, in the skies the situation was dire for the British, the worst period of the entire war. Despite Sir Douglas Haig's post-Somme appeal for an enlarged Royal Flying Corps, it was proving difficult to expand the Corps and supply new-generation machines. On the Somme Allied aircraft had been able to wander almost at will behind the opposing lines, but by March 1917 all this had changed. Having been outclassed in 1916, the Germans had made great technical strides. In the Arras and Vimy sectors a trip into hostile territory was acutely perilous, for Manfred von Richthofen's *Jasta* 11 controlled the skies. Numerically, the British were still superior, but the enemy had added twenty-five *Jasta* of superior machines to their establishment whilst the extra territory to be patrolled as a result of Operation *Alberich* and the occupation of extra French line had greatly extended the RFC's responsibilities. Although their machines were outdated, with the offensive looming there was a huge amount of vital photographic work to be done. The stolid reconnaissance craft were splendid tools for the job, but British protective escorts, machines such as the BE2c, FE2b and d, Sopwith 1½ Strutter and DH2s, were outclassed by the latest German scouts. During February and March 1917, when the greatest activity was required, squadrons in the sectors astride Arras were on average losing a machine and crew every day to the Albatross, Halberstadts and Fokkers of the 'Circus'. British pilots eagerly anticipated the new RE8, Sopwith Camel and SE5, but whilst they waited, technical inferiority meant that life expectancy was around three weeks. Indeed, in the five days leading up to Z-Day, 131 aircraft were lost, either shot down (seventy-five) or wrecked as a result of poor weather or pilot inexperience. Because of the impending offensive, however, the RFC were *forced* to be more adventurous than their opponents, seeking out and photographing targets for the artillery and potential problems for the infantry, and balloon busting. Mundane as it may seem, they were also put at a serious disadvantage by the weather, the prevailing westerly winds persistently nudging the flimsy machines into Richthofen's airspace. German fliers were seldom called upon to venture beyond the Allied line; there was no need, for to achieve their aims the British must inevitably come to them.

The new generation of scouts were to appear too late to make an appreciable difference at Arras. GOC of the Royal Flying Corps,

Dainville.
nach Wartus.
Abg.d'Amiens.
Montenescourt.
Wagnonlieu.
St.Nicolaskirche.
Gouves.
Agnez.
Str.nach St.Pol.
Duisans.
Su...

Str.nach Cambrai.
...nville.
Südl.Zitadelle.
St.Sauveur.
Bahnhof.
Arras.
Eglise des Ardents.
St.Sacrement.
Rathaus.
Friedhof.
Kathedrale.
Seminar.
Hafenhaus.
Bahn Arras-Douai.
Blangy.

Aufnahmestandpunkt: südl. Roeux. aufgenommen: 19.V.16. Brennweite: 120cm.

Above German observer practising air-to-air gunnery. BHK

Left German view of Arras from an observation balloon. The German lines are marked in blue, the British in red. HS M706 M10 Nr 405

Inset A balloon camera. BHK

Major General Hugh Trenchard, was all but impotent to improve the situation, rightly unwilling to allow delivery of the new planes until testing was fully complete. He expressed regret at the appalling situation his men had been placed in, and acknowledged and saluted the profound sense of duty towards their earthbound colleagues. Although the word 'suicide' was never mentioned, Trenchard often implied it at his gatherings, on one occasion in early April going so far as to admit that the aircraft now being used (FE2bs) were obsolete and unacceptable for purpose; he would find it difficult to take action, he added, if pilots refused to fly. They flew. As crews suppressed their fears and a growing resentment about the quality of the tools of the trade, so Trenchard was doing everything humanly possible to speed the arrival of the new 'buses'; until then, he said, the Corps must simply do their best. As Z-Day appeared on the horizon, the call for fresh intelligence became daily more raucous as requests for up-to-date aerial photographs flooded in from the various armies. Windows in the gloom were priceless and had to be exploited. Like a swarm of hornets, *Jasta* 11 waited.

IN THE SOUTH

On Allenby's right flank, General Sir Hubert Gough's Fifth Army (with elements of the Fourth) were given responsibility for the southern battleground. Their task was to attack the underbelly of the main thrust, break through around Ecoust, Riencourt and Bullecourt, form a defensive flank and drive northwards. Gough's sector was ostensibly a weak point in the German defences, for it was believed they had not had time to complete the Hindenburg fieldworks before the British appeared on the horizon. It caused local commander General Otto von Moser (XIV Reserve Corps, or *Gruppe* Quéant) to fall back upon a variation of the fixed system with a forward outpost zone. The topography, however, lent itself more than favourably to observation and defence. Sited on gentle rises, the villages of Bullecourt and Riencourt were especially dominant, the former being incorporated into the line as a heavily fortified, blockhouse-shaped salient standing proud of the line, whilst the latter, situated within the German support system, formed a formidable secondary target. For Gough to make progress northwards, both villages must fall. Bullecourt's salient was impressive, presenting uninterrupted fields of fire for kilometres to the west, south and east, much of it in enfilade. In all the villages of the area, there was ready made protection in the form of strengthened cellars and of course the ubiquitous catacombs.

What the First, Third and Fifth Armies might face by way of resistance was unknown until battle was joined. Certainly, the *Alberich* withdrawal had signalled a new and unexpected change in the way the German was waging war, but it was his propensity to shift tactics swiftly on a local basis that was most worrisome. Advanced though aerial photography and its interpretation had become, the results were incapable of revealing the plans of German tacticians.

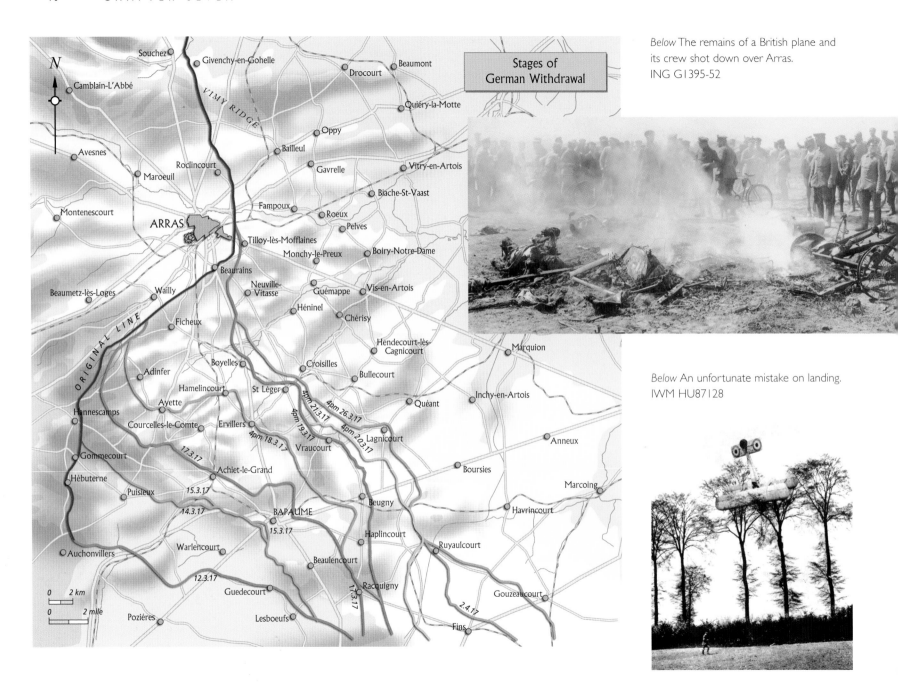

Stages of
German Withdrawal

Below The remains of a British plane and
its crew shot down over Arras.
ING G1395-52

Below An unfortunate mistake on landing.
IWM HU87128

Souchez
Givenchy-en-Gohelle
Beaumont
Drocourt
Camblain-L'Abbé
VIMY RIDGE
Quiéry-la-Motte
Oppy
Avesnes
Bailleul
Roclincourt
Gavrelle
Vitry-en-Artois
Maroeuil
Biache-St-Vaast
Montenescourt
Fampoux
Roeux
ARRAS
Pelves
Tilloy-lès-Mofflaines
Boiry-Notre-Dame
Monchy-le-Preux
Beaurains
Neuville-
Vitasse
Guémappe
Vis-en-Artois
Beaumetz-lès-Loges
Wailly
Héninel
Chérisy
ORIGINAL LINE
Ficheux
Hendecourt-lès-
Cagnicourt
Marquion
Boyelles
Croisilles
Bullecourt
Adinfer
Inchy-en-Artois
Hamelincourt
St Léger
4pm 26.3.17
Quéant
Ayette
4pm 21.3.17
Hannescamps
4pm 19.3.17
4pm 20.3.17
Courcelles-le-Comte
Ervillers
4pm 18.3.17
Lagnicourt
Anneux
Vraucourt
17.3.17
Gommecourt
Boursies
Achiet-le-Grand
Hébuterne
Marcoing
15.3.17
Puisieux
Beugny
14.3.17
Havrincourt
BAPAUME
15.3.17
Haplincourt
Warlencourt
Ruyaulcourt
Auchonvillers
Beaulencourt
Gouzeaucourt
12.3.17
1.3.17
Guedecourt
Racquigny
2.4.17
Poziéres
Lesboeufs
Fins

0   2 km
0   2 mile

CHAPTER EIGHT
Preparations

An offensive begins long before the first salvo of shells is fired. At Arras the period of preparation was almost three months – from the very date the decision was made to utilise the sector for attack. Such a colossal logistical enterprise was unlikely to escape notice, and in effect the Germans were able to watch from the air as the central nervous system was being installed.

In falling back to the *Siegfried Stellung* in the Arras sector, the Germans left a swathe of villages including Beaurains and Mercatel stranded in a 'new no man's land'. In places, the departure was discovered by patrols, whilst in others it was signalled by the enemy himself: expecting earlier British occupation, Germans guns began shelling their old lines. Quite often, however, it was simply chitchat that instigated action.

One morning there was a rumour that the Boche front line had been evacuated. I was detailed by the C.O. to go up and see what I could find out on our front [Neuville Vitasse sector], and discovered that the Germans had actually retired. Our Pioneers had got a communication trench over to the Boche line and I found that the Germans had blown up all the entrances to their dug-outs which were about every 100 yards along the front line trench. This demolition work had evidently been done very hurriedly, and in a number of instances, very ineffectively, so that with a little clearing I was able to get down one dug-out entrance and discovered that there was a continuous corridor right along the whole of that part of the front line with chambers off at different intervals. The first thing we had to do was make a rigid examination for booby-traps. I returned to H.Q. and received instructions to repair as quickly as possible the entrances with the least damage done so that our troops could occupy. I made a rough survey and found that with very little extra work I could connect the most forward tunnel that we had been driving with these dugouts, thus forming an underground connection between our support line and the German trenches. I persuaded the C.O. to put this before Army Headquarters, and it was decided to make the connection. Eventually I was able to make repair of about 2000 feet of damaged German dug-outs which connected up with the German rear lines, so that there was an underground communication between our lines and their rear line trenches. The Germans on our front had only retired for about a mile, and, in the early morning we could see them quite plainly out in the open strengthening their positions along the Cambrai road. Everything was now being rapidly got ready for the attack.
CAPTAIN STANLEY BULLOCK MC, 179 TUNNELLING COMPANY, RE

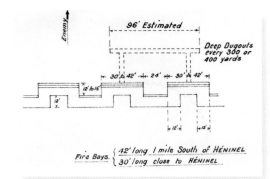

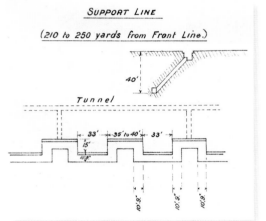

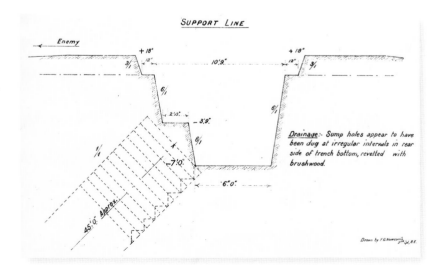

Previous page Trench raiding party awaiting the officer's order to go over. IWM Q4694

Left and below Royal Engineer drawings of Hindenburg Line trench, dugout and tunnel designs. The tunnel beneath the support line extended unbroken for many kilometres. AC

Right Typical German dugout entrance. Here, British troops check and occupy an evacuated system. IWM Q4390

Partly to identify the kind of protective work-ings Captain Bullock had found, across the entire battlefront trench raids were a common feature in the final month before battle. These miniature attacks were generally deplored by the infantry because the average casualty rate was high, more than 33 per cent, and the infor-mation gained often of limited utility. The purpose of raiding was to do as much damage as possible to enemy trench infrastructure; cap-ture documents, maps and prisoners; glean information on accommodation (dugouts and pillboxes) and weaponry; judge the extent, con-dition and capabilities of the enemy garrison; and note alterations in order of battle. Because, regardless of nationality, they usually 'sung', prisoners were a most precious commodity, and killing was deemed necessary only if capture had been ruled out as too perilous. Raids could also have a profound psychological effect: the very fact that one's enemy had managed to enter one's lines was deleterious to morale, making a garrison nervous for some time after-wards. They could be small – a dozen men – or several hundred strong, but all were extremely hazardous, with many never reaching the enemy trenches at all.

Although many a document had been

Above Hindenburg support line. Note trench width. AJ

Left RE section of Hindenburg support Line. AC

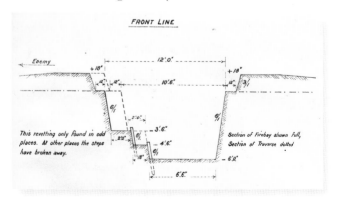

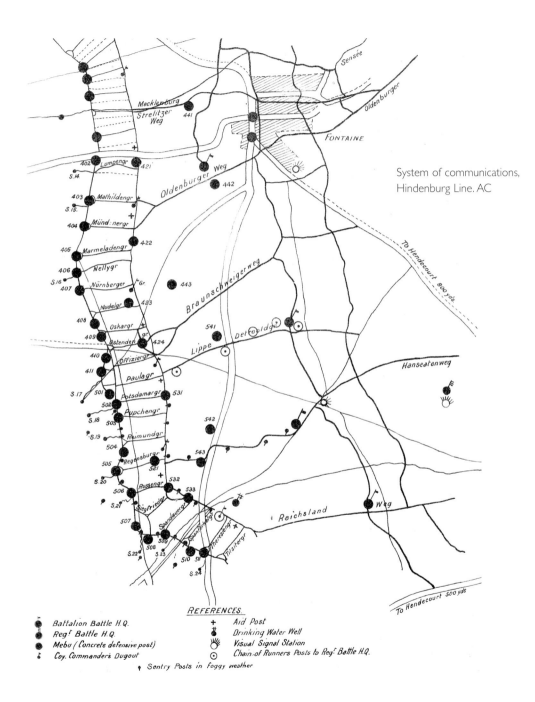

System of communications, Hindenburg Line. AC

REFERENCES.

Battalion Battle H.Q.	+	Aid Post
Reg.t Battle H.Q.		Drinking Water Well
Mebu (Concrete defensive post)		Visual Signal Station
Coy. Commander's Dugout	⊙	Chain-of-Runners Posts to Reg.t Battle H.Q.

Sentry Posts in foggy weather

found and captured that indicated not only the projected timescale for completion of the Hindenburg system, but also variations in its design, it was still essential to gather as much local intelligence as possible in order that infantry training for the attack could take the appropriate form. It was equally important for the artillery to know what kind of defences they were required to destroy, for certain features demanded the attention of certain calibre weaponry; for example, it was no use targeting concrete and deep dugouts with field guns. The Hindenburg Line was designed to be permanent and included: a host of hidden emplacements; dense and wide belts of barbed wire; an astonishing filigree of tunnels to safely and secretly move and accommodate troops; deep, strong and wide trenches; tunnelled dugouts; and underground command posts connected by sub-surface telephonic communication. During the period following the decision to construct it, every aspect of the original 1915/16 trench system was redesigned to counter the ever more devastating effects of artillery, and baulk the latest British innovation, the tank. This weapon, despite being slow and unreliable, announced the future, for once the 'bullet-proof cavalry' had been refined, and above all the machines could be deployed *en masse*, the threat was potentially deadly. Although somewhat less secure for the infantry, many German trenches were therefore modified to be marginally wider than a tank could safely straddle. Tank traps (camouflaged pits) and anti-tank guns were installed, roads and tracks mined, and trees and woods felled so that trunks lay perpendicular to the expected line of tank attack. This latter tactic slowed or stopped the machines at places where they became yet simpler targets for anti-tank weaponry, including mortars and field artillery. In absolutely vital addition, German infantry had recently been supplied with the first consignments of armour-piercing 'K' (*Spitzgesgeschoss mit StahlKern*) ammunition – a pointed bullet with a steel rather than lead core. Designed for use with standard Mauser rifles and the standard machine gun, they were more than capable of piercing the lean armour plate of the seventy machines, Marks I and II, then available on the entire Western Front.

The tank did not hold great destructive power. At this stage its real value lay in the alarm it created. Arras was only the third time the ironclad monsters had been faced, but by the end of the battle the Germans had gone a long way towards shedding the psychological fear. Because the Somme attacks, where the machines had first been employed, had gained ground, no tank had yet actually fallen into German hands. Until that time, not only was the design unknown, but there was little agreement on their true appearance.

BUILD-UP

It had been an awful winter. For weeks the thermometer sulked at or below zero, and when the thaw came at last it took nearly a month to emerge from the ground. Frost and snow returned time and again, making the pre-battle period long, trying and demanding maximum activity by all arms of the forces to meet deadlines, the first of which, it will be recalled, was mid-February. For the engineers, the permafrost-like conditions stopped all trench work and brought brick and concrete construction to a halt. Water pipes, so carefully installed, were seriously damaged, whilst storage tanks, reservoirs and troughs froze solid. As the Sappers

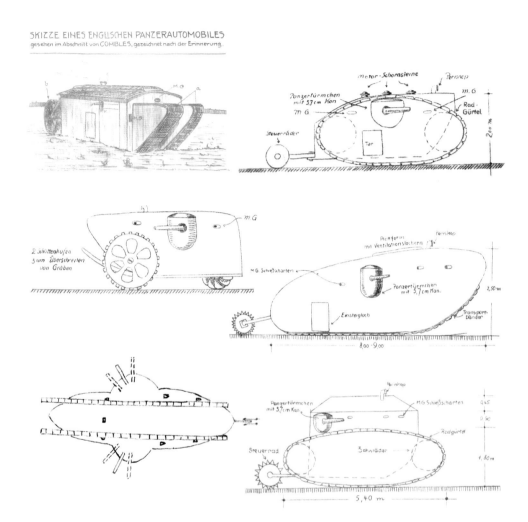

German sketches of tanks before the first machine was captured. BHK: 6 BRD Bund 16

struggled day and night with the effects of the weather, the infantry were in training. In the hinterland behind Arras, where the civilian population were still in residence and doing their best to continue the rhythm of food production, scores of thousands of troops were engaged in a now habitual pre-battle activity. Adequate tuition for battle as opposed to basic military training was one of the most difficult goals to achieve, simply because the nature of the war evolved at a faster pace than preparation could properly assimilate. The early war years and recently the Somme had robbed the British of so many 'practically educated' soldiers and leaders that there was a shortage of experienced men both in the line and behind it. Instructors with knowledge and the required communication skills were a rare commodity, and the shortage was reflected in the Staff too. The administrative tail of the Army grew at a far faster rate than the body, leaving many men, whose task was planning these great encounters, in positions of huge responsibility, but serious unfamiliarity with a swathe of new tactics, techniques and weapons. The fall-back position was simple: apply parade-ground drill procedures to practice for battle.

We had to march to Ambrines each day, a tiny village distant from Manin about five miles, where we constructed shallow trenches of two feet in depth and two feet in width to serve as a model for the purposes of practice. The earth was like iron, being frozen to some depth. Then it commenced to thaw with occasional sleet and snow, followed at last by a spell of heavy rains. Our lives were rendered a misery to us then. The fields in which we were digging were simply ploughed agricultural land so that they got into an indescribable state. As we tramped over them it was just one long, hard struggle to raise our feet one after the other from the suction of the gluey mud. All of France which we had not shovelled into sandbags seemed to be sticking to our boots.

So punishing was the terrible 'going' over those sodden fields that more than once I saw strong-looking men trembling and whimpering like kids. For days on end I never had a dry rag on me. Each day our clothes were soaked right through with rain and perspiration, our boots sodden, and before they could dry we were out in it

again all day. No fire was allowed in or near our billet, so that after cooling down on our return each day we sat tired, cold and shivering in our soaking wet things until bed time. Even then we had to lie in our wet things: the alternative was to lie naked under an Army blanket, itself cold and damp besides being stinking and dirty. All of us at this time contracted troublesome coughs which disturbed us very much at night so that we could get little sleep. A little cloud of vapour (steam) was always rising from each of us as we lay in our blankets, the warmth of our bodies drying our soaking clothes. The long drag to and fro each day, and the digging, made our feet tender and sore in the sodden state, and I suffered a good deal with rheumatism until I had worked it off each day.

The system of trenches we dug represented actually the system we were detailed to attack when the time should come. Every twist, every turn, every dugout or machine-gun emplacement was copied and correctly marked on large scale maps; each strongpoint was charted down and known to us, so that each man knew his own objective and what difficulties lay in his way to that objective. It was all very simple and beautiful in theory at any rate.The instant the General gave the signal a barrage of Stokes 11-pound trench mortars began to play upon the 'enemy' front line. In the real thing the T.M. Batteries had to dig in out in No Man's Land during the preceding night. In the practices live rounds were used and we had one or two narrow escapes when a 'dud' suddenly exploded in the middle of advancing troops, probably by being kicked or touched by someone's foot.

When this barrage ceased, the first wave, (in which I had my place) standing only 40 yards behind the explosions, started; closely followed by the second wave. This wave was called the "Moppers-up", their duty being to remain in the trench taken by the first wave to 'clear it up', killing any skulkers and investigating dugouts whilst the survivors of the first wave reinforced by the following 'storm wave' pushed on to further conquest ahead. Naturally those in the leading wave suffered, so for the purposes of practice men were detailed before-hand to drop out as casualties at a given point, the proper halts being made to time with the scheme of artillery barrages which played over the trenches and ground to be assaulted. These artillery barrages in our practice were represented by men stationed with raised flags. At a sign from the officer in charge the flags were dropped to indicate that the barrage, timed to a second, had lifted, at which instant the men who had been kneeling 30 yards behind the barrage 'rushed' forward (i.e. at a steady walk) with 'frenzied shouts', bayonets levelled for execution.

While the artillery barrages were 'on', the storming troops had to creep up, and stoop down on one knee just 30 yards behind the bursting shells waiting for the steel curtain to lift to the next trench. It was a very important point to bear in mind.

PRIVATE PERCY CLARE, 7TH EAST SURREY REGIMENT

Two of the Canadian divisions facing Vimy, the 3rd and 4th, had garrisoned the sector for months and were intimately acquainted with every square metre. The difference between these soldiers and their British counterparts was in communication. Instruction involved every rank taking part not only in practical exercises but 'schoolroom' teaching. The social chasms that existed in Britain and its army were here less marked, and everyone down to the private soldier was taken into confidence and given detailed instruction with the use of maps and models. Such practice was rare in the BEF and all too often men were sent into battle ignorant of the objectives or even the where-abouts of the enemy. The Canadians treated their troops not as a mechanical mass that reacted solely to commands, but as individual fighting units with a self-determination and initiative. This does not mean to say they were perfect – no army has ever reached that exalted

position, nor will one ever do so, for war is not predictable – but by intelligent education the troops were offered an improved chance of success and therefore survival. It must be borne in mind that even had a more enlightened regime existed, the sheer size of the British Army compared to those of its Dominion cousins made the task of comprehensive training infinitely more complicated. As the Battle of Arras loomed, the sum total of all Dominion forces was twelve divisions and one Brigade (South African); four divisions were Canadian. At this time, the British were deploying forty-eight.

It still being late winter, mud was a staple of the pre-battle period, and the infantry could march nowhere without the assistance of Sapper colleagues. Roads were a huge headache. There were few major existing routes, and as with all offensives the relentless passage of military materiel caused havoc with a granite-cobbled *pavé* designed for light agricultural use. Heavy wheeled traffic chewed it to shreds; maintenance and especially reconstruction was horribly labour intensive. Orders known as 'thaw regulations' that forbade movement when conditions were unfavourable were introduced, but nevertheless so great was the demand for supplies that many a critical highway had to be closed for several weeks for emergency refurbishment. In the First Army sector alone, over 650 kilometres of highway were repaired before the battle, and a further 160 within captured territory after 9 April. Eleven Quarry Companies and fourteen prisoner-of-war companies were engaged solely on the procurement of road metal. In the forward areas huge dumps of stone and timber were set aside, sufficient to extend selected routes (there were twelve in the Third Army area) into newly captured

British infantry working party return from a night's labours on behalf of the Royal Engineers. IWM Q1993

ground, terrain that was likely to be pulverized by artillery. These materials had to be brought forward by road, of course. In addition, the heavier the ordnance one employed, the more designed, maintained and robust one's transport infrastructure needed to be. Every piece of medium and heavy artillery had to be delivered to the battleground, first by rail, and then to its final battery position by road. And every gun had a limited range; once that limit was approached, reaching further objectives meant the weapons must be moved. Without durable roads long before and indeed during the battle, and the manpower and materiel to maintain them, guns were trapped and forward momentum compromised. That stocks of road-making materials, mainly stone, were in place before action was therefore almost as urgent as the delivery of shells themselves.

Field guns, drawn by horse teams, were the first to follow an advance, harrying the enemy as he fell back. Such weapons were light and manoeuvrable, but in the event of a deep penetration heavy calibre weapons such as heavy and siege batteries would also require forward relocation. Most were not pulled by horse or mule, but by tracked or wheeled mechanical units often weighing more than the gun itself. Tanks, too, a supreme mangler of any surface, could not be driven from Boulogne to the battle front, but required special flatbed railway trucks, special loading and unloading platforms at both ends of the journey, special depots, special servicing facilities (the 'battle' depot was at Erin), and of course functional routes to complete their approach to the SP – starting point. Being new and far from reliable, the more work the machines were required to do before action, the more likely mechanical breakdown, and the less likely their participation in battle. Movement was

thus kept to a minimum and approach routes were deliberately made as short as possible. Add guns and tanks to the almost limitless supply of other machinery, trucks, wagons, mules, horses and indeed human feet traversing this tortured part of Artois, and the strain upon transport infrastructure may perhaps be partly imagined. The most awkward sector was Gough's, in the south. Here, the German withdrawal had placed a colossal workload on the engineers, mainly Anzacs, who were required to service the battles against outposts now being prosecuted in front of the Hindenburg Line, whilst at the same time prepare for the coming offensive.

Fresh rail organization was agreed soon after the Calais Conference in January. It is worth noting what actually happened in the month leading up to 9 April. The British had requested 216 trainloads of ammunition; they received a remarkable 215. As for railway material, an equally remarkable eighty-eight of ninety-one loads were delivered. The stone requirement for roads was 206 trainloads; only 125 were provided, putting continuation of any initial battle success in jeopardy: should the initial attacks thrive and then the weather turn against the British, the results could be disastrous if roads were unusable. To the standard-gauge railways had already been added a network of lighter lines, but for an offensive on this scale yet more were needed, especially 'spurs' to supply ammunition to long-range guns that would not be required to move for a while. In these back areas, to install the infrastructure, Royal Engineer railway companies established new camps.

I was detailed by Sergeant Henderson to assist in the construction of a cook-house on the site of a new camp by the side of the railway, between a spur and the main line. A corrugated iron hut had been erected and our job was to fix up brick stoves for cooking. The first day was spent in collecting old bricks from around the vicinity. The same evening after a stroll, on the way home to the Cotton Mill, we walked along the track from Mt St Eloi to Maroeuil and on reaching the spur previously mentioned, by the side of the site of the new camp a huge shape loomed up in the darkness, which turned out to be a 12-inch naval gun on rail mountings. "There's going to be some 'doings' in this district" – and our prediction proved correct. Questioning the sentry as to whether the gun was in position ready for firing or only parked there, his answer was of a very non-committal nature. Next morning after the usual parade, presided over by the Orderly Sergeant, Corporal Ross (he of the lusty lungs), the bricklayers proceeded to the job. The 12-inch gun was seen to be manned by its crew, who were busy cleaning it. "Going to fire?" I asked one of the crew. "No, we are only resting here."

"If a Jerry plane spots that lot," I remarked to my companion, "we are in for a lively time." We settled down and soon were busily engaged in the construction of the brick ovens. During the morning the "Archies" (anti-aircraft guns) were in action and bursts were seen in the sky above us. A Jerry plane was spotted. "That's done it"! Jerry's seen this outfit. Hope we are not putting this up for him to knock down! Still, there's a war on and the troops want a cook-house. So we applied our labours again. A short time after there was a blinding flash, the ground shook as with an earthquake, and the cook-house collapsed on top of us. Extricating ourselves from the mass of corrugated iron we pulled ourselves together and found out the cause. The naval gun had started its share in the Battle of Arras, of which we were yet ignorant. Further work was suspended for the time, but on being informed that the Camp was shortly removing to the site by the gun, we had to start again with longer nails and past experience to work with.

Our usual routine was to proceed to the scene of our labours and ask the gun crew if they were going to fire. If so, we proceeded to the Y.M.C.A. Hut at Etrun for a spot of tea. If not, we carried on with the job, but watched them very closely.

CORPORAL THOMAS HERITAGE, 31ST LIGHT RAILWAY COMPANY RE

Quite how much damage the artillery would do to the landscape was dependent upon the outcome of the first few hours of fighting, which in turn was based upon the duration and effect of the bombardment. If initial infantry attacks were held up during the early stages allowing German counter-attack, more shelling would be required, and in consequence the ground would suffer over a broader area. A swift and deep advance, on the other hand, could restrict damage to a relatively thin ribbon of territory. Put simply, the greater the destruction by the guns, the more labour, materiel and time required to install a transport infrastructure that would allow the offensive to continue. A successful initial assault, therefore, was as much the prayer of the engineer as the infantry commander or gunner.

Germany's submarine campaign added a further heavy burden to engineers' preparations. Indiscriminate attacks now included hospital ships carrying sick and wounded soldiers back to Britain, so it was decided to increase accommodation in France and Belgium. Thirty thousand extra beds were called for and supplied, half for the sick and half for convalescent patients. The work was carried out by a mixture of Royal Engineers and civilian companies, with a deal of assistance from prisoners-of-war. Building the camps was in fact the simplest part of the task, for sites also required new roads, tramways, light railways, electricity and water supplies, a heating system, drainage and sewerage, laundries (the main site at Hesdigneul washed a

The big guns prepare. An 8-inch howitzer position behind Arras. IWM Q1990

million items per week), offices, cookhouses, accommodation for staff and incinerators. And of course the construction personnel themselves had to be accommodated and fed. From Arras to Calais, the resources of the Engineers, Army troops, and labour companies were stretched to breaking point.

INFLUX

No decent accommodation had been readily available for the huge numbers of troops that descended upon the sector. Just a few kilometres behind the lines villages were all still inhabited by the local population. The great depth of the *Alberich* withdrawal also allowed many refugee civilians to return once the area had been made safe.

We were billeted in the village of Blaireville. Here we occupied an old ruin, which had evidently been the quarters of some German officers before we arrived. From the cellars of this house we could walk back to their old front-line trenches in underground galleries for over half a mile without once coming on top. In fact one could go through the entire village underground in this way. The day after our arrival I noticed a French woman coming out of a garden nearby. She was carrying something in a yellow scarf and looking very pleased with herself. In answer to my enquiry she informed me that she had just dug up from her old garden the savings of a lifetime – several thousand francs. The Boche had occupied the village for nearly three years, but failed to unearth her little fortune. Many old residents had adopted the same means of secreting their money and recovered it after the German retreat. The relief of the French civilians at the retreating Hun was very marked. As one French girl rather curiously expressed it to me: "Boche partir finish wind up now."

CAPTAIN H.D. TROUNCE, 181 TUNNELLING COMPANY RE

As on the Somme, barns and any other vacant spaces were commandeered, repaired if necessary, and fitted with bunks. Mass conglomerations of timber housing and Nissen huts (more than 4,000 were requested) offered shelter for almost 100,000 troops.

It got so frightfully cold that on some days we could not carry on drilling with rifles, and we had orders to stay in the huts (which of course were unheated) listening to lectures on bombs, rifle-grenades, Lewis Guns, gas, bayonet-fighting, and the old stager 'care of arms'. Once the C.O. addressed us and entreated us to kill, kill, always to kill the Boche and to give no quarter. We were merely amused, and guessed such blather came from our bloodthirsty and valiant armchair critics and politicians at home who spent most of their time trying to convince young men that they were very fortunate in being of military age, and that they themselves only wished they were young enough to go. At any rate, we were not bloody enough men. He spoke particularly to married men, as the Council thought perhaps such men who were fathers themselves, when confronting the poor Hun asking for mercy, might think of little children who would be rendered fatherless, and consequently would not drive their bayonets home.

The huts themselves were really quite attractive (to us) at night. What I mean is that they appeared inviting to men in our circumstances, though to people unused to our kind of life they would have seemed anything but attractive. Dozens of candles lighted the hut, each man buying a stock immediately the battalion reached its billeting village and was paid out. Poor old Tommy always had to pay for his light and cleaning materials. It seemed quite cosy to be perched on one's bed, or half reclining, smoking, chatting, or listening to the jokes, songs and laughter going on all around. Generally, the conversation turned to the coming offensive. We were assured that the hitherto unrivalled bombardments of the great Somme battle were to be dwarfed by the massed gunfire now arranged. During our march all along the roads

leading to Arras we had passed numberless field guns and some huge monsters with their tractors rolling with deafening clamour towards the front. We saw some of the new 15-inch guns with their ammunition lorries. Three shells only constituted a full load for them, each shell weighing well over a ton.
PRIVATE PERCY CLARE, 7TH EAST SURREY REGIMENT

In the forward area, field companies and pioneers drew up complex schedules of work to be done before Z-Day. For example, with the assistance of infantry working parties, in eight weeks the technical troops of 9th (Scottish) Division completed the following:

· 3,000 yards of new communications trench.
· 1,600 yards new artillery trench.
· 4,300 yards of old communication trenches cleared and trench boards raised on A-frames.
· 2,800 yards of tramway cleared, track raised 18 inches in places.
· 1,000 yards of new tramway laid.
· 10 heavy trench mortar emplacements with 10 feet of overhead cover installed, with mined magazines for 200 rounds of ammunition
· 38 medium mortar emplacements, proof against 4.2-inch shells, constructed.
· 7 artillery observation posts (OPs) in Arras, and 7 trench OPs with mined dugouts.
· Telephone exchange at sewer exit in Arras.
· 1,500 yards of road cleared and repaired and three subways made for passage under road.
· 4,500 yards of infantry tracks made.
· 3,500 yards of artillery tracks made involving 35 bridges, most of which had to be strengthened.
· Overland tracks made along 4,500 yards of communication trenches.
· Pontoon bridge over River Scarpe repaired for pack transport.
· Additional water storage installed for 1,500

gallons, with a piped supply of 2,000 yards to battery positions.
· 74 cellars and cave in St Nicholas strutted, and 15 dugouts extended or improved.
· Three Brigade Headquarters made, one large enough for an advanced Divisional HQ.
· 4,013 bunks erected, 518 bunks repaired, 8 Nissen huts built and 15 cookhouse shelters erected.
· Billet made for 44 officers in a French Adrian hut.
· Brigade HQ made for 34th Division, and dugouts for 50th Brigade RFA and Signals in St Nicholas.
· Large number of articles turned out of the Divisional workshops including:
    70 camouflaged targets, 143 water carriers, 350 infantry track (sign)posts, 138 trench bridges, 260 printed notice boards, 30 direction posts, 100 artillery track posts, and 20 stretchers.

The engineers of every participating division produced a similarly impressive list. Much of the material to be stored ready for battle, such as the various types of signs for naming captured trenches and other features, direction posts for rapid erection in unknown territory and trench bridges for troops, animals and guns, was pre-prepared, brought forward, camouflaged and only uncovered the night before the attack. Note how much of the work listed was for the benefit of artillery.

In this land of little water, supplies in prospective captured villages were also planned, and material stockpiled and prepared for use. It was known exactly how many wells existed in each village. The 4th Division engineers, for example, knew that ninety had once existed in Athies, and forty-five in Fampoux. They would require finding, checking for contamination and putting into working order so that as the advance progressed water did not

A naval 'railway' gun, employed for the destruction of targets at long range.
IWM Q5217

have to be carried onto the battlefield from the rear areas – a lesson painfully learned on the Somme. Ten pack animals per battalion were allotted for the transport of water and food.

One of the most curious tasks put in hand involved another form of water. In the knowledge that roads and tracks were likely to present tasks of 'great magnitude', it was planned to utilize pontoon punts to transport wounded and other materiel on the River Scarpe. It was full of obstacles, so units were set aside before the battle to clear navigable passages. Of course, the punts had first to be made!

Although all this preparation was being carried out under the noses of the German observers, scores of chroniclers note how slight was the German response.

For at least a week before April 9th the volume of traffic in and out of Arras was very considerable. The flow was greater at night but was by no means confined to the hours of darkness. Most of it came through the Baudimont Gate, a massive structure divided by a central wall into two miniature tunnels; and there was no getting round the Baudimont Gate. The congested approaches within and without the gate, were perfect targets for shelling. By day, the road from the west was under direct enemy observation at Dead Man's Corner. There was camouflage netting on the north side at this point, but often the posts and netting were lying flat on the ground. It is quite impossible that the vigilant enemy was unaware of the prolonged concentrated movement, yet he let it pass with no stepping up of his shelling. Moreover, the constant noise of traffic must have been audible in the Hun front line, until such time as the noise and effects of our barrage made listening almost impossible for him – his planes were not grounded, however. The barrage began three days before zero and was continuous.
CAPTAIN L. GAMESON, RAMC, MEDICAL ORDERLY TO 71ST BRIGADE, ROYAL FIELD ARTILLERY

Arras's suburbs continued to receive a pasting, for it was here that German gunners believed shelling must be most profitable. With the underground work now in hand reaching a colossal scale, this was not at all the case: it was not only one of the safest areas of the battlefield, but the most recent work was taking the British up to the German lines themselves.

We were engaged on glorified Russian saps which had already been started by the New Zealanders, having been begun in the support trenches and taken to a depth so that they should have a cover of about 12 to 15 feet, and were now at a point just in front of our front line. If I remember rightly the distance between our front line and the Boche averaged a little over 200 yards, the nearest point being about 400 feet.

We were working on three tunnels two of which started in chalk whilst the other was in a kind of loamy clay, but they were all in this sandy clay by the time they reached the front line, so that there was practically no hard picking to be done and we could work quietly. There were various rumours that the Boche was mining opposite us, and though we had the usual listening time, and the men thought they heard things, I was never able to discover any signs myself. Subsequently we found that it was only a dug-out system the German had right along that front line, the sounds from which we evidently heard when we got within comparatively close quarters. We had to put bore holes with 6-inch augers for ventilation purposes after we passed our front line, and, of course, these holes had to be plugged up in day time so that the hot air could not be seen coming out of them, as this would be easily seen on a cold frosty morning, and would have given the game away to the enemy.
CAPTAIN STANLEY BULLOCK MC, 179 TUNNELLING COMPANY RE

Because of depleted oxygen levels inside the saps, 6-inch vents were driven vertically

through the roof to the surface to encourage a natural flow of fresh air, first for the tunnellers digging the saps, and later for troops awaiting the moment of attack. The same ventilation initiative had been successfully employed on the Somme the previous year, but a critical and very dangerous difference was realized. Whereas the Somme was a summer battle, Arras had been planned for winter, and during cold weather the vents turned into chimneys, the heat and moisture created by human exertion inside issuing from the vents as plumes of steam – in neat lines across no man's land! Night work could continue, but in the daytime the workings had to be ventilated mechanically. As usual the tunnellers were working against the clock.

The date of the attack remained a military secret, but early rumour fixed it at 15 April. As the subways neared completion, electric lights were installed and protected with expanded metal screens. Blueprints were placed at each entrance showing a plan of the subway including entrances, exits, battalion headquarters, dressing stations, cookhouses, etc., and infantry battalions were issued with detailed instructions for policing each subway and we realised we were approaching the climax of our work. The Tunnellers finally surrendered their subways to the infantry and the variety of units necessary to mount an attack on a scale sufficient to overwhelm positions which the Germans had considered impregnable.
MAJOR F.J. MULQUEEN, 182 TUNNELLING COMPANY RE

In the Arras *Boves*, sewers, cellars and saps, practice marches took place for all those units destined to use covered communication on the day of battle. At 8.00 p.m. on the night of 7 April, for example, the 4th Royal Fusiliers timed the various stages of their approach, from organization and leaving of their cellars to

entering the sewer, reaching the Auckland cave system, passing through it and exiting (through Number 5 exit) into the designated assembly position, Circular Trench. The progress of both the head and the tail of the column were timed so that coordination with units in front and behind was finely tuned. This was the period of maximum risk where, like the French, the capture of documents or leaking of information might lead to tremendous loss of life.

With all the precautions taken, there were no means of keeping the enemy's spies out even from the tunnel and caves. On more than one occasion we had the diversion of a 'spy hunt'. A breezy old Padre in khaki came upon us one afternoon in the tunnel wishing us good day and handing us each an English cigarette. He enquired with obvious interest about our work, what we were doing, what part in the attack we ourselves expected to take, when it was to be made, and (rather significant this) how many did we think could be housed in the caves, and many other 'leading' questions. After thoroughly pumping us and I'm afraid getting very accurate answers, he left us wishing us the best of luck. He wore the uniform of an R.A.M.C. Chaplain and we voted him a pretty jolly old boy! An hour or so later there was a hue and cry raised for this same gentleman. Great excitement prevailed, and an identification of every single individual in the tunnel at the time was made. The man was known to be still underground, and it was desperately important that he should never be allowed to return with all the information he had. Double sentries under an NCO were immediately posted at the exits with strictest orders to let no one pass out, not even a General. It was possible that he had more than one disguise at his disposal. Military Police were hurried up from Arras and a very thorough and systematic search of every known cavern began. Everyone in the caves and tunnel was organised to search, and eventually our jolly old Padre was discovered in an empty and unused cave wedged in a deep fissure

Above Traffic flow. Mechanised and horse-drawn transport are separated to allow other vehicles, troop columns and dispatch riders to use the central section. IWM Q2826

Right Underground communication around Arras' Petite Place. Note the connection between cellars and sewers at right. REL

in the chalk. His wig and make-up taken from him he would not be recognised as the man who had spoken to us in Chaplain's guise earlier in the afternoon.
PRIVATE PERCY CLARE, 7TH EAST SURREY REGIMENT

For ten days reliefs took place, the units selected for the assault leaving villages and hamlets in the rear areas and swarming into the city to take up residence beneath. A film cameraman and his assistant joined them, intending to capture the pre-battle atmosphere as well as the instant of the great attack. As always, the strange exhilaration and anticipation that comes with facing the unknown was in the air.

The day had been sunny but bitterly cold. The men were in very good spirits, anxious to go in, get it over, and come back again (if still alive) to rest. We all knew that some who marched out would never march back, but each of course thought this only of the other man. On the road we passed troops coming in the opposite direction to occupy the very huts we had left. They could afford to be cheerful and wish us 'the best of luck' in passing.

Long queues of motor lorries and General Service wagons laden with ammunition, picks, spades, barbed-wire and all sorts of paraphernalia for trench-making, and – most significant – hundreds of scaling ladders seen only in trenches in a big attack. Red Cross wagons full of stretchers caused much joking and laughing ("That's mine", says someone, "I always travel Pullman – easy-like!") As we progressed the traffic grew ever more congested. Fortunately no shell came over and we had the satisfaction of sighting at last the well-known archway called Baudimont Gate, which gave entrance to the city of Arras, without a single casualty. If the Boche had known of that five mile stretch of piled up vehicles of war and the thousands of waiting men, what a glorious opportunity he would have grasped of pulverising them, and what slaughter would have ensued. But he didn't.

A guide met each platoon and conducted it to its appointed billet in the vaults and caves over which the city is built. We took up our quarters, the old well-known ones underneath the wrecked museum, adjoining the ruins of the cathedral. They were pitch dark, damp, dirty and smelt strongly of age-old rat warrens, decay and rubbish, but from the beams and rotting timbers lying around we soon got a fire going which made it look more habitable; with all its unhealthiness it became a warm and welcome home to us. We were glad to be there.
PRIVATE PERCY CLARE, 7TH EAST SURREY REGIMENT

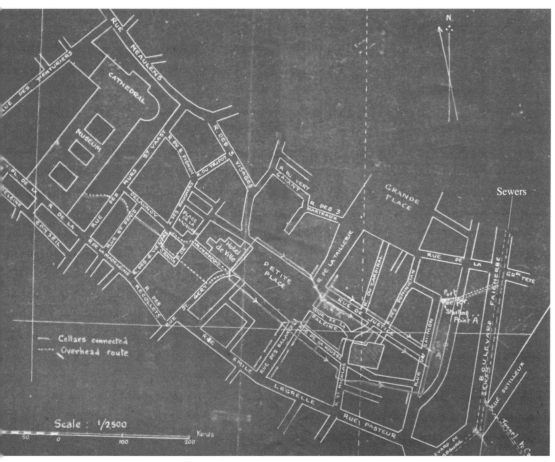

CHAPTER NINE
Countdown

Sir Douglas Haig was able to deploy four-teen divisions on the first day at Arras, precisely the same number as on 1 July 1916. In order to avoid a repeat of that event – a no man's land carpeted with British dead and wounded – the hugely augmented artillery with an almost unlimited supply of ammunition had to be employed in a different way. Like the Somme it was still required to pulverize trenches and destroy the sanctuary of shallow cover and dugouts, but much more importantly the era of the creeping barrage had now fully arrived. In 1917 an attack was being taught to, as 1st Canadian Divisional Commander, Major General Arthur Currie put it: 'follow the bar-rage as closely as a horse will follow a nosebag filled with corn' – in reality no more than 50 metres behind the curtain of shells. Only in this

One day, during the last week of March, we received our orders. As every movement was to be shrouded in secrecy, we did not even emerge from our cellars, lest the Germans might see us from the air. Instead we crept along them, passing from one to another, through holes knocked in the walls. Presently we came to some steps down. At the bottom we found ourselves in a large circular tunnel. A gangway of boards ran along one side of this electrically-lit passage, while along the bottom flowed a stream of water. We were in fact in the main drain of Arras. The war was full of queer experiences: but we had never imagined that we should be going into battle down the drain.

For a mile or so we trudged along this drain, emerging at length, much as Aladdin emerged, into a vast cave; only here the light was reflected not by jewels but by chalk. The caves (for there was a series of them) were fitted with every modern convenience: electric light, running water, braziers for cooking, a miniature railway and even furniture, though this consisted mostly of empty crates and petrol cans.

Here, in these caves, we lived for over a week. No sound reached us from the outer world. Very occasionally a small chip of chalk would drop from the roof, sign that a heavy shell had landed overhead.

From time to time we climbed to one of the exits debouching into the reserve trenches and took the air. From this part of the line we had a good view of the German positions and also of the effects of our non-stop bombardment. As far as we could see to the north and to the south, the German trenches were being pounded out of recognition. Great towers of earth were being flung up all along the eastern skyline and the air was full of whirring iron. Not much was coming from the German side.

LIEUTENANT ALAN THOMAS, 6TH QUEEN'S OWN (ROYAL WEST KENT REGIMENT)

YELLOW CROSS

BLUE CROSS

EHZ.17.

HZ.95.

GERMAN 10·5 cm HOWITZER
BLUE CROSS SHELL

FILLED:–
DIPHENYLCHLORARSINE – 413 gm.
BURSTING CHARGE :–
PICRIC ACID AND T.N.T.

YELLOW CROSS SHELL

FILLED:–
DICHLORETHYL SULPHIDE – 1360 ccs.
BURSTING CHARGE :–
PICRIC ACID – 23 gms.
MAX. RANGE – 7000

'T' SHELL

LACHRYMATORY SHELL
'K' SHELL

1. PARAFFIN WAX
2. LEAD RECEPTACLE
   FILLED:–
   BENZYL BROMIDE

KZ.14.

GERMAN 7·7cm GUN
UNIVERSAL PATTERN 1915

MAX. RANGE – 10000

FILLED
DIPHOSGENE – 317 ccs.

BURSTING CHARGE :–
PICRIC ACID

EKZ.16

EKZ.17.

BLUE CROSS SHELL

FILLED:–
DIPHENYLCHLORARSINE – 124 gms.

BURSTING CHARGE :–
PICRIC ACID AND T.N.T.

7·5 cm
LWM Zdr.

TEAR GAS

VOLUME 460 ccs.

Below A 'blind' British shell embedded in a wall at Blangy. AJ

Bottom Types of German gas shells. IWM Docs. 85/23/1

way could the infantry reach the enemy before hostile machine guns were brought into action. The closer one followed the curtain, of course, the greater the chance of injury through 'friendly fire', but as a result of the intensive training of gunners and infantry the risk of wholesale sacrifice should be dramatically reduced. Defective shells were something over which the gunners had no control. The problem had once been a serious one, but now manufacture and inspection had improved to the point where 'duds' were becoming rare. A shell was more likely to fail through faulty fuze-setting or adverse ground conditions than malfunctions traceable to munitions factories. It did not rule out bad batches.

Just before the Vimy show we had a lot of bad ammunition. A large percentage of our time-fuses were defective. With one of the bad fuses the shell burst at the muzzle of the gun instead of over the target [these are shrapnel shells]. That meant that the air in front of the gun was filled with a pint or so of shrapnel bullets about the size of small marbles travelling at the speed of muzzle velocity of the gun plus the momentum provided by the burst. In that cloud of lead there were also the big brass fuse that had malfunctioned to cause the premature burst, *and the shell-case. We ourselves were in a very unpleasant position. We were in the front row of seven lines of guns, and there were six batteries behind us firing prematures at us. All day and night the air above us was filled with the whine of shrapnel bullets from premature bursts and the howl of fuses and shell-cases. The only real protection we built in that position was in the form of thick sandbag walls behind the guns to keep out our own shrapnel.*
GUNNER C. BLACK, CANADIAN FIELD ARTILLERY

THE GUNS

The bombardment phase was intricately planned. On the Vimy heights the narrowness of the battleground meant that specific management was required: here, the German positions were to be subjected to utter annihilation.

Further south, the suitability, selection and treatment of targets was judged not by GHQ or Army, but by corps and divisional commanders taking advice from subordinates with an intimate acquaintance with their sector.

The artillery was divided into two types: guns and howitzers. 'Light' guns, 13- or 18-pounders, were quick-firing and employed for creeping barrages, wire-cutting (with shrapnel),

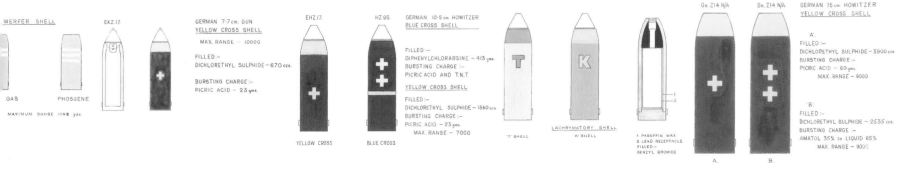

'raking' communication trenches and 'searching' areas with shrapnel; they were a highly effective anti-personnel weapon and could be used over open sights (on open ground as opposed to in gun pits) to fire at visible targets. These weapons and 13-pounder Horse Artillery (attached to the cavalry) were first to follow the infantry advance. The 4.7-inch or 60-pounders were classed as medium guns (in effect large field guns) and employed in a similar fashion to their smaller cousins. Greater range meant they could also be used to bombard communications centres, railways and roads with either shrapnel or high explosive. Heavy guns of the 6-, 9.2- or 12-inch variety had far longer ranges, to 15 kilometres and beyond, bringing observation balloons, villages and towns, dumps, railways and sidings into the equation. The key role of these 'heavies' was counter-battery work.

Howitzers were light – 4.5-inch and medium – 6-inch, both of which were mobile weapons, and drawn by animals. The heavier 8- and 9.2-inch, and super heavy 12 and 15-inch weapons required mechanical transportation. Although a more effective weapon against trenches because of their high arcing trajectory, a howitzer's role often overlapped that of the guns, but in general the medium to super-heavies were employed solely upon destruction of trenches, wire, strongpoints, gun-batteries and concrete emplacements. In addition, many of the medium and light weapons were capable of firing gas shells.

Wire-cutting was assisted by the new 106 'instantaneous' fuse that caused a shell to burst the very moment its nose-cap touched the earth, the fragments flying laterally to carry away entanglements.

To this category one might also add trench

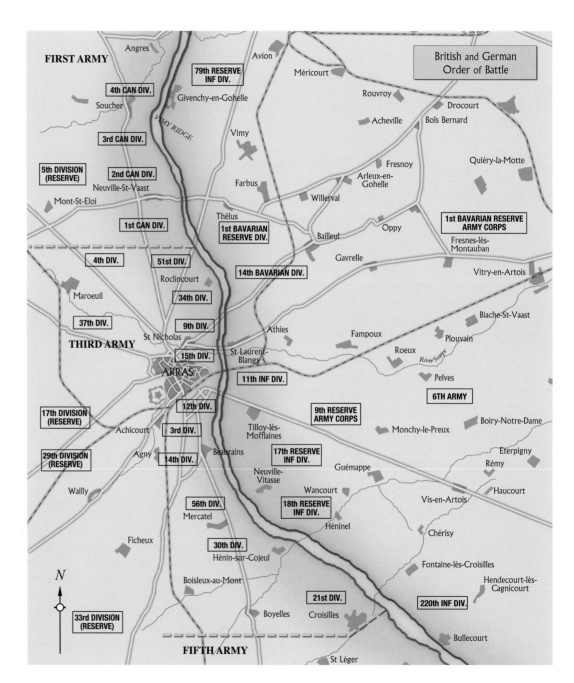

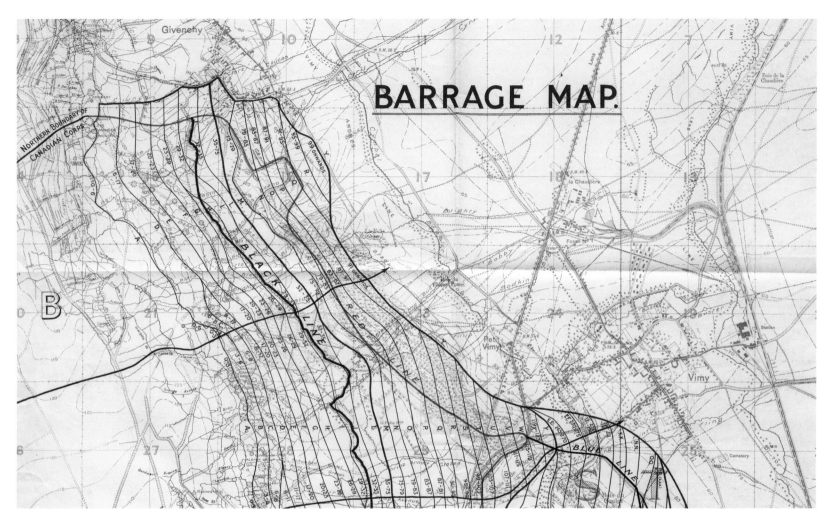

Above Section of a creeping barrage plan for the Vimy assaults. NA WO95-3884

mortar sections, a specialist organisation whose role was growing ever more important, not only for harassment and destruction (wire especially), but as a highly mobile means of delivering rapid fire to help overcome strongpoints, either in a trench line or in open ground, and for short-range incendiary and smoke work. One of the lessons learned on the Somme was that mortars could be incorporated into a tactic known as 'fire and movement', where Lewis machine guns and rifle grenadiers were employed to keep enemy heads down whilst parties of infantry and bombers infiltrated and neutralized. The basic types were light, Stokes 3-inch with a range of 350 metres, and medium, 2-inch firing up to 600 metres;

both were mobile. The heavy version, a 9.45-inch 'aerial torpedo', had a range of over a kilometre and was mainly employed for wire-cutting and general destruction. Both mortars and artillery had been made available in unprecedented quantities. Indeed, for the streams of infantry entering the battle zone, passing through the various gun lines was a heartening experience, and the affect upon morale – even at a distance – marked.

Montenescourt was about 10 miles from Arras, and it afforded us some idea of what the bombardment was to be on the sector to watch the gun flashes at night with the rumble of distant gunfire, ominous and continuous, in our ears. And at this time it was only the ordinary bombardment, not the real 'intense' bombardment. Several times a night we were awakened by the sound of the drumming of concentrated artillery, a sound never to be forgotten. The horizon towards the enemy line was aflame with flickering flashes like continuous lightning, marvellous to see, while the tremendous sound, vibrating the air where we stood ten miles away, filled one with awe. I used to stand with the gas sentry, both of us looking off to the fascinating sight, each thinking his own thoughts. We could sense the terrific concussions, all the earth and air seemed to be trembling.
PRIVATE PERCY CLARE, 7TH EAST SURREY REGIMENT

Without careful control of stocks, gunners would have had no difficulty expending the entire supply long before Z-Day. During daylight hours a restricted number of shells were fired, with pauses to allow for aerial photography and ground observation. To suggest the 'traditional' long bombardment was in the offing, observation balloon numbers were also restricted – a ruse that was noted by the Germans. Unless there were emergencies, by night shelling was less heavy, more sporadic,

and targetted upon areas where enemy infantry were known to congregate or travel. Nocturnal bombing by the RFC and machine-gun barrages firing long-range plunging patterns added to the mix. To hamper repairs, field guns threw shrapnel at enemy entanglements and delivered raking fire, disrupting reliefs and carrying parties to such an extent that food was taking up to six hours to reach the line. In places 'area destruction' was necessary: railheads and junctions, and suspected artillery and engineer dumps. Batteries were pushed to their limits.

6TH APRIL 1917

My Dearest Mother
No time for a letter these days – am shooting 14 hours out of the 24, and working out barrages and switches and lifts most of the other 10! Never was there such a bombardment – July last year was like pulling crackers to it!
Am awfully fit, and frightfully busy.
Much love from Boodles
P.S. The sucks are topping
P.P.S. Good work about America
P.P.P.S. No razor blades yet
MAJOR CUTHBERT G. LAWSON, 14TH BRIGADE, ROYAL HORSE ARTILLERY

Cuthbert Lawson's reference to America is a key one, for it was during the final countdown to Arras that President Wilson finally climbed off the neutral fence. The news could hardly have come at a more opportune time and it spread like wildfire.

On the 4th of April, we received news that America had declared war upon Germany. I thanked God in my heart that at last the English-speaking world had been drawn together, and I knew that the effect upon the Germans

Above Result of a British shell employing the instantaneous 106 Fuze. BHK

Below Hindenburg Line wire damaged by shellfire. IWM Q5286

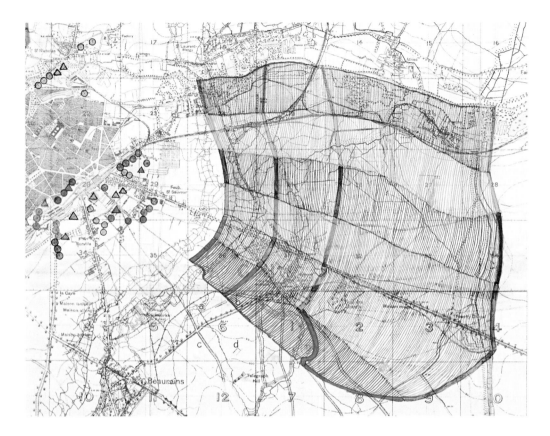

Above Creeping barrage zone plan for batteries of light and medium guns sited in front of the city. Each colour represents an artillery group, and each line an orchestrated 'lift' of the guns.
NA WO153-1144

Right Battery of German dummy guns. ING G1384-3

would be disastrous. I rode out that afternoon to give the good news to our men. I met a British Battalion coming out of the line, looking very tired and hungry. They were resting by the roadside, and I passed along and cheered them by telling them that the United States had now come in definitely as one of our Allies, and that I thought the effect would be the shortening of the war. America's decision could not have come at a better time. The year was opening out before us, and the initiative was coming into our hands. The prospect was bright and our men were keen for the encounter.

CANON F.G. SCOTT DSO, SENIOR CHAPLAIN TO 1ST CANADIAN DIVISION

The creeping barrage was to be mainly delivered by 18-pounder field guns. Although there were local variations, the general plan was that each 'lift' of 100 metres would take place every four minutes, the rate of fire being eight rounds per gun per lift, i.e. two rounds per minute. The signal that a lift was about to take place was a salvo of shrapnel alone, the air bursts offering clear indication to infantry. The guns would then deliver a 50-50 mix of HE and shrapnel until the next lift.

Whilst the creeper was in progress, a set of 'standing barrages' by heavier calibre artillery was to be dropped on certain points behind the enemy lines to deter the arrival of support troops, although the critical task of these guns was to continue counter-battery work and seek out hostile strongpoints, machine-gun posts, redoubts, command posts and dugouts, and communication hubs as they became evident to the FOOs (forward observation officers). In this respect the HAGs (Heavy Artillery Groups) were supremely important. Eight lined up for the battle: XIII, XVIII, XXVI, XLIV, LXX, LXXVI and 1st and 2nd Canadian. The Germans were well aware of the imbalance in firepower, and deliberately kept their 'powder dry' by keeping many batteries silent and well-hidden, defeating Allied flash-spotters (observers trained to take multiple compass bearings on the flashes made by a firing gun) and sound-rangers (a more technical method that utilized an array of 'electronic ears' capable of distinguishing, separating and locating the sound of hostile firing from ambient noise). These guns were being preserved for the battle proper.

The measures were effective: on 6 April only one of *Gruppe* Vimy's seventy batteries had been destroyed; the total at *Gruppe* Arras was thirteen of 352. What was described as a 'mountain of shell' appeared in German depots in Douai. This was all very well, but they still had to reach their destinations, and with the British pounding roads, railways, junctions and dumps, delivery was becoming ever more difficult.

As German reserves surged towards both sectors, there was indecision and disagreement on policy. OHL knew an onslaught was looming, but the battlefield boundaries were still unknown, so where should incoming units be most effectively deployed? Only Vimy was looked upon as a certain Allied objective. The confident Falkenhausen, utilizing lessons learned on the Somme, saw his defence as unyielding: in his opinion reserves need only arrive on the second day of the offensive. Crown Prince Rupprecht disagreed, advocating that *all* reserve units should be within striking distance – say 15 kilometres – before battle. Although Rupprecht prevailed and the orders were issued, it appears that through poor staff work they were carried out lethargically at best, and at worst, not at all. On Z-Day only the 17th Infantry Division had complied.

On 5 April, at a conference at Montdidier, General Robert Nivelle requested Sir Douglas

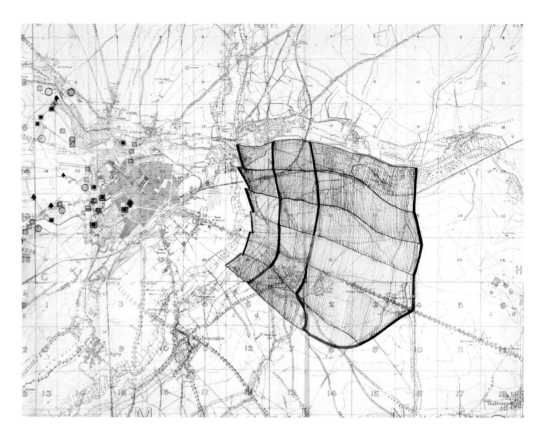

Haig to delay his attacks, asserting that two extra days would assist the French to better complete their preparations on the Aisne. Haig was reluctant, for his meteorologists were forecasting a change to more awkward weather. Twenty-four hours was as much as he dare offer. So be it, said Nivelle. The British and Canadians would now attack on Easter Monday instead of Easter Sunday, and the French on 15 April. British gunners were thus given a useful extra twenty-four hours to bludgeon the enemy and add further polish to their onslaught.

In places, the British were faced with massive entanglements making comprehensive

Above Barrage plan for batteries of heavy guns sited in and behind Arras. NA WO153-1144

obliteration difficult. Instead, concentrating their shot, the gunners cut dedicated lanes, leaving it to the infantry to widen gaps and create new ones – manual wire-cutting had been a part of pre-battle training.

In selected zones, gas was to play a major role in the battle. Deployed in enormous quantities in both cloud and projectile (Livens projector, shell and mortar) form, the scheme was designed to debilitate. Like the British, German gas protection was adequate, the latest masks offering security for about eight hours before requiring a refill; attacks were therefore designed to force the enemy to wear masks for lengthy periods, and time after time, affecting work and sleep patterns. The more often the alarm was sounded, the more aggravated and tired troops became. Two types of gas were employed: lethal and lachrymatory. When the attack was underway the area behind the first objective – the Black Line – would also be curtained off by gas shelling, forcing incoming German support troops to again don their masks. Although the Germans had a considerable supply of gas shells of their own – a supply they were keen to employ – they were persistently stymied by brisk westerly winds. There was no point in bombarding the British and Canadian forward positions because the gas would simply blow back across their own trenches. Targets were thus restricted to positions well behind the lines.

In the same way, the British barrage was equally dependent upon weather conditions. Several RA commanders were mixing smoke and gas shells in their 9 April concoctions. During the last week, they were able to test tactics on a small scale during a series of 'lightning raids' employed to gauge potential resistance on Z-Day.

Below Battery of Livens gas projectors. AJ

6TH APRIL

Maxwell came to talk about artillery support for one of the lightning raids. This came off at 5.57p.m. I watched it from a chimney behind the front. We put a box barrage of smoke shell round the front and support trenches of the German Front which materially helped to make the raid a brilliant success; but the success was over-shadowed, one smoke-shell killing six of our men as they went over the top.

7TH APRIL

I watched another raid. It was very successful. The artillery gave no indication of a raid and fifty infantry got over without a shot having been fired at them. The enemy observation was obscured by smoke shell as soon as the raid started. The raiding party returned with three prisoners of the 8th Bavarian Regiment.
BRIGADIER GENERAL SIR HENRY TUDOR, CRA 9TH (SCOTTISH) DIVISION

The question of deceiving an ever-vigilant and rapidly reacting enemy was crucial. On the Somme, where British tactics went through such an anguished and sanguinary evolution, it was found that the Germans not only launched counter-attacks against each and every Allied venture but, instantly noting variations, acted with speed, imagination and courage to make future use of similar plans wither at birth. For example, to counteract pummelling by British guns at Guillemont, the Germans chose to move men *forward* at night into no man's land, thus placing them in front of the barrage and safe from it. Not unnaturally, the British anticipated a *rearward* shift, and as a consequence the dawn attacks into territory where little or no opposition was expected were broken up with heavy losses. Surprise had been the key and few attackers reached the German line. Later, when the creeping barrage had come into regular if not habitual use, the Germans deployed their weapons on the very edge of British field artillery capabilities. In association with shrapnel, huge numbers of practically unassailable machine guns fired barrage patterns at long range, flooding the battleground with a fearsome barrier of flying lead. Ultimately, constant tactical variations slowed British progress on the Somme to such a degree that it was possible for the Germans to construct functional if primitive fieldworks faster than their foe was able to advance. The failure of so many Allied enterprises could not therefore always be blamed upon poor command or troop inefficiency: it was shrewd German thinking that so often rendered attacks powerless to progress.

At the same time as neutralizing enemy artillery, pockets of resistance needed to be identified and dealt with as soon as the first enemy positions had been occupied. This was the task of the aforementioned FOOs. They served two masters: first the artillery where they reported accuracy of gunnery (fall of shot) and the precise locations of fresh targets during the advance; and second the infantry, keeping commanders fully appraised of any local knowledge that might be valuable to present or future endeavours. Direct observation of this kind was critical, for despite advances in aerial photography and interpretation, the precise hostile content of the battleground could never be known. The extraordinarily widespread German use of underground and camouflaged cover meant that unexpected targets might present themselves at any time – activity that could only be perceived from the battlefield itself.

In order to have maximum control over action and reaction, as far as possible batteries were fired by orders emanating not from the commander stationed with his guns, but from the FOOs themselves, by telephone or buzzer.

In effect, FOOs were the true guardians of the foot soldier. Ironically, it was the task of the infantry, working under instruction, to install the communications that might save their lives.

A cable trench had to be constructed to take signal wires up to and over the front line. It was a deep but very narrow trench (6' 6" deep by 2' wide), one which was very awkward to work in. At the bottom of the trench when dug, cables were laid and the trench filled in so that there would be less risk of the wires being severed and communication stopped by shellfire. In a big action this communication is vital as is an artery in a man's body. The cable trench commenced away back behind the reserve line, was cut up through the support and front line and out as far as possible into No Man's Land – a ticklish part of the job this! Here the terminals of the cable were carefully protected and labelled and left ready to be connected up when our advance made it possible, the wire then being run out overground to our most forward post. Absolute silence and of course no smoking was the rule for all such working parties.

We had a tremendous job to get up the communication trench which for some reason was not duck-boarded like most. Owing to the depth of its gluey mud our feet were gripped in a powerful suction, and it was with the utmost difficulty we could withdraw them to take the next step. The muscular strain necessary was enormous and progress slow to a heart-breaking degree. We were to relieve another party who had been working since the afternoon, and we passed them in the trench on the way up. They were very distressed and exhausted, harassed by Minenwerfer [German trench mortars of various sizes] which kept both them and ourselves in a state of perpetual and wearing anxiety. I saw several poor fellows in the outgoing party in a state bordering on complete collapse, blubbering, shaking all over and sometimes wringing their hands like desperate children; indeed only kept from sinking down where they were in sheer despair

German wire on Vimy Ridge under British and Canadian shellfire. AJ

and surrender by their stronger and more determined comrades, who swore at, tugged at, urged and coaxed them to be game and continue the struggle.
PRIVATE PERCY CLARE, 7TH EAST SURREY REGIMENT

The effects of the British bombardment varied from sector to sector. By 6 April, on Vimy Ridge it was no longer possible to say that a defensive line existed at all: across a depth averaging almost a kilometre, the ground was a wilderness of craters. Likewise approach routes, communication trenches and dugouts had been effectively obliterated, the latter by heavy shells fitted with delayed-action fuzes. Shelter became ever more difficult to find. Because there was no great depth to the position, it mattered not whether a man was in the front, support or reserve line, for each was receiving the same brutal treatment. Every night the Germans struggled, digging, rewiring, draining, mending, only to have the work destroyed within hours. That great comfort, hot food, was absent, a failure that every commander knew was spirit sapping.

Already weak in numbers from the effects of the bombardment, scores of German troops were daily falling sick as a result of the ground conditions and nervous exhaustion; reports began to state that certain garrisons could no longer be called 'battleworthy'. The superiority in guns and mortars was achieving far more than Byng and Currie might have hoped.

By varying the intensity of fire, the effect was dramatically heightened. Shelling might slacken for a few hours, allowing the trembling defenders time to catch their breath; then there would come a sudden drumfire crescendo. And hidden inaudible amongst the burst and roar of high explosive were the plops of gas shells. Perceiving the day of reckoning approaching,

General Karl Ritter von Fasbender, commander of *Gruppe* Vimy, fired off some jingoistic encouragement to the troops, blaming the British for starting the war, exhorting every man to fight to the death whilst conceding not a metre of ground, and insisting that despite the situation none were cowed. All around he saw only steadfastness and courage; were not Richthofen's *Jastas* downing numerous enemy aircraft each day (this was close to the truth), and were not the guns simply awaiting the opportunity to smash the British attack as they always did? The message failed to reach many of Fasbender's men: on the wasteland that was the ridge they were effectively cut off from their own forces.

Unlike the first week of the month 8 April dawned clear and dry; it proved invaluable in allowing observers in the air and on the ground to survey the gunners' work. Attention could now be paid to insufficiently cut sections of wire, not only protecting the enemy front line but beyond, on the blue, brown and green lines.

On the Arras front operations against the outposts and villages in the Fifth Army sector continued right up to Z-Day. It was essential that hamlets like Ecoust, Croisilles, Hénin and St Martin were cleared to offer a suitable platform of attack when the whistles blew for Gough's part in the grand offensive. The nature of the fighting here – house-to-house and through village streets, protected by artillery and assisted by mortars and light machine guns – was quite different to anything that the majority of troops had experienced during the previous two years. Eventually, but not without heavy casualties, most of the German rearguard were pushed back close to the wire of the Hindenburg defences. OHL's aim had once more been achieved: by this final delaying tactic they had bought time to strengthen the new positions in preparation for the inevitable.

On Friday the 6th we shelled them pretty heavily and they were busy cutting lanes through the wire with light guns. The place was littered with our spotting planes and one got sick with seeing them downed, they seemed to last no time and the number shot down was very large. Gunners were all over the place, hurriedly making last dispositions and marking down last ideas, brigade bombers with working parties swarmed down the trenches, making dumps of thousands of bombs and accessories, R.E.s and more parties surveying and marking down things, dumping wire, pegs, etc. and in the night time a continuous stream of working parties bringing up T.M. ammunition, ordinary ammunition, rations etc., till you couldn't get around and the noise was like a sheep and cow fair heard at a distance. You'd have thought things never would disentangle themselves, and things like this were the usual episodes of those last nights. Bayliss, I and runner going round meet an NCO, asked him how many in his party, "9" says he, "Right ho, push along". We flatten ourselves against the trench wall, past come seventeen swearing Tommies carrying heavy loads, barging into us, falling themselves, shouting "Where's No. 7 Party" "Pass the word along there's no one behind Pte Atkins", the endless stream goes on and we get fed up with being banged with every three cornered thing under Heaven so collar the next NCO. "Who are you?" – "24th N.F, No. 14 Party", (the word has apparently never been passed down by the party before to let us through) – "How many men?" – "I should have 10, Sir" – "Alright, pass the word down to halt the party after that." We count five down and then start struggling down past the last five, find a blaspheming corporal wanting to know what ----- has stopped his ---- party. We mildly say "We want to get through", and push along past them. After going some 10 yards, meet another blaspheming NCO

Above 8-inch howitzer under camouflage in Arras. IWM Q7245

Below View of Arras between 'Cuthbert' and 'Clarence' (mine) craters near St Laurent Blangy. AC

who wants to know what the check is. We try to push past him and get hopelessly jammed with two men bearing a pole with ammunition slung on it. I tell Bayliss to get up on top and give me a hand, and we slither up, take a line and move off. Up starts the Bosch with machine-guns and we fall hurriedly back into the struggle again, and so it went on all night. It took me the whole night to get around our sector.
MAJOR BERTRAM BREWIN, 16TH ROYAL SCOTS

The caves and cellars were now packed with troops. Sir Douglas Haig was his habitually ebullient pre-battle self. The men, so the Official History states, 'had an air of confidence in their experience and training which he [Haig] had not seen during his inspections before the 1916 Picardy offensive'. It is worthwhile comparing Sir Douglas's pre-battle assessments of both the Somme and Arras offensives:

FRIDAY, JUNE 30 [SOMME 1916]
The weather report is favourable for to-morrow. With God's help, I feel hopeful. The men are in splendid spirits. Several have said that they have never before been so instructed and informed of the nature of the operation before them. The wire has never been so well cut, nor the Artillery's preparation so thorough. I have personally seen all the Corps Commanders and one and all are full of confidence.

SUNDAY, APRIL 8 [ARRAS 1917]
Yesterday I was all round the Corps in 1st and 3rd Armies who are attacking – I have never before seen Commanders so confident, or so satisfied with the preparations and wire cutting. To-day is lovely weather – so I hope things will turn out all right.
SIR DOUGLAS HAIG TO SIR WILLIAM ROBERTSON.

Whether Sir Douglas Haig's confidence would be fully justified and fully rewarded was subject

to how his enemy chose to respond. It was the last time during the war that the Commander-in-Chief's journal would display such confidence. His Despatch for 8 April includes the following piece:

SUNDAY, APRIL 8TH (EASTER SUNDAY)

Glass steady – fine night: slight frost: fine sunny morning. I attended Church of Scotland at 9.30 a.m. Rev. Mr. Duncan took the service. He spoke about the certainty of life hereafter, and prayed for us to be given an 'unconquerable mind'.

The troops too could attend services if they wished, but in somewhat different surroundings to Sir Douglas'.

EASTER SUNDAY 8 APRIL 1917

My dearest Mother,

A strange Easter this, in a very strange place. If you could see us you would be more than surprised. You have attended Communion today and it will have pleased you to know that I also took the Sacrament. Yes, the best of all services in a place somewhat removed from the surface of the earth in a dim light, big drops of water trickling from the roof on to my head.

It was 8.30 this morning and the communicants would not number more than 20. Three rows of men kneeling on stones over which sandbags were laid. In front of me was a Brigadier General, next a captain, then a rifleman. Next to me was another of our gun team, a little fellow almost twice my age. In civil life he is a Manager of a Flour Mill. I must not forget to mention the Altar. Two candles set on a Vickers-gun chest, the Chaplains white cloth set in front with the wine and wafers. Owing to peculiar circumstances I have had an excellent opportunity of attending Service this Easter. On Good Friday an evening service at 5.30. On Saturday morning communion at 10.30. Then again this morning. You see, we did not expect to be able to attend today, hence the service of

Saturday. Well Mother dear, you can bet I shall be glad to touch civilisation again. Fifteen days now without seeing a shop or civilian. Nothing but ruins. Can you imagine King Edward Street and Paragon Station, big hotels etc. skeletons of their former selves? It is a sight that tends to depress one. The weather is picking up and when the sun shines it fills the air with warmth. We do not get much of the singing of the birds. The indescribable din of the guns send them to more peaceful quarters. At times it gives one the most awful headache. The crash, bang, whizz, thump of guns and shells gets a bit feeding. Zep. raids are picnics. I have had 10 francs in my pocket for the last three weeks, but no chance of spending it, and there is three weeks pay to come. So, all being well when another week rolls by we shall make an attempt at a "spread" …

Well, little Mother, let this Easter cheer you and fill you with a hope that soon all will be at peace once more.

Give Dad this message also. My best love to the girls and John. Give Emilia an Easter kiss for me.

Your most affectionate son

Burton

RIFLEMAN BURTON ECCLES, 7TH RIFLE BRIGADE (WITH 14TH DIVISION, IN THE RONVILLE CAVES)

Another final Easter Sunday note from Haig, again to Robertson, is required, for it records a critical development that would affect all of 1917:

I hear Nivelle has had some trouble. Some of the French government wished to forbid the French offensive altogether; but Nivelle has gained the day. I think this indicates the instability of purpose with our French Allies! If anything goes wrong Nivelle will disappear.

British artillery observers in one of the craters illustrated on the previous page. IWM Q5095

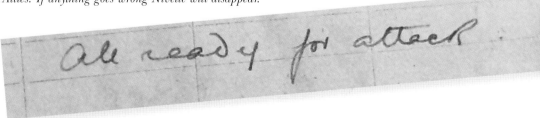

CHAPTER TEN
Osterschlacht North: Vimy Ridge to the Scarpe

On the 6th of April I had no doubt that a great British offensive was imminent at Arras … I begged the Group Headquarters to bring up their reserves nearer to the line in the area of the 6th Army. The last attacks at Verdun in October and December had confirmed the old adage that the right place for reserves is close to the firing-line. The "Defensive Battle" manual laid down that, in many cases on the front under attack, counter-attack divisions should be held in readiness in the second line to meet and throw back the enemy if he broke through the first line. The divisions which constituted the second and third waves were indeed moved up by the 6th Army, but on 8th were not close enough up. On the 9th, after a short but extraordinarily intense artillery preparation, our army encountered a powerful attack, led by tanks, on both sides of the Scarpe.

LUDENDORFF, *MY WAR MEMORIES*

The night of 8/9 April was something of a curate's egg. Clear at first, later it rained, snowed and blew. That the trenches were packed was perhaps fortunate, for 'herding' might at least have kept the troops slightly warmer. General Allenby had decreed that in order to save weight greatcoats (and packs) were to be left behind. Even without greatcoats, the essential encumbrances of battle were numerous and heavy. In addition to rifle, extra ammunition, a brace of bombs, gas mask, haversack and rations for two days, most were required to carry a pick or shovel, extra sand-bags or wire-cutters, all tools as critical to success and survival as the rifle.

350,000 troops deployed on the Third Army front, with another 30,000 at Vimy. Their feet turned the approach routes and assembly trenches into ankle-deep tracks of slime and mud-filled ditches. Tank crews were dismayed, for come the morning, conditions were likely to be precisely those they would most wish to avoid. Infantry commanders who were detailed to assist could only hope the machines would be of use, for few had ever seen them in action, let alone worked with them.

The final dispositions were as follows: lining up north to south on the Arras front were three corps, XVII, VI and VII. At first, VII Corps were to remain immobile because reconfiguration of the enemy positions in the sectors south of the Arras-Cambrai road meant that the trenches they looked upon as initial targets formed the *second* objective for their neighbours between the river and the road, VI and XVII Corps. To achieve a smooth unbroken line of advance, only after the Black Line (German front line) had been attained north of Beaurains would all three corps combine to assault the Blue Line. Three hours was allotted for the first manoeuvre, followed by an interlude of 3.5

hours for resupply and the moving forward of support. The engineers would be at work on roads at the earliest moment, as would their close colleagues, the signallers, putting in place the vulnerable tracery of cables. The next objective for all corps, the Brown Line, was to be kept under constant and heavy bombardment throughout the first phase, the extra five hours of bludgeoning, hopefully 'softening it up'. Beyond the Brown Line lay the final goal, the Green Line. This was certain to be an obstinate objective, for along its length lay the strategically

Tilleuls Neuville Acq   Berthonval. Fe. La Motte Fe.   Berthonvalwald.   Camblain. Villers Chatel   Villers au Bois   Schloß La

Mont St. Eloy. La Targette.   Bois des Alleux. Bonvalwald.   La Folie Fe

German aerial panorama of the Vimy Ridge. British/Canadian line picked out in red. HS M706 M10 Nr 366

important fortified villages of Fampoux in the north, Monchy-le-Preux in the centre and Guémappe to the south. As the Green Line was seen as the toughest nut to crack, it had been decided to employ a procedure that until this point in the war had never before been attempted. The battle plan as a whole universally incorporated a heavily practised tactic that came to be known as 'leapfrogging'. All attacks were separated into several phases, and for each phase battalions and brigades were given strictly limited objectives. As capture was taking place

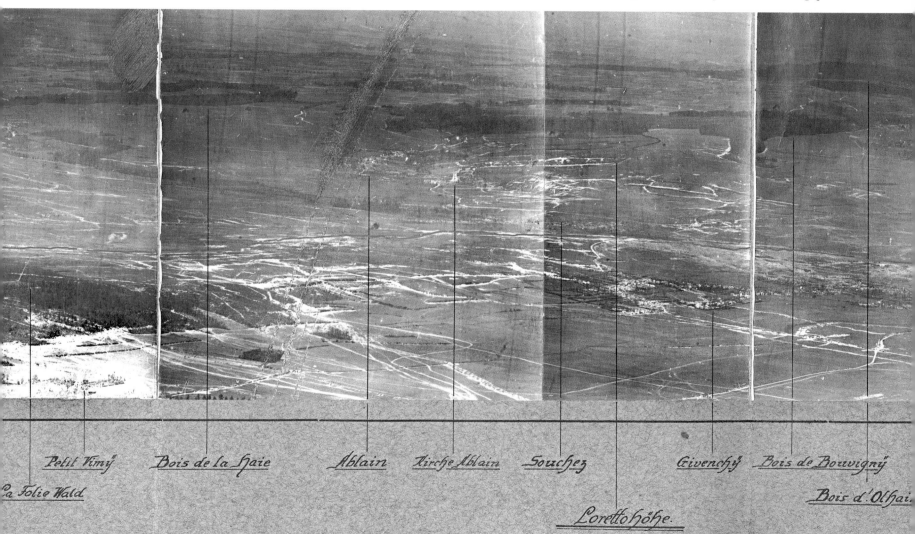

Petit Vimy   Bois de la Haie   Ablain   Kirche Ablain   Souchez   Givenchy   Bois de Bouvigny

La Folie Wald   Loretto höhe.   Bois d'Olhai.

fresh troops following on behind surged through to leapfrog the first attacking wave and assault subsequent objectives. The purpose was to maintain steady momentum to the final target and to have more than sufficient fresh troops upon arrival there for consolidation and the driving off of counter-attacks. For Arras' Green Line, however, the tactic was ambitiously expanded. Distances to the various objectives across the battleground as a whole were far from uniform. Having a greater depth of territory to secure, VI (Lieutenant General Aylmer Haldane) and XVII Corps (Lieutenant General Sir Charles Fergusson) were each employing three attacking divisions against the Brown Line; once it had fallen two fresh divisions would leapfrog and overwhelm an enemy frayed and battered by the guns. Once Monchy and Guémappe had fallen, Gough's Fifth Army would strike at the German solar plexus in the south.

Behind the lines, awaiting opportunities as they had done for more than two years, were the mounted corps. Two Cavalry Divisions (2nd and 3rd) were allotted to Third Army, one to Fifth (4th Indian), and another (1st) held in reserve for the use of First Army, or deployment wherever circumstances looked auspicious. Finally, the Army Reserve under Lieutenant General Ivor Maxse (XVIII Corps) consisted of three Divisions drawn from Fourth and Fifth Armies. Allenby had the use of sixteen divisions to pursue his surge towards Cambrai. In the morning, the guns *had* to deliver the perfect storm.

Easter Monday. April 9th 1917. Truly black Monday. A wretched awakening, pitch dark, cold, with a keen wind blowing. One can perhaps imagine the feelings of everybody that morning searching about in the darkness for equipment, chilled to the bone, half asleep, stumbling over other men's equipment and on top of all, the knowledge of

a very fair prospect of "pushing daisies up" before night fall. Equipment having been found it had to be disentangled – it has a hideous habit of getting itself into endless knots if laid down for a few minutes in the darkness – then waterproof sheets to be rolled and strapped to the belt at the back, water bottles filled from the water cart and numerous other odds and ends to see to.

Breakfast was ready to be drawn from the cookers by 3.30; it having been brought 'en masse' to platoons – here was another hopeless business trying to distribute boiled bacon to every man by the light of a miserable guttering candle, with hands stiff with cold and the wretched candle being blown out by the chill wind every few minutes.

Hot tea made everyone feel twice the man he was before, and by the time breakfast was finished dawn was breaking – a very cheerless sort of dawn, however. What a strange feeling there seemed to be in the air that morning, a lull before a terrible storm, for it wanted just one hour before the opening barrage. It was inexplicable this nervous tension; even the horses and birds seemed to be imbued with the knowledge that hell was to be let loose before very long. There seemed to be a strange hush hanging over every living thing, man, bird and beast. Dawn having broken the weather prospect looked decidedly gloomy; the sky was completely overcast with low rain clouds scudding above us. We were not to be disappointed in this at least for it poured with rain an hour or so later. At 4 o'clock the Battalion moved off, each man carrying his extra ammunition, rations for the day and an extra 'iron' ration – and, perhaps, a nervous sinking feeling in his stomach.

SERGEANT RUPERT 'JACK' WHITEMAN, 10TH ROYAL FUSILIERS (CITY OF LONDON REGIMENT)

THE BREAKING OF A BASTION

This Easter time we have had some very interesting talks in the church here. How excited all the line troops are about the offensive and are more optimistic than anyone.

Gruppe Vimy headquarters, Douai. AC

This mud and wet is enough to kill any fellow, yet in a trench how much worse it is. Something superhuman it means to be able to carry on under such stress. The traffic around here is getting as big as Albert was. How I long to be with Rosie again and to forget all about war, and yet I am well off. I pray that I may pull through …

Bombardment commenced and lasted all through the night. Saw a bunch of 3rd Division who hoped to go over at an early date. Had a good discussion at church on suffering. A bit better day but very cold. No mail so far … The traffic is a terror and goes on day and night. If some of the pessimists could come out here and see for themselves.

PRIVATE JOHN POUCHER, 9TH BATTALION, CANADIAN RAILWAY TROOPS

At Vimy, the primary mission of Horne's First Army was of course to safeguard the left flank of Allenby's thrust. Four Canadian Divisions and a single British Brigade lined up on the 7-kilometre front from Ecurie to Givenchy-en-Gohelle, to attack at the same hour as their Third Army comrades.

Having been occupiers for several months, most of the Canadians knew the ridge sector inside out; even the least experienced had been in situ for several weeks, so in combination with intensive training and the artillery firestorm, Z-Day was approached with some degree of confidence. The scheme was a simple one: a swift simultaneous surge by all four divisions of the Corps that would drive the Germans from the escarpment. In the key central area it was so steep that once over the edge the enemy would be faced with a choice: abandon the ridge and pull back to safer prepared positions on the Douai plain (the Vimy-Angres line), or, because the escarpment was hardly defensible, face annihilation.

The map on page 109 shows how in the area incorporating the summit about Hill 145, the Fischer sector, the final line to be gained on Day One, lay around 700 metres from the Canadian positions. Hill 145 had to fall because of its supreme observational potential, but also because it could be invisibly reinforced from the rear and both sides, and therefore employed as a foundation for counter-attacks. Rapid and decisive occupation was essential. Beyond, to the northern boundary of the battlefield, lay Bois en Hache (*Grosse Angres Waldchen*, to the Germans, a small wood that actually lay beyond the Souchez valley on the Lorette Ridge), and Hill 120, known to the British as 'The Pimple'. A mini-salient forming the northernmost section of the summit plateau, The Pimple was a menace for it had been deliberately sited to cover not only its immediate front, but the central ridge-top in enfilade. The capture of 145 would certainly be more difficult and costly if The Pimple was not also neutralized. Assisting the Canadians' attack here were the guns of the British I Corps, holding the line beyond the northern battlefield boundary but not taking part in infantry proceedings. Swinging their muzzles southwards 45°, they were to pummel the ridge, the eastern escarpment, and the German rear areas for eight days.

As the ground falls away from Hill 145 in the direction of the River Scarpe, no man's land can be seen to belly. In this sector the key objectives for the 4th Canadian Division were two fortified villages, first Thélus and then Farbus, the latter demanding a challenging 4-kilometre advance. Here, to achieve maximum effect, First Army and neighbouring XVII Corps gunners shared the significant targets. On the Canadians' southern shoulder lay the 51st (Highland) Division (Major General G.M. Harper), who although under Third and not

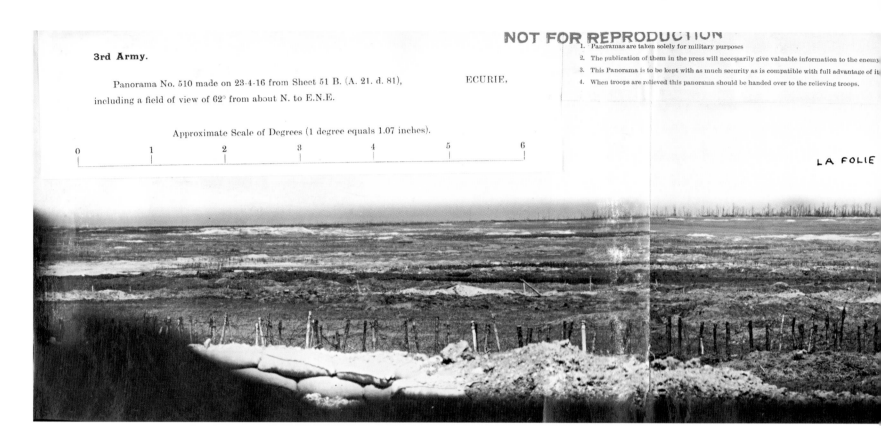

First Army command were clearly critical to Canadian fortunes. The remaining ground down to the Scarpe marshes and river was the responsibility of British divisions whose attacks, of course, must evolve at the same pace if success across the entire northern zone was to be complete. The attacking arrowheads of XVII Corps were the 51st, 34th, 9th and 4th Divisions; their endeavours will be described later.

By Y-Day, aerial photographs of the ridge had revealed the apparent complete obliteration of large parts of the forward enemy trench system, and widespread damage to the rear. Villages were easily observed, but harm to hostile gun batteries could not yet be gauged – that would only be revealed by the strength of the German response. Because XVII Corps observers were able to see partly behind the ridge, however, the gunners were confident they had damaged or destroyed known locations and much else; artillery HQs were comfortable that the infantry were receiving more high-explosive assistance than ever before. Deep dugouts were the greatest unknown quantity – it was a threat that could only be ameliorated by surprise in the timing of the attack, speed in its delivery, and irresistible troop numbers. There would certainly be problems here and there, but *all* the general signs were presently promising. German prisoners spoke of several regiments being so severely depleted that Allied commanders were coming to believe a troop advantage of three to one might not be implausible. In

Third Army Panorama 310 shows the open ground to be negotiated by 7th, 8th and 11th Canadian Brigade troops in their attack upon the La Folie sector. The need for subways is made clear. IWM

truth, it was probably greater. Some German supports were close by, sheltered in the lee of the escarpment and in the villages of Givenchy, Farbus and Vimy, but the majority of reserves and counter-attack units were billeted in places between two and five hours away. As the artillery had been supplied with ample ammunition to not only complete the bombardment but guarantee a blazing welcome for incomers, Byng, Currie and their divisional commanders were able to rest relatively easily at night. This time, it appeared that nothing had been left to chance.

APRIL 8TH 1917

Things are looking good. We have got a lot of new horses and everything is ready for a big smash. I am writing this on Easter Sunday. Though we are in France we had our eggs just the same. Our Captain brought them for us. This is Sunday April the 8th 1917 and the big smash comes off tonight. We were warned this morning that we had to carry our gas helmets at the Gas Alert. At 5 o'c the Infantry are going over tonight. We heard today that America has gone into the war. Things are looking good.
GUNNER EDWARD CULLUM, 2ND CANADIAN DIVISION ARTILLERY

During the night of 8 April, the troops moved quietly, smoothly and with minimal casualties into position. Deep beneath the flank of the ridge the subways admirably achieved their protective purpose, carrying thousands safely forward into the front line – and beyond through lanes cut in the wire to jumping-off

Obere Einteilung ist Teilstricheilung für
Feldartillerie, 360°=6400 Teilstriche.

Schacht 6   Civenchy-Wäldchen

The Pimple

Untere Einteilung ist ne² Teilung für
Fußartillerie. 360°=6100³/₁₀°.

positions scraped in and amongst the craters of no man's land. Leapfroggers remained under cover in the subways ready to filter swiftly out as soon as the first waves were in motion.

By 4.00 a.m. over 30,000 men awaited the whistle. Not a sign of German alarm had yet been recorded: they knew very well what was coming – but not when. In fact, some enemy units did notice unusual activity, but the severing of communication had been so complete and the devastation so widespread, that neither signaller nor runner was able to transmit the information in time.

My alarm clock went off at four a.m. on the great day of April 9th and I started off to see the opening barrage. It was quite dark. I went through the village of Ecoivres, past the Crucifix by the cemetery, and then turning to the right went on to a path which led up to Bray Hill on the St. Eloi road. I found some men of one of our battalions bent on the same enterprise. The sky was overcast, but towards the east the grey light of approaching dawn was beginning to appear. It was a thrilling moment. Human lives were at stake. The honour of our country was at stake. The fate of civilization was at stake. Far over the

Above A German view of the cratered northern end of the Vimy Ridge (left of image) from the Calonne sector. Part of the Lorette Ridge is also visible on the right. HS M706 M.9 Nr. 386

Below Ranges and targets for the various calibres of Allied guns

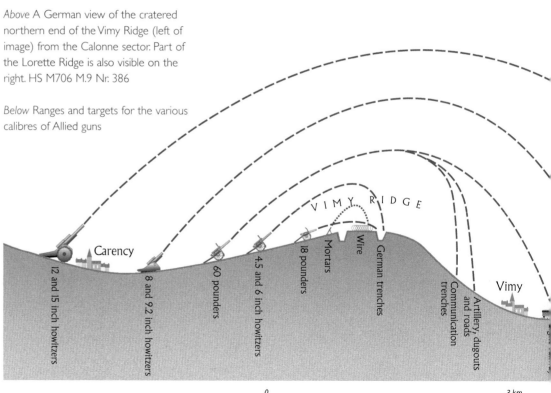

VIMY RIDGE

Carency

Vimy

12 and 15 inch howitzers

8 and 9.2 inch howitzers

60 pounders

4.5 and 6 inch howitzers

18 pounders

Mortars

Wire

German trenches

Communication trenches

Artillery, dugouts and roads

0   3 km

0   2 miles

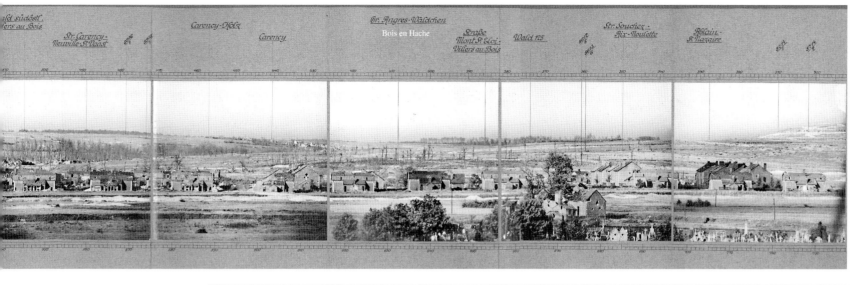

ald südöstl.
ers au Bois

Str. Carency-
Neuville St Vaast

Carency-Holz

Carency

Gr. Angres-Wäldchen

Bois en Hache

Straße
Mont St Eloi-
Villers au Bois

Wald 125

Str. Souchez-
Aix-Noulette

Rötain-
St Nazaire

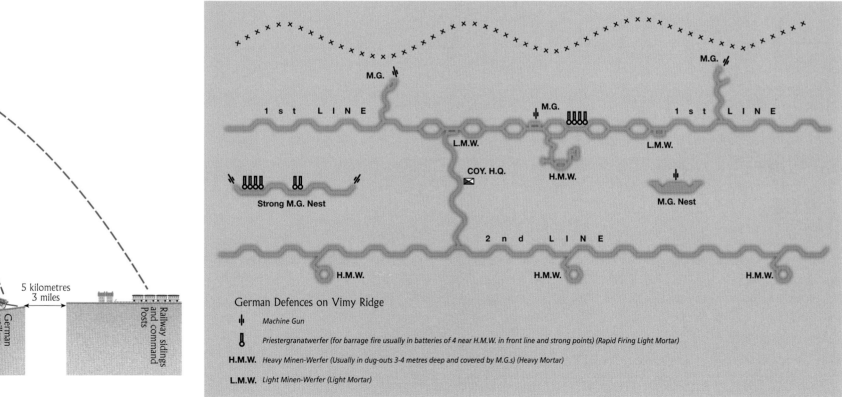

5 kilometres
3 miles

German artillery

Railway sidings and command Posts

M.G.

M.G.

1st LINE

M.G.

M.G.

1st LINE

L.M.W.

L.M.W.

COY. H.Q.

H.M.W.

Strong M.G. Nest

M.G. Nest

2nd LINE

H.M.W.

H.M.W.

H.M.W.

German Defences on Vimy Ridge

Machine Gun

Priestergranatwerfer (for barrage fire usually in batteries of 4 near H.M.W. in front line and strong points) (Rapid Firing Light Mortar)

H.M.W. *Heavy Minen-Werfer (Usually in dug-outs 3-4 metres deep and covered by M.G.s) (Heavy Mortar)*

L.M.W. *Light Minen-Werfer (Light Mortar)*

dark fields, I looked towards the German lines, and, now and then, in the distance I saw a flarelight appear for a moment and then die away. Now and again, along our nine-mile front, I saw the flash of a gun and heard the distant report of a shell. It looked as if the war had gone to sleep, but we knew that all along the line our trenches were bristling with energy and filled with men animated with one resolve, with one fierce determination. It is no wonder that to those who have been in the war and passed through such moments, ordinary life and literature seem very tame. The thrill of such a moment is worth years of peace-time existence. To the watcher of a spectacle so awful and sublime, even human companionship struck a jarring note. I went over to a place by myself where I could not hear the other men talking, and there I waited. I watched the luminous hands of my watch get nearer and nearer to the fateful moment, for the barrage was to open at five-thirty. At five-fifteen the sky was getting lighter and already one could make out objects distinctly in the fields below. The long hand of my watch was at five-twenty-five. The fields, the roads, and the hedges were beginning to show the difference of colour in the early light. Five-twenty-seven! In three minutes the rain of death was to begin. In the awful silence around it seemed as if Nature were holding her breath in expectation of the staggering moment. Five-twenty-nine! God help our men! Five-thirty!

CANON F.G. SCOTT DSO, SENIOR CHAPLAIN TO 1ST
CANADIAN DIVISION

The creeping barrage had twice been rehearsed (6 and 7 April) and all was ready for the performance. Grasping their lanyards, gunners waited to unleash a firestorm thirty times greater than the French had employed on the same ground two years before. Preparing for their own barrage, which was designed to further deter German supports moving forward from dugouts on the reverse slope of the ridge (the *Hangstellung*), machine-gunners checked

elevations on more than 150 weapons, ready to fire over the heads of the attacking troops. Everything was ready.

Replenished siege lamp, built up the fire. Called the guard in, enjoyed some hot cocoa, biscuits, cheese and "bully" while we discussed the coming show. Our officer warned me to awaken the men at 4.30 and gave me the lines for the first 5 barrages. The crew eagerly cleared the pit for action, got fuzes and gave the gun a last dab with the polishing rag and a feed of oil. Watches were synchronized at 5.20 and it was announced that the zero hour was 5.30. During the last half hour a strange quiet filled the place. Broken only by the pattering of the rain which now began to fall in a steady stream.
Are you ready number 1?
Are you ready number 2?
Five minutes to go.
4 minutes to go.
3 minutes to go.
2 minutes to go.
1 minute to go.
10 seconds.
5 seconds.
Whistle!!
We're off.

SERGEANT RAYMOND IVES, 13TH BATTERY, CANADIAN
FIELD ARTILLERY

At the very moment Sergeant Ives's battery fired their first salvo, a shelling frenzy began all along the line; every gun spoke, the medium and heavies drenching suspected enemy battery positions with high explosive and gas, whilst the smaller howitzers and field guns laid down the first of many lines of 'creepers'.

It was a wonderful sound. The flashes of guns in all directions made lightnings in the dawn. The swish of

Above Fixing scaling ladders prior to the attack. IWM Q6204

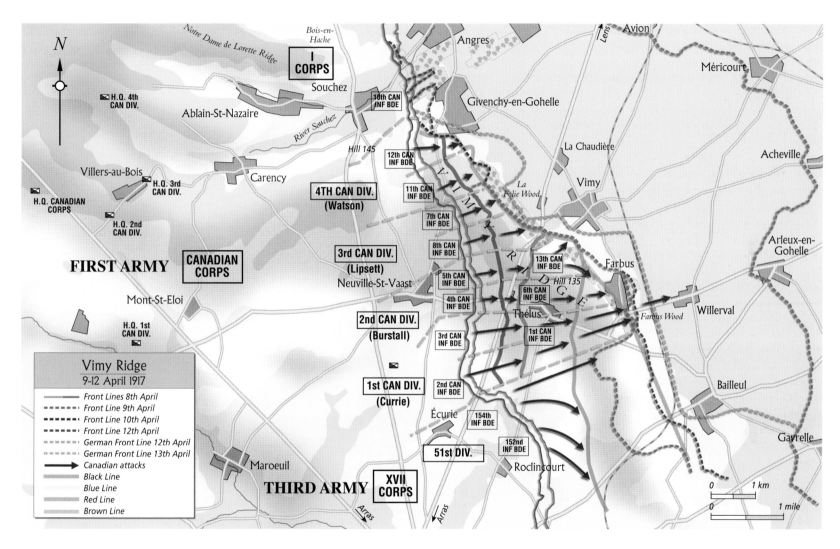

N

Notre Dame de Lorette Ridge

Bois-en-Hache

I CORPS

Angres

Avion

Lens

Méricourt

☒ H.Q. 4th CAN DIV.

Souchez

10th CAN INF BDE

Givenchy-en-Gohelle

Ablain-St-Nazaire

River Souchez

Hill 145

12th CAN INF BDE

La Chaudière

Acheville

Villers-au-Bois

☒ H.Q. 3rd CAN DIV.

Carency

4TH CAN DIV. (Watson)

11th CAN INF BDE

V I M Y

La Folie Wood

Vimy

☒ H.Q. CANADIAN CORPS

7th CAN INF BDE

☒ H.Q. 2nd CAN DIV.

FIRST ARMY

CANADIAN CORPS

3rd CAN DIV. (Lipsett)

Neuville-St-Vaast

8th CAN INF BDE

R I D

13th CAN INF BDE

Farbus

Arleux-en-Gohelle

5th CAN INF BDE

Hill 135

Mont-St-Eloi

2nd CAN DIV. (Burstall)

4th CAN INF BDE

6th CAN INF BDE

G E

Farbus Wood

Willerval

☒ H.Q. 1st CAN DIV.

Thélus

1st CAN INF BDE

☒

3rd CAN INF BDE

1st CAN DIV. (Currie)

2nd CAN INF BDE

Bailleul

Écurie

154th INF BDE

Vimy Ridge
9-12 April 1917

— Front Lines 8th April
---- Front Line 9th April
---- Front Line 10th April
---- Front Line 12th April
···· German Front Line 12th April
···· German Front Line 13th April
→ Canadian attacks
— Black Line
— Blue Line
— Red Line
···· Brown Line

51st DIV.

152nd INF BDE

Gavrelle

Maroeuil

Roclincourt

THIRD ARMY

XVII CORPS

Arras

Arras

0   1 km

0   1 mile

Above The results of Canadian Corps endeavours on 9 April 1917

shells through the air was continuous, and far over on the German trenches I saw the bursts of flame and smoke in a long continuous line, and, above the smoke, the white, red and green lights, which were the S.O.S. signals from the terrified enemy. In an instant his artillery replied, and against the morning clouds the bursting shrapnel flashed. Now and then our shells would hit a

German ammunition dump, and, for a moment, a dull red light behind the clouds of smoke, added to the grandeur of the scene. I knelt on the ground and prayed to the God of Battles to guard our noble men in that awful line of death and destruction, and to give them victory, and I am not ashamed to confess that it was with the greatest difficulty I kept back my tears. There was so

much human suffering and sorrow, there were such tremendous issues involved in that fierce attack, there was such splendour of human character being manifested now in that "far flung line", where smoke and flame mocked the calm of the morning sky, that the watcher felt he was gazing upon eternal things.
CANON F.G. SCOTT DSO, SENIOR CHAPLAIN TO 1ST CANADIAN DIVISION

Opposite the 3rd Canadian Division two heavy mines were blown, obliterating almost 200 metres of German line, crushing several dugouts and burying alive three sections of German miners. Across the entire sector Stokes trench mortars drenched no man's land with smoke, the robust north-westerly carrying it, the sleet and the fumes of explosions into the eyes of the defenders. Behind the curtain of shell bursts the Canadians rose from their sopping scrapes and stepped towards the inferno.

I looked ahead and saw the German front line crashing into pieces; bits of men, timbers, lumps of chalk were flung through the air and, blending with the shattering wall of fire, were the Hun SOS signals of all colours. We didn't dare lift our heads, knowing that the barrage was to come flat over us and then lift in three minutes. That queer empty stomach feeling had gone … I don't think anyone was scared … instead one's whole body seemed to be in a mad macabre dance … I felt that if I lifted a finger I should touch a solid ceiling of sound. I guess it was perhaps the most perfect barrage of the war, as it was perfectly synchronized. Then, suddenly, it jumped a hundred yards and we were away. I suppose we must have crossed the German front line, but I have no memory of it at all. Instead of a trench, there was only a wide, muddy depression, stinking of explosives.
CORPORAL GUSTAVE SIVERTZ, 2ND CANADIAN MOUNTED RIFLES, CANADIAN EXPEDITIONARY FORCE

From where we went over the top, it was impossible to know what was going on elsewhere. We were only concerned with our own small sector of the front. Remembering what had happened in our attacks on the Somme front, we were prepared for violent resistance. When zero hour came there was no rash charge, no dashing forward like a rugby scrum. We climbed out of the jumping-off trench, aligned ourselves with each other, and with a steady stride, rifles and bayonets at the ready, started towards our objectives. The German front line had just ceased to exist. There were several bodies lying in its ruins, and there was no resistance until we had passed it, and we were making for the second line. Then we came under fire from machine-guns

Above The infantry's greatest fear: a (triple) night-time mine blow. This one is German. BHK Abt.IV BS-N 63/5 31

in pillboxes on the hillside. Still we went forward, losing only a few men at this stage, until, as if from nowhere, there came a withering burst of fire from hidden machine guns well ahead of us. We were really into it now. We halted for a short time to get our breath and plan for the next move. Then a trench mortar group came along and sighted on the machine gun post, and secured direct hits on it, after which we again went forward, slowly and deliberately. There were some heroic pieces of action by some of our men, who, at great personal risk, went forward until within grenade-throwing distance of enemy groups and scattered them. When we finally reached the point at which we were to halt and allow other units to continue over our heads, we were surprised to find that we had been in action for three hours. It had been hard slogging but we had reached our objective.

PRIVATE MAGNUS MCINTYRE HOOD, 24TH (VICTORIA RIFLES) BATTALION, CANADIAN EXPEDITIONARY FORCE

Below British 6-inch medium range gun night-firing in the days leading up to 9 April. IWM CO1323

So effective was the artillery, and so unanticipated the attack, that the dreadful scenes witnessed the previous year on the Somme were nowhere replicated – the carnage was on the opposite side of no man's land. The Germans managed to produce many a machine gun from underground lairs, but few were brought into action before being overwhelmed by the leading wave. Bayonet-men followed hard on their heels and, as each dugout was identified, so was it neutralized. In places, the orders were 'no prisoners'. Despite the destruction and chaos, here and there information was reaching some German regimental and divisional headquarters. Normally, counter-strokes would have been quickly prepared, but on this occasion there was nothing anyone could do for it was all happening too quickly.

We had been there so long, we knew just where to look for Fritz, and we sure found him. We went out to our advance trench or what is better known as the 'jumping off trench', at 10 p.m. Easter Sunday, and were there all night until 5:30 Monday Morning. It was the worst night I have ever put in. It would rain awhile, then snow awhile. At 4:30 one of the officers came along the trench with the rum and I took a dandy and by 5:30 I was all nerve. As soon as our artillery barrage opened up, away we went, and all you could see was smoke, Fritz running and some whole ones, but mostly pieces of them, going up in the air. A person would naturally think that the very life would be frightened out of a fellow, but fear never enters your mind. All you look for is go ahead and blood. You just go insane and that is all. The noise of the artillery and the bursting shells get you going. It was a hell on earth. I got in one place where the whole bunch was cleaned out but me and I had to crawl from shell hole to shell hole, to find some more fellows and thus get at

The British barrage as seen from a German observation balloon. AJ

the Huns again. I got mine after about three hours' of fighting, and I threw off everything and started back and I made it. I do not mind the loss of my eye, but I am well pleased to save my life.

PRIVATE ARTHUR SOUTHWORTH, 87TH (GRENADIER GUARDS) BATTALION, CANADIAN EXPEDITIONARY FORCE

In the advanced German headquarter dugouts the only recourse was to burn classified docu-ments and get out to fight another day – there was no more fearsome a fate than to be trapped underground hearing the thump of Mills bombs, or even worse, phosphorus or smoke bombs, tumbling down the timber steps. Retirement – if one could – was the sole option, for under the circumstances salvation by counter-attack was more than unlikely. So rapid was the Canadian advance that even the

The Germans were hit with complete surprise. We were about 115 yards from them in trenches that had steps dug into the sides, and from there went over the top with bayonets fixed. Our artillery did a great job but it took them some time to silence the machine guns in the pill-boxes, which seemed to be the only German guns firing. All our casualties were caused by the machine guns. A sergeant right in front of me got hit by a machine-gun bullet and, as he fell, he nearly knocked me down. He was killed instantly. By his side were two dead Germans, one lying crosswise over the other. My first view of dead Germans, and it was pretty gruesome because one of the bodies was headless. I particularly remember one German popping up out of his trench with his hands up, pleading for mercy as I approached, giving him quite a scare with my bayonet. But he had no gun, so I motioned for him to go to the back lines where they were herding the prisoners, and I pushed on.

PRIVATE JAMES MACARTHUR, 13TH (ROYAL HIGHLANDERS) BATTALION, CANADIAN EXPEDITIONARY FORCE

German trench mortars located in reserve positions were only able to fire for a matter of fifteen to twenty minutes before they too were either pulled out or overwhelmed. The garrisons of advanced enemy dugouts both large and small were forced to surrender, the only resistance – fierce in places – coming from strongpoints, often concrete, to the rear of the shattered front-line defences.

Those lucky Germans who evaded the Canadian onslaught streamed rearwards carrying news of the loss to bewildered headquarters staff. Surprise had been complete.

Only in the northernmost sector of the ridge was the attack properly held up. After two hours Hill 145 and The Pimple were proving obstinate, and once the smoke had cleared concern over enfilade was realized. In both positions the Germans had labyrinths of tunnels and dugouts in which to shelter; indeed, it was from there that machine guns were now holding up the Canadians. The Hill 145 position occupied less than 200 metres of front, and although under pressure was still holding out strongly. The Pimple was smaller still, but by virtue of incorporating a brace of concrete emplacements (unsuspected); it was as yet entirely uncowed. Both commanded huge expanses of territory, the floor of the Valley of Death (Zouave Valley) some 4 kilometres away being well within range. The approaches were devoid of cover, save for shell holes and mine craters, and whilst subway schemes had been specifically designed to obviate these very problems, now the Germans were aware of the exits and had them pinpointed too.

It was known that parties of Canadians were close to the front and flanks of Hill 145 around La Folie Farm, but it was impossible to accurately plot their locations, so Major General David Watson (4th Division) felt unable to issue orders to smother the 16th Bavarians with high explosive. His own casualties were mounting, and resistance was at present too effective to employ Currie's fire and movement tactics. There was no choice but to continue the traditional frontal attack. The stronghold *had* to be reduced before reserves arrived from Givenchy and the *Hangstellung*, for history had proved all too often that expansion of the position by counter-attack was possible – the Germans were simply too adept at this. Fortunately, omens elsewhere were good. In the knowledge that his longer-range guns covered German approaches, that the ground at the rear of the ridge should be an inferno, that Canadian troop numbers were robust and that attacks on the flanks were continuing more than satisfactorily, it should only be a matter of time before resistance on the crest could be made to collapse. Watson elected to employ the patient option: Hill 145, he decided, would face his Reserve Brigade (10th) as soon as they were prepared, whilst the situation at The Pimple could be examined overnight. The day was going as well as anyone could have dreamed, but such success does not come cheaply and

casualties, though light by comparison to so many earlier encounters, were becoming a cause for concern.

We were kept busy cutting away clothing, to get at wounds; getting through the dirt and mud; wiping off the blood with solution; or painting with iodine, putting on shell dressings and bandaging. The early cases were chiefly the mild cases – i.e., the walking cases – the stretcher cases not coming in until later. From then onward we were kept busy practically for forty eight hours dressing continuously. I cannot begin to describe all the varieties of cases – rifle wounds, shell wounds, but no bayonet wounds. Fractures of all parts, from depressed fractures of the skull down to the bones of the foot. It was just a bloody jumble, heart breaking because you could not follow your cases through and give them rational treatment, covering the serious as well as the slight with a bandage hiding the dirt in the deeper recesses of the wounds and covering over protruding viscera with pieces of gauze. Some cases had been dressed by Heinies and these dressings invariably were tied too tight, one man's hand being swollen to double its size; one, a Hun with a wound in his neck, being almost strangled. The most serious cases did not arrive until the next day, that is, they had lain out in the cold and wet and snow for over twenty four hours, so you can understand their condition was deplorable. It is impossible for you to imagine how plastered they were with muck and corruption; cutting through the muddy clothing ruined all our scissors. Many were able to get shelter in the Hun dugouts, but of all the cases we saw it was surprising in what good spirits they were. Victory is in the air and it is a great stimulant.
MAJOR WALTER BAPTY, MEDICAL OFFICER TO 102ND (NORTH BRITISH COLUMBIA) BATTALION, CANADIAN EXPEDITIONARY FORCE

On the southern Canadian flank things could hardly have gone better for 1st and 2nd

Divisions. Casualties were minimal – far lighter than expected – and the creeper had been deployed in exemplary fashion. The guns did the work for the infantry, traumatizing the first- and second-line German defenders, who streamed back as prisoners through the advancing waves. As expected, it was the villages, bludgeoned but defensible and containing plenty of cover in the form of cellars and concrete, that caused the major hindrances. Despite the barrage, machine guns and snipers in and around Thélus hurt the 16th (Canadian Scottish) Battalion; the assault was broken into small parties, who by patient fire and movement only slowly silenced the guns. On this day, at least two Victoria Crosses were won in this way. As the advance surged on, so the gunners were required to follow.

At noon on the 9th we received orders to move to the top of the Ridge. The horses and limbers came up from the wagon lines and we started east on the La Targette-Thélus road. The road to, and a short distance beyond, Neuville St Vaast was passable; but about where the front lines had been, we became hopelessly bogged. After floundering and half-killing ourselves in that morass, we got turned around and regained the Arras road; then south to a junction near Arras, where we turned left and north. About where the road crossed the front line, again we were bogged. This time for good, and it was now blowing, snowing, and getting dark. I noticed both times it was nearly on the site of the front line trenches the mud was the worst. Possibly the two years of shelling caused that spot to be softer than others. We waited in the mud all night, no rations, nor water, for a soldier is a funny fellow. He will not carry the extra weight of iron rations or water unless made to do so. He will carry wine or rum in his water bottle, but not water in winter. The next day, I had eighteen horses and a hundred men with drag ropes pulling my gun through the mud. The shield acted as a

snow plough. It took all that day and most of the next day, to get the gun, and our battery, in action. Most of that time we had neither rations nor water. But one of the cooks got forward with tea rations in a sandbag that night, the night of the 11th. In one of the old cellars of Thélus, he managed to make some hot tea. Next morning, I saw the water hole where he had filled his tea dixies, for no water cart ever got to us at that time. This water hole was an enlarged shell hole, with a dead German in one end of it and several piles of human excreta in the water at the sides; it must have been a German latrine.

SERGEANT W.G. SMITH, UNKNOWN FIELD ARTILLERY UNIT, 2ND CANADIAN DIVISION

The grim conditions did not stop the infantry from sticking close to the timetable. The battle plan had also attached eight tanks of 12 Company D Battalion for the attack on the Thélus sector. Their task was to follow the 2nd Canadians into action at zero, and later catch them up to assist in breaking resistance around the village, the second objective. Throughout the preceding night tank commanders listened to the falling rain and sleet, and with each passing hour lost hope of a 'decent performance'. The geology had been studied, of course, and the worry now was for 30 tons of steel being able to traverse a surface that resembled a wet sponge. 'Bellying' was the problem. If this happened they were even greater sitting ducks than when travelling at the full speed of 3 miles per hour. Long before the crews caught a glimpse of the attack, all four commanders were walking ahead of their machines selecting the dryest and flattest route. The Canadian line was negotiated and the German front line, but then it became hopeless; despite being fitted with 'spuds' – track attachments that increased ground resistance – every machine nestled uselessly into the mud. None had fired a shot. All

The ruins of La Folie Farm, a key Canadian objective on the crest of the Vimy Ridge, as seen in February 1917. ING 40-75-19

that could now be achieved was for the crew to glumly dig the things out by hand (and under intermittent shellfire that caused almost a dozen minor casualties), return to base, carry out servicing and repairs, and hope for better conditions next time they were called upon. It took three days to extricate the tanks; they were then allotted to Sir Hubert Gough's Fifth Army.

Here and there the Germans succeeded in driving back the odd party of attackers, but with no flanking support their often courageous efforts were mostly in vain, for the breakthrough had been so swift and comprehensive that the Canadians were soon 'rolling up' parts of the third German line, i.e. fighting laterally along it. After dawn had fully broken, it had been possible to see parties of fleeing Germans clearly. Within two hours of zero breaches were discernible in several places between the ridge and the Scarpe River; that in front of the Canadian 1st and 2nd Divisions and the 51st Highlanders beckoned; tank assistance might not have been contemplated for a moment, but that of another corps certainly would have been – where were the mounted troops at this critical moment? The enemy were in confusion. Was this not the opportunity the Cavalry had for so long been awaiting?

Although Sir Douglas Haig and First Army commander Sir Henry Horne had written the cavalry into their scheme (the 1st Cavalry Division was waiting in reserve some 11 kilometres behind the line at Frévin Capelle), they had been omitted from the orders issued by the Canadian Corps. It was Horne's responsibility. Without being integrated with the guns there was no way they could be deployed simply because it would be impossible to alter the fire patterns of the scores of batteries now carrying out their task to the letter. Gaps were there and

German resistance was visibly and audibly withering by the minute. Whereas at the beginning of the attack the skies had been filled with SOS rockets, hardly any were now discernible, and still the advance continued behind the creeper at 100 metres every four minutes. Similar reports were flooding in from all parts of the line. Then the cavalry arrived: a single squadron of the Canadian Light Horse. The twenty-strong force galloped through into the Willerval sector and went into action against parties of Germans isolated by the creeping barrage. It was at the same time a heartening and depressing sight. Importantly, they had coped with the ground conditions; perhaps tomorrow might bring other opportunities.

As afternoon began to turn to evening the position was still unclear about Hill 145. Resistance had been growing, but Canadian HQ were well aware that they held almost all the trump cards; patience was still the key, and the present happy situation allowed for it. The opposing front lines, such as they were, still lay too close to each other for a sustained barrage, so mortars and machine guns were employed, the artillery playing on the German second line. Two companies of the Nova Scotia Highlanders came up via the subways to attack alongside elements of the 46th Battalion. Just as all the troops were ready and lined up in the trenches, the attack was cancelled. But the news failed to arrive and the assault began. Whilst a nervous brigadier held his breath and feared the worst, the Canadians carried the hill, driving the Germans from the ridge-top plateau to their third line at the very edge of the escarpment overlooking the *Hangstellung*. More prisoners streamed back. The conquest of the central sector of Vimy Ridge was completed the following morning at 4.30 a.m. when the entire

Above Canadian troops advance over the crest of the ridge. IWM CO 1159

Right The Thélus sector: objective of 3rd and 4th Canadian Brigades. IWM 3rd Army Panorama 519, 25.4.16

summit was stormed and found to have been wisely evacuated. On the afternoon of 10 April, the *Hangstellung* too fell into Canadian hands, although at a far heavier cost to 44th and 50th Battalions. Now all the lines to left and right could adjust and consolidate. The ridge was theirs – for sure. Just The Pimple and Bois en Hache remained, and they could wait until the troops had taken a well-earned break. With reliefs carried out, celebrations began.

The Highlanders of 51st Division were destined to struggle a little more than the Canadians because for the initial assault their commander, Major General G.M. Harper, had elected to use two brigades with an extra battalion each, instead of three full brigades; thus his attacking line-up was somewhat weaker than the northern neighbours.

Whilst those troops on the left flank of the attack stuck dutifully and correctly to the Canadian right, keeping formation and forging ahead, the rest of the Division were to become hopelessly mixed up and disorientated. Resistance was far fiercer in this sector and gaps appeared as soon as the attack began. Subsequent waves, ignorant of progress but all too aware of the streams of lead flying above the trench in an inauspicious direction, stuck to the plan.

At about 9.30 we left the dugout and set off to the end of the trench, keeping our heads very low to miss the hundreds of bullets with which the air was filled. It was now a case of follow my leader. At the end of the trench each in turn clambered out and over the top. It was then that we realised the saying that it was like "Hell let loose". One out of every three was shot down immediately on reaching the top of the trench. I remember the first thing I saw after leaving the trench was one of our fellows laid head first in a shell hole full of water with the whole of

Army.

Panorama No. 519 made on 25/4/16 from Sheet 51.B(A.23. c. 55.15) ...ding a field of view of 84° from about N. by E. to E. by S.

Approximate Scale of Degrees (1 degree equals 1.07 inches).

1   2   3   4   5   6

A.12.a.53   THELUS CEMETARY   BOYAU DES SALTIMBANQUES   THELUS WOOD   A.17 d.70.15   OP   A.12 d.8.9   A.23 b.53
THELUS CHURCH
THELUS-ROCLINCOURT   A.17 d.7.7

his legs bare from the top to the ankles. The ground was one mass of shell holes. After covering about 50 yards in short rushes with bullets whizzing all around we reached the first trench. Here were many wounded and killed along with a couple of R.A.M.C. chaps who told us that they did not intend moving from that trench for anybody. Having regard to the large number of wounded lying all around I thought this was not the thing to do and said so, but I suppose they were only human like the rest of us and not anxious to throw their lives away. After resting a few minutes to get breath we carried on down a support trench which was dotted every five yards with dead and wounded Germans in addition to several of our own. The mud in the trenches was nearly knee deep and made it very hard going. I soon abandoned my flag as it was impossible to use my rifle or bayonet and retain possession of the flag. We traversed many trenches which were very deep but did not encounter any active Germans except those wounded and killed. One German knelt in the trench rocking to and fro with his head in his hands – I do not know whether he was saying his prayers or pegging out. By this time we were hopelessly mixed up and in the trench along with two others and myself of our Battalion were Gordons, Argylls and 6th Seaforths. Along the whole front, troops were completely mixed up and it was impossible to say where each individual Company was or was supposed to be.
Private Stanley Bradbury, 1/5th Seaforth Highlanders

Problems arose as soon as the first enemy line had been overwhelmed. One platoon of the 4th Gordon Highlanders correctly adhered to the Canadian flank, whilst the rest of the battalion veered south, breaking the golden rules of maintaining formation and contact. The catastrophe was amplified by the neighbouring unit, 7th Argyll and Sutherland Highlanders, who swerved with them. A treacherous gap was formed. Worse still, when the Gordons on the

right discovered their mistake they chose to withdraw in search of support, rather than close the breach. Then, pushing forward again with the protective barrage long gone, they believed they had reached their objective, the Brown or Point du Jour Line. It was in fact just another portion of the Blue Line, several hundred metres short. The troops consolidated and settled in for the night, for no nocturnal operations had been planned. As a result a displaced fracture in the line appeared, the most dangerous of situations. Following the progress of 1st Canadian Division, Major General Arthur Currie was soon made aware of the problem and urgently contacted his British colleagues. It was agreed later that the severe early losses, especially in officers, plus the lighter establishment, but most of all inadequate staff work, had caused the breakdown: there was no excuse for officers or even senior NCOs in the line not immediately responding to what happened, unless they had been poorly instructed. As dusk

Above Canadian troops advance past a tank struggling with the ground conditions. IWM CO 1575

Above Part of the German Hangstellung on the rear slopes of Vimy Ridge. AJ

settled on 9 April the Brown Line had been secured by the Canadians at Farbus, and by 34th Division in front of Bailleul, who found resistance 'very feeble' at first, but encountered trouble from a railway cutting and a clutch of machine guns in the Blue Line.

It was too warm, and everyone lay doggo for awhile to consider the matter. I ran along Jog [trench] to see Warr, but he had slid forward to talk to Martin, commanding D [Company], so I pushed on and found Flett and Thurburn, the two other officers of B, told them what was happening and suggested opening with their Lewis gun, though the range was point-blank, and I would send up one of mine to give them a hand; dashed back and sent up a L.G. and found my men closing up on C. and D., dodging through shell holes etc. It was impossible to stop them, and perhaps just as well as we had a Battalion behind us, and C and D getting thin wouldn't mind a bit of thickening. It was very unpleasant getting up: the air seemed just alive, and one jumped, dodged and ducked, my runner and batman always

handy. Just as I got up to the scattered front line of C and D, I saw a very brave thing. Flett had got the Lewis gun fairly blowing the wood in, and the M.G.s were a bit upset: one stopped worrying us and made to turn on the L.G. when Flett jumped up and waving his men on, dashed at it. He was shot nearly at once, and young Thurburn jumped up and dashed off; he had a longer do and no doubt eased our way over. The M.G.s were worried over this new attack. And momentarily the fire died down and we were up and off, the whole lot together, C and D and myself and runners and my own company, racing (a good word through the mud), to catch up the rest and to get out of the inclement weather. We met a good deal of rifle fire, but my Lewis guns had been plastering the [railway] cutting top, and so had kept the Bosch down to the last moment, and we hadn't far to go before we were too close for Mr Bosch, and he disappeared and over we went.

To go on about Thurburn. I heard afterwards that he was shot through the shoulder, which didn't stop the lad, and he ran on and exchanged revolver shots with the M.G., but unfortunately was killed. The mix-up when I got to the top of the cutting was great, Bosch running about like rabbits up and down the line, and over the bank no opposition at all, and our own men had some lovely rabbit shooting; then up panted my Lewis guns, and the old Bosch got it real lively, some running for the barrage some 300 feet away and trying to run back again, when they found that so uninviting at close quarters to plunge through, throwing themselves in shell-holes, anything to escape the fire. Those in the cutting had all disappeared down the dug-outs, so we went down and put moppers-up on the job, and they just streamed up out of the shelters: they must have been packed.

The cutting ended in a level crossing and then ran into another cutting … and I saw a very pretty scrap going on. The Bosch was fighting quite well, and so were our men; one lot was working up to the level crossing and there was any amount of uproar. They were plastering the cutting with Lewis guns from a slope behind the

Izel-les-Equerchin Church

OPPY WOOD

Oppy

BAILLEU

Church

valley, and finally got such a volume of this that they were enabled to storm the cutting. Bosch came running out of it and ran into my Lewis gun and there were some quite lively scenes.

Warr had sorted out our men, and chased all Suffolks, and even Tynesiders, out of our sector of the cutting; these gay lads were on the loose and chalking the names of their Battalion on the dug-out entrances, and our men got fair mad with them and chased them. Warr's message to BHQ got there at 8.30, giving success at Blue Line.

Casualties: 2 officers killed (Flett, Thurburn)
6 officers wounded, 2A, 1B, 2D, 1C
310 other ranks killed, wounded and missing

Not much left! I went to see the "Bois", found the Bosch machine gunners all laid out by their guns, poor Thurburn only 20 yards from them. Prisoners streaming away westward, only too glad to go, sometimes shep-herded by a wounded Tommie, but mostly all on their own, and running like Billy-oh! – a fine lot of men generally, though some awful weeds amongst them. The weather brightened up about noon, and the sun actually shone for a while, and we dried in it, fairly ragamuffin-looking lot, all torn with wire and plastered from head to foot with mud. Felt awful hungry for the first time, so had a snack and a good pull of rum and felt much better and fit to tackle a soothing pipe.

The shelling was poor, from a Bosch gunner's point of view: I suppose the situation was too obscure, and we were too far forward.

MAJOR BERTRAM BREWIN, 16TH ROYAL SCOTS

Bertram Brewin's battalion consolidated their section of the Brown Line, but delays caused by machine guns allowed the Germans to regroup a little and it was dawn on 10 April before the

Fresnes Les Montauban

The Bailleul sector beyond the Canadian right flank was a Third Army (XVII Corps) target for 9 April. IWM First Army panorama number 111, 22 April 1917

objective was fully captured and consolidated. Frustration set in as soon as parties had completed their assault and were able to take stock. The omens were marvellous, but something vitally important was missing: the guns.

Spent the morning in tidying up our line, which was complicated, as we were facing north mostly across the place where the Tynesiders should have been; however, we met with no distractions, and at 11am Gavin and a patrol went out and found a battery of three 5.9s from which the Bosch cleared on sight, otherwise not a sign of Bosch for 600 ft East of us. What a pity, if only we had a few more divisions, and our guns could have come forward, we could have gone miles. The guns, we heard, were all bogged coming up, and of course when a few got fairly in, it stopped the whole lot. I <u>don't</u> wonder for the ground was bad enough for a man on his feet and what it must have

been like for gun teams and caterpillars I don't know.

Anyway, they couldn't come up, there were no reserves of troops, so we had to sit tight and watch the Bosch, in full view, calmly digging himself in some 1500 to 2000 yards away, and not a shot could be fired at him! It was galling.
MAJOR BERTRAM BREWIN, 16TH ROYAL SCOTS

Thankfully the 9th (Scottish) Division's efforts paralleling the River Scarpe were not similarly blighted. This unit, under the command of Major General H.T. Lukin, had been handed the task of making the furthest advance north of the river. On Lukin's front the Green Line burst away eastwards from the Brown, so the sector was one of those selected for a 'mass leapfrog', the 4th Division being detailed to pass through the 9th as the Brown Line was gained, and drive on to the final objective,

Fampoux. It was quite a challenge, for the village lay some 6 kilometres from the original jumping-off positions.

Another Division was to take the first 3 German Systems (Black, Blue and Brown Lines) then our Division was to go through and capture the 4th German System and then we were to go through and capture Fampoux and dig in about 300 yds beyond it. We marched at 5.15am – in a snow-storm to the Assembly Area about 5 miles away, where we had a hot meal and rum ration and picks and shovels were drawn. The last mile or so up to this place we were passing through continuous heavy guns and howitzers all firing hard; you never heard such a row. We passed streams of wounded, and dense columns of prisoners kept coming in. During our halt here we had one man hit by a stray bullet, Lord knows where it came from. We heard the Black Line was captured before we moved off (at 10.25am); we went up to the Athies-Plouvain road: gangs of Sappers and Pioneers were already hard at work on it. The enemy barraged the road and the 1st K.O. (Kings Own Lancaster Regiment) ahead of us lost heavily, but we kept a bit to the south, and got to the Blue Line (which had been captured in the meantime) with only one other man hit (2.40pm). The Blue Line was an enormous railway embankment, we sat on it and watched our heavies strafe Athies and the Highlanders take the place – just like a cinematograph – then moved on and got into our positions of readiness while our guns hammered the 4th German System.
LIEUTENANT COLONEL ALFRED HORSFALL DSO, 2ND DUKE OF WELLINGTON'S (WEST RIDING) REGIMENT

Unlike other attacks, these were to be protected by a creeper employing no shrapnel, just high explosive and smoke. Because the German lines here were widely spaced, shrapnel would have had no benefits on the uninhabited areas between, and therefore little effect on morale. A curtain of H.E., however, in its spouting, deadly and relentless approach not only engendered fear, but added far more greatly than shrapnel to the confidence of those following. The blinding qualities of smoke when one knew H.E. was approaching *and* a hostile infantry attack was underway, was also a 'great demoraliser'. This was the thinking of Brigadier General Henry Tudor, commanding the 9th Division artillery. His day did not begin quite according to plan.

9TH APRIL
My soldier servant called me early. I at once asked him the direction of the wind. He said the wind was east. That tears it, I thought. But when I looked for myself, I found that there was a moderate west wind, perfect for smoke-shell attack. My man explained that he meant that the wind was going towards the east!
BRIGADIER GENERAL HENRY TUDOR, CRA, 9TH (SCOTTISH) DIVISION

Tudor had put a great deal of energy, thought and experience into his fire plan for the 9th Division. The attack which it was designed to protect did not commence in the orderly fashion HQ was expecting.

The 12th Royal Scots were attacking on the right with the 6th Scottish Borderers on the left. The Scottish Rifles were taking on the second objective on the right, and we were for the second objective on the left. The best part of the Brigade assembled in the craters, and luckily the Boche left us severely alone. He seemed to suspect nothing: all was so quiet. Or was it a trap? How we wondered as we got into position. When our turn came to cross No-Man's-Land we found the most appalling mix-up of the division. Even at that early hour there were Highlanders who had wandered on my left, and also South Africans. Most of my people were too much to the right, and it was all one could do to get them back into their proper places in time for the advance on our second objective, the railway line.

A shattered railway cutting near Arras after British capture. Note dugouts in left bank.
AC

As we walked along we noticed Thorne, who commanded the 12th Royal Scots, lying dead. He was a fine fellow and, curiously enough, he had lost his brother, a wing commander, a few days before. Losses had been heavy, and we were getting it in the neck from M.G.s on the railway: it was at this time that poor Loftus dropped by my side, knocked over by a machine-gun bullet. We made him as comfortable as we could, but we had to get on, for the attack was just due to start. Then down the slope went that splendid throng of lads, and up they climbed to the railway close under our barrage. Nothing could stop them that day, though there were Boche machine guns everywhere, and skilfully placed too. In some cases they were placed in tunnels under the embankment. In that advance Jimmy, who commanded a company of the 12th Royal Scots, was wounded for the second time that day. Part of his hand was dangling, quite a nasty wound, and he calmly shot it away with his revolver. In the attack on the second objective, where he had no business to be except through his keenness to be in at the death, he was very badly wounded all round the groin by a shell, which burst at his feet. Though he was suffering agony he refused to be taken down on the stretcher till all his men had been first attended to. So great were his agonies during this waiting period that a sergeant twice prevented him from turning his revolver on himself.

LIEUTENANT COLONEL W.D. CROFT CMG DSO, 11TH ROYAL SCOTS

As it formed a part of the Blue Line, perpendicularly traversing the entire 9th Division frontage, the Royal Scots and Borderers also faced the task of clearing the cutting of the Arras-Lens railway. Cuttings were useful in defence but unwholesome in attack, riddled with dugouts and secreting many a machine gun and sniper. Brigadier General Tudor had also noted the poorly cut wire and had his field guns fire gas and smoke amongst the H.E., ceasing the gas as the infantry approached.

*Brigadier General Francis Aylmer Maxwell VC was shot by a sniper on 21 September 1917 while commanding 27 Infantry Brigade in the Ypres salient. Nicknamed 'The Brat', Maxwell won his VC in South Africa. He was looked upon as one of the most able commanders of the war.

They 'clambered through the wire to find the defenders sitting with their masks on, under the impression that it was just a gas strafe'.

We got hundreds of prisoners here. Railway cuttings are unpleasant neighbours in battle. They are too well shown on the map, and consequently they make excellent data points for Boche gunners: the railway on our second objective was no exception, and the Boche punished it thoroughly. So we got well out in front and consolidated there. We were allowed to dig in comparative peace until two low-flying Boche planes spotted us, and then the Boche gunners shortened on to us, and we began to suffer casualties which we couldn't afford. Shells sometimes play horrible tricks on their victims. I remember seeing one of our poor fellows get a direct, or nearly a direct, hit by a 4.2-inch. The body shot up into the air like a rocket, describing a complete parabola. And I saw a tiny speck come down from far above until it was near enough to recognise the head which was following the body. In the middle of our long halt at the second objective – we stayed there about four hours – we suddenly saw heavy columns of our infantry wending their way across the ridge to their assembly positions near the railway cutting. The Boche observers must have seen them too, for as one of the battalions crossed the ridge a 5.9-inch opened on them. The third shot found the head of the column, and that third shot must have caused at least thirty casualties.

At a Brigade conference held at the cutting to decide on which battalions were to assault in the third attack, Frank Maxwell* put the Scottish Rifles on the right, and we were on the left, supported by the Borderers, with what was left of the 12th Royal Scots in brigade reserve. Things were not too bright; for the 9th Division had a big gap on its right. But the wind was in the best quarter, and so the C.R.A. was able to put down a smoke screen which apparently gave the Boche the impression that we were using gas. Anyhow the result was that he cleared out in that quarter and enabled the advance to continue.

But we cast many an anxious look to the right rear

during the first half of the battle, for we could see with half an eye that things were not going quickly across the river. It was bitterly cold during that advance to our third objective. And we all of us expected to have a pretty tough opposition, for our artillery could not possibly have cut the wire which defended the Boche system round the Point du Jour. But as we advanced the Boche fire appreciably lessened, and as we approached that formidable belt of wire it died down altogether. Even the pill-boxes seemed to show no sign of life. What could it mean? Some trap, no doubt, and we set our teeth and went for the wire. It was a tough job getting through the wire, even with little or no opposition, and then we saw an inspiriting sight – a mob of Boches hareing away out of the trenches. It was too much for our fellows: with a wild view-halloo we were after them. It was too much for the Borderers, who raced us for the Point du Jour. What a sight it was when we got there! One could see half the world, and everywhere one looked were fleeing Boches. Victory, victory! Even far-away Monchy seemed covered with fugitives.
LIEUTENANT COLONEL W.D. CROFT CMG DSO, 11TH ROYAL SCOTS

The division might well have had the assistance of a brace of tanks had not all eight machines of No. 7 Company, C Battalion been knocked out by enemy action or succumbed to the boggy ground like their northern colleagues. On Colonel Croft's left the advance was sweeping forward, taking hordes of prisoners and conforming well with units to the left and right. The next objective, Athies, suffered the same fate as the railway cutting, being blown to brick dust before the creeper and the infantry arrived.

I was chosen to be the FOO (Forward Observing Officer) for the brigade. From a high perch in a ruined factory building I heard and saw the barrage suddenly come down on the German lines, which immediately gave a magnificent display, miles long, of rockets and coloured

signals, some of which looked like great theatre globes hurled into the air. I then set out, according to a pre-arranged plan, with ten or twelve signallers paying out telephone wire along the embanked railway line which crossed the valley of the Scarpe. Every 500 or 600 yards, I left two signallers behind to patrol and repair the telephone line, of which we carried a length of about 2½ miles. According to every precedent, this should have been ample, for the German trench system had never been penetrated in one day to such a depth. But quite early in the morning we had come to the end of our reels, and still there was British infantry ahead of us. So I went on, to find out what I could and then come back to report, for our telephone line was being kept in good repair without great difficulty.

On the hillside above the village of Athies I found a German battery still in position, and attended by an officer and a number of men who had not yet been gathered into the columns of prisoners whom I could see being shepherded back towards Arras. The remains of their half-eaten breakfast were still lying about, and the officer told me that they had been taken completely by surprise when our barrage came down and their communications were cut to ribbons by counter-battery fire. I next came across a British sergeant who assured me that he had been, with thirteen men, at least a mile and a half further on, and that there were no Germans left between us and the village of Fampoux.
LIEUTENANT HARRY SIEPMANN, 14TH BRIGADE, ROYAL HORSE ARTILLERY

Now it was the turn of the 4th Division. The Royal Scots could take a breather, but not before Brigadier General Maxwell had tried and failed to make further arrangements.

The telephone spoke to Frank Maxwell:
"Are the Boches on the run?"
"Yes."
"Is cavalry good business?"

"Yes, ten thousand times yes, but it must be done now. Too late to-morrow … Why can't we go on?" And so forth. Then the 4th Division came through us. They had been marching all day without the excitement of battle to buoy them up. On they went and disappeared into the Blue. What a victory! We had bitten in 3 miles into a strongly defended line held by the Boche's best troops, the Bavarians. On ground of his own choosing we had trounced him well and truly beyond the very shadow of a doubt. We all thought the war was over – and then a sniper hidden a few yards away in a shellhole shot one of our best officers! He died – that sniper.

Looking back was almost as fascinating as looking forward. For far below us lay Arras – poor, beautiful, mutilated Arras, lying down there in the hollow like a dead swan. Everyone asked his neighbour, "How the devil did the Boche allow us to exist in such a place?"
LIEUTENANT COLONEL W.D. CROFT CMG DSO, 11TH ROYAL SCOTS

The Brown Line on the Point du Jour ridge was now under 9th Division rule, and four brigades of field artillery were already on their way up. But no cavalry. Meanwhile, the troops of 4th Division were arriving to take the advance to the final Green Line.

On reaching the 4th System it was found that the wire was absolutely untouched by our artillery – there were only a few gaps in it left by the Germans and these were under artillery fire. There was a certain amount of confusion as we had to close in to get through the wire, pass through the other Battalions and then shake out again. However, we pushed on towards Hyderabad Redoubt passing through the German barrage. "B" Company was dropped at the Sunken Road and quickly cleared the dug-outs and occupied the trenches just east of the road and began to make "strong points". "C" and "A" Companies went on to capture the Redoubt. Here again the wire that entirely surrounded the place was unbroken

and there were only two gaps to get through. By the mercy of Providence both here and at the 4th System of trenches the Boche put up no fight at all, a few men with a machine gun could have stopped the whole Brigade and hung up the whole attack. We entered the Redoubt, No. 11 Platoon drop kicking a football into it and rushing in afterwards! Owing to the great depth of the trenches in the Redoubt and the confusion caused by only being able to get in by two gaps it took some time to reorganise. As soon as possible the dug-outs were cleared and seven officers and nine men captured. Consolidation was started outside the Redoubt and patrols and outposts began to go out. By this time, however (5.00 p.m.) the enemy were shelling the place pretty heavily and snipers and machine guns lying out in the open were picking off the men one by one. It was no use going on under these conditions, suffering unnecessary casualties, so the posts were withdrawn into the Redoubt, blocks were made in the communication trenches running towards the enemy and all efforts directed to consolidating the "T" heads that ran out from the Redoubt.
LIEUTENANT COLONEL R.T. FELLOWES, 1ST RIFLE BRIGADE

The advance from here was in artillery formation of Section Columns and was done just like a drill movement, every Section in its proper position moving steadily on. The German position was just over a ridge and we did not know we were so close to it when suddenly a hare got up and came dodging in and out of the columns. All the men cheered and watched it while the Bosch with his hands up came streaming out to us, but no one cared a damn for them compared to the hare. It was lucky the Bosch had the wind up as the wire was hardly touched and the trenches intact. From here we pushed on to Fampoux. On our right, South of the Scarpe, our attack had not got forward so well and the Bosch MGs kept going hard at us but I don't think anyone was hit, thanks to the very long range they were firing at. We had to wait some time for our heavies to paste the place. During this

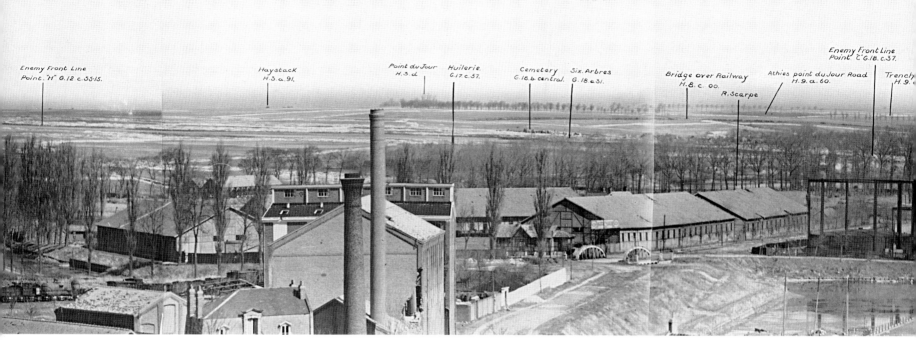

Enemy Front Line
Point. "H" G.12.c.35.15.

Haystack
H.3.a.91.

Point du Jour
H.3.d

Huilerie.
G.17.c.57.

Cemetery
G.18.b.central.

Six. Arbres
G.18.a.31.

Bridge over Railway
H.8.c. 00.

R.Scarpe

Athies point du Jour Road
H.9.a. 60.

Enemy Front Line
Point. "C" G.18.c.37.

Trench
H.9.

halt a few Bosch guns got on to us and a Subaltern was killed close to me and several men wounded (4.40pm). We fairly rushed the village, which was a very big one. Luckily for us the enemy was a bit on the run and it was not until we got near the far end that we had any fight-

ing; here we had to bomb them out of one or two houses. The Bosch made a stand beyond the village, holding a railway embankment on our right, several trenches, and a line of houses beyond, with MGs. Trying to advance to the Green Line we lost about 80 men and 6 Officers in

Above Segment of Third Army Pan. 507 looking eastwards over the Scarpe valley from Arras on 29 March 1916

3rd Army.

Panorama No. 504 made on 26-3-16, from Sheet 51 B. (G. 22. c. 8785), THE REFUGEES, including a field of view of 58° from about N.N.E. to E. by N.

NOT FOR REPRODUCTION
1. Panoramas are taken solely for military purposes.
2. The publication of them in the press will necessarily give valuable information to the enemy.
3. This panorama is to be kept with as much security as is compatible with full advantage of it being taken by our own troops.
4. When troops are relieved this panorama should be handed over to the relieving troops.

Approximate Scale of Degrees (1 degree equals 1.07 inches).

0   1   2   3   4   5   6

St Nicholas

British front line

Road to Gavrelle

German

British front line

(Railway over road)
4. 14. a. 03.

Athies L'Abbayette
H. 14. b

Railway Embankment.
H. 13'. d. 98.

Trench
H. 15. b. 64.

Athies–Fampoux Rd
H. 15. d. 43

Fampoux Church
Chimneys
Fampoux Station

Church
G 22. a. 82

Roeux

Below The view north-east from the Arras rooftops towards the high ground astride the Point du Jour and Gavrelle. IWM Third Army Pan. 504, 26.3.16

2 or 3 minutes. The survivors had to lie flat, any man showing himself the slightest bit being shot to pieces. I decided that without artillery support we could not push further so we dug in along the forward edge of the village (5.35pm). It was rather an anxious time for a bit as

south of the river on our right a heavy Bosch counter-attack had gone clear past and about ¾ mile behind us; and on our left where we were warned an attack was expected the rest of the Brigade had not come up into line. So we were just holding the forward end of the

St Laurent Blangy

German front line

Point du Jour

Road crossing
H. 8. c. 12

Railway embankment

village and a bit either side with both flanks in the air. However I managed to get a Coy of the L.Fs to join up on our left (8.00pm), and the rest of the Brigade came up into line – or rather part of them did – during the early hours of next morning and I got the KO [King's Own] who were in support to hold a bridge over the river for us (in our rear).
LIEUTENANT COLONEL ALFRED HORSFALL DSO, 2ND
DUKE OF WELLINGTON'S (WEST RIDING) REGIMENT

Fampoux and the high ground to the north were both solid, and another section of final objective attained. There were those who believed that the 4th Division leapfroggers could have been saved for later and that the 9th should be allowed to continue the attack on the Green Line themselves, for their blood was up and the fire of victory in their bellies. But orders were orders. There were many more who seeing the nature of the success and gauging its further tremendous potential wondered where on earth the cavalry had got to.

9TH APRIL

There were practically no enemy left to stop us and our infantry would doubtless have passed the valley of the chemical works [Roeux] and the next ridge called Greenland Hill. Infantry and cavalry should have been rushed up in support and a real breakthrough would have resulted. As regards the cavalry, I went to the Cavalry headquarters and enquired about the plan for them. I was told that they were to follow through south of the River Scarpe when the 15th Division had broken through. I asked if we were successful north of the river whether there would be any cavalry move to follow us up. I was told "No", that their orders were only to advance south of the river. I had always been taught that the cavalry was an army of opportunity. Here the opportunity was decided before it had occurred; which seems like putting the cart before the horse. The 4th Division advanced

and captured the Green Line which included the village of Fampoux, but here they stopped. Our headquarters are now much too far back.
BRIGADIER GENERAL HENRY TUDOR, CRA,
9TH (SCOTTISH) DIVISION

The remains of Vimy church. HS 06/6/25

Once more, there was much to celebrate. Tomorrow would surely bring a harvest of fresh opportunities.

CHAPTER ELEVEN
Osterschlacht South:
the Scarpe to Croisilles

8th. The Day Before!
9th. THE Day!

Good news came first – then bad news. Didn't hear our bombardment at 5 a.m. owing to the wind blowing in the wrong direction, and to the fact that I was asleep. Went into Duisans, and learned that we had the front system everywhere, but that our Brigade (45th.) were held up by the Railway Embankment, which is some 60 feet high. That meant that 'A' and 'B' companies were held up. Heard they were to try again at 12.15 p.m.

Saw about 1300 prisoners – poor specimens, particularly the officers. Couldn't rest all day, but looking for news. Thousands of cavalry passing through Duisans all day. Heard that the "Blue Line" was taken at 3 p.m. and then the "Brown Line" in parts. At 5 p.m. all objectives of Division gained, and 37th Division going through towards Monchy – the pivot of Vimy Ridge. Felt bucked but feared the casualties. All divisions have done beautifully. Far better than the Somme show. Poor Alan Whyte killed. Shankland and Eric Duncan wounded. Jock Stewart seriously wounded but still able to swear, which he did all the way down to the Casualty Clearing Station. Hunnybun got shell-shock. Went into my valise at 7 p.m. with indigestion.

Lieutenant Robert Mackay, 11th Argyll and Sutherland Highlanders

For Sir Edmund Allenby, it was essential that progress on the southern battleground mirrored that in the north, for here lay his axis of advance upon Cambrai. It was here too that he keenly wished to use the cavalry. The key objectives were Monchy-le-Preux and Guémappe, fortified villages that stood sentinel either side of the Arras-Cambrai road close to the Green Line. Both lay within the 4-kilometre-wide battle front of VI Corps. To crack these potentially tough nuts, Lieutenant General Aylmer Haldane had at his disposal 15th (Scottish), 12th (Eastern) and the 3rd Division, many of whom were comfortably billeted in the *Boves*. In reserve in the town cellars, ready to consolidate as soon as Monchy fell, were the 17th (Northern) Division. To the south was VII Corps under Lieutenant General Sir Thomas D'Oyly Snow. Faced with an attacking front composed mainly of the Hindenburg Line, their vital task was to produce a firm flank for Haldane's thrust, and a solid foundation for the assault of Gough's Anzacs on 11 April.

THE VALLEY AND THE TRIANGLE

Immediately south of the River Scarpe, the two leading brigades of 15th (Scottish)

Division under Major General F.W.N. McCracken had potentially the toughest assault of the day. The sector was narrow and held the knottiest of obstacles: Railway Triangle. Known to the Germans as the *Geleisedreieck*, the feature was formed by the conjunction of railways to and from Arras, Lille and Valenciennes. To traverse the Scarpe valley, when the line was built engineers constructed cuttings and high embankments. By 1917, these had long been fortified. The eastern embankment, protected by a strong trench known as the *Zwischen Stellung*, occupied the highest point. It commanded the ground both sides of the Scarpe, which it also bridged. The conglomeration was a fortress, and McCracken was therefore offered the assistance of two tanks. 45th Brigade's day began in organized fashion.

Reveille for the poor Jocks at 3am. Poor fellows, they seemed unwilling to start. We got up at 3.45 am and breakfasted "with a good 'eart". Our original time for leaving our own cellars was about 6.15 after the 91st Field Company RE. Time went on and the men enlightened the wait with a concert. Personally I sat on a box and tried to get to sleep. At 8 am we began to file along the cellars and picked up news on the way. The Black Line was taken with little opposition, but the Blue Line was holding out on the left behind Blangy and the Black Watch were badly cut up in getting through. Passed along the sewer and left mouth of sewer at 9.15 am. At the moment of exit it was raining, with a cold west wind. The air was rent with the steady roar of shells filled with rifle and shrapnel pellets. After a few seconds I did not feel acutely windy and in five minutes felt almost careless. An agreeable surprise. We crossed almost entirely in the open, passing crowds of Huns, some carrying our own stretcher cases. Nearly stopped a bit of shrapnel near Boost Trench. Now headed for the railway, following the 12 HLI just in front of us. They had 60 casualties, we had none. Several dead to left of railway. Got on railway and filed forward to OG1 [the original German front line]. A very hot corner that got much hotter as we turned south and passed along OG1. A weak barrage of 5.9s and plenty of HE shrapnel, some of it very close indeed. Windy stuff is HE shrapnel. Several dead Gordons in OG1. Got into an old trench and sat there

The view of Arras from the German lines on the high ground near the Point du Jour. BHK

Ronville   Bahnhof   Wasserbehälter   Ratha
              Station   Bel

until 11.30 with occasional reconnoitring. Had several near squeaks and a bit of shrapnel on my tin hat. Thousands of planes overhead, a few Huns among them. A tank came up behind us and passed over to our south spouting 3-inch shells – most impressive. And then one of the sights of the war. The Field Artillery came up and limbered up in 'no mans land' and began barraging, ear splitting din, especially from 13-pounder RHA gun. Frightful destruction of OG1 and complete destruction of five trenches.

MAJOR MARTIN LITTLEWOOD, 45TH FIELD AMBULANCE, ROYAL ARMY MEDICAL CORPS

To synchronize with 26th Brigade on the north bank, Blangy had to be cleared. The village was shared, the lines running through the ruins, in places separated only by a few metres of rubble. The proximity of opposing positions ruled out shelling in parts of the sector, so by way of compensation the RE had planted a mine to ease the way. The Sappers were well practised in the art, but this time they overcharged the chamber making the blow somewhat more powerful than expected. At 5.30, when the plungers went down, falling lumps of chalk caused a few casualties and not a little concern for the 13th Royal Scots already formed up in no man's land. Despite the mine, it still took two companies of the Battalion over three hours and the help of heavy mortars to break resistance in the village and head towards the Triangle. Troops of the same brigade utilized the engineers' other accomplishments to make their entrance.

Sunday, 8th April. Holy Communion in a cellar. We were told D day is to be tomorrow, Monday 9th April. We had tea, bread and boiled egg at 0400 hours. All was suddenly quiet. A nasty place for us to take was the Railway Triangle, a honeycomb of concrete forts. This was to get 250 15-inch shells and 200 12-inch shells to break it up. Then at 0530 hours a huge mine went up and a terrific barrage opened. We moved along our tunnel and found sappers cutting holes for us to emerge just behind the German front line, which we rushed from the rear meeting very feeble resistance and taking some very shaken prisoners. We then turned about and went on steadily but found the Argylls and Royal Scots Fusiliers were being held up at the Railway Triangle. Evidently the 450 shells were not enough! We had to wait

Süd Zitadelle   Egl. des Ardents   Kathedrale   Pte. du Hâvre   St. Sacrement   St. Nicolaskirche   Seminar   Nord Zitadelle

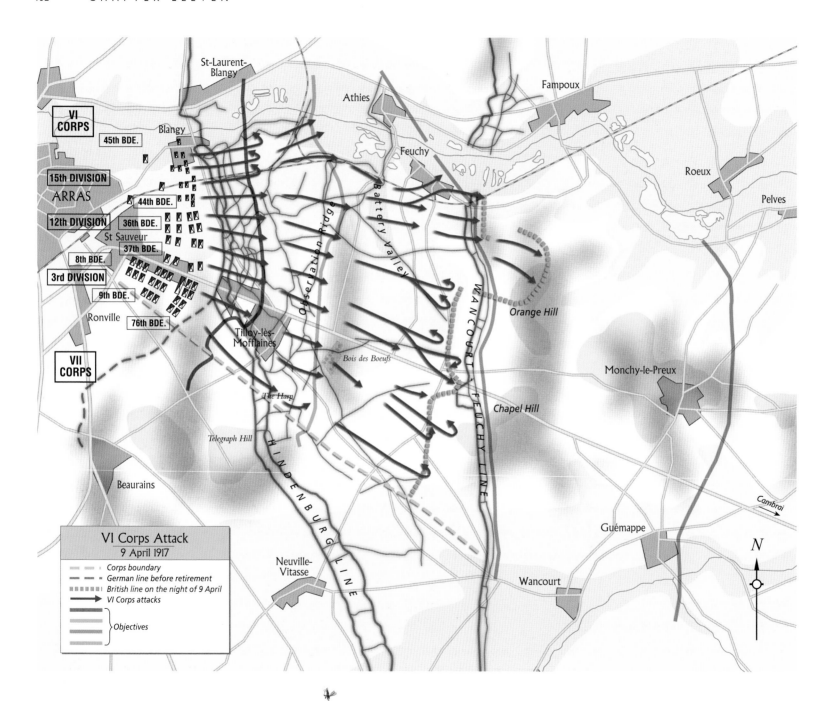

St-Laurent-
Blangy

Athies

Fampoux

VI
CORPS

45th BDE.

Blangy

Feuchy

Roeux

Pelves

15th DIVISION
ARRAS

44th BDE.

12th DIVISION

36th BDE.

St Sauveur

37th BDE.

8th BDE.

3rd DIVISION

9th BDE.

Observation Ridge

Battery Valley

WANCOURT

Orange Hill

Ronville

76th BDE.

Tilloy-lès-
Mofflaines

Bois des Boeufs

FEUCHY LINE

Monchy-le-Preux

VII
CORPS

The Harp

Chapel Hill

Telegraph Hill

HINDENBURG LINE

Cambrai

Beaurains

Guémappe

VI Corps Attack
9 April 1917

Corps boundary
German line before retirement
British line on the night of 9 April
VI Corps attacks

Objectives

Neuville-
Vitasse

Wancourt

N

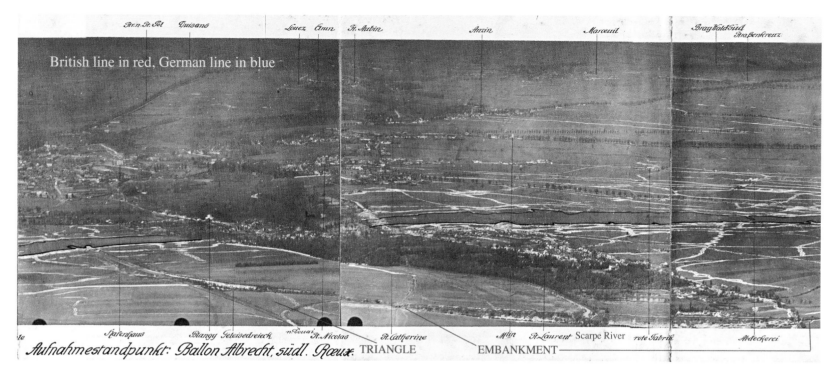

British line in red, German line in blue

Br.n.Fr.Pet   Duisans   Louez   Ennn   Ft.Aubin   Anzin   Marœuil   Bray Wald Süd   Straßenkreuz

le   Speterhaus   Blangy Geleisedreieck   n Douai Ft.Nicolas   Ft.Catherine   Mlin   Ft.Laurent Scarpe River   rote Fabrik   Abdeckerei

Aufnahmestandpunkt: Ballon Albrecht, südl. Rœux. TRIANGLE   EMBANKMENT

Above German aerial panorama segment showing the Scarpe valley, Blangy and Railway Triangle sectors, objectives of 15th (Scottish) Division on 9 April. BHK Rundbild VII No. 11

till they finally took it with bayonet and bomb. Then we all advanced rapidly and by 1800 hours had captured the strong Feuchy redoubt and the village. I was re-organising in the village when an extraordinary episode happened. A mounted Officer in the uniform of the Essex Yeomanry galloped into the village shouting "Get out quick, retire. The Germans are on you in great numbers, you have no chance". One of my subalterns, Donald Ross, a Canadian, at once shot him dead and we found he was a German Officer in disguise from his papers.
CAPTAIN PHILIP CHRISTISON, 6TH QUEEN'S OWN CAMERON HIGHLANDERS

Captain Christison makes the taking of the Triangle sound straightforward. It was not. Alongside 44th Brigade and protected by a 21-gun machine-gun barrage, the other battalions of 45th Brigade pushed up astride the railway towards the junction. At around 15 metres in height, the eastern embankment glowered over the valley. Gunfire was having little effect on it and casualties mounted as the infantry tried to nibble their way in. The lower southern section eventually succumbed in a few hours, but the rest was still spitting so much fire that it endangered the advance of 15th and 12th Divisions against Observation Ridge, the adjacent high ground to the south that protected the critically important Battery Valley. As the Triangle resisted, Major General McCracken saw the creeper advancing up the ridge – it could not be allowed to march away. Irregular measures were required and so he requested as many heavy and medium guns as possible to interrupt their fire patterns to target the Triangle. Thankfully, communications did not fail, and soon the embankment was lost amidst the dust and fumes. The tank Martin Littlewood saw may well have been 'Lusitania', which had also appeared at the Triangle to help break the deadlock. It was a long and very hard day of adventure for the crew.

Started from Citadel [rear of Arras] at 7.45pm. Bogged close to railway but got out about 1a.m. Attempted to tow another Tank out but failed. Received orders to proceed at 2 a.m. Arrived 100 yards from point of deployment at 4 a.m. when bolts connecting plate on back axle to extension shaft were found to be missing. Sent to Citadel for four bolts, receiving same about 8.30 a.m. Started for action at 9.30 a.m. crossing British and German front line systems over heavy trenches and shell holes in bottom gear without incident. Halted for 10 minutes to allow engine to cool. Caught up 44th Brigade just in front of Blue Line. Halted to clear water from Magneto. Heard that Brigade was held up. Fired two rounds of 6-pounder at machine gun in wood north of Railway at about 20.c.60.60. Heard no more fire from this gun. Received message from Brigade Major, 44th Brigade requesting reason of stoppage. Informed him we were filling up and would start in two minutes. Started engine and proceeded towards Blue Line. Half way over Sgt. Latham informed me that all Infantry were following, they arrived almost simultaneously with us, in fact too close to allow me to use my guns, and found the Germans with their hands up. Proceeded straight along railway towards FEUCHY REDOUBT, firing on same with 6-pounders and Lewis guns. Observed Germans evacuate this work, half running to the rear and half to the dugouts close to Railway Arch. Went on and inspected this Arch, firing on same with 6-pounders at anything resembling a machine-gun emplacement. Found we were now under our own barrage and were being shelled by an anti-tank gun. Went back up slope to see what had become of our infantry, found them on top and gave them the Green Disc signal. Turned and proceeded towards arch again. Observed an infantry signal from a party which had come up along railway and got to the arch. Sat outside the arch while this party took the Germans prisoners. Observed hastily abandoned guns lying along this valley. I then had to proceed S. about 400 yards and looked for a point at which I could climb the bank. Found the best place but engine was too hot to climb; all power had gone. Cleaned out Magneto which had been giving us trouble all through, the distributor being full of water every time we took it down.
SECOND LIEUTENANT CHARLES F. WEBER, OC TANK NO. 788 (LUSITANIA), BATTLE NOTES

Charles Weber's orders had been to help clear the Triangle from the rear, then turn and advance along the railway beyond Feuchy and assist the infantry by driving southwards down

Right Blangy village and the canalised Scarpe. SA

Below The Railway triangle sector under snow. SA

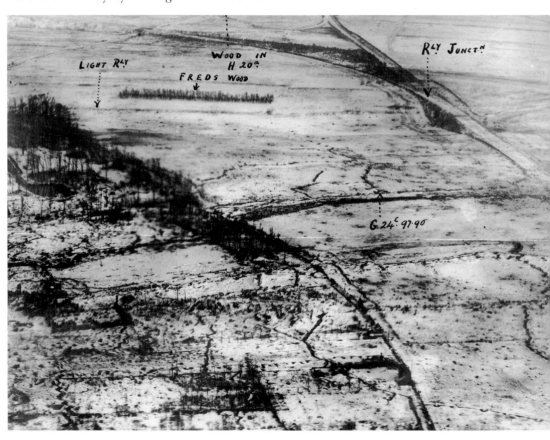

the Wancourt-Feuchy (Brown) Line. His sister tank had foundered, so 'Lusitania' was on her own. Given the strength of the first objective, the scheme was ambitious, but the crew managed to guide their machine among the pillboxes in the Triangle without either breakdown or being seriously hit – and with infantry following in their wake mopping up. It was a tremendous effort, at the same time saving and claiming many lives. The crew suffered no injuries, but were utterly strung out at the end of the day, a day that later held an honourable end for 'Lusitania'.

Started engine and climbed bank successfully. Found our Infantry were well over half way to the Brown line. Fired a few shells into trenches just north of the railway. Got into third gear and attempted to catch up infantry.

Observed them get over and into Brown line, so we swung half right along the line of barbed wire. Found on getting to point about H 28.c.40.70. that Germans were holding a small redoubt. Received signal from Infantry and turned in their direction. Germans retired. Informed that two snipers were out at the back of the line, turned in their direction and they came in with their hands up, an officer taking them prisoners. At this point the 15th Division ended, and we observed the Brown line extending South was not held by our troops. We proceeded for some distance along this line doing as much damage as possible with 6-pounder and Lewis guns. Seeing nothing of our infantry and being short of petrol, magneto also giving us a lot of trouble, I turned towards FEUCHY CHAPELLE. Had got about 300 yards when a Colonel requested me to turn back and help to take a trench. After explaining I was short of stores I agreed to do so. He assured me his men had orders to follow me. I got within 50 yards of trench, and found about 4 machine-guns were playing from same. Stopped and tried to silence these guns with shell fire. Believed we silenced two. Proceeded to within about 10 yards of barbed wire when my magneto absolutely gave out. We then opened a heavy fire along the trench with Lewis guns and 6-pounders, killing individual Germans with shells from the 6-pounders. Infantry failed to follow. Did everything we possibly could to restart engine, but failed. Decided to abandon car at 9.30pm. Did so, leaving one by one and bringing the Lewis guns. It is believed she was set on fire by a shell from one of our own guns, early in the evening of the 10th.

SECOND LIEUTENANT CHARLES. F. WEBER, O.C. TANK NO. 788 (LUSITANIA), BATTLE NOTES

With the Triangle largely subdued by 12.30, 45th Brigade marched on towards the Blue Line at Feuchy. Thanks to good counter-battery work, hostile artillery was weak and becoming weaker. Across the entire battle front the clearing skies were filling with aircraft, the RFC taking photographs and scanning the scene

Third Army Arras Cemetery Panorama
From: Sheet 51B G 29 b 2.7

St Laurent Blangy

Athies and Fe

Le Point du Jour

Valley of River Scarpe

Above Segment of a panorama from a British observation post looking eastwards across the Arras cemetery. IWM (no number or date)

below for rockets, flares and any signs that revealed British progress. The bombardment was marvellous to behold: a 15-kilometre linear arc of shell bursts. On the ground, it was also becoming easier for FOOs – both British and German – to see through the murk and guide their guns accordingly. In the hurricane of flying metal the job of airborne intelligence-gathering was a ticklish one. Given an awkward gust, the flimsy craft were likely to blow over even when on the ground; in the air, a heavy shell passing close by created a tremendous vortex. The resulting lurch could usually be recovered from, but even a glancing blow from a projectile – red-hot – could turn a plane to confetti, and now the heavens were full of them. Occasionally, aircrew would actually see heavier shells howling past.

The ground seemed to be one mass of bursting shells. Farther back, where the guns were firing, the hot flames flashing from thousands of muzzles gave the impression *of a long ribbon of incandescent light. The air seemed shaken and literally full of shells on their missions of death and destruction. Over and over again one felt a sudden jerk under a wing-tip, and the machine would heave quickly. This meant that a shell had passed within a few feet of you. As the battle went on the work grew more terrifying, because reports came in that several of our machines had been hit by shells in flight and brought down. There was small wonder in this.*
MAJOR W.A. BISHOP VC, FROM *WINGED WARFARE*

To gather information the RFC were forced to roam far and wide over enemy territory. Whilst pilots nervously scanned the skies around, observers squinted groundwards through the clouds and billows of bursting shells. What they saw around noon astride the Scarpe was pleasing.

The 15th Division were well on the move along the railway and heading towards Feuchy. As their frontage was narrow, the attack did not incorporate leapfrogging. 46th Brigade had been held in reserve in Arras, their task being to emerge from subterranean lairs in late morning to pass through 44th and 45th Brigades, and consolidate the Brown Line once it had been snatched. Advancing into battle from the Blue Line exactly on time at 12.50, two companies of the 12th Highland Light Infantry strode towards the crest of Observation Ridge.

Something of a surprise awaited us as we pushed on over the crest of Observation Ridge, for there on the reverse slope, not more than two to three hundred yards directly in front of us, were two batteries of German field guns that opened point-blank fire on us as soon as we appeared in view. It was something new and certainly very uncomfortable to find ourselves so close up to the muzzles of enemy guns in action; the range was so short that the flash of the guns and the explosion of the shells amongst our men seemed instantaneous. We were in extended formation, of course, but in the few minutes we were under that deadly fire several men were killed and a number terribly wounded. I remember catching a glimpse of my new batman, Don, with a gash in his neck that looked as if his head were almost severed, and beside him, standing stock still in his tracks and looking at me in a helpless sort of fashion, as if he wanted to know what I was going to do about it, was our mess cook with a spurting red mass of flesh on his shoulder where his arm had been. For the second time that day – and we had to decide quickly this time – we found our safest direction lay right ahead; in fact our only course in that situation was to rush the guns, which we did. We "ca'ed the feet from them'" as our Clydesiders put it, and I think we got most of the Boche artillerymen. They belonged to the 42nd Field Artillery Regiment.

After silencing the German batteries, we moved on across the narrow valley named in our maps "Battery Valley" (for very obvious reasons, as we had just discovered!)
CAPTAIN DOUGLAS CUDDEFORD, 12TH HIGHLAND LIGHT INFANTRY

Below Lieutenant Weber's Lusitania passes through the streets of Arras on its way into battle. IWM Q6419

With 36th Brigade (12th Division) entering the southern end at about the same time, Battery Valley was soon completely overrun. This was one of the greatest events of the day, for not only was it extraordinarily rare to reach the gun lines of one's enemy, but the British could now bring up their own artillery into the valley's shelter. Although a few German guns had managed to limber up and escape, sixty were captured, any undamaged weapons being swiftly turned upon their erstwhile owners.

The 12th (Eastern) Division under Major General A.B. Scott, had emerged from the Horseshoe Caves under St Sauveur to form up. It was this attack that the British had hoped but failed to film as a result of the camera crew being gas-shelled. Four tanks had been allotted to the sector. All made an entrance upon the stage, but none played a role, with two mired and the others set alight soon after the whistles blew.

The barrage lifted an hour or so before the attack was due to start. The silence when it stopped had to be experienced to be believed. But this, only for about an hour during which we all took up our position for the advance and awaited 'Zero'. What pathetic and strange incidents can be conjured up in such an hour. During the course of a dug-out inspection, a very young soldier, nothing but a boy, was found, alone, crying his heart out, frightened beyond all words and just hiding from the moment when we went over the top. How unbelievably terrible. His nerve had completely gone. It might so easily happen to anyone. He had to be persuaded to come out and take his place rather than stay where he was and later face arrest and the only possible consequences.

There were several inches of snow on the ground. Not the best of backgrounds for hiding our advance. Whilst waiting to go over I well remember an officer friend of mine coming along the trench to have a word with me. He had been out in France for a long time and was an old hand at these attacks. Strangely, when leaving me he held out his hand for me to shake and said, 'Good bye old lad, I have a feeling that this is it.' He was, from what I heard later, dead within minutes of that farewell. It was often said that this sort of premonition presented itself at such a time and the feeling was there that your number was up. An hour then of almost unbelievable and unbearable silence and suspense. Watches synchronised – every nerve stretched. Came the moment.

Lieutenant Arthur Worman, 6th Queen's (Royal West Surrey Regiment)

The 12th Division's sector was a strong one, but by means of Russian Saps the first wave of Norfolks and Buffs were amongst the enemy in

quick time. Worman's 6th Queen's, in the second wave, were to leapfrog.

It would have been reasonable to suppose, that with all that had gone before, no single Hun would have been found alive in their lines. By no means so. The majority may have been moved back but plenty had been left in the line.

Our turn came to go over, through the preceding wave as we had been taught, to our objective – the Hun line [in front of Monchy village]. On the way over, my faithful orderly happened to glance my way, saw blood oozing through the front of my tunic. I had been hit in the groin but, strangely enough, had felt nothing of it at the time, although later it proved to be quite a sizeable splinter of shrapnel which had got me. I have never concerned myself with telepathy or the supernatural, but on the night of Easter Day my Mother, then living in Croydon, awoke from her sleep, wakened my Father and told him that she had just seen me walk into their room in uniform but with a loose white bandage wound round my middle. A strange story indeed as I had only been hit that morning and would not have been reported wounded until perhaps some days later. My orderly covered the wound with iodine and applied my field dressing both of which we all carried. Our barrage of the previous days had torn the Bosche trench system to shreds. They had suffered heavy casualties in its wake, as witness those lying around when we got over who would fight no more. Indeed the Hun was trained to fight. This was brought right home to me when I was moving forward with my platoon to our objective. A Hun was lying on the ground just ahead of us, apparently very dead. I had passed him and was amazed that, with such life that he had left in him, he twisted himself over and fired an automatic pistol at my batman. He was fortunately too far gone to find his mark and it was his very last effort. But what stamina and what hatred.

Lieutenant Arthur Worman, 6th Queen's (Royal West Surrey Regiment)

Above Special bridges built by the RE to cross the River Scarpe permitting both foot traffic and barges. Note the height of the railway embankment in the background. IWM 5822

Below A German dummy field gun on the western slopes of Battery Valley. IWM Q5179

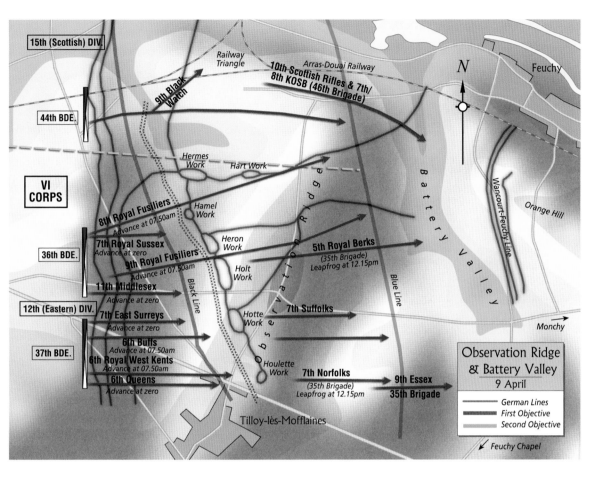

15th (Scottish) DIV.

44th BDE.

Railway Triangle

Arras-Douai Railway

9th Black Watch

10th Scottish Rifles & 7th/ 8th KOSB (46th Brigade)

Feuchy

N

VI CORPS

Hermes Work

Hart Work

Observation Ridge

Battery Valley

Wancourt-Feuchy Line

Orange Hill

36th BDE.

8th Royal Fusiliers
Advance at 07.50am

7th Royal Sussex
Advance at zero

9th Royal Fusiliers
Advance at 07.50am

Hamel Work

Heron Work

Holt Work

5th Royal Berks
(35th Brigade)
Leapfrog at 12.15pm

12th (Eastern) DIV.

11th Middlesex
Advance at zero

7th East Surreys
Advance at zero

Black Line

Hotte Work

7th Suffolks

Blue Line

Monchy

37th BDE.

6th Buffs
Advance at 07.50am

6th Royal West Kents
Advance at 07.50am

6th Queens
Advance at zero

Houlette Work

7th Norfolks
(35th Brigade)
Leapfrog at 12.15pm

9th Essex

35th Brigade

Tilloy-lès-Mofflaines

Observation Ridge & Battery Valley
9 April

— German Lines
— First Objective
— Second Objective

↙ Feuchy Chapel

On the Royal West Surreys' left flank were the 7th East Surreys, the leading wave of which had also spent time in the St Sauveur caves before their attack.

The divisions who were to lead the attack were all in the line and we knew that our reserves had been brought up and were bivouacking close to us underground – in fact literally under our feet. Anxiously we awaited the dawn. My own immediate neighbour in the dugout was a certain Lance-Corporal named Steele. He had received by the last mail brought up to us by the Orderly *Corporal, a parcel containing among other delectables a couple of bloaters from his native town, Yarmouth. Many were the jokes passed, and many the caustic remarks when these made themselves felt. They had evidently spent too long in the packing. 'Dead Fritzes' someone called them; others declared that they had been found 'hanging on the wire at Loos'. Steele answered all these gibes appropriately and at once commenced 'cooking' them by holding them on the point of his jack-knife over the very smoky flame of a lamp made on the spot by the insertion in the neck of his rifle-oil can of a piece of four-by-two. When they were sufficiently burnt – and smoked – he ate them amid much chaff and laughter. Whew! They did smell, but, as Steele said, he didn't know when he might get another chance. By that same post I received a postcard from Aunt L. displaying a bunch of roses and the words "With Easter Greetings" on it.*
PRIVATE PERCY CLARE, 7TH EAST SURREY REGIMENT

For Percy Clare's regiment, 9 April and subsequent days were to be ones of tremendous trial. His narrative of events (he came back into battle again in early May) are possibly the most extensive account extant today. As they offer an extraordinarily detailed picture of the varying character of action across much of the front on 9 April, they are here freely quoted:

Our platoon officer came to give the boys a last word of advice. McEvoy was quite a young man, probably not more than 25 or 26 and formerly a private in the Australian contingent; he had been wounded at Gallipoli. He somehow got to England, obtained a commission, and had been gazetted to the 7th East Surreys as a Second Lieutenant. He seemed to be suffering

British front line   German front line

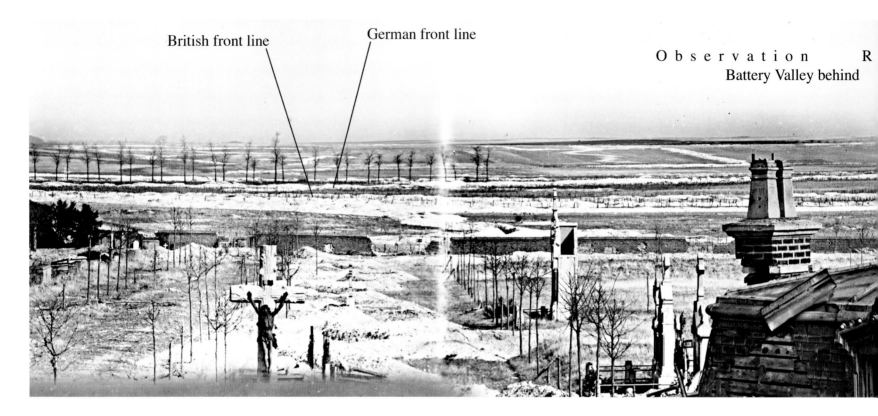

somewhat from 'swelled head'. This officer was really a transport officer, and as such his duties precluded him from participation in the attack, and consequently he was not present at any of our practices at Ambrines. McEvoy told the men that once Zero came and we got going, to go 'Hell for leather' for the Boche front line. Get there, said he, in the shortest possible time and so escape the Boche's protective barrage. In theory it seemed alright, but he had overlooked, or perhaps did not know, that our own concentrated fury of gunfire was timed to play for two minutes upon that very Boche trench after it had swept over No Man's Land 30 yards in front of us. In our rehearsals we had been trained to crouch or kneel 30 yards behind it when it reached the German trench, wait for two minutes until it lifted, and

advance steadily together at a walk keeping a good line and true direction. It is obvious that anyone following McEvoy's advice would inevitably perish under our own barrage. Corporal Steele and some others expressed their intention of following him. McEvoy also said he would unhesitatingly shoot with his revolver any man he saw stopping or hanging back, or seeking cover in shell holes, or going back unless severely wounded. True, he gave any man permission to shoot him if he hung back, but his threat was quite unnecessary, and the men received it in hurt silence. They were only glad to be given a chance to get to close quarters with the Hun instead of having to stand in a trench until invisible death found them from an invisible gun. McEvoy boasted that we had been set the task of carrying the first

Monchy le Preux

Above VI Corps' battleground for 9 April as seen from an OP in a house behind the OP behind Arras cemetery.

Inset Manoeuvring an 18-pounder field gun into position inside the cemetery. IWM Q6205

four lines of enemy trenches, but he would lead us to the fortieth if there were so many to take. Such bragging only proclaimed his inexperience and unfitness to command us in so important an action. Poor chap, he was killed before he got to the very first line through his rashness in running under our own barrage fire. Unfortunately, he took some others with him.

The battalion moved from the cave to the assembly trenches and prepared for the attack.

Each man had been given about a tablespoonful of neat whisky in a rifle-oil can, and we were now told to drink this. For some reason, on this occasion rum was not forthcoming and our officers were giving us the whisky at their own expense. "Two minutes" was passed down in a low tone amid dead silence on the part of the men, followed almost immediately by "One minute: get ready!"

The comparative quietness after the din of the bombardment especially during the last four days was remarkable. I did not feel nervous: I felt that, anyhow, my fate was not now in my own hands. I was anxious to get on.

"Now boys!" came faintly, and I saw the dark line of our parapet against the sky broken by bobbing figures while a confused murmur came to my ears. The men were muttering oaths and injunctions as they slipped on the muddy trench walls and jostled each other in their anxiety to get out. The crumbling trench wall gave way beneath my foot as I attempted to clamber out, causing

me to slip back. Moving slightly to the left to gain a firmer hold I found a team-mate, Prestwich, struggling up on his knees and hands. He was an awkward fellow. When I thought Prestwich was clear I threw my right hand up to get a good grip of the parapet. Now in this hand was the rifle with bayonet fixed. I felt the bayonet meet something, and simultaneously heard a deep "O –oh!". I looked up to see Prestwich, who in the darkness I thought was clear of the trench, slipping back with his hand clapped to his buttock. Poor old Prestwich: I am sure he must have had the distinction of being the first casualty in the attack. Lots of men would have envied him. The immensity of the sound, the concentrated crackling of over a thousand guns, batteries of trench mortars, mingled with the hideous din of innumerable machineguns from both sides was awe-inspiring beyond words. There was no want of light. The whole sky and earth seemed to have burst into flickering flames which ran like chain lightning for 20 miles along our front. Really I could have found it in my heart to feel sorry for the poor old Hun.

We had moved forward only a few yards when the German retaliatory barrage descended and the earth began spouting about us in miniature volcanoes. Our [Lewis] gun team moved shoulder to shoulder, anxious only not to get separated. This was not easy. We had progressed little when a German shell struck the butt of the Lewis Gun which was carried by a man next to me called Medhurst. It was a direct hit and the gun was instantly splintered to atoms. The burst of the shell blew me some yards and knocked down our section commander Corporal King, Medhurst and two others. Fortunately the 'blow' of the burst was expended forward in the direction in which the shell was travelling, and therefore away from us. Almost at the same instant, I felt another shell burst at my feet. Strangely enough I felt the force of the blow of the first shell in my mouth, and for a minute or two I thought all my teeth had been blown out. I was bruised and shocked, but recognising the peril I was in I picked myself up, secured the panniers of ammunition

which were lying close by, and went forward alone. I believed King and Medhurst to be killed. The only chance I had was to move from under their barrage zone; I had already absolutely forgotten all about the two minutes halt we were to make whilst our guns played upon the German trench.

I pulled myself together, rose and started. The din was prodigious and the smoke shrouded everything in an impenetrable veil except when the wind blew a rift momentarily. I was conscious of the terrific chatter of machine-guns which could not be located by sound; they seemed all around everywhere. I caught sight of bobbing figures and managed to rejoin the survivors of our wave just as they were moving forward to storm the trench. The enemy had scattered the ground of No Man's Land with spiked balls, balls of iron from which radiated three or four long sharp prongs. Put there to impede us they were not very effective except to further wound any who might be unfortunate enough to fall on them. Their barbed wire had been pretty well all 'skied' and strewn around by our barrage of 'toffee apples' [trench mortars]. The front storming wave in which I had my place was ordered not to stop in the first trench but leave it to be 'cleaned up' by the second or 'moppers-up' wave. Alternate waves were always 'moppers-up', theirs being the duty of remaining in the trench in order to kill all skulkers and survivors, clearing out the dugouts by the simple process of flinging down the entrance shaft a Mills bomb or a Stokes trench mortar. This was very necessary as bitter experience on the Somme taught us that the Germans stuffed their front line with machine-guns and men who, when the line of stormers has passed over the seemingly deserted trench, emerged to attack them from the rear, confident that their own rear was safe on account of the terrific barrage that their artillery put down between the lines.

9 April 1917. British infantry moving up in artillery formation. Note the troops in the trenches with sandbags draped on their shoulders for protection against the weather. IWM Q5115

Before reaching their first objective, the Black Line, the East Surreys had three more trenches in the German forward system to negotiate.

Clambering out of the trench which had offered practically no resistance we continued our advance on his second line. In front, great swirling clouds of smoke, reflecting the flashes and flares; dim ghostly figures in a half-stooping attitude moved in the smoke, only visible for a brief second so that one felt horribly lonely and helpless. Behind and in front the ground was alive with the bursting of shells – ours and their barrage. Shell holes appeared without one being able to distinguish the noise of the explosion which made it.

Again the barrage lifted and crept forward, while we rose to our feet and advanced with levelled bayonets. The resistance was greater than one would have expected after such a pounding from our artillery. In the portion of trench that I entered I found two stricken Huns very badly wounded from our shellfire. One was about 48-50 years of age I guessed; the other a mere boy possibly 20 years, bearing a remarkable resemblance to the other. I next noticed that their hands were interlocked as though they had determined to die together. It was easy to see that they were father and son, and deep compassion for them took possession of me. It distressed me to see them in such a case. In spite of the entreaty of our C.O., voicing higher commands, to show no mercy, I felt as sorry for them as I should had they been my own friends instead of my enemies. I would have stayed by them had it been possible to see that that they were spared and handed over to our stretcher-bearers.

The faces of those two fellows, so ghastly white, their features livid and quivering, their eyes so full of pain, horror and terror, perhaps each on account of the other. Their breasts were bare showing horrible gaping wounds which without doubt were mortal. One or two of our fellows passing by raised their bayonets as if to thrust them through when their cries for mercy were truly piteous. Plenty of men could be found who never bayoneted any but wounded Germans, and I stood for a few moments restraining any who in the lust of killing, and having in mind our CO's lecture, might thrust them through. Poor fellows, they were doomed. I had to go

forward. The third German trench was some way ahead, and our wave of attackers had dwindled so that reinforcement was necessary. This was effected by combing in half the moppers-up wave behind us. One of those was a man named Bean, a butcher by trade. I discovered from him that he had come across those two poor wounded Huns in mopping up and had thrust them both through the abdomen with his bayonet, not even troubling to see that he had really put an immediate end to their miseries. My indignation consumed me, and friends though we had been I told him what I thought of it and from this moment we had no use for each other. I told him he would never survive this action; that I didn't believe God would suffer so cowardly and cruel a deed to go unpunished. Bean himself was killed on 3 May, and it was I who first discovered his body. Before the third line, a formidable trench, we were led up a few moments to allow the flanking unit, who had got a little behind, to join up. As I looked back, crouching in my shell hole I could see in the rear wave after wave of infantry advancing in good order in spite of the frightful weather (it was snowing heavily now). These troops had issued from the tunnel under the old No Man's Land through the boring which had been blown when the battle first commenced. They were not yet wet like ourselves having been housed snugly underground. We were soaked to the very skin, and ankle-deep in mud. On my right I noticed Tilloy wood and village shelled by the British heavy guns.

The German support positions had now been reached. Here, one was likely to find greater numbers of underground shelters, and therefore larger hostile garrisons.

The dugouts of this trench were deeper and more spacious, which accounted for the number of survivors. The resistance was distinctly stiffer and we had to bomb our way along the trench in one or two places. It is a chancy business and a lot depends upon luck. In the next bay, *separated from you by the traverse only, are the Germans, anxious for a chance to bomb you. You lob your bomb or bombs over the traverse hoping they fall in the trench at the right spot, listen for the explosion, meanwhile dodging if you can any of theirs that are flung with similar hope and intent, and rush round the traverse immediately before they can recover, to bayonet or shoot any who are still inclined to show fight. Sometimes the bomb has done its work and you watchfully step over the mutilated carcases (if they are not mutilated it is better to make sure). If the bomb hasn't done its work, well it is left to your own prowess with the rifle, either its bayonet or butt, but you usually get the advantage if you are quick: you must arrive <u>almost</u> at the same time as the explosion, and you must shoot or bayonet any man still on his legs before he gets you. He has the advantage of waiting for your appearance. You are lucky if he is so shaken that his arms are up in surrender, but even so you have no time to see whether he has a handy bomb in his fist, and you generally shoot first and look after. A rotten business.*

The capture of one more trench would take the East Surreys and their flanking colleagues within reach of the Black Line – the first objective of the day.

The fourth trench reached, and we halted for a brief time to allow more supports to get up and reinforce us. Not many of the original wave remained, and those of us who found ourselves still unwounded were pretty well exhausted. Isolated Boche snipers were now very much in evidence, and although the enemy was in full flight for the time being, these pests held on to their posts very stubbornly and caused us many casualties. There is no truth in the legend that the German was anxious to surrender as soon as our men appeared. Why, otherwise, were all our gains so costly? Their snipers and machine-gunners never ran. Owing to resistance from these isolated strongpoints, the assault fell far behind the barrage, but these centres of strife were left and our people

pushed on between them so that being surrounded and far within the British zone they had eventually either to surrender or be wiped out with trench mortars or rifle grenades; all that I saw chose the latter after doing all the execution they could. At 12.30 after seven hours continuous fighting our sister Brigade, the 35th (we were the 37th) passed through our exhausted and depleted ranks and moved to the front. Here I found another Buffs man with a Lewis Gun but no ammunition, so we joyfully got together.

The 12th Division were to capture their Blue Line second objective at 1.05 p.m., at which point elements of the British field artillery (18-pounders) moved forward to the eastern edge of the Arras suburbs to carry the barrage further into enemy territory. Although he had not once been able to play his allotted part as a member of a Lewis gun team, Percy Clare's share in the 9 April action was now (almost) complete, the plan being for 35th Brigade to take the fight to the Brown Line and the 37th Division to the Green. Events did not unfold this way as the creeping barrage left the 12th Division behind. The troops emerged onto the plateau in front of Monchy unprotected. Hostile fire was by no means heavy and parties of Germans could actually be seen leaving the Wancourt-Feuchy line (the Brown Line), but the wire defending it was not cut. The guns had no time to attend to the wire and there was no hope of support from the right flank, for neighbouring 3rd Division troops advancing south of the Cambrai road had an even longer trek to attack their section of the same line. Soon, the Germans who had been seen abandoning their positions were back in the line. Facing them was a jumbled assortment of British regiments. Percy Clare's next duty was to find his unit and await fresh orders.

Above British cavalry moving forward. IWM Q1989

Left German dead in the front line. IWM HU16198

*It appears that Percy Clare's fears may have been borne out, for according to the CWGC database 22-year-old Lance Corporal Christmas James Steele (10503) has no known grave. He is commemorated on Bay 6 of the Arras Memorial to the Missing.

Prisoners were now streaming down the trench to the rear. They were being sent down without any escort, a fact which tempted about a dozen of them to clamber out of the communication trench and make a dash in the direction of their own lines. They were instantly detected and excited shouts appraised everyone in the neighbourhood. Swinging round our Lewis Gun we joined in the general fusillade and they were, every single man of them, shot down within twenty seconds. Seeing that in the excitement we as well as the others were firing across our own ground, and a good many of us were facing each other, there could be no doubt that some of our people somewhere were shot as well.

After this we hastened away to seek our own regiments, and eventually came across some of our men trying to locate a troublesome sniper. He was still well within the British zone. He had lain secure behind a fallen tree and was picking our fellows off one by one. He had killed outright six of our men including Captain [actually Lieutenant] Potter, the Company Commander of 'C' Company, Captain King of 'A' Company had been slightly wounded in the hand by him, and before he was overcome he added several others to his bag. He had plenty of opportunities with men coming up moving about in the open quite unaware of such a lurking enemy. Once located with certainty he was surrounded and rushed. He immediately put up his hands and cried loudly, 'Kamerad'. Needless to say all the 'Kamerad' he received was ten inches of British steel though his chest.

As the shelling receded, so the light artillery began their advance, engineers and signallers moved in to repair roads and tracks and extend communications, the Medical Corps arrived to create forward aid posts and dressing stations – and the clear-up of the battlefield commenced. For those whose day was over, there was just a little time to take stock before they were informed of the next challenge.

Nearby us was a heavy machine-gun emplacement, the crew of about ten men lying dead in a heap by the broken and upturned gun. They were horribly mutilated; all were killed by one heavy shell – a direct hit. The gunner was chained to the heavy tripod, and two suits of armour plate were lying by the gun. Just over the parapet was another heap of German dead, probably seven or eight; the bodies were flung one across the other and all the faces were a ghastly greenish-black colour. Several others were hanging in some still-standing barbed wire which protected the gun emplacement. These bodies and other dead round about were left where they fell for burial by the men of the labour and salvage battalions who would come later to clear the battlefield. A burial party was detailed to go back over the ground to find our own dead, to bring in where possible the identity discs and bury the bodies. I was included in this party, and during the afternoon until dark we worked hard digging graves through the deep snow. It was through this that I came to learn the fate of our platoon officer, McEvoy, and the others who had so foolishly run into our own barrage and perished. Some awful sights I saw, and yet they seemed to affect me not in the least: they might have been plants I was burying. I wondered at myself, that in such a short time I could grow callous. And yet I mourned the loss of comrades I had known so intimately, and daren't think of their folk at home at all.

We dug a row of shallow graves to take those we could move, an officer's 'more sacred corpse', McEvoy's, being amongst them. Captain King came along with the Chaplain to read the burial service over him. I did not hear the words said as I was some hundred paces away covering the remains of poor Steele* and eight men who fell with him. This lot were too mixed up and mangled to move; their bodies were all in a pile, and because of this and the shocking injuries which daunted me, I decided not to disturb them, especially as I was working alone and they would be difficult to handle. I therefore heaped earth all over them (they were all in the crater of the shell *that killed them), stuck four rifles in the ground by their bayonets, hung four shrapnel helmets on the butts and left them to be found and properly reburied by the burial party who would presently come along. I have often thought of that little group and where they now lie. No Chaplain gabbled over them.*

PRIVATE PERCY CLARE, 7TH EAST SURREY REGIMENT

German bodies were attended to by dedicated parties, 'Instructions for burying dead' orders having been issued before the battle. Each battalion was also required to collect 'intelligence' from enemy corpses. Normally, a party of three men under an NCO gathered half of the two-part identity disc (the discs were snapped apart on a serrated joint, the other half being buried with the body) along with any relevant papers, maps and letters, plus unusual equipment. The accumulated material, not unsurprisingly, was considerable, and was taken to the Arras Prison where it was sorted and despatched to the Intelligence Corps for translation, study, and, if suitable, use as propaganda. Excerpts from German letters recovered in this way can be found in intelligence notes of divisional war diaries, known as 'Comic Cuts'. The identity disc and personal items of no military value eventually reached the Red Cross who would arrange delivery to the German authorities. Families could expect notification of death or wounding within a fortnight, and receipt of personal effects about ten months after the event.

Long before the light began to fade on 9 April the battlefield was alive with men from those units whose duty it was to reinstall a functional infrastructure on captured ground, and to deliver the necessary supplies to the foremost troops. Conditions were as grim as many could remember.

The roads were now crowded with men of the Pioneer and Labour battalions with their thick-set navvy-like men, Army Service Corps, Royal Engineers, Artillerymen, Signals and R.A.M.C. The heavier guns were being hauled with difficulty and many curses and oaths from their pits. Limbers and mules with stores of all descriptions and ammunition were passing ceaselessly in both directions, their drivers hailing each other with jests and sallies instead of sitting stolidly glum on their seats as they usually did. Everyone was in good spirits – had we not got Jerry on the run at last? Most welcome sight to us then, perhaps, was a long line of cavalry on magnificent horses, arriving to bivouac under the low undulating ridges. Whilst we were on the road two Boche airmen buzzed overhead at a discreet height. They were met with heavy fire from our 'Archies'. The planes at last turned tail and made off towards their own lines, but I'm afraid they had plenty of interesting news to impart to their headquarters. The full moon behind the clouds and the snow-covered countryside rendered everything plainly visible. Even before we got clear of the road 5.9 shells began coming over to fall in the rubble and debris of wrecked houses fringing the road.

PRIVATE PERCY CLARE, 7TH EAST SURREY REGIMENT

The 12th Division had reached and vaulted the Blue Line and pushed on to the threshold of the Brown. On their left most of the 15th Division made greater gains, taking sections of the Brown Line and pushing well beyond – a splendid gain but awkward for their right flank, now adjacent to but detached from Clare's crowd, was held up.

Now it was the turn of Major General H. Bruce-Williams's 37th Division to enter the arena and complete the design by claiming Guémappe and Monchy. Strongpoints barring their way, such as the Railway Triangle and Feuchy Chapel, either had been or soon would be eliminated, the latter by the 9th Essex, but

Above A German reconnaissance aircraft heads east as dusk closes in. ING 150-87-259

Right A key objective: Monchy as seen from 'Refugees' OP across the Arras rooftops. IWM Pan. 505 (no Army noted), 1.5.16

delays and disorder in the earlier afternoon, combined with the fractured gain line between 15th and 12th Divisions had caused Bruce-Williams' leading brigades, 111th (objective, Monchy) and 112th, to be pushed up in a supporting role only. Before Monchy could be approached, the rest of the Brown Line had to fall, so his third Brigade, the 63rd, was ordered to pass through the 15th and 12th Divisions, and occupy part of Orange Hill. The three brigades, therefore, were no longer a cohesive attacking force. It was approaching 6.00 p.m.; wintry showers came on once more, hindering visibility on the ground and from the air, and the light was beginning to fail. Monchy and Guémappe were within touching distance and resistance there was still meagre. It was possibly the most critical moment of the entire battle. Opposite all the British divisions between the Scarpe and Monchy lay a lightly defended gap though which either infantry or cavalry could have swarmed. The cavalry were to hand, indeed some had already dashed up the Scarpe Valley and already made a highly successful foray. Sabres in hand, the Northamptonshire Yeomanry had surged along the railway through the 15th Division to reach a crossroads adjacent to Fampoux. Clearing snipers and isolated posts, they secured the bridges, a vital action. Some crossed the river and made contact with 4th Division troops in Fampoux village. The triumph was crowned by the capture of no fewer than six guns. There were sufficient mounted troops close at hand to take the fight strongly forward, and considerable

bodies of infantry in the sector to assist, mop up and consolidate. Daylight remained, still enough to make a serious impact, at least upon the thinly held Brown Line. But there was no communication and therefore no orders.

It was at 3.00 p.m. that 112th and 111th Brigades (37th Division) had been ordered forward from the devastation of the Blue Line over Observation Ridge and across Battery Valley towards the Wancourt-Feuchy line, ostensibly to pass through the 15th and 12th Divisions to attack Monchy-le-Preux.

It was perhaps 4 o'clock and the sun sinking low, when we received the order to open out into artillery formation, and advance over the ridge. On the true summit of the slope at last! But where was that inferno of crumping shells and smoke indicating the firing line? It was certainly far from being obvious. Very few shell holes seemed to be visible. Where on earth were the troops, supposed to be in front of us? Not a living soul was to be seen, not a single shell burst. Directly in front and ¾ mile away could be seen a line of strongly constructed trenches and just this side and running parallel with them, a roadway with a line of trees on each side [Feuchy Chapel-Feuchy road]. This trench system, we soon learnt, was the "Brown Line", into which we were to stroll, reassemble, and from there start our part of the business. It did not look like a battlefield but more like a piece of peaceful countryside. Here and there a hare could be seen coursing through the grass, evidently wondering what had brought such a host of Cook's tourists to that region. We wondered just as much as the wretched hares. "What is happening?" everyone asked his neighbour. Two miles off, over the undulating grassy country and beyond the Brown Line, could be seen a village crowning the summit of a circular hill, with its red-roofed cottages peeping out from amongst the green foliage of trees, altogether a very picturesque view. This village was Monchy – our objective – and our Battalion had to take it.
SERGEANT RUPERT 'JACK' WHITEMAN, 10TH ROYAL FUSILIERS (CITY OF LONDON REGIMENT)

Reports at this time stated that the Brown Line had fallen, but they were erroneous and misleading; it was only true of the narrow section

Above British aerial showing German island redoubts on Observation Ridge. Note the wire. SA

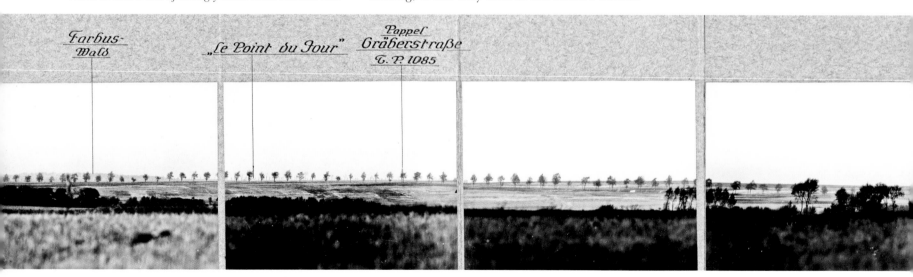

Farbus-Wald   „Le Point du Jour"   Pappel Gräberstraße T. P. 1085

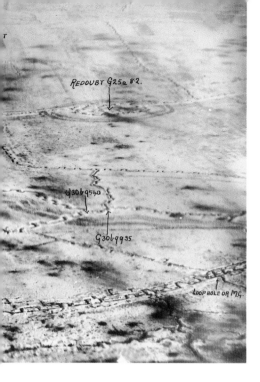

Below German view from the Wancourt Tower across 3rd Division's sector of attack towards Monchy. BHK Rundbild VII 20, October 1916

from the crest of Orange Hill to the river; elsewhere the line had been approached but not actually attacked. Battery Valley was now seeing the arrival of British gunners, and in order to properly ascertain the true situation 18-pounder battery commanders climbed Observation Ridge to view the scene. It was all too clear that the trenches shielding Monchy between Orange Hill and Chapel Hill were unconquered, but there was no barrage, so were they occupied still?

On starting on the downward slope to the Brown Line everyone was surprised to hear the all-too-familiar sound of a machine gun fired from somewhere in front; and still more so, when a few bullets whistled over our heads or cut through the long grass at our feet with a "Zipp". When another machine gun opened fire on us, Colonel Rice gave the signal for the Battalion to open into extended order. By this time it was getting dark and, what was much more to be regretted, beginning to snow. As the advancing line of men got nearer the Brown Line it became all too apparent that the machine gun fire came from the trench itself; so, obviously, the Germans still occupied it. We never found out what became of the division supposed to capture this trench before we put in an appearance; still, they were not ahead of us as per schedule so it was no use crying about it. Fortunately only about three machine guns and a few snipers seemed to be firing; had there been more we should have suffered heavier losses. By the time we reached the road running parallel to the German trench it was quite dark and snowing hard. Cover was difficult to find as there were very few shell holes. The road was about 100 yards from the trench, and just outside the impenetrable tangle of barbed wire almost as wide as a street and five feet high. Most of us by this time had taken cover from bullets in the gutter; it seemed useless to get nearer, for no man could cut a gap through the wire whilst being fired at from point blank range.
Sergeant Rupert 'Jack' Whiteman, 10th Royal Fusiliers (City of London Regiment)

There was no time to mount an assault upon Monchy or Guémappe. The endeavour was abandoned – and night fell. Critically, no plans

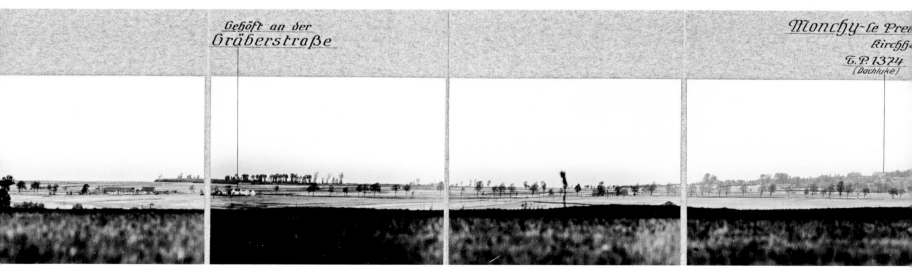

for nocturnal attacks had been laid here either, and therefore no pre-battle training carried out. Few night-time assaults had ever been launched as part of a major offensive, and most had ended in disaster; none had ever been attempted in such grim weather conditions. The villages would have to wait.

TILLOY AND THE HARP

VI Corps' right-hand unit, the 3rd Division (Major General C.J. Deverell), also had part of the Wancourt-Feuchy line as its objective. In front of the village of Tilloy-lès-Mofflaines it will be remembered that the German line had here pivoted when the Hindenburg Line positions were completed and the original trenches evacuated. Being at the very junction of the 'old and new' systems, the sector was a deep and complex tangle of field defences. It was also attached to one of the most formidable positions of all, The Harp, which it 'shared' with 42nd Brigade of the 14th Division (VII Corps).

A marvellous array of Russian Saps had been installed here, the most impressive being those associated with the Ronville Caves in front of Beaurains. Faced with the barrier of the Hindenburg Line, a potential net of forward outposts, dense wire, much concrete and unaccommodating topography, the troops of both VI, and on their right flank VII Corps, would be heavily reliant upon the guns. For this reason The Harp and Tilloy sectors were also given the lion's share of tanks, sixteen in total.

So important was this sector to the whole scheme that less than thirty-six hours before Zero a raid had been organized to ascertain the garrison strength and the results of the British bombardment on the German entanglements and fieldworks. A raiding party returned with

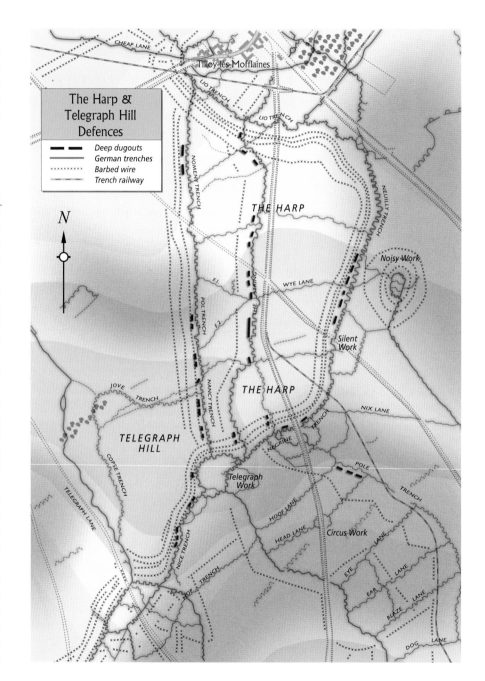

the heartening news that damage was widespread and wire pretty well cut. Prisoners were referred to as a 'measly lot'.

The 3rd Division got off to a good start, the first waves attacking both from advanced trenches and the saps. At less than a kilometre wide their frontage was unusually narrow, but the zone it was assaulting 'fanned' markedly beyond the German front line, extending at the Brown Line some 4 kilometres distant to almost twice its original width.

Four minutes to go!!! The platoon officer comes along just to see that all is well. Three minutes, two, one minute, then the earth seems to rock under our feet, the air is filled with the noise of flying shells as every gun on the British side opens out. It is deafening, but we take no notice. 'Over you go', and we scale the parapet and steadily cross the open ground to our first line trench

Below Advanced British trenches dug in the northernmost 'hinge' of ground vacated by the Germans at Tilloy-lès-Mofflaines. The new German line is formed by the Harp; their original line is marked at left in red. REL

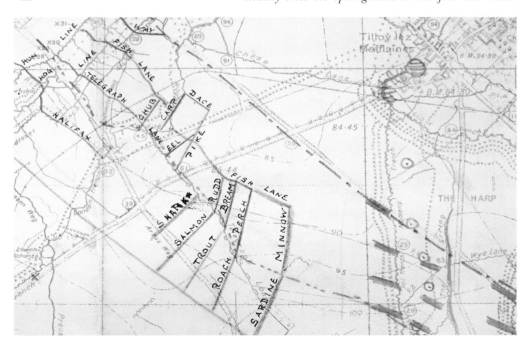

from which the 1st Gordons have already gone. Across the trench by bridges and on to 'No Man's Land'. In front is the German 1st line trench, myriads of lights rise and fall. Red, green, orange colours. Golden rain. All appeal to his artillery to concentrate on us. Looking again at the enemy trench we see great spouts of flame and earth as shell after shell falls accurately in or nearby the trench. Nothing on earth can live in such as this. Around us, almost deadened in the terrible din, Fritz's shells are exploding as he vainly endeavours to stay our advance. Now and then a man falls dead or wounded but we take no notice, but our casualties are slight for the terrible bombardment is too much for the enemy machine gunners who are either killed or cowering down a deep dugout. We reach the first line, now almost battered out of recognition and here we see a mopping-up party of the Jocks clearing the dugout and sending the prisoners back to our lines. Now on again to the second and third lines which have been taken without much resistance, and here for a short space we halt. Everything has gone well so far and now we are waiting for our barrage, which is playing on the wood, to lift before we do our part and take the wood. On the right edge of the wood can be seen a few of the enemy, and shots are exchanged. We now move on again to the centre of the wood.

PRIVATE GEORGE CULPITT, 10TH ROYAL WELSH FUSILIERS

Following the plan precisely, a single battalion of the Gordon Highlanders took the German front line. Ahead lay three parallel sets of trenches, all associated with Devil's Wood. The Somme fighting had engraved upon the hearts of many a British Tommy the fact that woodland and trenches spelled peril, but although the garrison here was significant there was little opposition: heavy shellfire followed by the metronomic perfection of the creeping barrage had caused many of the enemy to bolt towards the greater sanctuary of the village.

Our shells are now falling with clockwork regularity on the German 4th line which runs along the far side of the wood and which is our objective. A ten-minute wait close under our own barrage and we move forward again to our objective. No resistance meets us for the Hun has long since left in an endeavour to seek safety further back. A few dead lie in the trench but no living enemy is there to meet us and we occupy the position, and commence to consolidate in anticipation of a counter-attack. We have achieved our mission without resistance and at comparatively slight cost to ourselves. We now have time to breath fully and to take stock of our position which is a good one: in front nearly 1000 yards away lies the village of Tilloy on which our barrage is now concentrated, and a little nearer in front of the village is an enemy trench, deserted as far as we can see.

PRIVATE GEORGE CULPITT, 10TH ROYAL WELSH FUSILIERS

The trench was populated only by dead and wounded, but Tilloy itself was a different story, the ruins of the village and adjacent park being strongly fortified. Leapfrogging, the 2nd Royal Scots and 7th King's Shropshire Light Infantry (8th Brigade) began the delicate process of assault, and after an extended period of rifle-bombing and Lewis-gunning, the stronghold was encircled and gradually reduced. Helping them out were a welcome brace of tanks.

Tilloy.   Sergeanten-Wäldchen.   Str. Arras-Cambrai.

Above Segment of a German panorama taken from within the Harp defences in March 1917. Troops are at work on the wire entanglement that crosses the image. British guns were most destructive in this sector. AC

Our tank was a part of No 9 Coy of C Battalion and, preceded by a heavy creeping barrage, we reached the enemy front line in about one hour. From there onwards the ground became very difficult. However we did manage to get along engaging the enemy and had the satisfaction of taking part in the capture of Tilloy. We had some good shooting at machine guns in protected cellars and it was good to see the infantry taking over surrounding the enemy. Unfortunately we ran into a very bad patch on the outskirts of Tilloy and became stuck with the tank resting on its belly and the tracks going round uselessly. Almost simultaneously, or so it seemed, we were hit by a shell smack on the gun mounting between the officer and driver in the front cab. Fortunately it did not explode but went straight through

the tank and out at the back doing slight damage to some of the machine gun ammunition stowed in racks between the exhaust pipes of the engine. No-one was seriously wounded – just one or two smacks, but as might be expected we were all momentarily rather shaken. Our officer was new to the tanks, and I was the only one of the crew who had previously been in action in a tank. When we had somewhat recovered our composure, he held a conference as to what should be done. We had of course a big hole in the front of the driving cab, which would be an excellent mark for enemy machine guns, and I could only suggest that as I knew there was a square steel plate at the back of the tank by the radiator which could be unbolted, taken off and fixed over the hole with some stout wire. This would cover up the defect

but needless to say offer little or no protection from machine bullets hitting the cab. It was a very uncomfortable job with the tank a sitting target, and there were plenty of shells exploding in the vicinity, apart from some machine-gun bullets. The next task was to get the tank unstuck. Whilst looking for some suitable wire to fix the plate I had noticed a length of iron railings lying loose and suggested we get this under the track in the hope that it would help the machine to lift itself out of the morass. Two more men were sent out to help us get this length of iron railings under the track. The engine started and the moving tracks drew the fencing underneath and slowly the tank became clear. Whilst we were fixing the plate over the hole, a German dashed out of a nearby ruin and tottered up to us and dropped on his knees with his hands in the air begging for mercy. He did not appear to be wounded but was in a bad shell-shocked condition and deathly white. I motioned him to proceed and the poor fellow did so on his hands and knees towards Arras.
GUNNER WILLIAM DAWSON, TANK C50, NO. 9 COMPANY,
C BATTALION, HEAVY BRANCH MACHINE GUN CORPS

The second machine, C41, performed the same service by tracking north of the village before trundling on eastwards in the wake of the infantry. There lay another dense belt of wire beyond Tilloy, and then a block of woodland known as the Bois des Boeufs. Only these two features shielded the Wancourt-Feuchy (Brown) line some 2 kilometres beyond the wood. Between the Bois des Boeufs and the Brown Line lay a single undefended trench, a switch line called the *Wittelsbacher-Weg* that connected the southern end of The Harp with Feuchy Chapel, a strongpoint lying just in front of the Brown Line on the Cambrai road. The barrage patiently made its deadly way across.

On our front there has been no hitch and as far as we can gather everything has gone well all along the line.

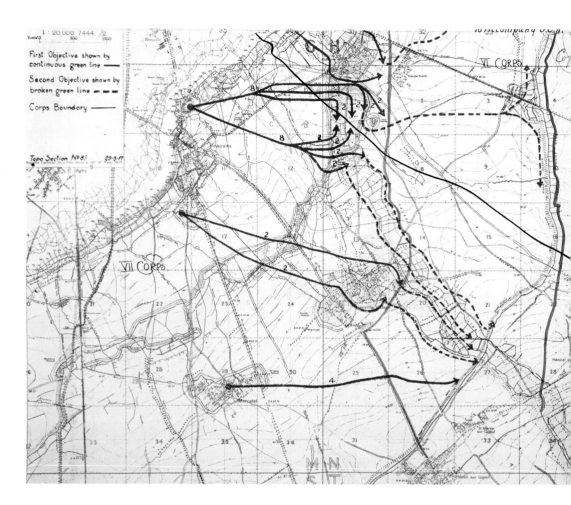

Two hours pass uneventfully and now behind us can see the advanced line of the 8th Brigade coming to carry on from where we left off, to take Tilloy Village and some ground behind. Our machine guns suddenly start on the right and we hastily turn our attention in this direction. Through a gap in the enemy trench we can see the Boche hatless, without equipment or rifle, running for his life, but not many of them get away for they run into our barrage or are caught by our machine gun fire. By this time the advanced line of the 8th Brigade has nearly reached

Above Tank objectives for 9 April against the Harp, Telegraph Hill and Neuville Vitasse. Adjusted German lines highlighted in pink, evacuated lines in red. NA WO95-1869

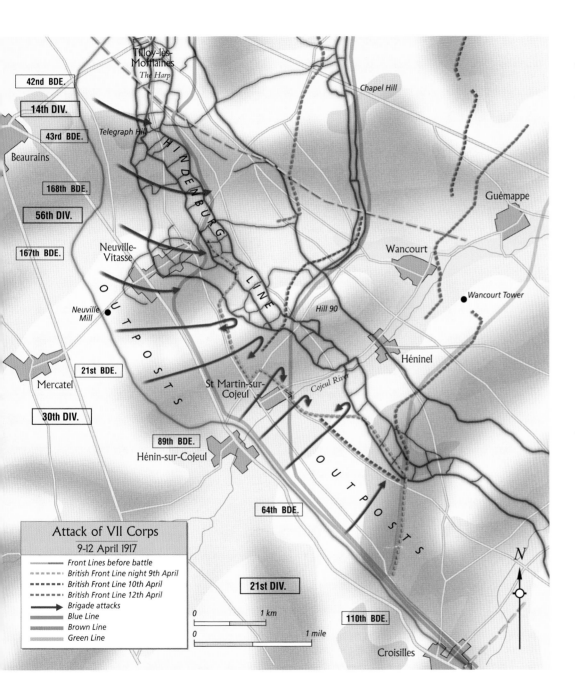

Attack of VII Corps
9-12 April 1917

Front Lines before battle
British Front Line night 9th April
British Front Line 10th April
British Front Line 12th April
Brigade attacks
Blue Line
Brown Line
Green Line

0 _____ 1 km
0 _____ 1 mile

our trench and after a short halt to get into line they go forward across the 1000 yards of open country to the village. We are now spectators of the battle which is taking place in front of us, and which we watch eagerly. They reach the trench without difficulty and then go forward to the ruins of the village. Here they are lost to sight to reappear at intervals among the piles of bricks and stone which were once houses. Again our attention is drawn to the right for here a sharp scrap is taking place. It transpires that there is a sort of Brigade Headquarters and here we captured an entire German Staff. A short time elapses and now the scene has changed for we see the Germans coming back, but without arms for they are prisoners, 20 or 30 in a batch in charge of one or two British Tommies. Some mere lads, some old men, a few well set up, well-built chaps and here and there a haughty officer walking with his nose in the air. Once more the noise of battle lessens for a time, the advance is stayed according to programme. By 10 a.m. the Germans have been driven back over a mile and are almost out of range of our light guns, which are now busy limbering up and moving forward to take up a position in the open. Soon on our right and left we see our batteries gallop into action, swing round, unlimber and after a few sighting shots once more proceed to harass the retreating enemy.

PRIVATE GEORGE CULPITT, 10TH ROYAL WELSH FUSILIERS

Apart from one or two isolated pockets of resistance, the remaining German garrison of the village and park eventually elected to surrender rather than perish, about 140 soldiers emerging with their hands in the air. By this time the advance had moved on, local commanders comfortable that any delay at Tilloy was safe to be left to moppers-up. Two battalions of the 76th Brigade leapfrogged, and surged forward through the wire and on towards the Feuchy Chapel, a redoubt that was soon to delay attacks to north and south. George Culpitt's attention had been attracted by events at The Harp. Here, tanks were 'liberally' deployed, the greatest concentration on the entire Arras and Vimy battlegrounds. The Harp was especially problematic for tanks because of the greater trench width and variable fire-bay designs. It had received a prolonged extra-severe battering by the heavies, leaving the ground particularly 'spongy'. Four of C Company's tanks bogged long before Zero and well behind their own lines, succumbing to the soggy Crinchon valley despite the efforts of engineers to firm the passage with timber and woven matting. Some machines were later extricated, but not in time to assist in the attacks. Five only, including William Dawson's (and Lieutenant Weber's 'Lusitania' at The Triangle), appeared at Zero for action between Tilloy and the River Scarpe. The tanks were supposed to work in pairs, crossing the trenches perpendicularly then turning north and south, 'rolling up' the German line. Seven of the ten ditched before reaching the enemy trenches.

3rd Division's attack was believed to be moving along well, but communication with Brigade Headquarters was only intermittent, and this was to become a typical and hampering problem during the first era of fighting across the southern battlefront: in order to avoid the kind of crippling casualties seen on the Somme, battalion commanders had been required not to advance with their troops but remain in command posts. In this way they might be slightly out of touch with the attack, but not with the parent brigade. It will be noted how many soldiers' testimonies mention being able to see events taking place many kilometres distant; this is possibly all that stood between success and failure for the British, for on 9

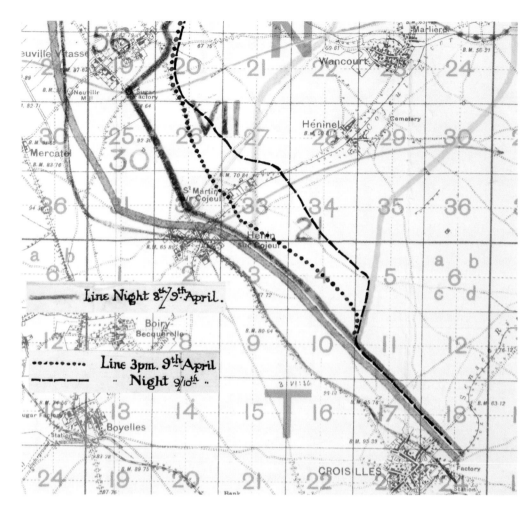

April commanders generally remained in sheltered posts in the valleys from where nothing of the fast-moving battle could be gleaned directly. Had they elected to follow progress in person, the captured ridges and crests offered grandstand panoramic views upon which tactical judgments could be reached with minimal delay or indeed no delay at all. Gaps could be seen, opposition gauged, deficiencies

Above Part of a British Narrative Map VII showing 30th and 21st Division gains on 9 April. NA WO95-363

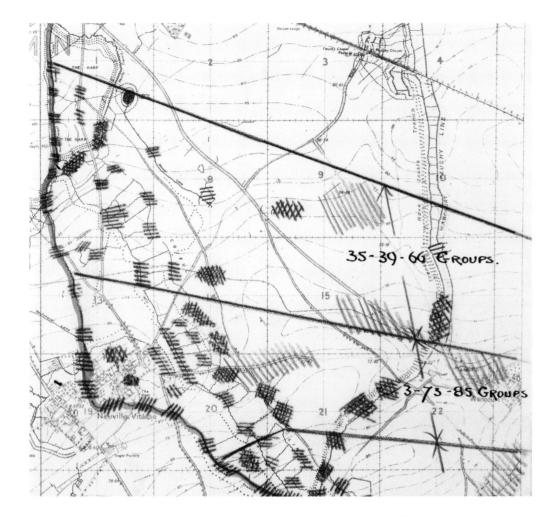

35·39·66 GROUPS.

3·73·85 GROUPS

Above Segment of British artillery map showing heavy artillery targets in the Neuville Vitasse sector. NA WO95-1869

behind the three villages of Guémappe, Wancourt and Héninel. At the southern extremity the Black, Blue and Brown Lines meet, and for a distance of some 2 kilometres actually form one and the same objective. Snow's command formed the right flank of Third Army's endeavours for 9 April; two days later the battle front would be extended another 16 kilometres south and east by V Corps and I Anzac Corps.

Along the entire front, VII Corps faced powerful Hindenburg Line fieldworks. So strong was the bastion that General Snow felt that an element of shock might be injected if he attacked in sequence from left to right, i.e. the 14th Division was to jump off at 7.30 a.m., the same time as its neighbour the 3rd, with the brigades of each successive division attacking at a later time, concluding with a 4.15 p.m. assault by 64th Brigade (21st Division) in the far south. In a way, the timings were academic: if the Germans held out at The Harp and Telegraph Hill the entire plan would crumble, for the two features occupied such dominant positions in the landscape, commanding not only the immediate attacking front, but almost every square metre of ground from Observation Ridge to Neuville Vitasse in enfilade. The final key aspect to Snow's 'echelon attack' idea was that his guns, supported by extra artillery from 'inactive' divisions, would have more time to bludgeon the immensely deep and strong belts of wire guarding the German line.

The 14th Division's attack commenced slightly late at 7.34 a.m., two hours later than their northern neighbour, the reason being the dog-leg in the enemy line at Tilloy. One third of The Harp was their responsibility, plus Telegraph Hill. Although the troops were unaware, the first stage of their assault was

noted and faults rectified – in an instant.

The duty of Lieutenant General Sir Thomas D'Oyly Snow, commander of VII Corps (14th (Light), 56th (London), 30th and 21st Divisions), was to annexe the rest of the Wancourt-Feuchy position to the point where it joined the Hindenburg Line. This, however, was his Brown Line; the final Green Line ran considerably further east traversing the heights

especially hazardous, for the topography meant that the creeping barrage fired by low-trajectory field guns would barely clear the heads of the attacking waves! According to the gunners' calculations, the difference between shell and helmet was estimated as just 'a few feet'. It would therefore be especially important to follow the instructions given in training.

Destruction of wire by gun and mortar had been audaciously augmented during the night by manual cutting parties. The gaps appeared adequate, but the ground had been churned into a sloppy mass of earth, wire, timber and chalk. Surprisingly, given the sector's importance, at Zero German defensive artillery fire was weak, which helped the first wave jumping off from newly dug advanced trenches to overtake a couple of tanks and pick up the 'skirts' of the barrage.

The 14th Division's action was assisted by ten tanks of C Battalion and four from D which crushed more wire and kept hostile heads low, although it is interesting to note that the respective reports of the tank companies and those of the brigades to which they were supposed to be attached do not conform. 42nd Brigade diaries are somewhat at odds regarding the tanks' contribution, noting, '...failure of the Tanks for the second time in the experience of the Brigade'.

The brevity of the British bombardment had fooled many of the garrison, for large numbers of Germans were found still sheltering in the many dugouts (see map on page 150), believing the shelling to be a part of a longer artillery preparation. Widespread demoralization was reported.

There's stacks of dead and wounded which we temporarily ignore because of dug-outs here and there which

would account for so many live Fritz and, apprehensive, alert, small gangs of us move in and commence to bomb them out. First, however, we give them the chance to come up: give them a shout, from the majority no response – the silence of a tomb, which some are about to become. So safety pins pulled, I count one, two, three, let fly and if you want a ghastly eerie sound, listen to the bombs explode at the foot of dug-out shafts. Those that survive come stumbling up in droves; several show that they want to fight. There's a free-for-all melée, bayonet jabs, shots, and eventually what is left is a set of stupified and cowed men, many like jibbering lunatics. They are quickly and roughly searched, not merely for souvenirs

Above Tanks C21 and C26 advance beyond Tilloy. IWM Q6298

Right Barrage map of Neuville Vitasse attack (REL) and (inset), Neuville Mill. PC

but hidden weapons, any doubtful cases having their belts removed for the very simple reason that you're unable to do much damage if obliged to lurch along holding up your pants. The bulk of the Boche laid dead on top were look-outs, suicide squad blokes, doomed and condemned to death whilst gangs of them sheltered down below. We winkle, we survey, reform and press on. Some of the German casualties are ghastly to behold, some motionless, face down, others grotesquely huddled flat on their backs gazing skyward out of sightless eyes, all bloody, some bloodier than the rest. A few of them still breathe, muttering 'wasser, mutter, wasser', whilst everywhere around a junk heap of discarded blood-stained equipment.

PRIVATE FRANK HARRIS, 6TH KING'S OWN YORKSHIRE LIGHT INFANTRY

Both the Harp and Telegraph Hill were in British hands by 11.00 am. The 56th and 30th Divisions were faced with the unattractive prospect of capturing one of the larger villages of the region, Neuville Vitasse, situated immediately in front of the Hindenburg positions, plus, half a kilometre beyond, the smaller hamlet of Héninel. Neuville was a fortress a little like Bullecourt, the Germans having created a salient of its boundaries. To front and sides were dense belts of wire; to the rear, protected by further thick entanglements, the Hindenburg Line. From the Neuville salient enfilade fire was possible to north and south, hence the need to narrow no man's land with advanced trenches. There were also outposts to deal with. The most notable and dangerous, Neuville Mill, lay outside the wire 200 metres from the nose of the salient. It was no ordinary mill, but a concrete blockhouse armed with machine guns. On the night of 7 April four men of the Manchester Regiment had been killed whilst patrolling nearby; they had not been the first, and the position was seen as a major obstacle to progress in thirty-six hours' time. It was therefore given its own tank (believed to be either D1 or D2) which on 9 April neatly fired a 6lb shell through an embrasure, killing nine, capturing four, and permanently neutralizing the hazard. The ground in the Neuville sector was a little firmer; if they could reach the sector without mishap there was a chance the tanks might be of 'material assistance'. The going for the infantry was less advantageous – it had not been

r Cojeul.   *II. Stellung.*   *Heun*

Above Scene of 30th Division's attack towards Héninel and Wancourt north of the Cojeul valley, showing the Hindenburg Line defences (right) and the village of St Martin (left). Neuville Vitasse can just be seen over the ridge in the centre of the image. BHK Rundbild VII 19, 4.3.17

possible to pay Neuville as much artillery attention as the defences deserved.

Like Gough's Fifth Army a little further south, parties of the 30th and 21st Divisions had been obliged to eliminate outposts that formed the Blue Line in this sector. Prisoners later stated that they had been instructed to hold the posts 'at all costs' until 18 April. St Martin, a fortified hamlet, fell to 2nd Bedfords at 1.30 a.m. on Z-Day, whilst others were overrun or the garrisons driven back to the main line. Several were still in place, however, when time ran out; whatever was left would have to be dealt with at Zero.

Shortly after midday the two brigades of

56th Division advanced down the ridge east of Beaurains, their objectives being the northern outskirts of Neuville first, the Hindenburg Line second, then on to the Wancourt-Feuchy line – the Brown Line. Their final target here was just a 330-metre section of trench. Thanks to vigorous British counter-battery fire the German defensive barrage was again weak, which was fortunate because on the long and open slopes the troops presented the most perfect targets for shrapnel. The left-hand brigade, 168th, managed to struggle through the entanglements with the help of a tank, and although some parties fought their way across the Hindenburg Line trenches and into the open ground

Sto. nach Heninel.

Siegfried-Stellung auf Höhe 89.7 im Plan. Qu. 7405.

beyond, linking with 14th Division neighbours well forward, a substantial number became bogged down in a Hindenburg Line bombing dispute that was to continue throughout the coming night. Similar to the attack of the 51st Highlanders, the line became fractured and disjointed. On their right, contact was kept with 167th Brigade who slowly but grittily fought their way into and through Neuville, reaching the Blue Line late at 4.00 p.m. The formidable Neuville Vitasse trench prevented progress when 30th Division attacked in mid-afternoon. On the low ground the wire was found to be almost undamaged and prospects for the infantry soon looked bleak. With the tanks fail-

ing to forge a route, they dug for cover in the open. In places hostile machine-gun fire was serious, in others minimal; observers later suggested that the German entanglements had been so dense and deep that some defenders could not actually see – and therefore shoot – through it. As the attack ground to a halt, shrapnel thinned the ranks to the point where, even had breaks existed, the force was too weak to make any impression. To the left the troops could see the successful attack on Neuville; to the right, up on the high ground, the 21st Division faced the same barrier. Elements of 64th Brigade found two or three breaks and managed to annexe a short portion of the first

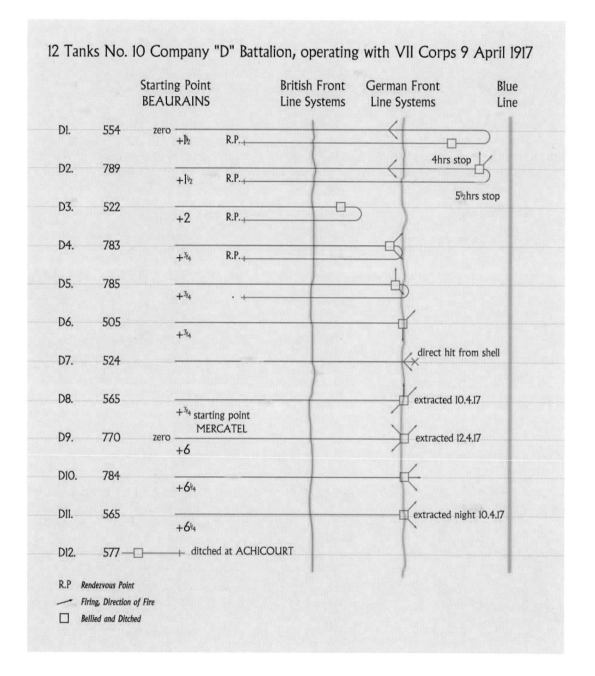

12 Tanks No. 10 Company "D" Battalion, operating with VII Corps 9 April 1917

		Starting Point BEAURAINS	British Front Line Systems	German Front Line Systems	Blue Line
D1.	554	zero +1½ R.P.			
D2.	789	+1½ R.P.		4hrs stop	
				5½hrs stop	
D3.	522	+2 R.P.			
D4.	783	+¾ R.P.			
D5.	785	+¾ ·			
D6.	505	+¾			
D7.	524			direct hit from shell	
D8.	565			extracted 10.4.17	
D9.	770	+¾ starting point MERCATEL zero +6		extracted 12.4.17	
D10.	784	+6¼			
D11.	565	+6¼		extracted night 10.4.17	
D12.	577	ditched at ACHICOURT			

R.P   *Rendezvous Point*

⟋   *Firing, Direction of Fire*

☐   *Bellied and Ditched*

Left Schematic showing D Tank Battalion results on 9 April

Below A ditched 9 April tank being dug out by engineers and infantry. IWM Q6431

Left British cavalry moving forward through Arras on 11 April. IWM Q2825

Below Wire protecting the village of Neuville Vitasse. SA

Hindenburg trench, but no more. The panorama segment shows the formidable wire protecting the first objective of this division. Here, the 9 April battleground ceased.

It was a mirror image of the first day of the Somme: great progress in the north, minimal gain in the south. Despite the lack of success, there was serious German alarm. Expecting the onslaught to continue, they began pulling field guns and trench mortars away to safer position behind the Wancourt-Feuchy line.

*From our perfect O.P. we could see great confusion on the roads behind Héninel, and our set programme being over at 5 p.m., we were able to engage some glo-*rious targets – roads congested with gun limbers, retreating Huns and vehicles of every sort, all went into the hash together. The Hun asked for war, and now at last he is getting it in good measure, heaped up and overflowing.*

MAJOR NEIL FRASER-TYTLER DSO TD, 150TH (COUNTY PALATINE) BRIGADE, ROYAL FIELD ARTILLERY

And up on Telegraph Hill the cavalry arrived to take advantage of the situation.

We were not brought up until 1 p.m., when we marched via Wailly and Arras and formed up on the western slopes of Telegraph Hill. It was a vile day and as cold as could be. There were occasional snowstorms, and the wind was like ice.

As we emerged from Arras on to the flat piece of ground between the town and Telegraph Hill, we passed General Greenly and his staff standing by the roadside with a lance and pennon stuck in the ground to represent Divisional Headquarters. He wished all the officers good luck, and I really thought we were going to achieve something. But we were not taken any farther than Telegraph Hill. The infantry objectives had not been gained and it would have been criminal to launch ten thousand cavalry against a trench line defended by wire.

'AQUILA', WITH THE CAVALRY IN THE WEST

The close of day was within sight. Now, the technical troops had twelve hours of heavy toil ahead. As snowfalls intensified during the evening, Sir Edmund Allenby issued orders that the remaining Brown and Green Line objectives must be taken the following morning. The troops south of the Scarpe were to jump off at 8.00 a.m.

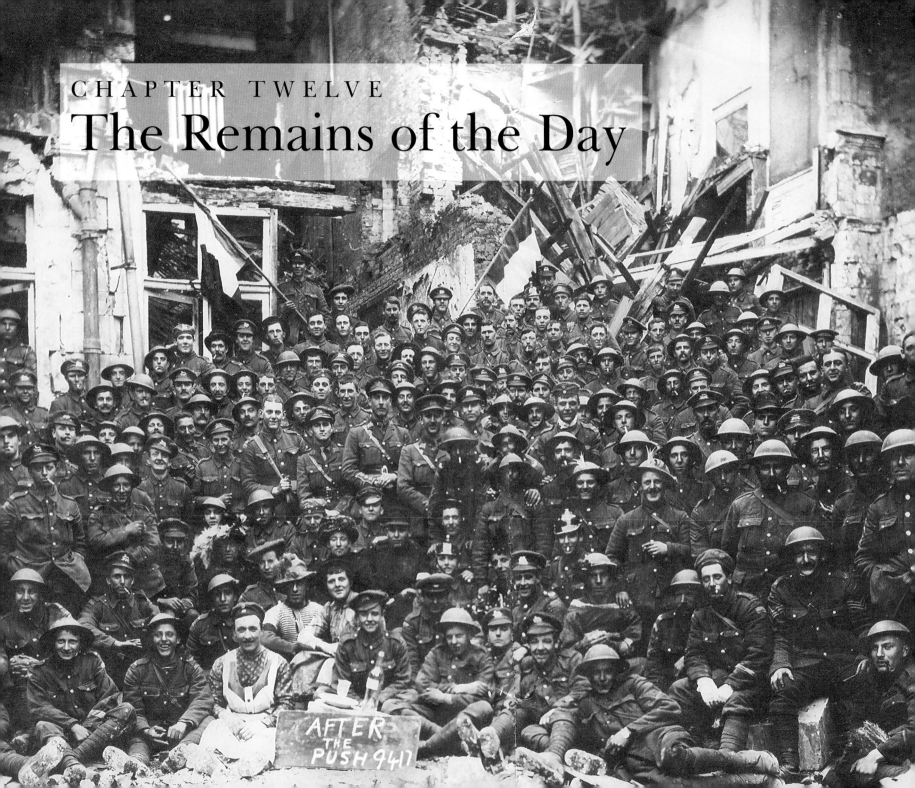

CHAPTER TWELVE
The Remains of the Day

AFTER
THE
PUSH 9417

Our burial parties were hard at work collecting the bodies of those who had fallen, and the chaplains were with them. I met some of the battalions, who, having done their part in the fighting, were coming back. Many of them had suffered heavily and the mingled feelings of loss and gain chastened their exaltation and tempered their sorrow. I made my way over to the ruins of the village of Thélus on our left, and there I had my lunch in a shell hole with some men, who were laughing over an incident of the attack. So sudden had been our advance that a German artillery officer who had a comfortable dugout in Thélus, had to run away before he was dressed. Two of our men had gone down into the dugout and there they found the water in the wash-basin still warm and many things scattered about in confusion.

Our signallers were following up the infantry and laying wires over the open. Everyone was in high spirits. By this time the retreating Germans had got well beyond the crest of the Ridge and across the valley. It was about six o'clock in the evening when I reached our final objective, which was just below the edge of the hill. There our men were digging themselves in. It was no pleasant task, because the wind was cold and it was beginning to snow. The prospect of spending a night there was not an attractive one, and every man was anxious to make the best home for himself he could in the ground. It was wonderful to look over the valley. I saw the villages of Willerval, Arleux and Bailleul-sur-Berthoult. They looked so peaceful in the green plain which had not been disturbed as yet by shells. The church spires stood up undamaged like those of some quiet hamlet in England. I thought, "If we could only follow up our advance and keep the Germans on the move," but the day was at an end and the snow was getting heavier. I saw far off in the valley, numbers of little grey figures who seemed to be gradually gathering together, and I heard an officer say he thought the Germans were preparing for a counter-attack. Our men, however, paid little attention to them. When I started back I met our Intelligence Officer, V.C., D.S.O., coming up to look over the line. He was a man who did much but said little and generally looked very solemn. I went up to him and said, "Major, far be it from me, as a man of peace and a man of God, to say anything suggestive of slaughter, but, if I were a combatant officer, I would drop some shrapnel in that valley in front of our lines."

CANON F.G. SCOTT DSO, SENIOR CHAPLAIN TO 1ST CANADIAN DIVISION

Left An evidently delighted group of 12th West Yorkshire Regiment celebrating their triumph of 9 April in Arras. JB

It is interesting to note Canon Scott's vision of 'numbers of little grey figures' as if no one else had noticed the activity. There was reason, for it may have been an almost singular image: beyond the Vimy Ridge lay a fissure in the German defences almost 3 kilometres wide. It was filled during the night of 9/10 April, in places deliberately, in others, not. Counter-attack troops (from as far away as Lille) were ordered forward to retake Hill 135 and push back the Canadians about La Folie Wood and Hill 145. Scheduled somewhat optimistically to deploy in mid-afternoon of the 9th, they actually arrived after dark and during a blizzard. Fortunately for the Canadians there was also confusion in dispersal and orders, and the Germans did not attack but simply reinforced weak points. One party required to assist Hill 145 by assaulting from The Pimple moved into position about midnight but were defeated by the conditions, the darkness, the snow and the mud; it was almost impossible to move. Perhaps a Canadian machine-gun crew heard German cursing, for it was said that a single burst was sufficient to extinguish the danger. Other units simply lost their way. The counter-attack threat became more minimal as the night wore on.

Excepting the right flank of VII Corps where the Hindenburg Line wire was at its strongest, there were gaps and weaknesses in the German lines across the entire battlefront. It would be at least another twelve hours before the first sizeable bodies of reserves could arrive, and being early April those next twelve hours would be enveloped in darkness. Where resistance existed it was diaphanous, requiring only a gentle heave to crumble to dust. But no one heaved because it was not part of the scheme. Whilst the Canadians gazed upon the void before them, the gap opposite the 51st Division

OUVROY Ch.   ACHEVILLE Ch.   DROCOURT Ch.   BOIS-BERNARD Ch.   BREWERY
U 20 A6·1

was wider still, the flimsiest of German protec-tion stretching almost to Fampoux. In the latter sector the greatest advance of the war to date had been recorded: an extraordinary leap of more than 5½ kilometres. Across the river in front of Guémappe and Monchy the door was still ajar. Only south of Telegraph Hill had there been any semblance of a coherent German defence. As a result of the situation to the north, even here preparations were in hand to evacuate parts of the Hindenburg defences. Should it be necessary, Crown Prince Rupprecht had the unfinished Drocourt-Quéant Switch to fall back to, but after the triumph of *Alberich* it would be a disheartening move and one that he zealously wished to avoid. At OHL, few were to sleep that night.

9TH APRIL

Some of our advanced divisions gave way. The neigh-bouring divisions which stood firm suffered heavy losses. The enemy succeeded before noon in reaching our battery positions and seizing heights which dominated the coun-try far to the east. The counter-attacking divisions were not there to throw the enemy back, only portions of the troops could be brought up by motor transport. The situ-ation was extremely critical, and might have had far-reaching effects if the enemy had pushed further for-ward. But the British contented themselves with their great success and did not continue the attack, at least not on April 9th. I had looked forward to the expected offen-sive with confidence, and was now deeply depressed. Was this to be the result of all our care and trouble during the past half-year? Had our principles of defensive tactics proved false, and if so what was to be done? I was not at

FRESNOY

Above Part of First Army Panorama P109 (IWM) made on 10 April 1917 from Thélus Hill showing the Canadian view beyond Vimy Ridge.

Inset Canadian troops look down upon the prospect of Vimy village. IWM CO1351

that time able to get a clear view of all the details of the battle. I sent for officers who had taken part in the conflict in the front line, and by means of conversations with them and telephonic communications gained the impression that the principles laid down by G.H.Q. [OHL] were sound. But the whole art of leadership lies in applying them correctly. Moreover, a division had failed here which had previously enjoyed a high reputation. April 10 and the following days were critical. The consequence of a break through of 12 to 15 kilometres wide and 6 or more kilometres deep are not easy to meet. In view of the heavy losses of our men, guns and ammunition resulting from such a break through, colossal efforts are needed to make good the damage. It was the business of G.H.Q. [OHL] to provide reserves on a large scale. But it was absolutely impossible with the troops at our disposal and in view of the military situation, to have a second division immedi-

ately behind every division that might possibly fall out. A day like 9th April threw all calculations to the winds. The end of the crisis, even if new troops were available, depended very largely, as it generally does in such cases, on whether the enemy, after his first victory, would attack again, and by further success aggravate the difficulty of forming a new line. Our position having been weakened, such victories were to be won only too easily.

LUDENDORFF, *MY WAR MEMORIES*

As an invisible sun set on Easter Monday 1917, the greatest offensive opportunity of the war had gone begging. Now the British would toil through the night to try to prepare a platform of attack for the following day. Field Marshal Paul von Hindenburg, with Ludendorff at this time, had this to say of the day:

The evening report of this 9 April revealed rather a dark picture. Many shadows – a little light. In such cases more light must be sought. A ray appeared, though a tiny flickering ray. The English did not seem to have known how to exploit the success they had gained to the full. This was a piece of luck for us, as so often before. After the report I pressed the hand of my First Quartermaster-General [Ludendorff], with the words: "We have lived through more critical times than today together." Today! It was his birthday! My confidence was unshaken. I knew that reinforcements were marching to the battlefield and that trains were hastening that way. The crisis was over. Within me it was certainly over. But the battle raged on.
HINDENBURG, *OUT OF MY LIFE*

In hindsight, Hindenburg was being perhaps a little too ebullient. What had happened to the carefully laid-down elastic defence-in-depth schemes formulated since the Somme? Why had they failed so dramatically? The answer was devastatingly simple: at Arras they had not been put into effect. Investigations revealed that too many commanders had elected not to follow orders, and when the attacks came had their men fall back to the next line of defence to await the *Ablösung*, the reserves, among them the specialist counter-attack units. In most sectors, therefore, the Germans were still employing the rigid linear defence as employed the previous year on the Somme. Hence the widespread British and Canadian breakthroughs – the immensely augmented British artillery had planned their patterns of fire to break this very system, and succeeded admirably. It was also undeniably the reason for the heavy German casualty count, averaging a sombre 35 per cent. Had the system of outpost zones with lightly held trench lines been employed, the outcome might have been radically different; confirmation of this could be

perceived in places where German troops had been driven back and forced almost by default to form individual pockets of resistance: a machine-gun here, a nest of snipers or bombers there. British assaults, although not halted, were considerably slowed, and a noticeably greater number of casualties sustained. Crown Prince Rupprecht was furious. Not only had orders been disregarded, but requests to have reserves held between 2 and 3 kilometres from the front had been ignored, and now he and his men were forced to nervously wait, not knowing if British night attacks were pending. As a direct result, Sixth Army commander General Freiherr von Falkenhausen lost his job

On 9 April, the British had been effective, but benefited from the good fortune of facing an enemy whose defensive structure was neither one thing nor another. The First Battle of the Scarpe would undoubtedly resume on Tuesday, 10 April, but in what manner? How would both sides respond? It appears that the day had been so extraordinarily refreshing for the British that most observers (i.e. those not in the line or installing new infrastructure) were understandably more content with the present than concerned about the future; it was a spectacular day, a rare moment deserving of celebration, and newspapers across the Empire would be full of dramatic and dazzling reports in a few hours time. Sir Edmund Allenby, judging by letters to his wife, might be said to have been just a little too 'full of himself'.

10TH APRIL

My Mabel,
I had really a very big success yesterday. I won, all along the line, killed a host of Boche, and took over 7000 prisoners. Also, I have captured anything between 30 and 60 guns – but they have not yet been counted in. My

Above German prisoners being shepherded to the rear on 9 April. IWM Q5122

Below In the 'cage'. IWM Q5150

losses were not very great, and the Divisions are all in great heart … A Corps of the Army [Canadians] on my left also did a good attack; took the positions aimed at and caught 3000 or more Boche prisoners. We have, at last, brought off what I have been working at all this winter. My Staff have been splendid; and the operation which required the most complicated and accurate calculations worked like clock-work. Not a hitch anywhere. My artillery were brilliant, and the German guns were smothered from the start. The battle is not over, as we are still on the tail of the Enemy, pressing and capturing their rearguards. For the present my Head Quarters are where they were.
Your Edmund

True, scores of guns were in British hands and more than 10,000 prisoners sat in the cages, but it had not worked like clockwork, and there were a host of hitches. At the same time as Allenby was writing the note to his wife, Colonel Fritz von Lossberg would be touring *Gruppe Arras*, speaking with commanders, assessing local situations, and hoping that the combination of poor weather outlook and the fractured nature of the advance astride the Arras-Cambrai road would cause the British to struggle in not only bringing forward guns and stores, but also in deciding exactly what to do next. More attacks were inevitable, but would they be wholesale or piecemeal? Having noted that many an assault had reached a certain point, then stopped despite there being little or no resistance ahead, the natural conclusion might be that no British reserves were in place to follow up the advance, i.e. it was perhaps unanticipated. If there were no reserves ready for battle on the first day, there would almost certainly be none for several days to come. OHL, Rupprecht and von Lossberg all banked on piecemeal British action, certainly in the

short term. They therefore needed troops on the battlefield (there were a full five divisions in reserve) and guns to support them – fast. At the same time a new form of defensive structure and mentality was required. Fortune had smiled upon the British and Canadians, but time was on no one's side.

For the cavalry, 9 April had been a frustrating day. News had only slowly filtered back to the various headquarters, and it would be later noted with the deepest regret that opportunities – the greatest of the war – had been presented on a platter by the splendid endeavours of the infantry. Despite the weather and the ground conditions, between The Harp and Vimy Ridge the enemy had been rattled. The infantry had been in a position to attack the Brown and Blue Lines in front of Monchy and Guémappe, but instead of action there was discussion. Orders to attack Monchy had been quite plain, but once the opportunity had been presented, commanders came to the conclusion that it was just too late in the day.

MONDAY 9 APRIL 1917
One of the best days for the British Armies in the war. At 12 noon the 2nd and 3rd Cavalry Divisions were moved up east of Arras and waited there for a chance to advance. The attacks were going so well that, at about 2.00 pm, they were ordered to move east with the idea of getting in to the Valley of the Sensée. Up to this point all had gone well, but the Boche lines running through Feuchy Chapel to the River Scarpe proved to be a harder task than was at first thought. The wire was very thick and had not been cut. This delayed the attack and this line was not taken till about 6.00 pm. The attack of the 7th Corps south of Arras was not so successful and the Hindenburg Line here held out quite successfully. There appeared no chance to use the Cavalry that evening, so it was brought back: the 2nd Cav. Div. into Bervines

between Agny and Wailly, the 3rd Cav. Div. north-west of Arras between the main St Pol road and the Scarpe River. As regards the Cavalry, the day was disappointing, if the Feuchy line had gone, I think the Divisions would have gone through and probably made a bag of guns.
BRIGADIER GENERAL SIR ARCHIBALD HOME DSO, BGGS, CAVALRY CORPS

General Home was choosing his words carefully. It is true that the line in front of Monchy was knotty, but elsewhere other marvellous chances had gone begging. The Feuchy line had in large part been broken on VI Corps' left and it was weakly held elsewhere apart from at Chapel Hill on the Cambrai road. There were soldiers like Frank Maxwell bellowing 'It must be done NOW', into the telephone, but yet again poor communication meant that by the time this and many other desperate appeals reached the ears of headquarters staff, opportunities had passed. The Northamptonshire Yeomanry – a single squadron – had shown what was possible.

Given the appalling ground conditions and the fact they were still practically prototypes crewed by neophytes, the armoured cavalry – the tanks – had actually performed pretty well. There had been several instances of truly useful action, and few were left in any doubt of the inspirational effect a tank could have on the infantry. Now the Heavy Branch Machine-Gun Corps had arduous work ahead, unditching bellied, damaged and broken-down machines and getting them back for refit – they were urgently required for the next stage. Although many felt rather crestfallen, there was good reason for crews to take heart, for they had been defeated more by the ground conditions than hostile action. If a full complement had reached the battlefield, the difference could have been

marked. But disappointment was soon swept away by the need to plan the next attack.

OPENING NIGHT

(April 9th.) It was quite dark when we arrived finally at the trench which was our halting place, and I felt a very weary man as I dumped my load and went along its deserted length to find company. The night was bitterly cold, with every now and then flurries of snow brought on a keen north-east wind. We had no greatcoats and our clothes were cold and wet as the snow melted on them. The only dugouts in the trench were occupied by the officers and signallers, but having regard to the rigour of the weather they permitted the men, as many as could, to sit on the steps leading down the shaft and to cluster round the entrance. Those who could not squeeze in had to make the best of the worst outside. Our little party who had been down to Ritz Dump (to bring up elephant shelter sections) arrived back after all the available space on the dugout stairs and at the entrance had been appropriated, and so found themselves in for a very uncomfortable night. It snowed frequently and it was impossible to sit down, much less lie in the trench. I kept on my full battle order equipment for the sake of the warmth it seemed to give, but I sorely felt the terrible exposure and torturing lack of sleep. I cannot convey the degree of hardship we endured at this time and can only wonder how we survived it.
PRIVATE PERCY CLARE, 7TH EAST SURREY REGIMENT

On the battlefield, the night of 9 April was foul. Those who had fully gained their Green Line objectives or come to rest upon the Brown Line were more likely to find comfort than others, for these positions were associated with German trenches and therefore dugout accommodation.

At 7 o'clock we are relieved by the other two Companies in our trench on the edge of the wood and return to a

Above Consolidating captured trenches.
IWM Q1995

Left A wounded man is lowered into an
underground dressing station. Q1996

dugout in the German 2nd line where we are to spend the night. Black bread, coffee, tinned horse, sugar, cigars, cigarettes, fell into our hands, and were speedily made use of. The black bread did not find favour, but the coffee was good warmed on one of his patent cookers of which there were some thousands lying about. The tinned meat (horse flesh) was not so bad and was speedily demolished. By the time we had investigated every corner of this large dugout it was well on towards midnight, so we turned in for a short rest for we did not know what the future might hold for us. It had been a good day's work.
PRIVATE GEORGE CULPITT, 10TH ROYAL WELSH
FUSILIERS

Being well behind the original German front line, dugouts associated with the Blue and Brown Lines were almost astonishing in their luxury, but few troops were able to take advantage because so much of the new British line lay in open ground between German positions: accommodation here was either short sections of battered trench or sopping shell holes. The line had to be consolidated and garrisoned at all times, for there were no guarantees against nocturnal counter-attack. In the meantime company and platoon commanders crept about seeking disoriented troops. On its own the snow might have been bearable, for men were not unused to harsh conditions, but the wind chill added an extra dimension of discomfort. It sapped the life from many a man and beast.

There were no German night attacks, for the nerve of the opposing commanders had been shaken: the manpower was not available, and at the end of a chaotic day they were just as unsure as the British and Canadians exactly where their enemy lay. Attending to the wounded was now of paramount importance. A trickle of casualties had begun arriving at dress-ing stations before the attack began, men wounded or injured during assembly, like Percy Clare's pal, Prestwich. As soon as the whistles blew, the trickle increased exponentially according to how quickly casualties could be evacuated from the field. The first attention one received was from stretcher-bearers, men who commanded the highest respect. Their job was simply to get a wounded man off the battle-field to the battalion medical officer who would have quickly selected a suitable place for his Regimental Aid Post (RAP). The immediate first aid given on the battlefield was restricted to treating haemorrhage and splinting broken limbs. Both conditions were life-threatening, the first for obvious reasons, the second being associated with shock: if a bad break was not splinted, the pain and further damage caused during evacuation could easily be fatal. Morphine and tetanus antitoxins would also have been administered, especially if it was per-ceived that evacuation might be some time in happening. A man was expected to treat him-self for 'minor' wounds, using the dressing every soldier carried inside his tunic.

The attacks generated huge numbers of prisoners, who were pressed into British service, very often becoming a vital link between the field of battle, RAPs and the more comprehen-sively organized dressing stations where more comprehensive treatment was carried out. The military 'hospital' was the Casualty Clearing Station, a fully equipped and usually large per-manent facility, with a staff that included nurses. At the RAP a man would have a label attached to his tunic. Upon it the nature of his wounds was noted, making subsequent treatment more rapid. Along the line of evacuation all informa-tion had to be recorded: a man's arrival, a description of his wounds and actions taken, where he was sent and by whom. The pressures of recording were intermingled with those of treatment and demands for more kit, the dressing stations being the nearest repository to the battlefield.

In a nook left between the end of the stretcher racks and the exit from the shelter was set a small collapsible table whereto were pinned a map of the district and a more detailed one of the trenches, both together making up the board on which you played your own special little game of chess against unforeseen circumstances. A clip took in all the "chits" from the M.O.R at the various R.A.P.s [Regimental Aid Posts], chronologically arranged as they came in, and marked with the hour of receipt, by the Sergeant-Clerk who sat beside you. Each message was supposed to have the hour of its dispatch written on it by the sender: fifty per cent of them never had. Many were soaked and barely decipherable – medical handwriting is somewhat peculiar at best, especially when written in indelible pencil which had "run". Many demands were indefinite – "more stretchers", "more bearers", "more dressings"; others asked for impossible and exaggerated quantities. Here your knowledge of the sender's mentality had to come in, and you discounted the requests of the M.O. who thought too imperially, and dealt with him on more parochial lines.

All the time you were jotting down a running tale of how things progressed, your literary efforts interrupted by visits here and there to lend a hand in dressing cases and loading cars; or by interviewing messengers and supervising the issue of stores in response to indents, and seeing that other indents were going back at once for fresh supplies.

Then your map had to be kept up to date as the regimental aid posts changed when the battalions advanced, and all such changes had to be duly notified to the A.D.M.S. [Assistant Director Medical Services]. Altogether you were the head of a somewhat irritable family, whose nerves, after some hours of it, were apt to get a bit jangled: knowing, too, as regards yourself, that you were the certain recipient of criticism, both from those above and those below you in rank, for all that went wrong; and at the very least expected to remedy the unexpected with the speed of Hermes and the patience of Job.

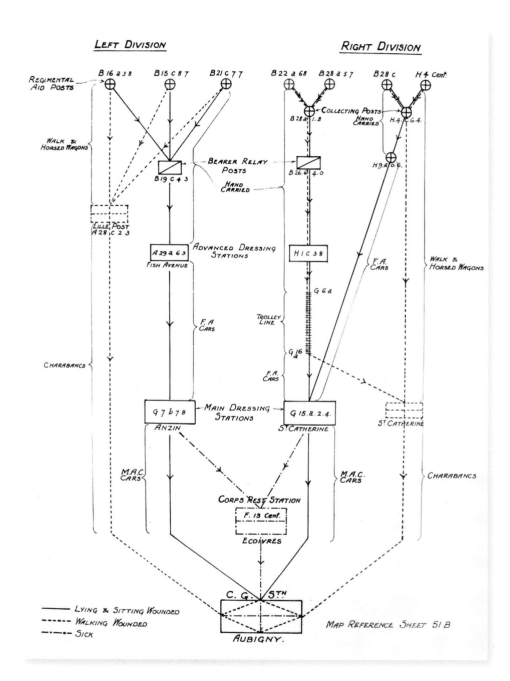

But, above all, your metier was to "cock your bonnet and whistle", to be a "good humorist", and to preserve throughout all your troubles the placid, enigmatic smile of a Mona Lisa.
LIEUTENANT COLONEL DAVID RORIE DSO TD, 1/2ND (HIGHLAND) FIELD AMBULANCE, ROYAL ARMY MEDICAL CORPS

Medical personnel worked on through the night until the battlefield was 'clean', struggling with the inevitable congestion on roads and tracks as a new infrastructure was installed. It was fatiguing work. Prisoners could not be employed in the forward areas at night because of the chance that they might slip away, but their assistance in dressing stations was essential to ease the burden of work. Most were more than willing to help for they knew that food and drink were likely to be supplied.

It would have been an unmentioned source of gratification amongst experienced troops that the Arras battle was taking place before the 'fly season', the Army's battle with sickness- and disease-carrying insects becoming a heavy burden from early May to October. As the lists of dead arrived at headquarters dugouts, the thoughts of company commanders were already turning towards letters informing families of their loss. This was an unwritten duty. Although, it might take several weeks for a personal letter to be written, the responsibility was seldom shirked. The great care with which such letters were composed is most poignant.

Left Schematic showing the system of evacuation of wounded employed at Arras and Vimy. AC

Below A British working party prepare for another gruelling shift on the repair of roads and tracks.
IWM Q1616

Mrs B.P. Richardson
Grenfell
Sask(atchewan)

Dear Mrs Richardson,
You have doubtless been informed through official channels of the death of your son Charles, and I am writing just a few lines as his platoon officer to give what comfort you may receive from the exact particulars. We had reached our objective early in the morning with small losses, but by mid-day were subjected to heavy bombardments by enemy artillery. Charlie was with his men when a large shell burst close at hand inflicting the injuries that proved fatal. We had him well cared for and made as comfortable as possible in a captured dugout. I visited him constantly and did what I could to ease the pain. He was wonderfully cheerful and displayed marvellous endurance. It was morning again before it was possible to obtain stretchers to carry out the more serious cases and the wait was too long. I was with him when he died – he was calm and apparently unconscious of his wounds – he just slipt away.

I trust you may be comforted in knowing that his life and death were glorious examples worthy of the highest praise.
Ever sincerely
Gerald W. Guiore Lt.

Meanwhile, throughout the night fresh troops seethed into the city, nervous and eager for news of the day's proceedings, for come early on Tuesday they would be part of the next act.

The Major in charge read out the laws concerning looting as we were about to march into the city of Arras. I admit I had got the wind up to be once more in the danger zone for I had been some months out of shell range and I was very depressed in consequence, as there were signs in plenty to prove that the enemy could shell this district with ease. The first sight of the place realised my worst fears. It was a nightmare city from beginning to end, every feature of which was calculated to 'put the wind up' anyone who witnessed it. The first glimpse was of shattered houses, trees with branches lopped off by shell fire, gaping shell holes. As we marched into the city, which we did in small groups or parties, the signs and havoc became much more pronounced. Large buildings partly demolished, many of them smoke blackened, roads littered with rubbish, barbed wire entanglements, camouflage netting stretched across dangerous roadways as a screen from enemy observation, danger notices and direction posts strung out, one at each corner, ponderous guns belching forth their messengers of death and destruction from artfully hidden emplacements in the squares; all these tended to have further effects upon nerves strung to high tension. We were halted for a short space under the shelter of a great municipal building and the sights that we had a short leisure to gaze upon absolutely beggared description. This roadway was crowded with soldiers steadily marching along and, coming from the opposite direction, was a continuous stream of wounded, blood be-spotted humanity. The sights sickened me from their very persistence. Yet the most amazing feature of it was that these wounded appeared to be cheerful, as if glad to get out of the inferno beyond at such a price. As I gazed at this remarkable scene, a building at the end of the road was blown up by a German shell, the wreckage flying to a stupendous height and a pall of black smoke and falling debris obscured the end of the road for some minutes. The smoke had hardly cleared when another building further over to the left was blown up. All our nerves were in such a state by now that it was a positive relief to get the order to move on. We passed by the blown up building and came in view of the railway station, an amazing sight of shattered glass, brickwork and ironwork, a glaring monument to the utter madness of warfare. We branched along some side streets the houses in which were shattered with shells and shrapnel and down one of these streets a trench was made. It appears as if a lull had occurred in the battle as there was now

v. Arras

Rœux

n. Pelves

v. Wancourt

n. Boiry - Notre Dame

n. Boiry - Notre Dame

No 14

n. Guémappe

n. St. Rohart

30.7.15

Monchy.

Above An aerial view looking north over Monchy towards Roeux and the River Scarpe. HS

Overleaf A composite German panorama showing types of Allied soldier held in the prison at Douai where many men captured during the Arras' actions were interrogated before being moved on to PoW camps. The captions are taken from the original. ING G 1375-S1

comparative quiet, and I was fully expecting we were to follow this trench, but instead we branched off down a side track and at last we came to a dug-out into which we filed. To my great surprise this dug-out was the entrance to a series of underground caves of great dimensions and to my further surprise I found them electrically lighted. It was absolutely the greatest surprise I had struck since my arrival in France. Here we were snugly quartered under the city whilst enemy shells were pounding it mercilessly. No sounds of battle permeated down here and the only discomfort was the water which dripped from the chalk roof continuously, making the floor very slippery. But we got our oil sheets out and made ourselves as comfortable as possible, smoking and chatting and we managed to get to know how the battle was progressing from an R.A.M.C. Corporal who was dressing some wounded in one of the caves, as these subterranean chambers were never used for an advanced aid post. It appeared that the 112th Brigade had driven the enemy from the adjoining village and they were now following up the retreating enemy. We were, of course, elated at this news.

SAPPER R. BRIGGS, 153RD FIELD COMPANY, ROYAL ENGINEERS

CHAPTER THIRTEEN

Not Much Doing

Left A German officer watches the sun set on another day at Arras. ING G 3547a-218

Below Segment of German map showing the trench system protecting Bullecourt

The mood in the Canadian and British HQs in the early morning of 10 April was one of surprise, joy, but hardly frantic brainstorming activity. There was a general atmosphere of astonishment at the previous day's events. This time it was nothing to do with an enemy retreat/withdrawal and propaganda was almost unnecessary – 9 April was indisputably triumphal, the best offensive day of the war. In places, the Germans had been most certainly on the run. And herein lay a problem: given the novel circumstances, who was qualified to appreciate properly the situation and plan the next move for the infantry to 'put it across' the enemy today as effectively as they had done yesterday?

With the central battleground ostensibly prepared, Sir Hubert Gough prepared to throw his I Anzac Corps (Lieutenant General Sir William Birdwood) at the underbelly. Had his artillery been strong enough to weaken the Hindenburg Line defences by 9 April, this attack too would have taken place in conjunction with Allenby and Byng's, but observers had noted with concern the continuing density and depth of wire. More attention from the guns could only be beneficial in achieving the required pincer movement for the infantry were to breach the line in the Bullecourt sector, thus allowing the 4th Cavalry Division to sweep through and link with their comrades south of the Cambrai road.

Anxious to be in the fight, 'Thruster' Gough was swayed by a novel idea. As success after success unfolded on 9 April, Lieutenant Colonel J. Hardress-Lloyd, commander of D Tank Battalion had appeared at Fifth Army HQ with a proposition devised by Major William Watson, OC of 11 (Tank) Company, that outlined the prospects for a single-division infantry assault on a narrow front led by all eleven available machines. Don't make the mistake of offering the Germans easy targets by sending them in piecemeal, he said, for the original plan had been to employ them in widely dispersed pairs; as guns had been in short supply for wire-cutting, why not let the tanks perform the same duty? After they had crushed and breached the wire, and begun the process of rolling down the enemy trenches, the infantry could use the gaps and swarm through.

Above all, the deployment of a cluster of tanks on a strictly constrained battlefront meant that even if some were knocked out or ditched, there should still be a generous number to frighten the wits out of the German defence.

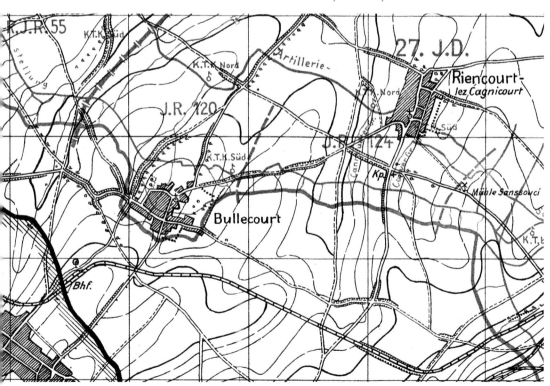

Despite there being only a matter of hours to plan the attack the idea appealed to Gough, who selected the 4th Australian Division for the venture, with the 62nd British Division; the former would attack with tanks east of Bullecourt, the latter west, pincering the village. Zero was the following morning at 4.30 – about ninety minutes before sunrise.

In hindsight, the idea of using a dozen tanks as the foundation for an assault, and in the dark even on a narrow battlefront, appears almost absurd, especially given the ground conditions. Valiant though crews undoubtedly were, the machines could hardly be relied upon to reach the jumping-off point, never mind lead a potentially lengthy attack. In fact tanks had *never* led an attack before. But, explained Gough to a concerned Birdwood and Anzac Corps chief General Staff officer, Major General C.B. White, this was all part of the surprise. The attack would go in.

The tanks set off for the front after sunset on the evening of 9 April. From the shelter of Mory Copse, it was 6.5 kilometres to the battlefield. Orders were issued to the two respective divisions, and at 1.00 a.m. the Australians began to form up in no man's land to await the tanks. The two attacking brigades of the British 62nd Division also prepared, buoyed by the news that the neighbouring 21st Division had pierced the Hindenburg Line some 4 kilometres to the north. They were not informed how small the incursion was, nor that the troops were isolated. More erroneous intelligence then suggested that Bullecourt might have been evacuated. The troops on the ground knew it plainly had not. During the night the village was subjected to a liberal dose of phosgene gas by Livens Projectors, and shelling with H.E., the latter

continuing until Zero to cover the noise of the approaching tanks. The British were to await a signal indicating that Australian troops were actually in Bullecourt before launching their assault. In preparation, the apprehensive commander of 185th Brigade, Brigadier General Vigant de Falbe, asked 2/7th and 2/8th West Yorkshires each to deploy three patrols in advance. Behind a barrage shield, the troops were to approach the enemy trenches at Zero and gauge resistance.

As the clock ticked towards 3.30 there was no sign of the tanks. Nor at 4.00 a.m. At 4.15 a message arrived from the guide: snow and darkness had hampered their progress, but they could be there in about ninety minutes. It was too late; the attack was quickly cancelled, with the order to clear the field reaching the still prone and sopping troops at 5.00 a.m. Almost 6,000 Australians then crept back to safety without attracting German attention. But west of Bullecourt the cancellation order failed to reach the British patrols, some of whom had already managed, as instructed, to negotiate the entanglements and move towards the enemy positions. The intrusion was soon detected, and troops both inside and outside the wire were flayed by machine guns. Falling back, they sought the shelter of a sunken lane which was promptly shelled by British artillery. The patrols suffered 162 casualties.

News of the Bullecourt washout quickly reached senior ears. At a midday meeting of commanders in Albert it was agreed to try the same ploy again tomorrow, for Third Army intended to attack Vis-en-Artois, Fontaine and Chérisy. Tank commanders assured everyone that they would be in position on time. An hour and half earlier there had been an even higher-level meeting.

German troops march through the village of Oppy to reinforce garrisons in the Arras sector. AJ

About 10.30 I saw General Allenby and Horne at St Pol. They each explained the situation on their respective fronts. The Canadian Corps had consolidated its front and captured Hill 145 with 32 Germans out of a garrison of 300. Patrols have been sent to Vimy village and Willerval. Canadian Corps has now taken all its objectives. The Third Army is attacking Monchy-le-Preux at 12 noon from the northwest and west. I urged on Allenby the importance of keeping the Enemy on the move during the next 24 hours, before he can bring up reserves to meet our advance. If the Third Army is held up from the west of Monchy-le-Preux, I urged Allenby to push forward on the north of the Scarpe and then move southeast in the rear on Monchy so to turn the Enemy's flank.
SIR DOUGLAS HAIG, DIARY ENTRY, 10 APRIL 1917.

The exigency in Sir Douglas Haig's words is evident. The predicament of General Sir Henry Horne's First Army was a happy one and held little concern at GHQ; his task was to complete the final brushing of German forces from a few small pockets still, firmly consolidate, install a fresh infrastructure, and drive on if and when the time was ripe. Once lost, the Germans were certainly going to struggle to retake the Vimy heights via the eastern escarpment route, and the idea that the Canadians would *ever* relinquish the ridge was fantasy. Vimy could be considered safe.

It seems hard to believe Allenby would not have had Haig's sentiments constantly in mind throughout the entire four-month planning process for Arras, especially when discussing and setting the several objectives for Z-Day. The Commander-in-Chief made suggestions, but because of the ancient and continuing antipathy, there was no meeting of minds, and certainly no vigorous discussion and formulation of ideas. One might imagine that the Third Army staff would by morning not only know the precise whereabouts of their various troops, but be fully prepared with strategies for the next series of offensive steps. They were not. Instead they deferred, waiting for orders from Olympus.

On this day the reins were quickly handed to von Lossberg who believed that order and coordination might still save the day, not least because his enemy had chosen not to attack during the night of 9 April. Had they done so, the outcome would almost certainly have proved disastrous. What the actual British objectives might have been on the first day was academic; Sixth Army Command knew the British would attack again – but the longer they delayed, or could be delayed, the better. The character of the next assault might very well decide the battle. Germany's defeat *had* to be restricted to a single day only – 9 April. This was von Lossberg's challenge.

The weather continued as foul as ever. Fruit trees may well have been in blossom, but these last throes of a long and cruel winter were truly wicked. The squalls of the previous day had now turned to blizzards and the wind freshened again, increasing the chill factor.

The British were determined that the enemy be kept under the severest possible pressure, but how was this to be done, and where? A spot of propaganda was required, but not for Press consumption. Third Army headquarters despatched a telegraphed communiqué to all corps commanders:

The Army Commander wishes all troops to understand that Third Army is now pursuing a defeated enemy and that risks must be freely taken. Isolated enemy detachments in farms and villages must not be allowed to delay the general progress. Such points must be masked and passed by. They can be dealt with by troops in rear.

In the north, the Canadians had reduced Hill 145 overnight. They were now left with the capture of The Pimple and Bois en Hache, simply a matter of time and careful planning. For the troops on the ridge, dawn on 10 April was a revelation. Thousands of Canadians gazed from the heights across the wide Douai plain to a land of fields and spires. The sun chose to make a brief appearance, turning the view from misty grey to vibrant green and white. Somewhere down there, German staffs were preparing to evacuate the comfort of *Gruppe* Vimy headquarters, buildings occupied for over two years, whilst some 60 kilometres away tremors passed along the corridors of *Gruppe* Lille. It was too late for the Germans to mount counter-attacks against the ridge. The bastion was lost. Horne and Byng knew it too. What was to come next?

It was not possible to advance safely along Allenby's main axis on a narrow front basis. Action north of the river in the Roeux and Greenland Hill sectors, and south of the Cambrai road against the heights behind Wancourt was required, so that should attacks on Monchy and Guémappe be held up, pressure could also be exerted from both flanks. This meant assaults by troops of three separate corps and the heaviest possible artillery presence. Given the achievements of the previous day, the Roeux assault looked distinctly promising for the 4th Division, now firmly established in Fampoux. On their left confusion still reigned on the 51st and 34th Divisions' fronts: it was not known to what extent the Germans had been able to reinforce the ungained portions of the Brown Line during the night.

Lieutenant General Sir Charles Fergusson suggested a cavalry attack out of Fampoux through Roeux and on to Greenland Hill might pay dividends:

The impression that I formed from General Allenby's attitude preceding the battle was that he was far more interested in the possibilities south of the Scarpe than in the operations north of the river – the Senseé and Cojeul area was where he hoped to break through and use the cavalry – more than once during the first few days fighting on the 9th I asked that cavalry should be moved up ready to push through on my front, but he did not seem sympathetic, to say the least of it. The Commander-in-Chief came to my headquarters at Aubigny in the evening of the 9th, I think between 6 and 7pm, when we knew of the capture of Fampoux, and he asked me whether the cavalry was being pushed on. I told him that I had represented the opportunity, but that none had been allotted to me. He seemed annoyed, and used my telephone to speak to General Allenby. Of course it was not until the following afternoon that a Brigade arrived, far too late to be of any use.

I am not criticising – there is no doubt that Cavalry could have gone through on the evening of the 9th, if they had been on the spot then, but I doubt whether they would have got through next morning. To have been on the spot on the previous evening would only have been possible had the possibility of their use been envisaged early in the day. Even then I doubt whether one Brigade, let loose on the Douai plain without any definite objective, would have done more than create some temporary discomfort and local confusion. It would hardly have affected the position in Roeux and on the Scarpe. That however is a matter of opinion. Of course, if a whole Cavalry Division could have gone through on the evening of the 9th there are endless possibilities as to what might have resulted. But could such a possibility have been foreseen?
LIEUTENANT GENERAL SIR CHARLES FERGUSSON, COMMANDING XVII CORPS

The heavier guns were not yet ready to lay down a bombardment, but several field artillery brigades were available. The sector was not believed to be heavily garrisoned, and there

Digging in. British troops seek cover from the enemy and the elements. IWM Q1168

was sufficient infantry support to follow up such an action. The operation order, to the 1st Cavalry Brigade, was issued at 11.45 a.m.; they had around 10 miles to travel. Enthusiasm for the plan spread and it was developed further: Greenland Hill having fallen, the 1st Cavalry Division would annexe a host of surrounding villages including not only Plouvain and Gavrelle, but Vitry-en-Artois, some 7 kilometres from Fampoux. In the meantime a strong two-brigade infantry assault upon the Gavrelle-Roeux road was cancelled in favour of smaller-scale fighting patrols designed to 'tidy up' the sector in preparation for the cavalry.

That the Germans had rectified their deficiencies during the night was now made immediately clear to the British, for the moment one fighting patrol appeared from Hyderabad Redoubt (*Polen Werk*) on the ridge north of Fampoux, a ferocious and unexpected storm of fire cut down two platoons of the 1st Somerset Light Infantry. The story was the same in the valley below where machine-guns in the fortified chemical works adjacent to the railway soon made continuation of initially lucrative probing by elements of Brigadier General Carton de Wiart's 12th Brigade suicidal. The first of the cavalry arrived at 4.30. They had nothing to do but wait. At 5.30 the Germans had the audacity to mount what appeared to be a counter-attack. Although quickly broken up by field guns firing shrapnel, it showed very clearly how the environment of battle had radically changed in just twelve hours. Without heavy artillery the route to Greenland Hill was barred. To crown the discontent Fampoux came under shell and heavy machine-gun fire.

We were warned to attack the buildings in front without a barrage. Fortunately I told our Brigadier that it would

be simply murder to take men out to do so, and they then said the cavalry would charge the trenches between us and the buildings and we go up in support. However the cavalry jibbed and nothing happened. Luckily our G.S.O.1 came up to see the situation and I took him round as much of our front line as it was prudent to get to; by an especial mercy the enemy was barraging every street with MGs and really pasting the village with H.E. and it rather impressed the G.S.O.1 who even told me he thought it foolhardy to move about the village but I rubbed it in that the infantry had no choice.

LIEUTENANT COLONEL ALFRED HORSFALL DSO, 2ND DUKE OF WELLINGTON'S (WEST RIDING) REGIMENT

It was dusk, time had once again run out and the 1st Cavalry Brigade retraced their steps to bivouac in Athies.

For XVII Corps 10 April was but the palest shadow of the previous day: although the line had been straightened a little and some 'missing' sections of the Green and Brown Lines occupied, there was nothing to celebrate. No pressure at all was put on enemy garrisons holding the ground north of Monchy; indeed, the inverse was the case: hostile fire across the Scarpe River valley disrupted British attacks to the south – precisely what commanders had wished to avoid. Having waxed long and lyrical on the 9th, in his diary for 10 April the one man whose troops might have been expecting to force further breaches, 9th Division artillery commander Brigadier General Henry Tudor, chose to write just five words: 'There was not much doing'. It was all too true.

THIRD ARMY – SOUTH FLANK

Across the Scarpe valley in the VI and VII Corps sectors the day began in similar fashion, with commanders trying to identify where their troops lay shivering. In the far south an unpleasant bombing battle had been conducted throughout the night of the 9th/10th. It resulted in a stretch of Hindenburg Line between Neuville Vitasse and the battlefield boundary being annexed by 56th Division, but not enough to allow the thwarted 30th Division on their right to benefit further. Small nocturnal jabs had also been made at the Wancourt-Feuchy trenches, again without gain. Lieutenant General Snow's line lay irregular and broken, so for him it was simply impossible to agree to Allenby's orders for an 8.00 a.m. assault. Even discounting the likelihood of counter-attacks, the earliest opportunity for effective action would perhaps be towards midday, almost halving the daylight hours for the cavalry. There was nothing Snow could do: with fighting continuing throughout the night with bomb, bayonet and rifle butt, he had weary men in unknown locations, so the drawing up of an artillery barrage plan was out of the question. If anything was going to be gained in his sector on Tuesday, he needed not only time, but initiation to begin elsewhere – on his left flank, Haldane's VI Corps. To assist Snow it would require sufficient pressure astride the Cambrai road to make the enemy relinquish ground to the south, voluntarily or otherwise. Like Allenby, Haldane was forced to issue orders without actually knowing beforehand whether units could comply. Despite the conditions, at first light low-flying 'contact' aircraft, distinguishable from the ground by a black band painted on the underside of each wing, noted the locations of British troops below. A Klaxon horn helped to attract attention, at which time men were required to light red flares. The results were either passed back by wireless, or flown back and dropped at 'report centres' to be swiftly taken to Corps and artillery HQs. Visual signals received by stations on the newly captured hills added to the picture, and in this ways commanders slowly discovered the whereabouts of their men. What the RFC

Str. ARRAS - CAMBRAI   Höhe 93   Waldst. 1 Klm nordwestl. MONCHY

Wancourt Tower

failed to spot was the approach of large numbers of German reserves.

An 8.00 a.m. attack from VI Corps territory was equally impossible, so piecemeal assaults simply to keep the enemy busy were made between the river and St Martin, going in at different times according to when units were prepared. More comprehensive assaults were planned for 14th Division on the part of the Wancourt-Feuchy line that the tired 56th Division had failed to conquer the previous day largely because of machine-gun fire from Hill 90 (see panorama pages 214-215); it protected much of Wancourt's western quadrant. The attacks would receive all available artillery assistance and begin behind a creeper when the main barrage lifted at 11.45. Two brigades, 43rd and 41st (in reserve until now), assembled for the attack, the latter detailed to leapfrog the former as soon as the protective line had fallen, and assault both the village and water tower-capped ridge beyond. The troops were slow to form up, and about 12.15 the action began. The Hill 90 guns again raked the first

waves before they finally managed to enter the Wancourt-Feuchy Line. In the snow and confusion assaulting parties drifted northwards partly into 3rd Division territory, so when the leapfroggers arrived to skirt around Hill 90 towards Wancourt, there was no sign of 43rd Brigade. The same guns then restricted *their* movement until snow obscured them as targets. Eventually a link was made, but no further progress achieved. In the hope that the line would be carried, after an awful night in the open far behind the lines, the cavalry and horse artillery had again been called forward.

I think that night was the most miserable I have ever spent. I slept behind my saddle, but in the morning I was covered with snow from head to foot. The horses had all been clipped out during the winter and had no rugs, so that they suffered terribly. Many died. The cheerfulness of the men under conditions like this is positively amazing: one never hears a murmur, except various uncomplimentary remarks about the weather. At dawn the next day I was woken up by two of them shouting some humorous

Segment of a German panorama taken from near Bullecourt. It was the high ground seen here that the British and Australians hoped might be excised by attacks from the south. Note Wancourt Tower. HS M706 M.10 Nr397

MONCHY·le·Preux
FONTAINE·lez·Croisilles   Kapelle a. d. Str. Bullecourt-Croisilles   Schornstein CHÉRISY
                                                                            Kirchturm CHÉRISY   Hr· FONTAINE-BULLECOURT   B. du. VET
                                              Waldst· auf Höhe 76   Waldsh·auf Höhe 76
                                    Waldstück 800m·südöstl·v·d·Mühle(südöstl·Monchy)

remarks at each other at the top of their voices. At two o'clock we were brought up again and sent on to the jumping-off point which was between Neuville-Vitasse and Wancourt. This was an unpleasant journey. The leading troops were met with heavy machine-gun fire from the village [Wancourt], which emptied some saddles and did considerable execution amongst the horses; but the chief danger was from the German gunners on the ridge behind, who had us in full view for several hundred yards before we reached the valley we were making for. As it happened, a heavy blizzard came down just as the advance began, and this must have shielded the leading troops from view, but the rest of the brigade must have made a fine, if a fleeting, target seen against the snow. There was one cross-road which I shall not easily forget. A battery of field guns was beautifully ranged on to this. The brigade was scurrying down the hill at a fast pace with fifty yards' distance between troops. I saw one troop receive a shell right amongst them; and for a moment they were lost in smoke. When the smoke cleared away I saw a mass of mangled men and horses. I have grown accustomed to the sight of blood, and of men with limbs blown off, but a badly wounded horse is one of the most revolting sights I know. Regimental headquarters got through with only two casualties. My own mare "Kitty" was very excitable under fire and reared right up when some shells dropped near us, almost unseating me and knocking off my steel helmet. If the Huns had fired more shrapnel, the casualties would have been very heavy; as it was they fired almost entirely H.E., a large proportion of which were "duds". The point we had now reached was the infantry front line; and the Huns were just over a little rise. It is extraordinary how a small valley will hide a large force. Here was a brigade of cavalry with its R.H.A., etc., absolutely hidden in this small fold in the ground.
'AQUILA', WITH THE CAVALRY IN THE WEST

Hill 90 was a thorn in Snow's side. Under the covering fire of any and all available weapons, the 8th Rifle Brigade were ordered to mount a dedicated attack. That too came to naught. As soon as it was safe to do so, the mounted troops and the horse artillery slipped back towards Arras. None had fired a shot in anger or drawn their sabres. The battle was already beginning to resemble the latter stages of the Somme and this feeling was reinforced by the final action of the day, a German counter-attack that at dusk bombed the 21st Division's 64th Brigade from the Hindenburg Line on the southern flank of the battlefield, a line they had struggled so bitterly to enter. For a brief period the British pondered their own counter-attack, but so swiftly were hostile machine guns brought into action that there was no hope of regaining the positions. Again, all too Somme-like. The elements of 64th Brigade may have been isolated anyway, but because it was the first loss of ground of the battle the blow was deeply felt.

As darkness enveloped the battlefield, VII Corps' gains were unexploitable, therefore offering little assistance in VI Corps' bid to take Monchy and Guémappe – an absolute necessity.

CENTRE GROUND – TUESDAY

Despite the foulness of the weather and a night of extreme discomfort, the optimism of Lieutenant General Aylmer Haldane's VI Corps troops was still warm thanks to what had been achieved the previous day. No one was in any hurry to mention the fact that objectives had not been attained at any point south of the river, indeed many would not have been aware of it.

When the 37th Division passed through us that morning in full battle order for the attack, we watched them with the cheerful interest and satisfaction of men who had already accomplished successfully their own particular share of the work, and who now could look on at their

Above More German support troops arrive in the sector, 12 April 1917. AJ

Below The cavalry suffer whilst awaiting an opportunity. IWM Q2212

leisure while others took up the job. But our part of the show was by no means over, as we later discovered, although at that moment we may have fondly imagined so! Our commanding officer with the adjutant and myself accompanied one of the support waves of the 37th Division over Orange Hill to watch the progress of the attack, and also to get a good view of Monchy-le-Preux and the valley of the Scarpe beyond. Monchy stood on a knoll of rising ground, and at the time we first saw the village its red roofs appeared almost undamaged by shell fire; a pretty place, with a large chateau-farm on the northern side surrounded by fruit orchards that were then a mass of pink and white blossom.
CAPTAIN DOUGLAS CUDDEFORD, 12TH HIGHLAND LIGHT INFANTRY

The importance of Monchy cannot be overestimated. Occupying an elevated plateau above the plain, it was invaluable for observation. The village was sprawling, defensible from walls, windows, roofs and gardens, and from it radiated many a sunken lane swarming with dugouts. Those to the east of the village, being invisible to the British, simplified supply and reinforcement. They now screened troops, weapons and stores, and repeated bitter experience had revealed such features to be *always* costly to attain. The village was served by seven, with another half dozen connecting routes. On the approaches from Observation Ridge, there was hardly a square metre of ground that could not be seen.

At 1.30 a.m. orders came to move at once and take up another position ready to support the 15th Division (H.L. Infantry) in an attack at dawn on the Bosch lines which had held them up the previous day. Heavy snow fell all the time until 8 a.m. when we were told that the enemy had retired on our fourth objective, leaving isolated strongpoints here and there, especially on Orange Hill and Chapel Hill. At 9 a.m. we formed for the advance on Monchy-le-Preux, our final objective, with the front wave lining the Chapel road and facing Orange Hill. Great excitement was now aroused by the appearance of about 20 batteries of R.F.A. and 6-inch guns from Battery Valley, who were to co-operate with our 37th Division, now leading the attack. The 3rd Cavalry Division also came up at 10 a.m. and formed up on our left flank. The Bosch hadn't seen us yet.
LIEUTENANT L.S. CHAMBERLEN, 13TH RIFLE BRIGADE

Divisional Headquarters had been moved forward at Allenby's request. Four were to take part: 3rd, 12th (Eastern), 15th (Scottish) and 37th Divisions, the same as the previous day. The first two were ordered to integrate with VII Corps' plans, attacking the still intact Wancourt-Feuchy Line at around noon. The 37th were already in position about Orange Hill (astonishingly, Allenby was unaware of this until the morning of the 10th). Before the main bout of the day, however, the undefeated section of the Wancourt-Feuchy Line had to fall in both VI and VII Corps sectors, and 12th Division had a nasty obstacle to overcome in the form of the redoubt that nosed out from this position towards Feuchy Chapel.

The plan was as follows: having eradicated the redoubt the 12th Division were to capture Chapel Hill; all three brigades of the 37th would then leapfrog and attack Monchy – they had spent the night on the battlefield. Meanwhile, on their right a combined 3rd Division/VII Corps assault would take the Wancourt-Feuchy Line, keeping pace, protecting the right flank, and enveloping Guémappe. In the left sector between Orange Hill and the river, the 15th Scottish should use the territorial advantage they had already gained and 'turn' the enemy by driving down behind him in the direction of Monchy.

The redoubt at Feuchy quickly fell, and Chapel Hill was found to be devoid of Germans – an excellent start.

We advanced right through the centre of the resting cavalry. They were awfully excited and keen with the prospect of seeing action – this was to be the first and last experience for many of them. Passing through them quite cheered us up, for their cheerfulness was infectious. I well remember some of them saying to us, 'Give us covering fire, boys, when we pass through you at Monchy.'

On reaching the higher ground beyond the cavalry, the whole countryside lying between us and Monchy was visible. Monchy was about 1½ miles away. A few hedges ran down from the village on the flat and on the lower ground slightly to the left was a small wood. With these exceptions, the ground we had to attack over was just even, grassy country, but at that time all covered with snow. Monchy itself looked very picturesque; all the houses and trees were untouched by shell fire, and the red tiled roofs showed up here and there through the mantle of snow.

As we passed down the slope on to the flat, the whole Battalion opened out into extended order. On our left and right, long lines of men could be seen advancing in a general line with us. The Arras-Cambrai road was now only about ¼ mile to our right, and the lines of men extended some distance to the other side of it, and showed up black against the snow. A few German shells began to fall about us, and their machine guns commenced as soon as we came over the ridge and were seen from the village. Neither the shells nor machine gun bullets worried us much at that moment, for the artillery fire was spasmodic and the machine guns some distance away – and the day was yet young!

The question still on everyone's lips was "Why is our artillery not shelling the village?"
SERGEANT RUPERT 'JACK' WHITEMAN, 10TH ROYAL FUSILIERS (CITY OF LONDON REGIMENT)

The 37th Division had been handed almost the same orders as the previous day: one brigade

✝ Wancourt   ✝ Mt. St. Eloy

Telegraph Hill   The Harp   Thilloy

(111th) to capture the village, the other two to cover the flanks. Monchy was far from empty of Germans. The village was being shelled by a few British heavies, but no creeping barrage plan had been drawn up. The moment the troops crested the final rise at 10.45 they came under heavy fire.

From now on the advance became a matter of running from one newly formed shell hole to another, each of which smelt horribly of hot suffocating gases from high explosive shells. At every step nearer the village the machine gun fire became more intense and we began to lose men; this had the effect of making everyone take all possible cover so that progress became slower and slower, and when about 300 yards from the bottom of Monchy Hill the 10th Royal Fusiliers and the 13th Royal Fusiliers – who were on the immediate left of the 10th – became completely held up, due entirely to the terrific machine gun fire. Anyone who attempted to leave one shell hole for another would have a hail of bullets projected round or into him. Any control over the Battalion was now impossible for orders could not be passed along. Companies and platoons became hopelessly mixed up and scattered about, taking cover wherever possible; two men in one shell hole, six in another, perhaps a dozen in a natural fold in the ground – anywhere to be under cover from those deadly machine gun bullets. A slight ridge extended from the right of the village along which a sunken road appeared to run from Monchy to the main Arras-Cambrai road. It was from this road, with its high banks on each side, that most of the machine guns seemed to be firing. A machine-gun is like a rifle inasmuch that it has a smokeless discharge so that it is very difficult to locate: the only means of approximating the position is by the report which resembles that made by a child dragging a stick quickly along a fence of iron railings.
SERGEANT RUPERT 'JACK' WHITEMAN, 10TH ROYAL FUSILIERS (CITY OF LONDON REGIMENT)

The chaos that had ensued on Monday was being replicated. No matter which face of the village one approached, the German response

Segment of German panorama taken from Wancourt Tower (Fasbender Turm) on 31 October 1916 showing the observational capabilities northwards to the Vimy Ridge. From here, flash-spotting of British gunfire was possible around an arc of over 200 degrees. BHK Rundbild VII/18

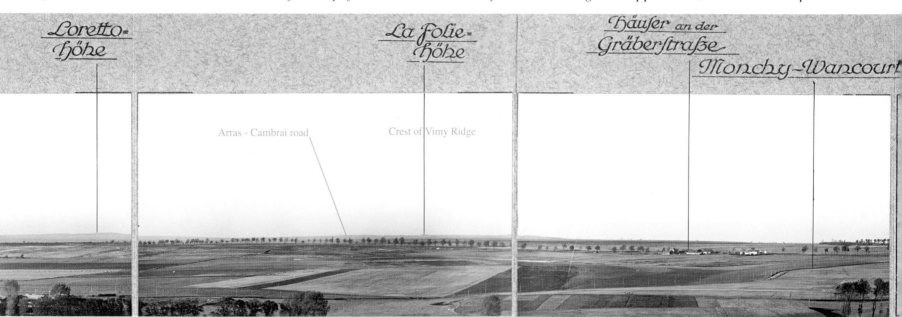

Loretto-Höhe   La Folie-Höhe   Häuser an der Gräberstraße   Monchy-Wancourt

Arras - Cambrai road   Crest of Vimy Ridge

was the same. For the cavalry to make any move into the valley would have been suicidal. Their original orders had been to attack at any time from 7.00 a.m.; 11 o'clock was the next suggested hour. Erroneous reports of British troops being seen in Monchy put the cavalry on standby at 3 p.m. The several brigades dotted across the landscape were coming under ever-greater shellfire, and being immobile were suffering from the snow and wind chill. A single foray was made north of Monchy, the troopers of the Essex Yeomanry fortunate in being able to abandon their charge and return beneath the cover of a blinding snow squall. The troops had advanced almost a mile, which was no mean feat, but not a moving soul was now to be seen in the white fields below the village. Time was slipping by.

No orders of any description came from the "powers that be"; no one dared even to show his head so that it was madness to expect runners to distribute orders from the Colonel. This was life to be sure, and death too, if one was not careful, for here we were lying perished in shell holes with no prospect of anything hot to eat or drink for perhaps days, and worse than anything else, the whole frontal attack on Monchy held up by invisible machine guns.

Away on our right things seemed to be much the same as with us, for on looking out of our shell hole we saw a platoon of the York and Lancs regiment suddenly rise out of the ground and, forming into fours, run towards the village; they had gone but a dozen yards or so forward when their numbers seemed to literally melt away under the machine gun fire which they had attracted; the few that were left standing saw that to advance was hopeless, so went to earth in the nearest shell holes. From start to finish this little incident occupied a matter of 3 minutes yet in that short time they must have lost 15 of their number out of a total of 23

or thereabouts. It must have been 5 o'clock when Nature quite unexpectedly came to the rescue or so we thought at the time. The snow had been falling in flurries for the last hour, but suddenly it began to fall thicker and thicker and in a few minutes a regular blizzard set in, hiding the village, the road, and everything beyond a radius of 20 yards from each person. This was the chance we had been waiting for to get across the 300 yards and right in amongst the Germans with bomb and bayonet before they had time to realise what was happening. Under cover of he snowstorm. we dashed forward and must have covered 150 yards when the screening blizzard thinned out as suddenly as it had commenced, revealing the whole Battalion running forward. We were able to see the village again, so the Germans were able to see us, with the result that immediately all their machine guns in the sunken road and the village opened up, and frightful was the havoc made in our ranks. Our poor chaps fell like ninepins and all round figures were stretched out, dead and wounded in the snow.
SERGEANT RUPERT 'JACK' WHITEMAN, 10TH ROYAL FUSILIERS (CITY OF LONDON REGIMENT)

For the survivors, there was no choice but to dig for their lives, wait for dark, wait for orders and wait for rations.

Nightfall found the 10th and 13th R.F. front line still west of Monchy and 40% laid out. The K.R.R.C. had lost 200 out of 500 and we, 80 out of 500. The Bosch had us absolutely taped and we had to halt and dig like moles or die. As soon as I got my fellows settled in and established a signal station in a convenient shell hole, which Brooker dexterously manipulated and increased, I took Sergt. Champion and visited the companies and K.R.R.C., but not the R.F's. We nearly lost ourselves in the darkness and snow, but after numerous shaves from bullets etc. we discovered all we wanted, chatted to various fellows and riflemen here and there. We then

Above Quieter times in Monchy. A German band plays for soldier and civilian during the summer of 1916. AJ

Right German light machine-gun crew on the outskirts of an Artois village. AJ

returned to our own Hqrs. Company and I left Sergt. Champion with L/Cpl. Brooker and went to see Col. Pinney and report. He, Archbold and Pidsley were in H.Q. (an 8-inch shell hole) close by – and Rfn. Davies, Richardson (my servant), Frankish (Pinney's servant) had made tea for us – joy!! I was feeling pretty well chilled to the bone, soaked, and deuced hungry. So a tin of bully, a few biscuits (our last) were devoured, and so we tried to sleep a bit in turn. <u>Question</u>:- Would C. Coy. (ration carriers) arrive before dawn when we should inevitably advance again?

LIEUTENANT L.S. CHAMBERLEN, 13TH RIFLE BRIGADE

Most of the cavalry started the long trek back to Arras as the light began to fail, but by virtue of the fact that the attacks were to be pursued at first light the next morning, certain mounted units remained on the battlefield. It was a murderous decision. Whilst the afternoon attacks had been underway, British airmen had at last spotted the most serious event of the day: regiments of German reserves filing into the battle front.

Sir Douglas Haig was keen to see General Haldane for a verbatim report on the day's doings. Haldane, however, acting upon concerns from several quarters, had gone forward to encourage his divisional commanders to place headquarters yet nearer the battle zone to further improve communication and command. The C-in-C moved on to cavalry HQ in Duisans, and about the same time in the afternoon as the infantry were being driven to ground in a blizzard in the valley below Monchy, he spoke with General Kavanagh, commander of the Cavalry Corps. Kavanagh noted with concern that 'the infantry were not as far forward as he had been led to believe'. But the infantry could not possibly have done more. They were in limbo.

It became dark to a pitch-black intensity; hours passed but no orders came until sometime during the night our Company Commander Captain King came to tell us we were to fill a gap between two units that had lost touch with each other in the fields below Monchy. We went cautiously forward until we reached the face of a gentle slope of the eminence upon which the village stood. Here we again sank into shellholes which were well within easy rage of the numerous machine guns which raked every hollow and shell hole in the fields beneath. How we stuck it I don't know. Of all the bad nights I ever spent in France, this one was easily the worst. It blew an icy blizzard all the time, and the machine-gun fire prevented anyone rising to walk about to get the blood circulating. I had not slept at all for six days and nights, and was in that state of apathy when it didn't matter a rap to me whether I lived or died – I just didn't care. Anyhow, it seemed that the next morning would see us all as corpses. In spite of my sufferings I found myself lapsing into unconsciousness, dozing for few minutes now and then. My toes, ears and fingers were an agony. The Medical Officer came round once, creeping from shellhole to shellhole warning men not to go to sleep in the snow. He got more curses than thanks. Captain King himself too crawled from hole to hole trying to keep up the spirits of the men with words of entreaty and encouragement, and giving some a sip from his brandy flask as long as his supply lasted. His own servant was in a shellhole near the one I was in and I saw Captain King take off his trench coat and cover the sleeping man, whom he couldn't awake.

PRIVATE PERCY CLARE, 7TH EAST SURREY REGIMENT

It is not known how many men failed to awake after this dreadful night. Entirely lacking shelter, in the valleys between the ridges scores of cavalry horses succumbed to the bitterness of the night. The question now was: when morning came, who would be called upon to attack?

CHAPTER FOURTEEN
Back to Business

General Haldane Commanding VI Corps also came to see me. He had been close to Monchy.
His difficulty was to get Commanders of Divisions to go forward, and take control of the operations.
They had been accustomed to sit behind trenches and command by the aid of telegraph. Now their
wires in the open soon get broken, and they lost connection with their brigades who are fighting.
He had seen all the Division Generals of his Corps and felt things were moving better.

SIR DOUGLAS HAIG. DIARY, WEDNESDAY 11 APRIL

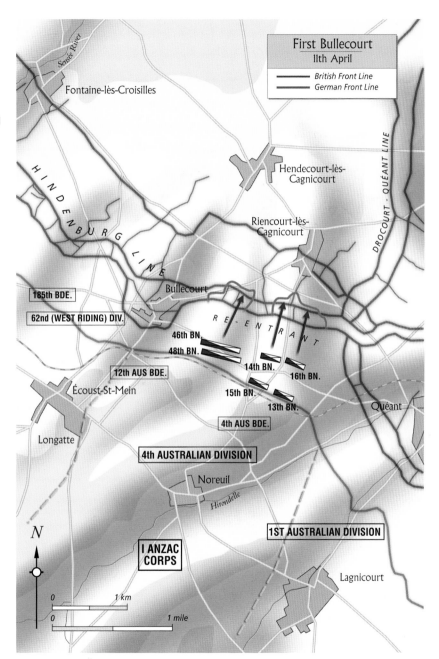

First Bullecourt
11th April

―――― British Front Line
―――― German Front Line

Fontaine-lès-Croisilles

HINDENBURG LINE

Sensée River

DROCOURT - QUÉANT LINE

Hendecourt-lès-Cagnicourt

Riencourt-lès-Cagnicourt

Bullecourt

RE-ENTRANT

185th BDE.

62nd (WEST RIDING) DIV.

46th BN.

48th BN.

14th BN.

16th BN.

12th AUS BDE.

Écoust-St-Mein

15th BN.

13th BN.

Quéant

4th AUS BDE.

Longatte

4th AUSTRALIAN DIVISION

1ST AUSTRALIAN DIVISION

Noreuil

Hirondelle

N

I ANZAC CORPS

Lagnicourt

0   1 km

0   1 mile

It is possible that on the morning of Wednesday, 11 April that Sir Edmund Allenby was battling the impulse to admit that his offensive was disintegrating. As he breakfasted, the Germans were concentrating fresh troops and guns along the entire Third and Fifth Army battle front; that was no longer in doubt. In terms of future aspirations, the hours before the sun next set were as important as any that had passed in recent days. No British staff officer would have dreamed of opposing the day's attacks, but already the foxhunting aphorisms had vanished: the chase was over, for the British hounds appeared to have lost the scent. Both Haig and Allenby (the former was actually in Arras on this day) were anxious to maintain a grand offensive outlook, for local attacks against a coalescing enemy were proving worthless and dispiriting. It was essential to rekindle new momentum and the only way to achieve this was by using all arms on the widest possible front: the same front as Tuesday.

Snow's VII Corps gathered themselves up. Again, fighting had continued throughout the night; should it have proved unsuccessful, starting at 6.00 a.m. on Wednesday, the 21st and 30th Divisions would complete the capture of the Hindenburg Line. Lancing the Hill 90 boil was still the responsibility of Major General Hull and his 56th Division; Major General V.A. Couper's 14th (Light) Division was to snatch Wancourt plus its tower, whilst Guémappe was the objective of Major General C.J. Deverell's 3rd Division. The 37th, 12th and 15th Divisions of Haldane's VI Corps again undertook the advance to the Green Line beyond Monchy. Today, however, there was the added and very important drive of General Sir Hubert Gough's I Anzac Corps at Bullecourt. As for Greenland Hill, this was XVII Corps country, the 4th

Division being commissioned to eliminate fire across the river valley that had hindered the previous day's actions around Monchy; unless tackled now, it would delay all further eastward advances. Behind the battlefront the entire Cavalry Corps was preparing for action wherever opportunity beckoned.

Monchy glared down. Once more British troop dispositions had to be ascertained before orders could be issued. It was now forty-eight hours since the whistles of Z-Day had sounded. For at least the last fifteen hours German reserves and guns had streamed into the region, sealing leaky ranks, cementing gaps and nestling into new battery positions. At von Lossberg's request the construction of a new defensive line was begun. It was to run from the high ground behind Wancourt, through the two woods east of Monchy (Bois du Sart and Bois du Vert), to the village of Pelves on the River Scarpe. Primitive though it may have been, it was no longer splendour and longevity that mattered but the practicality of a position, who garrisoned it, and how those men were trained to behave. On Wednesday, 11 April it was Australians who would begin one of the most bitter days of fighting of the war.

FIRST BULLECOURT

The night passed with slow feet, while my tanks were crawling forward over the snow. The Brigade-Major re-wrote his orders. Officers and orderlies came in and out of the cellar. We had some tea, and the General lay down for some sleep. There was a rumour that one of the tanks had become ditched in climbing out of the road. I went out to investigate, and learned that Morris's tank had been slightly delayed. It was, unfortunately, a clear cold night.

When I returned to the cellar the Brigade staff were making ready for the battle. Pads of army signal forms were placed conveniently to hand. The war diary was lying open with a pencil beside it and the carbons adjusted. The wires forward to battalion headquarters were tested. Fresh orderlies were awakened.

MAJOR W.H.L. WATSON, D BATTALION, HEAVY BRANCH MACHINE GUN CORPS

There was nothing now to be lost by bowling Gough's troops fully into battle, so on 11 April two separate ventures were intended, one north and one south. Allenby appears to have still believed that he was dealing with a form of open warfare, but the two attacks were of the pure, old-fashioned siege style, with the added appeal of ultra-modern technology in the form of tanks. If the latter attack only partly succeeded, it would certainly greatly assist the former; if it fully succeeded, the cavalry waiting behind both sectors might link to do great things.

Sir Douglas Haig was now a great admirer of the Anzacs, noting how much the Corps had improved in recent months. Their training would be critical at Bullecourt, for the 1,500-metre battlefront consisted of a wide re-entrant (a 'dent' in the line as opposed to the 'bulge' of a salient), the defences and wire of which had been by use of the contours designed to funnel attackers into machine-gun crossfire. The hope was that as the *Wotan Stellung I* (Drocourt-Quéant Line) coupled with the *Siegfried Stellung* (Hindenburg Line) just to the east, the loss of Bullecourt and Hendecourt might force the Germans into falling back across the Third Army battlefront.

This time there was to be no initial British involvement, just two brigades (12th and 4th) of the 4th Australian Division (Major General W. Holmes). Birdwood was again discontented with the plan, but in the face of GHQ enthusiasm kept his concerns to himself. A 62nd

Top three images Concrete German gun positions sited inside farm buildings. AJ

Left A German OP tower built inside a cottage. IWM Q5137

Division assault on Hendecourt was to follow. The first attack was scheduled to commence at 4.30 a.m. and there was again snow on the ground. Not only had the Australians never before worked with tanks, but the accepted wisdom at this stage of the development of armoured tactics was to attack at dawn when targets were at least becoming visible. It was known that the Germans had installed anti-tank measures, and a host of mobile gun batteries existed in the Bullecourt/Riencourt sector, many mounted in concrete emplacements built into cottages and farm buildings; they too would be hindered by darkness. Although the defenders, 124 (Würtemberger) Infantry Regiment had fought against neither foe before, it is possible that they feared Australian troops rather more than tanks, for it was rumoured, or possibly even circulated as 'encouragement', that Diggers did not take prisoners.

Assembled once again in no man's land, the troops awaited the arrival of the tanks. German *horstposten* – advanced listening posts secreted within the entanglements – record hearing them around 3.00 a.m., but the Australians actually both heard and saw the approach from a distance, as red hot sparks flew from the exhausts. They were to pass through the waiting troops, then the first two waves would follow.

In the early hours of the morning of the 11th ... the troops of the 4th Brigade, arriving from all directions, under cover of the darkness, assembled in a sunken road. Out in front 1000 yards away over a gradually rising plain ... somewhere, was the Hindenburg Line. Beyond it lay the villages of Riencourt and Bullecourt. The attack was arranged to proceed in four lines or waves, each to be some half a minute behind the other. Snow began to fall at about 3.30 am. Zero hour – the hour for jumping off was 4.30. Punctually at that hour, after grim and silent handshakes of farewell, and perhaps with some foreboding of the result, the first wave clambered up over the side of the sunken road and commenced on its forward move.

SERGEANT WILLIAM GROVES, 14TH BATTALION, AUSTRALIAN IMPERIAL FORCE

As far as is known, for accounts do not concur, only two tanks actually made it to the wire. It appears they entirely failed to make any pathways for the infantry, which makes Australian success in negotiating the forest of thorns and breaching the line in two places all the more astonishing. By daylight, but leaving scores of dead and wounded in and on the wire, strong elements of both brigades had gained entry. At a given signal they were supposed to have benefited from a box barrage, i.e. a protective screen of shells falling 200 metres ahead and on both flanks to deter the approach of German supports. It did not materialize, the gunners being erroneously informed that both infantry and tanks had pushed ahead into the zone upon which their guns were ranged. General Birdwood believed it, however, and forbade the barrage. In doing so he sealed the fate of the Australians, for the only guns to fire were those already ostensibly engaged in counter-battery and distant harassing fire – except for the German artillery that was showering no man's land with shrapnel and H.E. There was no way forward for support troops and no way back for the marooned attackers. Further reports said the Diggers and even a tank were in Bullecourt, the communication – also flawed – reaching 62nd Division HQ. Birdwood pleaded for British help with an attack on Bullecourt's western flank. Fortunately Lieutenant General

Herbert Fanshawe understood the impossibility. He had been awaiting confirmation, for in anticipation of orders to attack his advanced companies were already on the battlefield; they had sent no messages regarding fighting in the village, only that the wire was still uncut and that Bullecourt was evidently still in German hands. To attack now would simply lead to a massacre. More than thirty men were already dead as a result of hostile shellfire, so Fanshawe called his troops in. They sustained sixty-three further casualties in returning to the British line. If not in Bullecourt and Hendecourt, where were the tanks?

At last the reports began to dribble in. There were heavy casualties before the German wire was reached. The enemy barrage came down, hot and strong, a few minutes after zero … Fighting hard in the Hindenburg trenches, but few tanks to be seen … The enemy are still holding on to certain portions of the line … The fighting is very severe … Heavy counter-attacks from the sunken road at L.6 b. 5.2. The news is a medley of scraps. Soon the Brigadier is called upon to act. One Company want a protective barrage put down in front of them, but from another message it seems probable that there are Australians out in front. The Brigadier must decide. One battalion asks to be reinforced from the reserve battalion. Is it time for the reserve to be thrown into the battle? The Brigadier must decide.

They have run short of bombs. An urgent message for fresh supplies comes through, and the staff captain hurries out to make additional arrangements. There is little news of the tanks. One report states that no tanks have been seen, another that a tank helped to clear up a machine-gun post, a third that a tank is burning. At last R., one of my tank commanders, bursts in. He is grimy, red-eyed, and shaken. "Practically all the tanks have been knocked out, sir!", he reported in a hard, excited voice. Before answering I glanced rapidly round the cellar.

These Australians had been told to rely on tanks. Without tanks many casualties were certain and victory was improbable. Their hopes were shattered as well as mine, if this report were true. Not an Australian turned a hair.
MAJOR W.H.L. WATSON, D BATTALION, HEAVY BRANCH MACHINE GUN CORPS

Upon reaching the headquarters dugout the recalled British 185th Brigade patrol leaders were able to reconfirm that Bullecourt was most definitely still occupied by Germans. Faulty intelligence, however, had already reached the ears of Sir Hubert Gough; it said that both Bullecourt *and* Riencourt might be in Australian hands. Being a cavalryman, at 9.35 Gough had ordered the mounted troops forward to the railway embankment. It took only a short while to discover the truth of the situation, and with surprisingly few losses that venture too had been abandoned.

The tanks had failed in what they hoped to achieve, and now the guns were not assisting. All that was left for the Australians in the Hindenburg Line was to attempt to get home. Hostile bombing attacks had already commenced on the flanks, and the Diggers were just about holding their own. Lewis-gunners foiled German approaches from the direction of Riencourt, but it was the bombing that troubled battalion commanders. A couple of late-arrival tanks arrived to draw fire for a while, one of which helped supports of the 47th Battalion to bring forward much-needed ammunition and water as well as their precious selves.

Almost two hours before Gough had sent in his cavalry, supplies were reaching a seriously low ebb. The peril of the situation dawned on Australian 4th Division headquarters staff and at 11.00 a.m. the box barrage finally appeared, several hours too late. Its

Above A knocked-out tank on the Bullecourt battlefields is inspected from a distance by nervous German troops. HS 0615/19

Below A stricken tank near Riencourt. AC

purpose now, however, was to assist troops to get *back* not forward. Those who had not already been cut off were told to retire as best they could: it was every man for himself.

'Back to the old front line,' called Imlay, as a bloodied messenger raced in. I glanced round the trench as I swung my [Lewis] gun on my shoulder. Bright mess tins lay about. There was half a loaf of bread with an open tin of jam beside it, and bloodstained equipment lying everywhere. The dead sergeant still lay on the parapet. Other dead lay limp on the trench floor. Wounded sprawled or sat with backs to the parapet, watching us with anxious eyes.

'You are not going to leave us?' asked one of me. I could not answer him, or meet his eyes as I joined the party moving down the sap. For some reason I felt that the guilt of deserting them was mine alone.

Here was a tangle of dismembered limbs and dead men. The air was heavy with the reek of explosives. One man, with his foot blown off, leaned wearily back. He had a Mills in his hand with the pin out. He would not be taken alive.

Our party – about sixty strong, with our two remaining officers – spread along the German front line, men with ready bombs and bayonets on the flanks. No other Australian force was left in the Hindenburg Line.

Our shells still screamed about the parapet. When this fire died down the might of the German Army would fall again on our outflanked few. Between us and our line stretched masses of brown wire, and fifteen hundred yards of bullet- and shell-swept level land, over which for a long time no messenger had lived in attempting to get across. Wounded men stood or sat silent on the upper steps of deep dugouts. I leaned on my gun, pondering the utter hopelessness of the position.

Word came from the left flank, punctuated by bomb bursts, 'Enemy bombing back. We have run out of bombs.' All stores of German bombs had been used up by our men. An officer's voice called clear, 'Dump every-

thing and get back.' Discard my beautiful gun? They mightn't give me another!

Our few unwounded climbed the parapet. Heavily I started to climb the steep trench wall where a shell had partly blown it in. I looked up to see Bill Davies standing on the top amid the bullets, with hand extended to help me up. A vast indifference settled on me, as I stood on the parapet. Three yards out a man lying over a strand of wire called, 'Help me, mate.' I put down my gun and tried to heave him into a shell hole. He screamed with pain as I heaved, so I stopped. 'I can't do anything for you, old chap,' I said, and hoping that I would be forgiven the lie, 'I will send the bearers back.' 'Thank you,' he said. I picked up my gun and walked on. A shrapnel from the enemy flank churned the ground just in front, as I picked my way through the wire. A piece of shell fragment cut my puttee tape, and dropped the folds round my boot.

In complete indifference I trudged over the field, making the concession of holding the gun flat so as not to be too prominent. A man reaches a blasé stage after too much excitement. Once I thought of settling down and blazing defiance at the enemy with my last solitary magazine. But the thought of our wounded in the track of the bullets made me refrain.

Five-point-nines burst black on either hand, and futile bullets zipped about. They could do nothing to me. Silly cows to try. Someone ought to tell them. I sheered across to have a look at a burned-out tank, around which shells burst regularly. It was still smoking hot.

The sunken road containing battalion headquarters was not far off. A little tremor ran through me.

We laboured at the stretchers till darkness fell. The cold of the night would claim the rest. One man we found wandering in circles, blind from the shock of a bullet that had creased his head. He walked beside me with his hand on my shoulder, trustful as a little child, while we struggled along with another man on the stretcher.

LANCE CORPORAL GEORGE MITCHELL, 48TH BATTALION, AUSTRALIAN IMPERIAL FORCE

As the exodus began, catastrophe was amplified, for not only were German machine-gunners prepared for this very eventuality, assisted by the shape of the re-entrant to employ converging enfilade fire, but Australian shells were dropping short making the Diggers run a gauntlet of both hostile and friendly fire. In the Hindenburg Line, the news was bad: the box barrage had fallen *between* the two lines held by the Diggers, leaving those in the furthest position pinioned. Cornered groups battled on until they could fight no further. Almost 2,000 were captured, the highest number of the war for the Australian nation (Sir Douglas Haig was given the figure of 400, which he noted in his diary). 4th Brigade alone listed 2,339 losses from an establishment of 3,000; the total casualty count for the day almost touched 3,500. It was one of the most shambolic examples of poor and disjointed command of the war. Ironically, later in the day both sides readily agreed on an unofficial truce to clear the battlefield of dead and wounded. German losses were said to be around 750.

Who was to blame for the debacle that was First Bullecourt? Principally, the Australians blamed the tanks. None could deny that closer cooperation was required, but it was so early in the evolution of armoured warfare that it would have been miraculous if things had gone according to plan. Having seen the fate of many of the fifty-one casualties out of Number 11 Company's 103-strong starting crews, few infantrymen would have willingly swapped places. Of the eleven machines deployed, only two did not perish on the battlefield. A brace are believed to have got into the Germans lines, one on the left finding the outskirts of Bullecourt, the second veering right towards Quéant, entering the Hindenburg Line and eventually being

literally shot to pieces by armour-piercing bullets, leaving just three survivors. Five machines were hit by enemy shellfire.

Others blamed the gunners for failing to deliver the box barrage. And then there was the distorted intelligence – such a common and costly occurrence. Finally, there were the 'shorts' on the return across no man's land. Once distilled, however, certain things may be said to account for the catastrophe: General Hubert Gough's decision to attack the re-entrant in the first place appears to have been hasty, the principal mistake. It was an allegation that Gough himself was later to acknowledge. Above all, however, it had to be admitted that the Germans had delivered yet another outstanding defensive performance. It should have surprised no one, and the Diggers later spoke of their respect for the way the enemy had fought. There were few enough left to speak of it.

At ten that night our relief battalion arrived, fit and strong. We moved out in a weary file in the teeth of wind and sleet. At length we came to a factory by Vaulx. Through glassless windows we could see a number of men round little fires. On going in, we found that they were survivors of other battalions in the attack. We pulled out window frames and made a fire. I went out and filled our dixies with snow, broached our iron rations, and made tea. Then we collected bags and German greatcoats, and made a bed. Fierce and completely terrible were the tales those men told in matter-of-fact sentences.

The following afternoon we drifted in to the battalion. Two officers out of twenty-one and about forty men out of six hundred in the actual attack were still on their feet. A pitifully weak company was all that remained of the proud, strong unit that had marched that way a few days before. The other battalions of the brigade cheered us as we marched. That night in Bapaume we sat

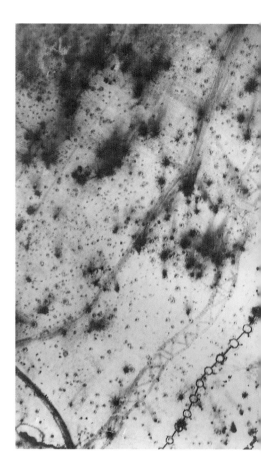

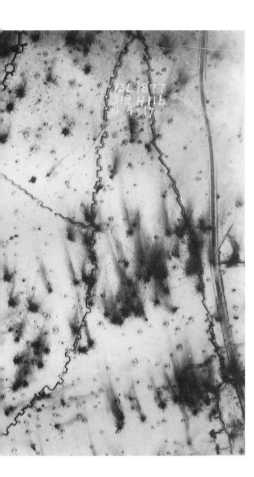

British aerial view of German defences in the Oppy sector. Taken on 11 April 1917, it shows the ground conditions on this day. The strength of the wind can be gauged by the 'drift' of the earth thrown up by the explosions. AC

through a picture-show. It was strange and unreal to watch slapstick comedies with minds not yet detuned from battle. A few days later we stood on parade while 'Birdy' delivered some of his 'usual'. Then he spoke of our losses. "These have not been in vain," he said. Officers – hard faced, hard-swearing men broke down. From the silent other ranks came a deep feeling of warmth and sympathy, a feeling that endured as long as the flame-racked years, and beyond.

LANCE CORPORAL GEORGE MITCHELL, 48TH BATTALION, AUSTRALIAN IMPERIAL FORCE

Even after the drubbing Fifth Army staff retained the opinion that their enemy was about to relinquish the Bullecourt salient. More patrols were reluctantly sent out by 185th Brigade to reconfirm that which earlier expeditions had already reported. And more casualties ensued.

One last misfortune befell the Fifth Army on 11 April 1917: two tanks fell into enemy hands, the first of the war. The result of the action could have been even worse without them, but the Australians could not have cared less; next time they were called upon to share a battle with tanks they refused, and not politely.

Gough was unimpressed with any of the post-morteming. He was determined to have another crack at Bullecourt, and as soon as was feasibly possible, for events further north were to ease whatever misgivings or culpability he might have harboured. Support also came from an unexpected source. On the night of 11 April, Sir Douglas Haig received a wire from Robert Nivelle, now in the final stage of planning for his offensive. It included the line, 'Franchet will attack tomorrow, Micheler on 15th and Pétain on the 16th; advise you strengthen General Gough and attack towards Quéant.' If Gough's ego needed an extra puff, this was it. He

immersed his staff in planning a much heavier blow against the Hindenburg Line.

MONCHY-LE-PREUX

Platoon after platoon of infantry were waiting to move up in the opposite direction, and, as we passed them some who had arrived from other sectors enquired of us what it was like "up there" – meaning the line. "Its a hell, ain't it?" they said. "We heard about Monchy; it's another bloody Ypres they say."

ANONYMOUS

Almost every battalion in the northern sectors received their operation orders for 11 April ridiculously late. Having spent the night scraping and scratching, the news arrived variously between 3.30 and 5.00 a.m.: attacks to begin at 6.00. From first light the troops watched the grey skies fill with aircraft, the British again seeking information on how close the previous day's attack had approached Monchy. Between the snow showers it was not difficult for aviators to see muddy shell holes and fragments of trench as dirty smudges in the white carpet below. The tracks of officers and NCOs creeping from spot to spot were evident, as were the pre-dawn traces of fresh troops moving into jumping-off positions. There was no line. Some knew more about their target than others.

After a week of these dress rehearsals, with which everyone was fed-up, the name of the real village to be attacked was divulged to all senior N.C.O's; "No junior ranks were yet to be told", they said. It was Monchy-le-Preux. One can imagine the rush for maps to find the place and having found it the thoughts that would be passing through each person's mind. "What has that village in store for me?" In a matter of a few days details of the final attack on the village were issued to senior

Str. Bullecourt – Croisilley
Westrand VIS-en-Artois
BOIRY NOTRE-DAME

Str. Bullecourt – Elough

BULLECOURT

HENDECOURT-lez-Cagnicourt   Kirchl. DC
Scharnt westl-DURY
L'Espérance Fme Kreuzung ROUTE NAT⁰
Mit südl- Bulle.

N.C.O.s; small street maps – strictly confidential – were given to platoon sergeants, who were provided also with photographs, some taken from aeroplanes, and some taken in the streets themselves, showing German soldiers lolling about the estaminets – or inns – and strolling about the streets, for Monchy was then used as German Divisional H.Q. and rest billets. These details were truly wonderful, the size of large cellars and their positions were marked on the maps, how many men each would hold and approximately what size of shell it would take to make the cellar roof cave in. All the particulars, photos, etc. must have been obtained through our spies under the direction of the Intelligence Dept. This was all the more wonderful when one remembers that Monchy was at that time 5 miles behind the Hun front line. At the end of a week all senior N.C.O.s had so studied the maps that

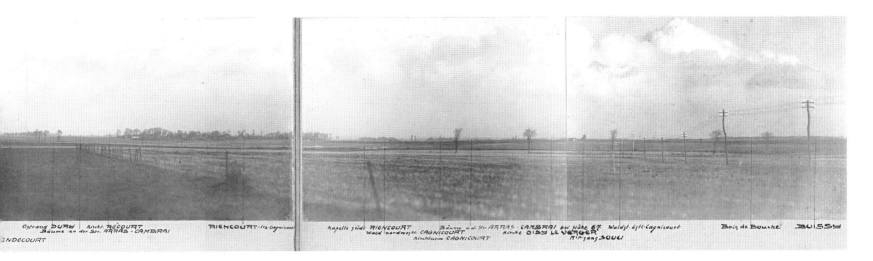

Above The Australian section of the Bullecourt battleground east of the village. The railway embankment from which the troops attacked runs across the image beyond the mill. HS M706 M10 Nr 396

each could sketch the position of the principal streets, size of cellars, etc, from memory. Having reached this stage the Battalion had orders to move nearer Arras.
SERGEANT RUPERT 'JACK' WHITEMAN, 10TH ROYAL FUSILIERS (CITY OF LONDON REGIMENT)

These troops were probably better acquainted with the village than many of its German incumbents, for numbers of Bavarian reserves arrived just hours before the British attack of 11 April. During the night engineers had managed to repair and reopen the Arras-Cambrai road as far as Feuchy Chapel, an extraordinary accomplishment that would eventually facilitate the supply of hot food, ammunition and other stores. Not least, they had brought forward hundreds of trench bridges for the use of cavalry and horse artillery. As for the guns, they were still struggling to make headway in the mud, and quite unable to guarantee the infantry a barrage of the optimum weight at the optimum time.

Major General H. Bruce Williams was under no illusions about the importance of this day and the task his men faced, placing all three brigades of the 37th Division in the line. On his left lay the Scots of the 15th Division, ordered to push on to the Green Line, isolating Monchy from Pelves; on his right facing Guémappe, two brigades of the 3rd Division under Major General C.J. Deverell. On the north bank of the Scarpe, 4th Division troops would parallel their endeavours with the capture of Greenland Hill. Zero-Hour was twice delayed, for the guns were not ready. The 15th Division's initial attack was a muddle.

We resumed our advance in a blinding storm of snow and sleet, the 46th Brigade on the right, and the 45th Brigade on the left, with the 44th remaining in reserve. The morning was dark, and because of the driving snow the visibility was so bad that we could see only a short distance ahead of us, so that it was very difficult to keep touch with the adjoining units, and we had to depend mostly on compass bearings for our direction. In another way the lack of visibility was all in our favour, as it screened the first stage of our advance from view of the German artillery, whose shelling was so haphazard and erratic that we were able to progress for a long distance with comparatively few casualties until the snow began to clear. As we drew near to Monchy, even before the village appeared in view to us, we could hear a great clacking of machine guns and rifle fire from that direction, from which commotion we knew that the assault was already being pushed home by the leading waves of our brigade. The snow gradually cleared when we were still

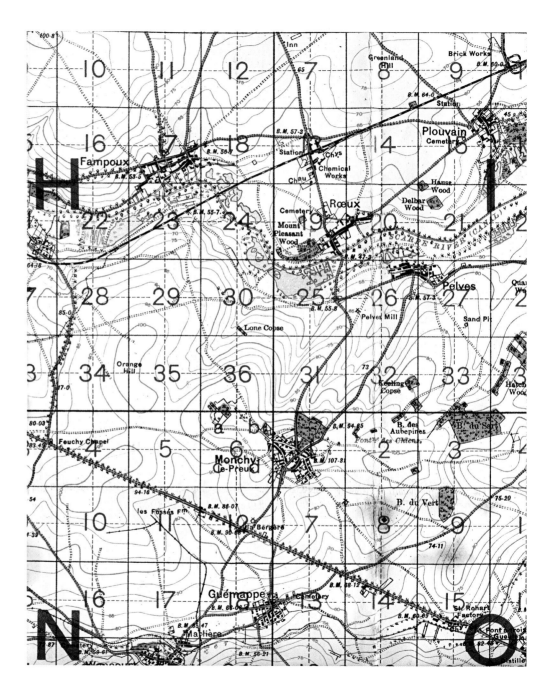

Above Loopholed walls being used in 1914 in the same way as the defenders of Monchy employed them in April 1917. AJ

Left Section of British 1:40,000 map showing the critical contour relationship between Monchy, Guémappe, Fampoux and Roeux. AC

some seven or eight hundred yards from Monchy, and as the visibility improved we discovered that almost the whole of the brigade had converged on the village, and that a large part of the 45th Brigade also, which should have advanced with its left flank on the banks of the Scarpe nearly a mile to the left, had veered on to the same objective. To lose direction to that extent, they must have executed almost a complete right wheel in the course of their two mile advance through the snowstorm. Perhaps it was the attraction of the rising ground on which Monchy stood, the tendency always being to proceed direct up the face of a slope, but in any case their wheel brought them up against the blank loop-holed walls on the north side of the village, where they suffered terrible casualties at the hands of the German machine gunners and riflemen. Part of our battalion joined in the attempt to take the place by direct assault and to clear the enemy from house to house, but they lost heavily in doing so, as did also those battalions of the 37th Division that pushed into the streets of the village, which were swept by fire from the house windows and from every street corner.

Captain Douglas Cuddeford, 12th Highland Light Infantry

The wheeling was disastrous, ruling out the severance of the connection between the villages, and inadavertently putting a deal of added pressure on Monchy. In the centre, with only a few hundred metres to the outer edge, 111th Brigade were almost certain they would be relieved before zero. Having attacked the previous afternoon, and spent the night digging for dear life, the exhausted troops were strewn all over the place.

By 4.30 a runner and his mate came from 'out of the blue' with orders to Captain Shutes. They could hardly have been worse; 'over the bags in half an hour for another attack on Monchy'. Oh the helplessness of it all: unable to take the village on the previous afternoon yet here we were about to attempt it again this very dawn and with many less men than before. But what did it matter! What did anything matter now! Soon after we got these cheerful orders some one hailed out of the darkness enquiring for the 10th Fusiliers. Since we did belong to such a Regiment long ago, when things were different and we were humans and everything was not cold, hunger and death, one of our party replied and a few minutes later about 50 others of our Battalion joined us. It was very cheering to learn we were not after all the sole survivors of the poor old Battalion. All sleep was now out of the question and everyone set-to cleaning rifles. At about 4.50 a.m. another party came up from H.Q. with rations of bully beef and biscuits. Amongst the rations was a jar with 'S.R.D.' on it but unfortunately there was no time to open and distribute it.

At about 4.30 a.m. CSM Mellings dug a hole and buried this jar, thinking perhaps that a future date it could be unearthed and enjoyed!

Sergeant Rupert 'Jack' Whiteman, 10th Royal Fusiliers (City of London Regiment)

Over on the right of the village, elements of 112th Brigade (37th Division) were also to attack early – with the aid of a handful of tanks. The tree-lined Cambrai road should have plainly indicated the correct axis of advance here, but again Monchy acted like a magnet, the troops drawn towards the outer houses. It may have been something to do with following the tanks.

The Official History says that, 'All the tanks taking part in it were put out of action, but it is doubtful that Monchy would have fallen without their aid.' Here, perhaps more than on any

other occasion during the Arras battles, tanks were to play a truly critical role. Having struggled through the night to reach Feuchy Chapel, six machines prepared for action. Three were to track north around the village, and three south. Although zero was twice postponed, no one informed the tank crews; they advanced shortly after 5.00 a.m. One machine quickly foundered in the slush and another was foiled by a broken track. The remaining four struck out from Les Fosses Farm for La Bergère, where they were to turn north toward the village. In their wake came the infantry (possibly elements of the 11th Loyals (North Lancashire) and 11th Royal Warwicks), also uninformed of the changes to zero hour. A German account of this action reveals the effect tanks could have if they were fortunate enough to actually reach the enemy.

The advancing Tommies were 600-800 metres away. Suddenly we heard a shout from 3 Kompagnie: 'There's a tank on the right of the road!' We stared aghast as slowly a tank crept towards us. At fifty metres we opened fire with rifles and machine-guns and about thirty metres away it suddenly veered right towards the Bavarians. We clapped and cheered! But our celebrations were a little premature. The tank turned back towards us and advanced. We hoped the wide ditch at the side of the road would stop it. Little did we know of the capabilities of a tank. It entered the ditch and tipped acutely to the left and remained there for one or two minutes but he straightened himself out and crossed the road towards us, repeating the ditch crossing manoeuvre on the other side. Then the tank moved to within five metres of the right section of the 1st Kompagnie and stopped without firing. Now a concentrated fire from 1st and 3rd Kompagnies was directed at the tank, hand grenades were thrown and some brave men got up and advanced from their positions. At this moment the tank tracks began to move and the crew opened up with a murderous machine-gun fire which was slowly directed along 1st Kompagnie trench. Those that were not killed instantly screamed as they lay there wounded. Lieutenant Hardow gave orders to clear the trench to the left towards 3 Kompagnie, but the tank was already on them too. Then the panic started, everyone from 1 and 3 Kompagnies jumped out of the trench and ran the fastest race of his life, pursued by the merciless tank machine-gun fire which cut down many men as if it were a rabbit-shoot. The troops that ran wildly from the enemy were experienced soldiers, and they only stopped running when they reached the lane from Boiry to Guémappe about a kilometre away.

RESERVE INFANTRY REGIMENT 84, HISTORY

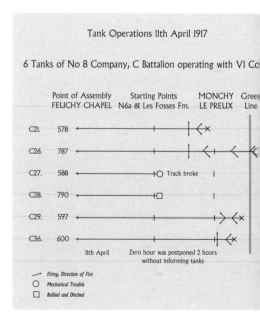

Tank Operations 11th April 1917

6 Tanks of No 8 Company, C Battalion operating with VI Co

	Point of Assembly FEUCHY CHAPEL	Starting Points N6a & Les Fosses Fm.	MONCHY LE PREUX	Green Line
C21.	578			
C26.	787			
C27.	588	Track broke		
C28.	790			
C29.	597			
C36.	600			
	11th April	Zero hour was postponed 2 hours without informing tanks		

╱ Firing, Direction of Fire
◯ Mechanical Trouble
☐ Bellied and Ditched

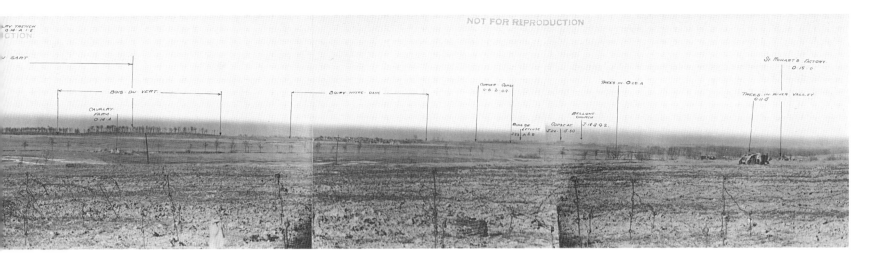

(image annotations: LY TRENCH ... CTION; U SART; BOIS DU VERT; CAVALRY FARM O·14·A; BOIRY NOTRE DAME; BOIS DE LETLUSE ·23·A & B; CORNER COPSE O·6·2·69; COPSE AT J·22·d·50; BELLONE CHURCH J·18·d·92; TREES IN O·20·A; ST ROHART 8 FACTORY O·15·C; TREES IN RIVER VALLEY O·11·d)

Hour the Tank started for action: 3.30 am

Hour of Zero: 4.45am

Extent and nature of hostile shell fire: Shell fire heavy – practically no shrapnel. Machine gun fire not excessive.

Ammunition expended: Approximately 40 rounds (6-pdr)

Casualties: Nil

Position of Tank after action: 0.19.b.05 (approx)

Condition of Tank after action: Unserviceable; both tracks broken, probably from direct hits; also on fire.

From battle notes of D Battalion Tanks

The account above may well refer to tank C30 commanded by Second Lieutenant Ambrose, the post-action report noting that it came in for a battering from machine guns, grenades and armour-piercing bullets, and that resistance was at times from very close range. C30's action ended when a shell scored a direct hit on a gun sponson. Of the seven crew, four were killed and two wounded, but the tank kept firing its Lewis gun, distracting the attentions of German troops. C29 under Second Lieutenant Toshack avoided the *melée*, and at La Bergère veered left before coming under fire from several points. After a few minutes it burst into flames, probably hit in a petrol tank. Three men escaped. Lieutenant Salter's C21 cleared the Germans from trenches near La Bergère, informed the infantry (who occupied them) and tracked northwards towards the village, probably along Hussar Lane. It appears that this tank may have been hit by friendly fire, for six of the seven crew were killed or wounded when shell fragments pierced the thinly protected rear of the machine. These three tanks had played a critical role in drawing German fire, but the fourth managed even more. Second Lieutenant Johnston's C26 attacked at 5.00 a.m. Heading west of the village

it successfully eliminated machine-gun positions and trenches before turning north and then east. By this time a sporadic British barrage was falling, and C26 was cruising amongst it. She avoided the shells but her engine expired, leaving the crew to abandon ship taking Lewis guns and ammunition with them. The 37th Division assault was taking place at the same time.

At 5.o'clock, without any fuss or excitement, we climbed out of the trench. There was none of the romance usually connected with 'going over the top' – no stirring strains of martial music, no colours flying in the breeze. None seemed to care what happened that morning, everyone was mentally and physically finished, as we advanced mechanically in a long line for a hedge which stretched away to the right from the little wood in front. There seemed to be a surprising number of troops advancing with us both on the left and the right. Being out of sight to the Germans everything was quiet until the hedge was reached, but on the line breaking through it things in general began to hum.

Oh yes! The Huns were still in the village. It was fairly light by then and the scene of the previous afternoon's 'blizzard rush' could be plainly seen. It is strange what a wonderful tonic machine-gun bullets are to tired troops! Before passing through the hedge everyone vowed they did not care if they were killed there and then, in fact they hoped they would be; but on reaching the other side of the hedge everyone ran to the nearest bit of cover of any description; the few shell-holes available were soon filled to capacity with men who still seemed to have plenty of energy and the joy of life left in them.

From this stage onward the 10th Royal Fusiliers became hopelessly mixed up. Men belonging to other regiments mysteriously put in an appearance amongst us and kilted Jocks poured from the wee wood now on our left. This mixture of Battalions had not advanced far before being again held up by the murderous fire – but not for long as we soon found out. The machine-gun fire which was doing a lot of damage seemed to be coming from a little two-storied red-tiled cottage on the left, standing by itself on the outskirts of the village. Then it was that Corporal Scales – the Lewis gun corporal of 'C' Company – did an excellent piece of work, thereby saving dozens of lives; lying prone on the ground he trained a Lewis gun on this house but was immediately ordered by one of our officers not to fire because our men were in it. Scales, without looking round to see who the speaker was, consigned him to a definite place and opened fire. Window panes flew in all directions as his bullets poured into an upstairs window. He evidently saw something there that no one else did for immediately all firing ceased from that quarter.

Sergeant Rupert 'Jack' Whiteman, 10th Royal Fusiliers (City of London Regiment)

In the next bound, assisted by the appearance of tanks, the Fusiliers were among the houses.

There appeared to be no Germans in the trench at the foot of the hill but there was great activity amongst those in the sunken road on the right; they could be seen running up and down, the tops of their heads being just visible; the tank making in their direction was evidently the cause of their excitement.

At this stage another strange thing happened

which turned the whole tide of events in our favour. All firing from both the village and the sunken road abruptly ceased. There was no need then to hug the bottom of shell holes and within a few minutes the surrounding fields were a mass of running men all centring on Monchy. Before the tanks had reached the bottom of the slope they were overtaken and passed by the Infantry. There seemed to be only one street leading down the hill from out of the village in our direction and everyone made for that. Entering the village there seemed to be a representative of almost every regiment in the British Army! Along the street and up the hill the crowd surged, as one sees issuing from the gates after a football match. All bayonets had been fixed but I don't think anyone had occasion to use them. It was not until the top was reached that we realised that the village was ours. Yes, really ours after sacrificing all those lives to get it! It was practically deserted but almost every house showed signs of a hasty retreat; in some, coffee was found simmering on the stove and in quite a number the table was laid for a meal.

Sergeant Rupert 'Jack' Whiteman, 10th Royal Fusiliers (City of London Regiment)

The mixed bag coaxed their jubilant way into Monchy, perhaps more by luck than judgment all arriving around the same time. A pleasing spectacle met many an eye.

There, running across the snow with coat-tails flying in their eagerness to get Monchy well and quickly behind them, were numbers of black figures. They were the late garrison of the village, the ones responsible for creating such havoc in our ranks during the last two days; Huns flying for the Fatherland. This sight was far too tempting for some of us and fully 80 men raced off down the hill in pursuit, stopping every dozen yards or so to fire off a couple of rounds at the retreating black figures. I was amongst this party and after racing through the wood, where a few prisoners were taken, we came out on

German 1915 aerial photograph looking beyond Monchy and its protective lanes towards the valley where the cavalry formed up for their assault. HS

to the barren flat at the bottom of the hill. Up till then everyone had lost their heads, and it was not until the Germans had reached the ridge in front that we realised that there was still a war on, for a murderous machine-gun fire opened up from the ridge and laid out a lot of our pursuing party. The Huns had evidently reached pre-constructed trenches on the ridge and were determined to make us pay dearly for having followed them.
SERGEANT RUPERT 'JACK' WHITEMAN, 10TH ROYAL FUSILIERS (CITY OF LONDON REGIMENT)

The infantry's orders were to notify the cavalry, then push on to the Green Line beyond the village, organize fresh dispositions, and consolidate according to circumstance. Whilst a score of runners took messages back, the houses and especially cellars had to be properly cleared. It was not a task to be rushed.

Suddenly things became quiet, and it looked as if the Germans had pulled out of Monchy. As the only Officer forward I took a patrol through the town which seemed deserted and at the far end I could see German parties retreating and horsed-teams coming up and taking out guns about 1,000 yards away. I came back by a side street when suddenly Private Kay, my runner shouted: "Keek at yon" and hurled a grenade into an estaminet. About 25 frightened Huns poured out, unarmed, and gave themselves up. They proved to be ordnance personnel who had been told nothing and had no idea what was happening. Things were now very quiet, except for the sound of the odd shot from a sniper. Why was nothing happening? Where were the Cavalry that were to go through? There were neither trenches nor wire beyond Monchy and I could see right into Pelves and that Fampoux had been taken on our left [Fampoux was already in British hands]. It was all good open rolling country. I felt frustrated. I went over to the Middlesex of 37th Division but they had no orders to go on and were pretty shaken I thought. I could now see the whole

Cavalry Division drawn up in squadron columns on the rear slopes of Orange Hill, a magnificent sight. I went back to battalion H.Q. told Colonel Russell the situation and was told we had done our job well and the Cavalry were about to go through.
CAPTAIN PHILIP CHRISTISON, 6TH QUEEN'S OWN CAMERON HIGHLANDERS

The quiet that Captain Christison mentions was not to last; it only endured until the Germans established that Monchy was unquestionably lost. It was at this time that one of the most controversial events of the war took place. There had been heavy snow showers all morning and, having spent several dreadful nights in the open, the cavalry were ready and eager to get into action – anything to get the blood circulating. At 8.30 a.m. three squadrons moved forward.

During a lull in the snowstorm, an excited shout was raised that our cavalry were coming up! Sure enough, away behind us, moving quickly in extended order down the slope of Orange Hill, was line upon line of mounted men covering the whole extent of the hillside as far as we could see. It was a thrilling moment for us infantrymen, who had never dreamt that we should live to see a real cavalry charge, which was evidently what was intended. In their advance the lines of horsemen passed over us rapidly, although from our holes in the ground it was rather a "wormseye" view we got of the splendid spectacle of so many mounted men in action.
CAPTAIN DOUGLAS CUDDEFORD, 12TH HIGHLAND LIGHT INFANTRY

Aircraft were flying and messages being passed. Many were reaching German gunners. Some planes were not only passing messages, but dropping aerial darts on the static British, flighted steel daggers that could pass cleanly through helmet and man alike. South of the Cambrai road the 3rd Dragoon Guards advanced to attack astride La Bergère where the tanks had lately been, and where some lay crippled. Machine guns from the right flank near Guémappe stopped them in their tracks. The troopers dismounted, sent back the horses, took cover, and became infantry. A second squadron followed suit with the same result. Adhering to orders, on the north side of Monchy the Essex Yeomanry and 10th Hussars swarmed off Orange Hill and pushed east before wheeling south and cantering into the village using the cover of the houses to shelter from increasing machine-gun fire from their front and left flank. Both made for the sanctuary of the central *place*. It was not only fire from Hill 100 that was causing the problem, but *again* machine-gun fire from across the river valley. Soon the threat was from artillery. The cavalry could not remain in Monchy as there was no cover for horses, so they struck out north-eastwards to attack the enemy from the Pelves and Roeux roads. On emerging from the houses fire was so intense the troopers wheeled their mounts and headed straight back. Adjusting patterns and ranges, German gunners now formed a box barrage around the village, preventing both inward and outward passage. Inside the high-explosive frame of the box they fired salvo upon salvo of shrapnel.

There was a chaos of regiments, none knew where the rest of his own Battalion had got to. The streets were littered with dead, wounded and screaming horses, and the steep gutters running down the hill flowed with blood. Many of these poor wounded creatures were shot by our chaps to put them out of their misery. The scenes in that village were too horrible to put on paper. The three regiments of cavalry which had entered Monchy, composed of the Royal Horse Guards, the 10th Hussars and the Essex Yeomanry lost their ill-advised leader, General Buckley Johnson [Bulkeley-Johnson] and over 500 horses. The cavalrymen themselves did not suffer so heavily since they were able to take cover in cellars and dug-outs whereas the poor old horses had to remain unsheltered in the streets.
SERGEANT RUPERT 'JACK' WHITEMAN, 10TH ROYAL FUSILIERS (CITY OF LONDON REGIMENT)

The Royal Horse Guards, seeing the predicament, attempted to reinforce their colleagues. Although reaching only the western outskirts, they were inside the box: a brave but doomed action. With several infantry parties forging a line eastwards, the village was now not strongly held, and fears of counter-attack during the chaos encouraged the British to send in support from the 15th Division on the left flank. In the mistaken belief (a single unconfirmed verbal message was accepted as factual) that Pelves was in British hands, these men too were cut down. On the right the British were still some 300 metres back but still advancing; on the left there was not a soul to be seen. Under machine-gun fire from the Bois du Vert, Bois du Sart and Hill 100 (*Termiten Hugel*), the troops dug for all they were worth to establish

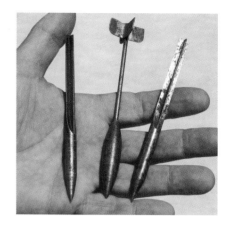

Above Aerial darts or *flechettes*. Image courtesy of Johan Vandewalle

Below The cavalry huddle against the wind and sleet whilst awaiting the call to attack Monchy-le-Preux. IWM Q5163

a defensive barrier. No German trenches existed here, so it was a question of deepening shell holes to make defensible posts. Reaching the Green Line was entirely out of the question. As the new dispositions were not yet known to the British artillery, 'friendly' shells then began to fall between the posts and the village. Contact aircraft from both sides were out in force, some German observers sounding klaxons to make the British light flares and reveal their locations. And Richthofen's scouts attacked the columns of horses being led from the Monchy fighting zone. Shelling grew heavier by the minute, and at around 2.00 p.m. groups of grey-clad figures could be seen accumulating in the distance. If this meant counter-attack, the British were gravely ill-prepared. Dismounted cavalry were a welcome addition to the ranks,

The British had managed to construct a salient in which they were pinned down. On the right the new line cut across the Cambrai road just in front of La Bergère, a meagre 800-metre gain. Guémappe was also reported captured by another erroneous message, but it was still firmly in German hands. Fire continued across the Scarpe valley, so Roeux and Greenland Hill were still obviously unconquered. Attacks were planned and cancelled, as it became clearer that the enemy were in strong possession of key objectives. Between Monchy and the river the situation was acute – across a front of almost 3 kilometres the

infantry were between 1 and 2 kilometres short of the Green Line; any further attacks could not hope to succeed without a parallel advance by XVII Corps on the far bank. No definite orders had been issued regarding the timing of Major General Lambton's 4th Division assault in this sector. Apart from patrolling, nothing was to happen north of the river until noon, seven hours after the first assaults had gone in at Monchy. Although the two assaults were supposed to jump off together and thus be mutually supporting, Lambton wisely decided that a bombardment of several hours' duration was necessary before his men attacked. This, not the fate of the division on the south bank, was his priority. Because of uncut wire on Lambton's left, a plan for a simultaneous 51st Division attack on a small unconquered section of the Point du Jour line was cancelled until the evening. It gave Lambton's three brigades a narrow frontage to assault without cooperative action on either flank. Monchy was already under attack by the time his Brigade began moving to their jumping-off positions. Whilst the 12th Brigade were able to keep under cover until the last moment in Fampoux, elements of the 10th were seen and fired upon whilst moving in to the sunken lane north of the village, then shelled when forming up in the trenches about the Hyderabad Redoubt. The attack from this hill entailed an open approach of between 1 and 2 kilometres towards the railway crossing.

We were then told that our barrage was starting at noon, so we knew when we'd begin. The road we were then on was called "Sunken Road" and as we went forward, the height of the bank protecting us on our right got less and less, so that by the time we had got to the top, we had only a foot or two to crouch down behind. We had to advance by small rushes, or on our hands and knees, the enemy machine guns spitting just above our heads. When we had got our proper positions and distances, we waited until the barrage started; then over we went. When our barrage began the enemy machine gun fire was about trebled, and I wonder yet how our fellows managed to get through it, because the bullets seemed to be going over and about my head by the hundred. I kept my steel helmet well down over my face and my head down, rifle with bayonet fixed slung over right shoulder, and my spade in my left hand as a protection for my throat. I had got about 300 yards when something struck me on top of the head, and I fell flat. I was stunned for about 10 minutes and when I put my hand up expecting to find a gash in my head, lo and behold! there was nothing but a small lump about the size of a shilling. I ventured to take off my helmet because the bullets seemed to be flying at a higher range and found that a bullet had penetrated my helmet, followed the curve of the crown inside, and found a way out over my back or shoulder. It gave me a bit of a shock at first to think of the narrow shave I'd had. By this time our chaps were a good bit ahead, so I got up to go on the way again, but only got 50 yards or so when down I went again with a bullet through the right knee. That settled it that time – no more going on for me. I began to think what was the best way to get back, but found I couldn't crawl because the bone was broken. I managed to get part of my iodine and field dressing on, and then, with the help of my shovel placed the right foot and leg on the top of the left, and with entrenching tool handle as a splint, wound my puttees round both my legs, binding them together. When I had fixed that I found that I could, with difficulty, crawl a little by lying on my back, reaching back my hands and

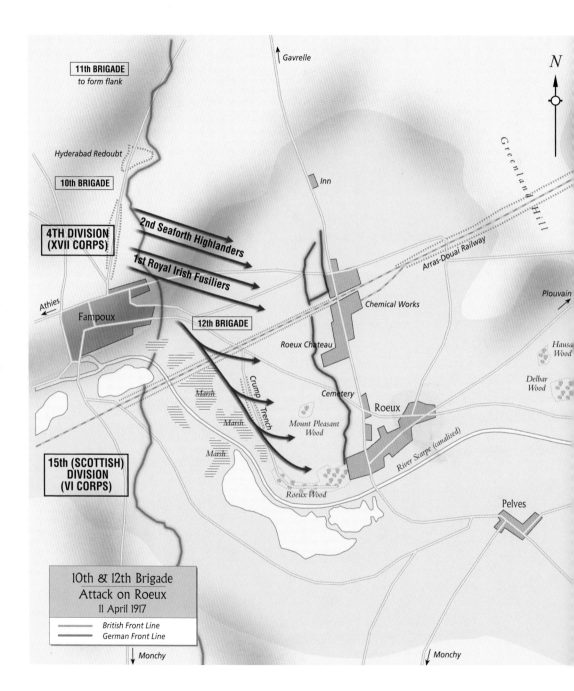

10th & 12th Brigade
Attack on Roeux
11 April 1917

British Front Line
German Front Line

pulling my legs after me. I had barely got 100 yards when I had to give it up as hopeless. I came across another fellow who was wounded lying on his face. In the afternoon the snow began to fall, so I put my water-proof sheet over me and lay patiently waiting for stretcher-bearers to come. They came over once or twice but took some cases from further down the field. We lay, and lay, still the snow came down, but no sign of any-body. When night drew on and lights and flares went up I thought we'd been forgotten about altogether, but at least they did come about 12.30 at night, and I was taken to the 1st Dressing Station in the village we had passed through. The first thing I got was a cup of hot Horlicks Malted Milk, which I did enjoy.

PRIVATE JAMES STOUT, 2ND SEAFORTH HIGHLANDERS

Parties of 2nd Seaforths and 1st Royal Irish Fusiliers approached to within 200 metres of the first objective, the ground about the railway and Chemical Works, but being thinned and ragged were forced to retire. Observers noted that the buildings were damaged but still defensible, the bombardment clearly having failed to subdue the garrison or their reputed thirty-plus machine guns. 10th Brigade had lost two-thirds of its fighting force in a matter of ninety minutes. Of the 432 Seaforths who attacked, 375 became casualties, many of the dead lying in neat rows. The fire had been so vicious that leapfrogging battalions were unable to reach those whom they were supposed to pass through. Alongside the Scarpe marshes the advance against Roeux village and Park was similarly thwarted. In capturing around fifty prisoners, 12th Brigade annexed a little ground of no practical use. Within two hours the entire operation had been defeated. General Lambton ordered a second attempt to at least secure the first objective, but with widespread chaos, streams of wounded to attend to, an effective

hostile barrage and just handfuls of traumatized men to carry out an attack against an undented, well-entrenched and well-organized enemy it is perhaps just as well that his orders failed to reach Battalion Headquarters until it was too late. They could not have acted upon them.

The 1st Cavalry Brigade, ready and waiting at Fampoux, remounted and retired to Athies, unemployed and unemployable. At the end of the day the new positions in the sector roughly corresponded with the Green Line objectives for 9 April, and the Roeux marathon had begun. It was these failures that compounded the difficulties at Monchy where, as the light faded, the situation was only slowly becoming less opaque.

As dusk was falling we saw a runner coming towards us from the direction of Monchy. We watched him, wondering what his news was. We hoped he would tell us we were going to be relieved.

'The Colonel's compliments, sir, and 'e would like to see you at seven o'clock at 'is 'eadquarters.'

'What's the news?' I asked.

'Dunno wot the news is, sir,' replied the other, 'but I reckon as our cavalry boys 'ave copped it up at Monchy.'

'How do you mean?'

'Reckon you'll see wot I mean, sir, when you goes up there.'

With a quarter of an hour in hand I left Gilbert in charge of the company and started off for Monchy, the runner showing me the way.

'For God's sake get us relieved,' Gilbert said, as I departed, 'The men are all in.'

I said I would do what I could. In five minutes we were at the foot of the village. As we turned the bend of the road to go up the hill, I stopped. The sight that greeted me was so horrible that I almost lost my head. Heaped on top of one another and blocking up the road-way for as far as one could see lay the mutilated bodies of our men and their horses. These bodies, torn and gaping, had stiffened into fantastic attitudes. All the hollows of the road were filled with blood. This was the cavalry.

As I learnt afterwards, when our horsemen had gathered in Monchy the Germans had put down a box barrage round the place – the four sides of the barrage gradually drawing inwards. The result of this shooting lay before me. Nothing that I had seen before in the way of horrors could be even faintly compared with what I saw around me now. Death in every imaginable shape was there for the examining. I walked up the hill, picking my way as best I could and often slipping in the pools of blood, so that my boots and the lower parts of my puttees were dripping with blood by the time I reached the top. Nor, I discovered on my way up, were all the men and animals quite dead. Now and then a groan would strike the air – the groan of a man who was praying for release. Sometimes the twitch of a horse's leg would shift the pattern of the heaped-up bodies. A small party of stretcher-bearers, obviously unequal to their task, were doing what they could to relieve the suffering.

I found the Colonel in the cellar. He was now in charge not only of the battalion and of the whole brigade, but also of the situation generally. He had, characteristically enough, assumed command of it on his own initiative, and when I arrived he was telling a battery commander where and when he was to fire his guns. It was a gloomy place, this cellar. It was lit by two candles and smelt of death. The only cheerful sight in it reposed on a table in a corner – an enormous ham. It was the only thing that any of us felt like attacking.

Lieutenant Alan Thomas, 6th Queen's Own (Royal West Kent Regiment)

Here and there on the Monchy battlefield the clear-up began, the snow falling on dead and wounded alike. Many froze to death before help could reach them. Once the new positions were considered safely garrisoned and consolidated, parties went out to search for fellow comrades.

While the snow was falling, and we could move about more freely without being observed by the Boche machine gunners and snipers, some of us went out to give what help we could to the many wounded men lying about in the open. An extensive orchard belonging to the big chateau-farm on the north side of the village was full of dead and wounded men of our 45th Brigade. Several units of that brigade in their first attack during the morning had swung round against the north side of Monchy, and in the snow beneath the masses of blossom on the fruit trees in that big orchard their dead and wounded were lying in heaps and rows. To add to the horror of it all, since the attack in the early morning in which these men had fallen, the Germans had heavily shelled the orchard and vicinity at the time the cavalry were retiring round that side of the village. As we moved through the orchard in the falling snow, wounded men on every side were shouting and blowing whistles to attract attention, but only too many of them lay like still hummocks of snow. I remember one of these hummocks heaved and cracked open on our approach, as a poor kilted highlander turned over at the sound of our voices. His bare thigh was only a blackened stump, but he complacently and without a murmur accepted the cigarette we lit for him. He, and a great many others of the wounded, must have died that day from loss of blood and exposure. It was a pitiful sight; the sort of thing that made one rage at the utter futility of it all.

Captain Douglas Cuddeford, 12th Highland Light Infantry

The Germans made no attempt to retake Monchy on 11 April, leaving its capture an achievement, but as a solitary glow in a dark day; by evening discontent and frustration had subsumed any earlier elation. Rightly, soldiers of all ranks were asking who was to blame for such appalling leadership.

Hill 90, the great sticking point in VII Corps area, continued to hold up progress,

Above and left Casualties of the successful attack against Monchy. IWM Q3955 and Q42028

Below British weapons captured by the Germans on 11 April. AC

projected assaults being poorly supported by a shabby artillery barrage. Attacks against Wancourt were stopped in their tracks by a set of pillboxes concealing machine guns, each covering gaps in the entanglements. The concrete was barely pockmarked by British shelling. The bombing battle therefore had to go on. Deadlock was at last broken by 167th Brigade (56th Division) which with the help of four D Battalion tanks broke into the junction of the Hindenburg Line and the Wancourt-Feuchy Line, finally splitting the enemy. Bombing was then redoubled, northwards towards Wancourt, and south towards the Cojeul River. The bombers of 169th Brigade were soon to occupy Hill 90 and push down towards Héninel in the Cojeul valley.

On this day the Arras offensive seemed to shed its short-lived guise of open warfare. By dusk it seemed that the trench-brawl had begun again. The British Official History chose to compare the casualty figures for the first three days of Arras with those sustained on the first day of the Somme, 1 July 1916: they were approximately 13,000 against 57,000. In the two cases, the nature of the fighting, preparation and character of the opposition had been quite different. Whether this evaluation was made by Allenby or Haig is not recorded, for the offensive was disintegrating. It was what was happening to individual actions within the wider confrontation that now caused concern. British commanders had to find a way to stop the slide back towards attrition by regaining at least a semblance of 9 April.

Those lucky enough to be relieved that night headed back to the sanctuary of Arras, a town changing its nature by the minute. Although still well within range of hostile shellfire, it was no longer under observation, and with German guns largely preoccupied elsewhere molestation became more haphazard each day. Every house and cellar was in use, by signallers, troops preparing to move forward, filthy and shambling men just out of the line, and groups of walking wounded. Ambulances and ammunition columns passed through; there were busy dressing stations and headquarters dugouts. The relieved simply wanted somewhere dry to sleep – and some hot food, a genuine luxury.

I was relegated to the rear when the battle opened on April 9th and I set up a rear H.Q., with two runners, in a cellar in the Grand Place of Arras, with a telephone and instructions not to move; of furniture there was none but a telephone and a cold stone floor, nor were we comforted to hear the "boom" of the arrival of long-range German shells; otherwise we heard nothing of the ensuing battle. Then the rain turned to snow which did not prevent our Brigade from advancing five miles. On April 12th (it might have been the 13th) our Brigadier and the Brigade Major reappeared dirty, unshaven, cold and famished. None of us had eaten for two days and something had to be done. Foraging round, we found an old cookhouse. There were two or three tins of Pork and Beans (standard Army ration), a little flour, a jar containing some mouldy mustard pickle and some salt. The whole lot went with water into an old cooking pot and was stewed over the fire we had made. So there we were, the Brigadier, the Brigade Major, a lance-corporal (myself) and two sappers of the R.E., all very dirty; with four days growth of beard, squatting round a blazing fire, warm at last and enjoying the most delicious stew that ever was! The war might have been 500 miles away instead of five. I also learned what a splendid savour a little mustard pickle can give to a stew.
LANCE CORPORAL FRANK MULLIS, 63RD BRIGADE STAFF, 37TH DIVISION

CHAPTER FIFTEEN

Something for the Weekend:
Thursday to Saturday, 12–14 April 1917

12TH APRIL

My Sweetheart,

I have your letters of 9th and 10th – three in all – I enclose a charming letter from Lord French. Will you send a copy of it to my mother, and keep the original? I was delighted with it. My advance goes on, and we gain ground gradually. We captured 11 more guns last night. My total of guns must now be over 100. The success of the first day was greatly due to the good shooting of my Artillery.

Weather conditions are awful. Last night and this morning some 6 inches of snow fell; but today is warmer and it is thawing fast. The Cavalry nearly got a chance yesterday, but it did not quite come off. Wire and machine guns stopped them. Brigadier General Bulkeley-Johnson, commanding a Cavalry Brigade, was killed and his Brigade suffered somewhat severely. I don't think that any of your friends were hit. Some of the tanks did good work. One youth took his tank into a village and destroyed 6 machine guns. Then his tank was hit by a shell, and set on fire. All his crew were wounded or killed, but he got out with a Lewis machine gun, drove off two attacks by parties of Infantry, and came away unhurt.

Your Edmund

LETTER FROM GENERAL ALLENBY TO HIS WIFE MABEL

Left British wounded await evacuation at Tilloy-lès-Mofflaines. IWM Q6195

Like the execution of the cavalry at Monchy and the Bullecourt fiasco, the shocking state of the troops received no mention in Allenby's letters to Mabel, nor in the British press. There was no escaping the fact that with each passing day the picture was becoming darker for the British and brighter for the Germans. 9 April had been a calamity for the latter, and later a Court of Enquiry was convened to lay blame at the door of those who had failed to carry out Ludendorff and Rupprecht's orders, a failure that had resulted in more than 20,000 casualties and the loss of well over 100 guns in the first three days.

Haig and Allenby were in a quandary. The C-in-C would probably have liked to have drawn a line beneath Arras and begun afresh elsewhere – in Flanders perhaps. It would have been an excellent strategic move, keeping the enemy guessing where the next blow would fall whilst still in the process of shifting guns and reserves to Artois. Such a path was of course impossible.

There was no choice but to continue at Arras, for a contract had been signed with the French, now possibly on the threshold of great things on the Aisne. Nivelle and indeed the French nation were mightily impressed with what was happening in Artois. Politically as well as militarily it was essential that the British tried to rekindle and maintain the pressure and momentum of 9 April. The question was, how might this best be accomplished? The golden opportunity of Tuesday 10 April had passed, so what now did Haig and Allenby wish or need to achieve strategically? Cambrai had to remain the objective, even if in name only, and Haig made this perfectly clear to General de Vallières, Chief of the French Military Mission, who on the 11th had called in on his way to French GQG. A promise was a promise.

Were British commanders capable of coming up with plans that would dispel the atmosphere of intellectual bankruptcy that was spreading swiftly down the chain of command to troops in the front line? Must the British keep the enemy occupied and be drawn ever more deeply into attrition, or save their resources for Flanders? They were in dire need of another 9 April.

Thursday the 12th was another black day for Third Army, although it actually began brightly for VII Corps. Overnight fresh troops had been brought in to continue bomb and bayonet actions, and the following morning progress could have been described as spectacular were it not for the fact that it was to a great degree assisted by decisions outwith British control.

Third Army.

Panorama No. 55? made on 29.4.17 from N22.C.95.40.
including a field of view of 26° from about

1. Panoramas are taken solely for military purposes.
2. The publication of them in the press will necessarily give valuable information to the enemy.
3. This panorama is to be kept with as much security as is compatible with full advantage of it being taken by our own troops.
4. When troops are relieved this panorama should be handed to the relieving troops.

Approximate Scale of Degrees (1 degree equals .70 of an inch).

0   1   2   3   4   5   6   7   8   10

Arras - Cambria Road.   Bois du Sart.   Bo

Shovel Trench. N

Monchy le Preux.   La Bergère N. 12. O   Trench Corner. N. 12. C. 72.

At 9am the Lieutenant Colonel of the 18th Manchesters gave orders for the attack. The men were surprised – they were exhausted and the trenches were in a bad condition. The lads got into the front-line and communication trenches by bombing. The Germans, using aerial torpedoes and hand-grenades, evacuated their own trenches and fled to the North. This offered a good target for the Lewis guns of "C" Company. The guns were placed on the top of the trench and they inflicted about a hundred casualties. All objectives having been gained, the Queen Victoria Rifles (56th Division) established touch with our left flank and a battalion of the 21st Division came forward to support us. Over 1700 yards of trench was captured and very heavy losses were inflicted on the enemy. It was found impossible to carry the line further forward for though the enemy was very disorganised our

Western houses of Hancourt. N.23.A.

Guémappe in Hollow.

Trees on Cambria Road. O.14.A.

Trees of Cemetery. o.16.b.

Edge of Wancourt Ridge. N.24.

Road Corner. N.8.c.8.

Trench in N.25.o. Central.

Trees near St Rohart's Factory O.15.c.

Railway N.24.8.

Trees North of Remy. O.18.A.

Above Third Army Panorama 554 (IWM) taken on 29 April 1917 from the carbuncle that was Hill 90. The picture shows how the hill commanded the approaches to Monchy and the objectives beyond, Guémappe, Wancourt and the heights south-east of the Cojeul valley.

chaps were extremely fatigued. In two dug-outs were found twelve wounded men of the 21st Division who had been captured the previous day. They had been bandaged and given food and drink by their captors. Ten prisoners were taken – four of them wounded. Many more would have been taken if the battalion had been fresh enough to gather the full fruits of victory. Owing to the thick mud rifles became choked – it was impossible to bring them to bear upon the enemy as they fled across the open. Trench guns and machine-guns were captured and large quantities of ammunition. One hundred of the enemy were killed in the open while thirty were found in the fire trench. The support-trench was thickly strewn with dead. Our casualties were six killed and twenty-seven wounded.

Private Paddy Kennedy, 18th Manchester Regiment

Hendecourt–Dury   ✝ Cagnicourt   ✝ Chérisy   ✝ Hendecourt–lez Cagnicourt   ✝ Riencourt

This was the Wancourt sector. The result of the Manchesters' action was to force the Germans to relinquish a full kilometre of Hindenburg Line, a stretch that had been selected for yet another 21st Division attack. The Hill 90 threat disappeared during the night and soon there were reports of an exodus from Héninel; another message said that resistance from Wancourt had all but dried up. The enemy had departed from a considerable wedge of territory along the Cojeul. As Haig and Allenby had hoped, the pressure had paid off. Could they be encouraged into further retirement? At the end of the day VII Corps were everywhere on the Green Line except on the heights overlooking Wancourt and Guémappe, a ridge crowned by a large stone water tower. Known to the Germans as the *Fasbender Tour*, it was probably the finest observation position on the Arras battlefield (see panorama above).

To the north, only the Guémappe sector now prevented a clean linear connection with Monchy le Preux. To say 'only' Guémappe gives the wrong impression: on 11 April the 3rd Division had been able to advance just 200-300 metres towards the village. It too was a stronghold, but perhaps there was now little need to do more here, for the enemy were clearly flagging – if Wancourt Tower and the northern tail of the ridge were gained, and a further advance made astride Monchy to the range of wood-capped hills beyond, then Guémappe would be left in a perilous pocket and almost certainly vacated in the same way as Wancourt. The tower was first captured on 15 April.

To our left was the village of Guémappe with the remains of a tank near by. We were astonished to learn that this was the front line. A quite untenable position on the reverse slope with the remains of a water tower just in front and no obvious enemy in sight. We discussed the situation and considered this position quite unsuitable. We also learnt that the Germans were still holding out in the village of Guémappe and had machine guns enfilading

Above The German view looking south-east from the Wancourt Tower on 31 October 1916. Note haystacks. BHK Rundbild VII/18

Right With agriculture continuing almost until the battle, haystacks were employed as OPs by both sides. AJ

ntaine -
3 Croisilles   ☩ Lagnicourt   ☩ Ecoust   ☩ Croisilles
☩ Bullecourt   St. Mein

the trench, which was foolhardy with no traverses what-ever. Colonel Robinson said 'come on we had a better investigate'. He led the way and I followed with the revolver drawn and ready for action as we approached the dilapidated building. No glass in the window and doors adrift. On reaching the building we peeped over the sills and found it was apparently empty so we climbed through the window and went through the back and looking out from broken windows we could see about 20-25 yards away from us the Germans busily digging themselves in and fortifying the remains of the tower. They did not appear to have any sentries and were just digging as hard as they could. We returned as quickly as possible and the C.O had made up his mind and imme-diately said to Darlington. 'Mr. Darlington, fix bayonets and take the tower'. Then turning to me said 'Get back to H.Q. Tell brigade the situation and get the artillery here at once. I want a barrage round that tower'. Whilst I was getting back Darlington's men rushed forward with fixed bayonets and the Germans ran for their lives. They took the tower and its environs and the only casu-alty was Mr. Darlington himself who received a bullet through his neck and the next and only time I saw him again was as he lay on the stretcher being carried back to the dressing station. Darlington's platoon immediately started to prepare the defence of the position and later the front line was joined up.

SECOND LIEUTENANT SIDNEY GREENFIELD MC,
6TH NORTHUMBERLAND FUSILIERS

Wancourt Tower was recaptured in a counter-attack the following day. A period of exchange had begun.

Far away in the northernmost corner of the 9 April battle front, a pre-dawn attack on the last two strongholds, the Bois en Hache and The Pimple by the British 73rd Brigade (24th Division, I Corps) and Canadian 10th Brigade respectively, finally swept the Germans from the entire length of Vimy Ridge. Crown Prince Rupprecht of Bavaria had been proven right: any notion of retaking the ridge was foolish and the garrisons of these last two sectors should have been quietly withdrawn on 10 April. By mid-morning on the 12th only a few men had departed; the rest were dead, wounded, or on their way to Canadian prisoner cages. Indeed, Rupprecht's systematic retirement scheme was exactly what Snow's VII Corps troops were witnessing at Wancourt, Hill 90, and Héninel. It was not a retreat.

On the same morning Canadian observers began to report a more general German emigration in the direction of Douai, huge fires on the plain below and to the north in front of Avion and Lens signifying the demolition of stores that time decreed could not be saved.

To many it appeared a promising development, but the ploy devised in a meeting in Tournai between Rupprecht, von Lossberg, Falkenhausen and Chief of Staff General von Kuhl was a simple one: Vimy was lost, but behind the ridge there still existed two more robust lines of defence. If the Canadians could be tempted from onto the plain, then the process of installing fresh infrastructure would have to begin all over again, but with a greatly elongated chain of supply – an exposed chain that was visible and vulnerable to artillery, no longer deficient in number. Rather than defend from imperfect positions at the foot of the ridge, the Germans pulled back to the 'premium' defensive fieldwork of the Oppy-Mericourt Line. How the Canadians reacted now would indicate their future aspirations: if they stayed on the ridge, there were probably no plans for further advances, certainly not in the short-term; if they came down, however…

ROEUX

Sir Edmund Allenby elected to continue to 'nibble' on Thursday, ordering limited but substantial attacks to deter German consolidation whilst preparing for a more extensive push when more guns were 'up' within the next few days. With the various villages and hills along the Cojeul valley having been occupied soon after dawn, VII Corps troops spent the day consolidating gains and making plans to assault the final section of the Green Line on the Wancourt Ridge, especially the tower, to rid themselves of an awkward dog-leg that now existed in their line. On their left the 3rd Division (VI Corps) need do nothing against Guémappe until the ridge was cleared. Across the Scarpe, despite pleas for a 24-hour delay, Lieutenant General Fergusson's XVII Corps were ordered to capture Roeux as soon as was feasible to relieve pressure upon VI Corps in the Monchy sector. Objectives again included the station and the Chemical Works; with these in British hands, Roeux village would become untenable, although this too was targeted. Fergusson was troubled, cabling that he could not possibly attack until later in the day – 5.00 p.m. at the earliest.

Leaving the survivors of the previous day's action (Seaforths and Royal Irish) in their forward scrapes and shell holes, three brigades (26th, 27th and South African) of 9th Division would advance under cover of smoke, pass through their ranks and engage the entire sector.

Neither the troops nor the guns were in any state to make an attack. Although the day dawned dry and bright with cloudless blue skies, having been in the line for three days and nights, men were chilled to the bone, many requiring to be lifted to their feet then vigorously 'massaged' to promote blood circulation. The clearer weather had brought out swarms of reconnaissance aircraft with their habitual accompanying scouts. It was the first real opportunity to properly photograph the battle

Above The battle beyond the ridge begins. Shells falling around Gavrelle. IWM CO1353

Right Plank roads. Canadian engineers creating a fresh transport infrastructure to pursue the offensive. IWM CO1261

front for the artillery, but time was too short to plan a satisfactory bombardment.

12TH APRIL

The headquarters command moved forward. I moved with it. It seems that the 9th Division had been rushed in to take the trenches which the 4th had not been able to capture. The whole thing was so rushed because it was expected the Heavy Artillery would have polished off the Hun. I had not had time to get my telephone settled. Our infantry moved forward over open ground for 1,500 yards before the barrage started; this was because I did not know the plan or the ground. In this battle [Arras], as at Neuve Chapelle and Loos, it was demonstrated that, if the first attack is successful, it is vital to send up supporting troops immediately. For an hour or two anything can be done; but the Boche soon rallies; and any further attack must be thoroughly prepared like an original attack before the enemy has been able to pull himself together.

BRIGADIER GENERAL HENRY TUDOR, CRA 9TH (SCOTTISH) DIVISION

The failures of the previous day were haunting the British, especially the *loss* of ground between Monchy and the Scarpe, offering yet clearer views and fields of fire across the valley. The attack on Roeux went ahead regardless. It was watched by Lieutenant R. Talbot-Kelly, a 9th Division FOO:

I went forward about three-quarters of a mile to the crest of a ridge to observe a local attack by the Highland Brigade [sic] on the Roeux Chemical Works. The attack started in bright sunshine; the noise of the supporting barrage being largely drowned by the strong gusty west wind which muffled the sound to everyone upwind. Almost immediately the assaulting infantry ran into German machine-gun fire from guns shooting at very long range across the Scarpe from the south. From where

I was sitting in a half-dug German reserve trench the noise of the German machine-guns was completely inaudible, and, as I watched, the ranks of the Highlanders were thinned out and torn apart by an inaudible death that seemed to strike them from nowhere. It was peculiarly horrible to watch; the bright day, the little scudding clouds and these frightened men dying in clumps in a noiseless battle.

TALBOT-KELLY, *A SUBALTERN'S ODYSSEY*

To avoid forming up in Fampoux, which despite the previous day's disaster was again included in operation orders, 27th Brigade (under Brigadier General Frank Maxwell, mentioned earlier in relation to calling the cavalry forward on 9 April) had assembled well behind the lines and out of enemy sight. The decision, however, presented them with an open downhill advance of around 1.5 kilometres which like the previous day emanated from the area about the Hyderabad Redoubt. It was this action that Talbot-Kelly observed. He may not have known that the 17th had relieved the 15th Division in the area of his OP and that Brigadier General C. Yatman, commanding 50th Brigade, had received orders to attack the ridges protecting Pelves – the positions from which cross-valley fire had cut up the attacks. The irony was that Yatman decided to delay his assault until an hour *after* that of the 9th Division. If they had attacked together, the outcome might have been a happier one. More ironically, when Yatman's troops did advance, the occupants of the German forward posts took to their heels in front of 6th Dorsets. The final irony is that having taken the ground (retaken, in fact, it having been lost on the 11th) they were then forced to relinquish it because of cross-valley fire – from Greenland Hill.

The attack against Roeux village took the

Rœux   Windmühle Plouvain   Plouvain   Selves
       Fresnes

v. Arras

n. St. Rohart
n. Cambrai

n. Guémappe

No. 50   5. II. 16

Monchy.

Left The two key sectors for the latter half of April: Roeux and Monchy. HS

Right Looking south over Roeux village and the River Scarpe; the Arras-Cambrai road crosses the top of the picture. HS

Neuville-Vitasse

n. Cambrai

as

N° 4

17. VII. 15

Roeux.

low ground bordered on one side by the railway and on the other by the Scarpe marshes. Against advice, the South African Brigade formed up in Fampoux village, and received a hurricane of shelling for so doing; thinned, they then advanced far behind the creeping barrage, which itself had commenced beyond the German front line – parts of which were either new or previously undetected. A screen of smoke disappeared with the creeper. The attack was described in the Brigade History.

The attack was timed for 5 p.m., when our guns opened fire. Unfortunately our barrage dropped some 500 yards east of the starting-point, and behind the first enemy line of defence, so that the South Africans had a long tract of open ground to cover before they could come up with it. Our artillery, too, seemed to miss the enemy machine-gun posts on the railway embankment, which, combined with the flanking fire from the woods in the south and the south-east and from the direction of the inn, played havoc with both the attacking brigades. The result was a failure. A gallant few of the South Africans succeeded in reaching the station, a point in their objective, where their bodies were recovered a month later when the position was captured. For the rest, only one or two isolated parties reached points as much as 200 yards east of the line held by the 4th Division. But as a proof of the quality of the troops, it should be recorded that before the attack was brought to a standstill, the casualties of the 2nd Regiment, who went in 400 strong, amounted to 16 officers and 285 men, while the 1st Regiment lost 2 officers and 203 men, and the 4th, 6 officers and 200 men.

BUCHAN, *THE HISTORY OF THE SOUTH AFRICAN FORCES IN FRANCE*

The advance averaged around 400 metres, making the endeavour a disaster worse than that of the 11th. It would have to be done all over again.

RELIEF

The long-awaited British relief took place overnight and on 12 April: four fresh and up-to-strength divisions for the sector south of the river, the 33rd, 50th (both to VII Corps), whilst in the VI Corps sector the 15th (Scottish) and 37th Divisions were replaced respectively by the 17th and 29th. The 14th and 30th Divisions went to XVIII Corps in reserve. North of the Scarpe, XVII Corps were not relieved until later, but their territorial responsibilities were reduced by First Army taking over the line from Farbus to Gavrelle, shortening Third Army's battle front by 2 kilometres.

Much was going to depend upon how quickly the fresh divisions would be required to go into action, for none of them knew the ground. At a meeting in St Pol on this day, Sir Douglas Haig's appreciation of the situation showed that he was well aware of the challenges now facing the two Army commanders, Horne and Allenby.

I pointed out that the Enemy had now been given time to put the Drocourt-Quéant line into a state of defence and to organise positions on our immediate front. He has also brought up a large number of guns. Our advance there-fore must be more methodical than was permissible on Monday night and Tuesday after the victory. Then great risks might have been made without danger because Enemy had been surprised and had no reserves on the spot! Now we must try and substitute shells as far as pos-sible for infantry.

SIR DOUGLAS HAIG, DIARY, THURSDAY 12 APRIL

Haig was also advised of the frightful battlefield conditions the troops had faced and were still facing, the guns having created such devasta-tion that movement everywhere was gruelling, and surviving without hot food and drink was a terrible ordeal. He solicited Allenby to give reliefs as much time as possible to acclimatise before action. Sir Henry Horne suggested that perhaps there had been too much shelling on 9 April! He also believed that the 'frontal attack had become … the easiest task'. Arras was clearly not an average battle, and there was food for thought at every turn. The final such dish of the day was a message from General Nivelle who wished to notify the British that due to bad weather his attacks would again be delayed – by twenty-four hours. Would that be acceptable? There was no reason for the British not to accede once more.

It was at this time that Sir Douglas Haig began to take a more personal controlling interest in events in Artois. His diary for the fol-lowing day, Friday the 13th, begins with the passage, 'I left Heuchin by motor at 10.00 am and visited HQ Third Army at St Pol. I told Allenby to arrange his advance steadily and sparing the infantry as much as possible; and that I would arrange the next general attack of the First, Third and Fifth Armies, in combina-tion, for Tuesday morning.'

Sir Edmund Allenby's hand was gently being lifted from the tiller. During the same trip

Above Address to German troops in a Roeux farmyard. BHK Abt.IV BS-N 10/2 677

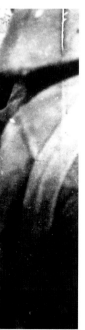

Left Digging out a British soldier buried by a shellburst. IWM HU96188

the C-in-C paid his first visit to the battlefields, scaling Telegraph Hill to view Monchy and the Wancourt Ridge. On the way he took time to look 'at the heavy artillery which were all ready to leave their emplacements in the banks of the Beaurains road and advance to new positions further forward. It is fairly easy work moving these great heavy guns nowadays by means of tractors. The real difficulty is getting the large amount of shells forward.'

The heavies were Haig's great hope. As he had just seen for himself at The Harp, they were capable of outstanding destruction. All the troops had to do was get the guns in position and feed them.

As evening approached, new arrivals were better prepared and equipped to face another bitter night, for they at least carried greatcoats. For the unrelieved units north of the Scarpe, the last few days were taking their toll. On the 34th Division front beyond the Point du Jour, for example, they had endured the physical and mental exhaustion of battle, followed by a long period of inactivity in wet and freezing trenches. There had been a few patrols to maintain, and some minor unopposed forward movement of the line had been reported, but for the most part it was a question of waiting for orders and praying heartily for relief. The trenches were deep in mud and slush, and men were beginning to suffer from exposure and trench foot. The latter was not just debilitating but a criminal military offence with serious implications for the officer whose duty it was to make certain his troops avoided it. In such conditions they were helpless.

Their feet were giving a lot of trouble; standing continuously in the slushy mud would knock most men's feet out. Mine I had rarely felt and certainly they had never been warm since Monday morning. Stephenson wrote out a stiff letter to Brigade, saying that the men were nearly at the end of their tether. It rained heavily all afternoon and evening and when Stephenson went round at 11pm he came back very perturbed over the state of the men. They were caving in and very exhausted: the mud and strain had fairly knocked them out. I went round about 3 am. I was shocked at the men, and the officers said they had the greatest difficulty to keep the men awake and feared some would die of exhaustion: they, the officers, were wonderfully cheery, and as I had a water bottle of rum with me I was very popular.

Stephenson was so upset over the men that he sent me direct to Divisional H.Q. with a free hand to say just what I liked, and also a letter for the G.S.O.1. – Brigade had sent us a message that Division could make no promises as to relief. It was a relief to get a real walk and be able to pick your way. I got on the Arras–Gavrelle road at the ridge top and had a very nice walk back to Arras, though the mud was appalling. Guns stuck at every point. You've never seen such a sight, and so many guns hors-de-combat. Got into Arras about 10am. I was a sketch, torn to ribands, and mud from head to foot, not a wash since Sunday afternoon.

Saw Brain G.S.O.1 and gave him Stephenson's letter. Oh! he said, your men have done splendidly: tell Stephenson so, and they are alright now, as there are no more operations for your brigade! I said it wasn't operations, but pure exhaustion that was knocking us out and that we couldn't go on. Brain pooh-poohed it, so I got wild and told him I hadn't seen a Brigade or Divisional Staff Officer beyond the Blue Line (the railway cutting) and that they knew nothing about it. He got quite huffy and wanted to tell me he knew all about things, so I flatly contradicted him and told him I would pilot him out to see for himself, as he wouldn't believe either Stephenson or myself. Nicholson, the Divisional General apparently had heard some of my trouble and came in. He was very amused at my appearance and I don't wonder: was awfully good and made me stay to an early lunch and then said Brain should go back with me; Brain didn't seem at all optimistic. Nicholson was charming and wanted to know what I was doing up there, and all about things. Then Brain and I set out on horseback, rode to the Point du Jour. He was not so cocksure when he had got there, but Stephenson insisted on his going to the line and just as they got to the trench two poor lads died in front of them. This straightened Brain up at once, and he said: "That's quite enough for me. You must be relieved," and set off back. The men perked up when we could give them some hope of relief and were soon pounds better; the rations were of course still cold but we got a bit of rum into them.

At 5pm the troops on our right attacked again and the Bosch shelled us unmercifully, luckily not for very long. They shelled us heavily again at 9pm. Had a nice birthday!

MAJOR BERTRAM BREWIN, 16TH ROYAL SCOTS

For Brigade HQ to allow such things to happen was the true crime, and it was far from an isolated occurrence. By forcing his superiors to come forward, Brewin was fighting a similar crusade to a host of other officers striving to connect commanders with the realities of the battlefield.

Along Vimy Ridge on the night of 12/13 April, the Canadians lay equally cold and equally uncomfortable, but considerably more contented. It had been the finest four days in the nation's military history and would be forever written into international chronicles as a feat of arms of the highest calibre. Overnight the events were reminiscent of old-fashioned positional warfare: plenty of flares, the odd burst of fire and much digging, draining, wiring, sandbag filling and cursing. By first light on Friday morning, however, scouts had returned carrying the news that the opposing trenches were almost certainly empty, the Germans appearing to have withdrawn dur-

ing the night. Indeed they had. The Canadians would be encouraged to follow, bringing their Bulldog spades and artillery with them, for Byng instantly ordered a general but cautious advance. The battleground was to widen once again.

The Roeux problem was playing upon the mind of the Third Army staff. The verdict was to ignore it for the time being and concentrate on progress elsewhere: at Monchy and the Wancourt Ridge. A good drive from here to the valley of the Sensée River should make the southern sectors of the Hindenburg Line opposite V Corps and I Anzac Corps vulnerable, if not untenable, and at the same time exert pressure upon Roeux and Greenland Hill. In fact, if Allenby was going to continue to pursue further triumph there was no other avenue but this. The Germans, still in firm control of the skies, observed developments. With the Canadians still to come down onto the plain, a stalemate north of the Scarpe, and the recent rout of the Australians at Bullecourt, there was little doubt in the minds of *Gruppe* Arras where their enemy would next try their hand. It had to be astride Monchy, for that salient was by no means yet safe, and Rupprecht and von Lossberg knew it would require offensive not defensive action to make it so. Guémappe and the Wancourt Ridge were 'untidy' sectors; they too would certainly be targeted at the same time. Two days of anarchic battle ensued, fought by ill-prepared troops on ground few were acquainted with.

Infantry Hill and the ridge crowned by Bois du Sart and Bois du Vert were the key British objectives beyond of Monchy. Take these and the village could be properly consolidated, and the devilish problem of cross-valley machine-gun fire expunged. To

Right Looking into the teeth of the British attacks in the Monchy, Wancourt and Guémappe sectors. Note the condition of the ground compared to earlier aerial photographs of these sectors. AC

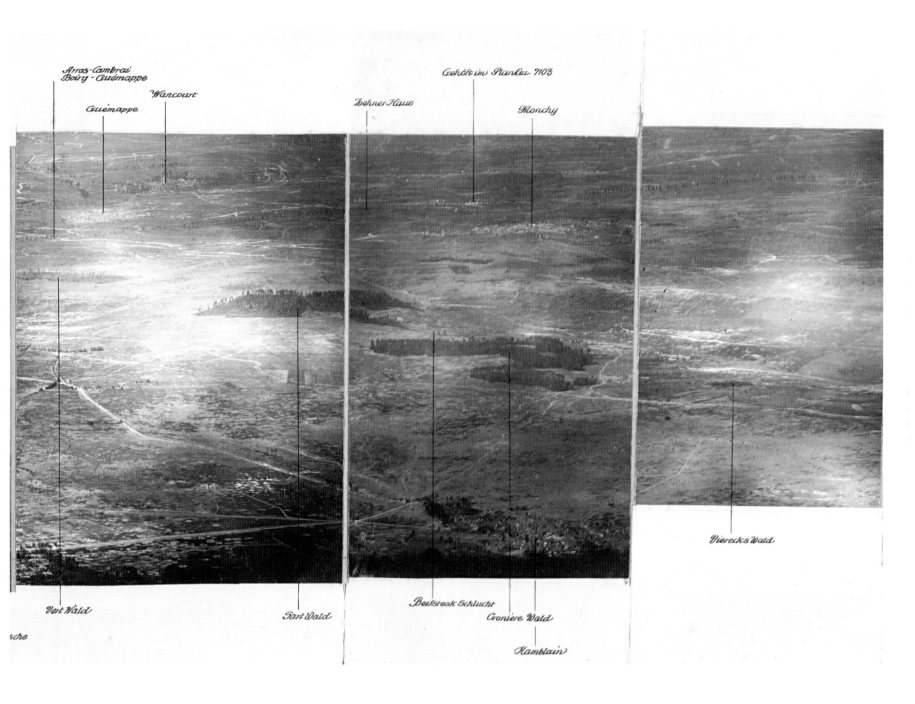

Arras-Cambrai
Boiry - Guémappe

Guémappe

Wancourt

Zehner Haus

Gehöft im PlanQu. 7103

Monchy

Vert Wald

Tart Wald

Beefsteak Schlucht

Croniere Wald

Kambtain

Vierecks Wald

sche.

leave them would be to invite counter-attack.

Major General Sir Henry de Beauvoir De Lisle's 29th Division only arrived in Arras late on the afternoon of 12 April. A proud unit with a notable pedigree, they would have attacked on the 13th if required, but De Lisle counselled that postponement would offer a greater chance of success. Corps commander Haldane agreed: the Division would take over the Monchy sector during the coming two nights and attack on the 14th. The incomers quickly came to realize how undefined the positions were. Few could say where their flanks lay, or even how close the enemy were. Except for Guémappe, the same unhelpful circumstances pertained across the entire Monchy-Wancourt battlefront. Part of the reason was that von Lossberg had already established a mobile defence in the form of dispersed pockets of resistance. Recognizable trench lines were no more.

On 13 April, 50th Division attempts to snatch Wancourt Tower were foiled, largely by lack of familiarity with the battleground. The Divisional Commander had requested an attack on Guémappe to support his own actions against the ridge, but it did not materialize until too late. In a nutshell, the first assault was stopped by enfilade fire southwards down the valley from the village, the second by enfilade fire northwards from the ridge. The plight of 6th Durham Light Infantry who attacked the tower was described in their unit history.

At night detailed orders were received for an attack at dawn, the Battalion's frontage being near Wancourt Tower. At 1 a.m. on the 14th April the men moved to the assembly position in the dry bed of the Cojeul River, with the 8th Battalion in support and 5th Border Regiment in reserve, the 9th Battalion being already in a line just south of Guémappe. The original orders had now been considerably altered, and zero hour arrived before fresh orders had been circulated to the Companies. The result was that at 4.30 a.m., after moving in file from the assembly position to a bank, some 200 yards in front, the Battalion advanced under a barrage in four waves of Companies, W being front and Z in rear, with no orders except a rough indication of the direction.

As they advanced they were met by very heavy machine-gun fire from the front and from Guémappe in their left rear. W and X Companies reached the ridge 500 yards from the starting point, and passing down the other side, were not seen again during the day. Y and Z Companies also reached the ridge, but could get no further. Later they were joined by the 8th Battalion, which was also held up. The fighting then died down, but apart from one brief message from X Company no trace could be found of the two front Companies, and the casualties in the remaining two were very heavy. To add to the confusion, the 56th Division on the right had lost direction, and men of the London Regiments were everywhere mixed with those of the 50th Division.

Over 50 per cent of the leading 6th DLI companies were lost. It was as if nothing had been learned on the Somme, 9 April had never happened, and the minds of commanders had become a tactical wilderness. At Monchy, meanwhile, because the post-11 April attack clear-up was underway and wounded still being extracted, De Lisle's men were making poor progress with the relief, and it was soon clear that the brigades selected to attack, the 87th and 88th, would not both be ready for dawn on Saturday the 14th.

What was to happen here was inexcusable in a host of ways. Only two 29th Division battalions, 1st Essex and the Newfoundlanders, were available for the assault. Before first light they formed up in a newly dug assembly trench east

Above Vulnerable British field guns firing in the open behind Monchy. IWM Q2017

Below Advancing across open ground near Arras. IWM Q5102

of the village; flanking units were distant and disconnected on the left, and not yet in place on the right. In the village, no one was on hand to close the gap in the line created by their advance. The prime objective was Infantry Hill. Having acquired it, patrols were to enter the woods and copses ahead and ascertain whether enemy troops were present. This was extraordinary in itself, for it was heavy machine-gun fire from this very ridge that had so recently helped to crush the Roeux attacks. For reasons best known to himself, Allenby appeared to be under the impression that the Germans may have vacated. By ordering a two-battalion assault, he was not only driving a perilously narrow wedge into hostile territory, but dangerously expanding the already vulnerable Monchy salient. To attack in such a limited fashion without support and almost entirely uncoordinated with the assaults on either flank, was one of the most bizarre decisions of the battle.

Before Zero-Hour, Guémappe was subdued by bombardment. The troops jumped off at 5.30 a.m. Initially, as was so often the case, there was success when the 23rd Bavarian Infantry Regiment on the horns of the attack fell back, either in panic or more likely by design. Most of Infantry Hill was in British hands for 7.00 a.m. – ostensibly, a tremendous feat. Before anyone could catch their breath, however, the riposte began, with counter-attacks on all sides. With no help on the flanks and artillery assistance impossible, there was no recourse but to flee. The Essex and Newfoundland troops suffered over a thousand losses. The Bavarians then proceeded to launch their own assaults upon Monchy itself. The time was now around 10.15. For five hours the meagre village garrison – less than a dozen men led by the Newfoundland CO, Lieutenant

Colonel James Forbes-Robertson – held the village. Had it not been for their astonishing tenacity, assistance from the right flank by the 4th Worcesters and the quick reaction of British gunners in dropping a powerful and sustained protective barrage behind the Bavarians, blocking routes of communication and supply, Monchy may well have been overwhelmed. Ironically, the foremost enemy troops were confined to the very trench from which the British attacks had been launched at dawn. The artillery, directed by observers on Orange Hill, showed some fine gunnery, dispersing the sequence of counter-attacks emerging from the two woods. The gravity of the situation at Monchy remained unknown for some time. Eventually, acting upon a message from Forbes-Robertson's adjutant, at around 3.00 p.m. the meagre defence was augmented by elements of 2nd Hampshires who, not actually knowing the nationality of the occupiers, approached gingerly from the north-west.

There was no territorial gain or loss on the day, as during the night both sides reoccupied their previous positions. It was as if the Germans had simply arranged a demonstration of what they were capable of – and what was to come. Afterwards, von Lossberg may well have looked upon the Monchy attack as a pretty successful first test of his 'active defence', and perhaps a turning point.

It would clearly have been advantageous if a British surge east of the village could have been combined with attacks upon Guémappe and the Wancourt Ridge, and it was in this respect that accusations of disjointed and befuddled thinking soon arose, not least in the mind of Sir Douglas Haig. There was no good reason for Third Army not delaying the action a further twenty-four hours, by which time sectors could have been properly garrisoned and more guns available for mutually supporting attacks on a wider front. Furthermore, Nivelle had donated extra time by once more delaying his own offensive. Haig was deeply dissatisfied, but he knew there was time for urgent reconsideration whilst the French launched their enterprise.

The disorderly events of 14 April brought to an end the first phase of the Battle of Arras. Final reliefs took place and the battle front settled into a period of preparation, principally by the engineers, for whatever course of action was decided. None could guess.

Friday, April 13th, we were ordered back to the Blue and Black Lines, and after dinner to the Roclincourt valley. We went back as far as the crest of the Vimy Ridge (or continuation thereof which ends just above Fampoux and the Scarpe), in a communication trench, a fearful heart-breaking walk, mud well up to the knees and real sticky chalk mud at that. We were the last to go, as we had to wait until the incoming Battalion had taken over all our line and we had received the magic words from each company "Relief complete". It was always rather a strain later on, on relief nights, awaiting that message. The Bosch was very knowledgeable as to reliefs, and we never knew if he would come over right in the pandemonium of "half in, half out", with all the C.T.s chock-a-block and everyone thinking much more of relief than the Bosch. It was piteous to see our chaps: lots of them could only just hobble and some were being carried down on a pal's back: their feet were in a dreadful state. We had lunch at the railway and then over the Black Line and down to Roclincourt valley, where we were apportioned a very draughty dug-out, not a downstairs one, but one dug into the side of the hill with two entrances: still it was <u>peaceful</u>. Sturrock had whiskey and soda for us and we pledged the 16th R.S. in a Royal Drink. We slept there that night, and next day tidied and cleaned up, shaved and generally

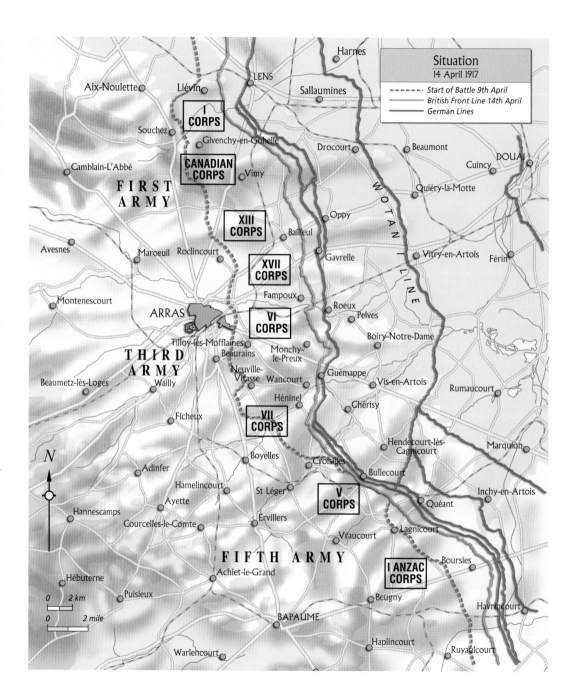

became respectable again. Nine-tenths of the men had cut the skirts off their greatcoats – not good for the coats but quite excusable, seeing that the tails got so heavy with mud that no man could carry them. There was an awful shortage of equipment and Lewis gun ammunition drums were missing by the hundreds. It was a very quiet day and after lunch I went over and did the attack on my own. They had tidied up wonderfully, heaps of salvage all over the place and all our dead from the early phases were laid outside a big crater, in which they temporarily buried the whole lot – rather a staggering lot to see, poor lads, when they were all collected. There were some damned civilians looting dead Bosch of odds and ends, so I scared them with a couple of shots from my revolver, and they ran like hares. It was sickening to see them, and some of the Bosch were pretty well stripped.

MAJOR BERTRAM BREWIN, 16TH ROYAL SCOTS

Brewin's 34th Division were at last relieved by the 63rd (Royal Naval) Division on 14 April. In deference to the efforts of both First and Third Armies, the period was later given two titles by the Battles Nomenclature Committee: the Battle of Vimy Ridge, and the First Battle of the Scarpe.

The following day, Sunday, was the eve of the French offensive. Personal attacks and secret briefings against Nivelle were now worthless: if he prevailed, the prize was immortality; if not, it was obscurity. Anticipation and indeed belief throughout the corridors of power in France and Britain was soaring.

We were very hopeful. This state of mind I have seen on the eve of every offensive, but rarely so intense as in this year. On the marked map in our office we studied the objectives and allowed ourselves to be carried away by our own imagination. We dreamed that the barrier was broken at last, marked the progress northwards and felt a foretaste of the joy that should be ours if the results came up to our expectations. In spite of our *knowledge that the whole path of the offensive was strewn with difficulties, we expected a miracle. That famous moment which was to see the enemy's heart fail him, and the beginning of the rout, was it to come now? I fancy that the whole of France was in the same state of expectancy. The war was drawing out intolerably, it was essential to put an end to it, every one would have given ten years of his life to see the dawn of victory. This war psychosis has been aptly called 'obsidional fever' [siege fever]; no phrase could better describe it, and I fancy that no Government would have been strong enough to stop the impending offensive. General Nivelle, however great his responsibility, was subjected to the instinctive pressure, the intoxication of this great mass of Frenchmen, enervated by delay, who awaited the miracle and demanded the end of the nightmare at any cost.*

JEAN DE PIERREFEU, DRAFTSMAN OF DAILY PRESS COMMUNIQUÉS AT FRENCH HEADQUARTERS

On 15 April, Sir Douglas Haig stepped in and called a halt to present planning at Arras. It was getting all too familiar, not only for the C-in-C but others too. Indeed, written representations had been made by three divisional commanders (De Lisle, Wilkinson and Robertson) expressing profound disagreement with actions that, as the Official History puts it, 'exposed the attacker to concentrated fire upon his flanks', i.e. costly piecemeal ventures. As if to emphasize the point, a substantial surprise attack took place on this day – the surprise was that it was German.

15TH APRIL
The weather was unfit for our shoot, the clouds were at about 1,000 feet and it was raining heavily. We decided to have a look at the line instead, and if the weather cleared to carry on with the shoot. On the way we heard heavy rifle fire about 4,000 yards behind the front line

and saw considerable numbers of our troops in extended order, obviously in action. Further inspection revealed that the enemy had launched an attack against the Australians who were on our right and facing Quéant, and that they had been driven back to the point where we heard the rifle fire. We heard afterwards that the initial surprise of the German attack was so complete that they were able to destroy a battery of 4.5-inch howitzers by hand. One brigadier is said to have fought in his pyjamas. By the time we had appreciated the situation it was about 0600 hours. No other aircraft was up at the time because of the weather, and but for the chance suggestion which led to our setting out to look at the front line, we too would have been on the ground at Courcelles. Under these circumstances it was something of a field day for us. There were infantry targets everywhere for, confident that the weather was keeping aircraft away, the Germans seemed to make no attempt at concealment. We commenced sending Zone Calls and soon obtained replies from the artillery. Occasionally there was an opening for the machine gun, but most of the time W/T cooperation was the more important work. We did silence one machine-gun nest and had the satisfaction of seeing our infantry overrun it and capture the guns. By 0830 the enemy had been forced back as far as our front line, where he broke and fled back across No Man's Land for the gap which had been cut in their wire during the night. We saw great congestion at these points. It was like a crowd struggling to rush through a narrow door. Our machine guns and field guns were firing into the mass and caused many casualties.

Second Lieutenant Wilfred Cox, 15 Squadron, Royal Flying Corps

Early on the morning of Sunday, 15 April almost 16,000 German troops penetrated the 1st Australian Division defences, intent on further deepening the re-entrant between Quéant and Bullecourt, and more. It was not just a raid but a major assault, and entirely unexpected.

Forward posts and trenches were cut off and surrounded and the Germans retook Lagnicourt, a village they had been driven out of on 26 March. With the front lines overrun, the Australian defence fell to reserves, HQ personnel, non-combatant troops and the few who had managed to escape the storm.

Stretching along a diagonal crossroad near the junction was a rag-tag group of HQ Johnnies – clerks, signallers, cooks and batmen – who I bet had not fired their rifles in anger so far in the war. They were facing whole battalions of the German Army. If we had known then that there were twenty-three German battalions altogether against only four battalions of ours we may have been more worried. The Germans were getting closer all the time. They would soon be only 300 yards away, which is well within the limit of accuracy for most riflemen. Unfortunately the HQ staff were not experienced rifle shots and, even with the welcome addition of our company, I didn't know if we had enough firepower to repel such a horde. My company were waiting patiently for the word from the 12th Battalion HQ to start firing. However, the HQ staff were getting anxious. I was quite impressed with the way a battle hardened little lance corporal was keeping the inexperienced staff steady. He refused to give the order to fire even though some of the men had turned their heads and were looking back at him imploringly. The one-striper simply ignored them or signalled them to keep their eyes to their front. He continued to walk up and down behind the line, keeping them steady by the sheer force of his will. The tension for them must have been unbearable. Then the veteran lance corporal, obviously seeing the danger on our left flank, said to his men, 'If you have any German souvenirs on you, you'd better throw them away now. You won't want to have them on you if you're captured.' That suggestion did not calm their fears any, but gave us all something to think about for a few moments. I know I quickly threw away a watch I had taken off a dead German in a previous engagement.

When I looked back to the front the German advance appeared to me to be much closer than before, a little over 100 yards, nor spread out ten yards apart as we were when we advanced but massed together for moral and physical support and making easy targets. My thoughts were interrupted by orders from both sides of me: 'Range 100 yards. Fire', and the silence was shattered. Every rifle to the left and right of me discharged almost simultaneously as every man had long since picked his target and aimed his weapon.

Large holes began appearing in the German ranks. Their walk slowed and then stopped altogether 100 yards away. This was a mistake as they now presented an exposed, stationary target. They had no shell holes to dive into as they had had on the Somme. Then they must have realized that there was no fire coming from our right, where a road stretched north-east to Lagnicourt, and so the part of the line that was in front of us began to swing across in that direction.

When we saw the German line move to our right I wondered if they were going to get around our position but I needn't have worried. I found out later that, before we arrived, Colonel Elliot had 'borrowed' a machine-gun and crew from one of his companies that was nearby keeping a lookout for any German aircraft. He had placed it on his right flank on the road to Lagnicourt. This gave it a commanding view of the battlefield across our front and right down to the next road junction; we didn't know it was there, until now. The distinctive sound of the machine-gun opening up was a very welcome one to us and caught the Germans by surprise. It was a bit like an ambush but I don't think it was planned. The withering fire coming across from the right had caught a whole battalion of the enemy in a crossfire – enfilade fire as it is called. However, the machine gun was rather isolated and vulnerable to a determined attack and it was starting to come under fire from some courageous Germans nearest to it. Fortunately their post

was at that moment reinforced by the remnants of a platoon coming back along the sunken road from Lagnicourt, who had attempted unsuccessfully to enter the village. These men then added their fire to that of the machine gun. The German line then crumbled and the advance was abandoned altogether.

PRIVATE ROY RAMSAY, 3RD AUSTRALIAN FIELD AMBULANCE

The attack penetrated deeply, as far as the battery lines, and five guns were destroyed before the Germans were driven back. Many other weapons were later found to have demolition charges in place, but the enemy engineers selected for the task had apparently been so intent on souvenir-hunting they had failed to blow them. According to prisoners this had been one of the primary intentions, the principal tactical objective being to so disrupt the Australians that further strikes against the Hindenburg Line would be delayed. An angry Rupprecht felt that more could have been accomplished had the various commanders been flexible with their scheme and not imposed such strict objectives. Planning had necessarily been rushed and had not several German supporting units arrived late for the enterprise, the outcome might have been serious for Gough and Birdwood. Casualties were 1,010 Australian and 2,313 German.

The same day, whilst awaiting news from the French, a conference was convened at St Pol where all three Army staffs discussed plans for the next thrust at Arras. In the north, First Army were back in the frame, being assigned the breaking of the Oppy-Mericourt line and the capture of Gavrelle; in the south, Gough's objectives were Riencourt and Hendecourt, which meant another attack astride Bullecourt, whilst between them Allenby's Third was to overrun the Sensée valley, and excise

Greenland Hill and the Bois du Sart-Bois du Vert Ridge to a line beyond St Rohart's Factory, a sugar refinery on the Cambrai road near Vis-en-Artois. There was, however, still some essential line-straightening to do first, namely on the Wancourt ridge and at Guémappe.

The value of the Wancourt Tower is illustrated by the panorama segment taken from this location (see pages 216–217). Between 14 and 18 April, the ruins became a shuttlecock.

About April 16, 1917, Lieutenant Colonel F. Robinson of the 6th N.F. discovered the enemy approaching the ruined buildings on the Wancourt Tower Hill, and promptly ordered a platoon to attack them. This plan succeeded admirably and the Tower and house were captured. The place was of vital importance to us as it commanded direct observation on all the roads leading to our part of the front. On April 17 the enemy shelled the Tower with 8-inch howitzers – generally a sign that he meant to attack sooner or later. The Tower contained a formidable concrete machine-gun emplacement, facing of course our way, but by General Rees' orders it was blown up by the Engineers. Sure enough the enemy attacked the Tower that night, and at an unfortunate time for us, for the 7th N.F. were in the process of relieving the 6th N.F. in the front line, and it was a vile night, with a blizzard of snow.

The German attack succeeded in driving our men out of the Tower and buildings, and though several bombing attacks were made that night to recover the position it could not be done.

CAPTAIN FRANCIS BUCKLEY, 149TH INFANTRY BRIGADE STAFF, 50TH (NORTHUMBRIAN) DIVISION

The 'demolition attack' by the engineers was a curious exercise, and worth recounting by an eyewitness.

The Fusiliers were holding a line just this side of the building, the Boche a hundred yards beyond it. It was

feared that the Boche might attack any moment and re-establish their machine-gun in the emplacement. Brigade, therefore, asked us if we could blow up the whole building and Littlewood went to have a look. The infantry said it was impossible to get there by day, the whole hillside being as bare as a plate with Guémappe just beside it. It was not even certain that there was not a post of Boches behind the house. Littlewood, however, walked straight up the hill alone and into the emplacement at two o'clock in the afternoon! He measured up the whole place, then came back, fetched a party of sappers and walked back again. About eight of them walked straight up across the open, carrying boxes of guncotton, laid the charge, lit it and ran down the hill again, without a shot being fired! A very gallant performance for the enemy were only about two hundred yards away. McQueen and I went up to a battalion headquarters near Heninel. We could see Wancourt Tower on the opposite slope. We were feeling a bit anxious, when who should appear plodding along but the whole demolition party, Littlewood in front, looking as solemn as a judge. He was followed by Sergeant Bones and Corporal O'Connell. They told us all had gone off well. To my horror, I saw that not a man of the party was armed. There was so much explosive to carry, that they had left their rifles and bayonets behind. Nice fools they would have felt if they had met half a dozen Germans, and it was about even betting that they would.

LIEUTENANT JOHN GLUBB, 7TH FIELD COMPANY, ROYAL ENGINEERS

The poor weather that had dogged everyone since Day One failed to improve, forcing postponement of any wider offensive until 23 April. During the period of relative calm between the first and second battles of the Scarpe, von Lossberg further injected his active defence serum into the troops. Heavier artillery was augmented and relocated out of reach of all but the longest-range British weapons such as the

Royal Engineers transporting stone and ammunition by barge and tram along the banks of the Scarpe. IWM Q5828

6-inch naval gun; only twenty-four were available in the Arras theatre and this had been noted by German plotters. By moving into an ever-narrowing pocket, the British were also forced to concentrate their batteries (indeed everything) in areas far smaller than the manuals recommended. It gave German gunners many an opportunity, with even unobserved harassing fire proving effective. Counter-battery operations were based upon aerial observation, which was not a universal forte.

The vital importance of committing the full force of our heavy artillery to disrupting the deployment of the enemy's artillery in advance of an expected major attack was clearly recognised. Aerial photographs enabled us to observe the build-up of the enemy's artillery in great detail and to predict when the enemy's next major attack would take place, almost to the day. Unfortunately, owing to poor visibility and inexperience on the part of the flyers assigned to these missions (of which more later), it was only possible to carry out planned shoots against individually identified targets on a small number of days. During the comparatively quiet period between the 14th and 23rd of April, for example, it was not possible to concentrate the weight of our artillery on counter-battery work, and we were only able to carry out observed destructive shoots on two batteries. When ground-level observation of enemy battery targets was not possible, rather than allow the enemy artillery build-up to proceed completely undisturbed, we resorted to map shooting, supplemented by frequent sudden bursts of fire by day and by night to disrupt the emplacement of guns and the bringing up of ammunition. This undoubtedly achieved a certain measure of success, as the enemy had massed his many guns in a relatively confined area and he was obliged, due to the difficult ground conditions, to use the roads to bring forward supplies of ammunition, and these were kept under especially heavy fire by our large-calibre flat-trajectory artillery.

'ARRAS: LESSONS LEARNED', BAVARIAN ARMY

Testimonies abound with examples of the growing effectiveness of German fire. The British dilemma was how to deal with it from their present positions.

18TH APRIL 1917

My Dearest Mother
I have only been able to get postcards off lately as life has been and is most frightfully strenuous. I'm glad to say I've changed my position a few hundred yards – the one I wrote last from was christened "Hell Valley" we had such a rotten time there. One night they shelled us with gas, 3 Batteries as hard as they could pelt for 5 mortal hours, putting in a burst of shrapnel and H.E. occasionally during the process to catch anyone who might be out trying to get a breath of fresh air. He put over a direct hit into our cook house, wounding our cook, and gassing 3 of the 4 servants pretty badly, my own amongst them, so you can imagine how uncomfortable we were without cook or servants!

The same shell wrecked most of the Mess stuff, and absolutely did in my toilet outfit, including my beautiful ivory-backed hair brushes I've had such a long time. Next the wily Hun started deliberately ranging on us with 5.9" by aeroplane observation – his mastery of the air here is complete, and I shouldn't like to say how many of our planes I've actually seen brought down in the last week. Anyway, the fellow ranging on us flew backwards and forwards about 500 feet above us and the 5.9" battery having found the range opened destructive fire – not only on my battery of course, the valley was full of us, and he swept up and down. We all had a lot of casualties, and I had two guns destroyed, and three others hit by splinters though still serviceable – and that night we left hurriedly for our present destination – mighty glad to be quit of Hell Valley, where amongst others I left my two best sergeants. An hour after we left the little hole in the bank we used as a Mess, and in which I always slept, took a direct hit from a 5.9 and disappeared entirely!

However all this is merely an incident – the battle

is a real good show, and far the nastiest knock the Hun has ever had.
Much love from Boodles
MAJOR CUTHBERT G. LAWSON, 14TH BRIGADE,
ROYAL HORSE ARTILLERY

The passage about roads in the Bavarian 'Lessons Learned' report is especially important, for in those sectors newly occupied by the British no routes could cope with the movement of guns, caterpillars and heavy horses that the advance had demanded. At the end of the first week railheads had been brought up to Arras, facilitating repairs by the delivery of stone and timber to the engineers' 'doorstep'. The Sappers were already hard at work installing light railways to all points forward – the transmission of shells being paramount. Going 'off-road' on the battlefield was not an option; thousands of Sappers were permanently engaged in repair, bridging and draining major and minor routes. Unless absolutely necessary, the infantry were not at liberty to utilize roads to traverse the battlefield; they followed special tracks, some laid parallel to the main routes (such as the Arras-Cambrai road), others tracing the many mediaeval byways that everywhere criss-crossed the landscape. The unexpected territorial gain of 9 April helped the engineers, for a vast amount of useful enemy materiel that would have been destroyed or removed had the advance been slow or repulsed fell into British hands.

Our stay in Wancourt has enabled us to see something of German works and customs. It is notorious that the German army and nation is organized to the last degree of perfection. In addition, they are in enemy country. Not only are they not like us, at every moment considering the interests and wishes of their allies, but it is part of their policy to cut down and carry away everything. They are thus able to cut down immense quantities of timber, and exploit the local resources to the utmost. There were three German dumps of materials in Wancourt and Marlière. One at the west end, containing chiefly timber, wooden frames, with also corrugated steel shelters. Another, in Marlière, also contained quantities of timber, together with brushwood faggots, hurdles and fascines. A third dump, south of Wancourt bridge, contained an immense amount of steel reinforcing bars and concrete stores. These were probably largely used for the construction of their big defensive lines, like the Hindenburg Line, which are full of concrete. Wancourt contained a great number of mined dugouts, as also did every bank and sunken road in the area. The diligence with which the Germans make mined and concrete dugouts is well known. There was also a good deal of Decauville tramway and derelict trolleys lying about. A main tramway line ran from Guémappe to Marlière and to all the above dumps

The Germans also have an excellent scheme for notice boards. Most of the houses round here had white walls on which they painted the name of the village and the direction of the roads. The letters are four feet high and can be seen a quarter of a mile away. On a wall in Wancourt was a huge notice, This road is passable for infantry and artillery between sunrise and sunset, provided no enemy balloon is up. *All the German dugouts in Wancourt were neatly notice-boarded, saying* 20 Manner, *or whatever it might be. The German graves round Wancourt were not collected in a cemetery, but were sited here and there, presumably where the men fell. All, however, were marked by neat black and white crosses, with the inscription,* Hier ruht ein tapfere deutsche Krieger, *here lies a gallant German warrior. I also saw several equally well-kept graves, inscribed* Hier ruhen zwei tapferen franzosischen Soldaten. *Compared with all we hear of Hun barbarities, this impressed me favourably.*
LIEUTENANT JOHN GLUBB, 7TH FIELD COMPANY, ROYAL ENGINEERS

Tramway simply adapted for the transportation of wounded. IWM Q6226

THE NIVELLE OFFENSIVE BEGINS

If the British were unsure of the form their next action at Arras might take, minds were swiftly and sharply focussed by events on the Aisne. The French were delighted with the British and Canadian achievements, for the Arras offensive had surely consumed large numbers of German reserves who might otherwise be facing the *poilus*. But time after time intelligence had confirmed the build-up of German forces in Nivelle's area of attack. The fear was that an advance might be made at huge cost only to be brought to a halt after 10 or 20 kilometres – another Somme. The declaration of General Pétain's concerns was influential: 'General Nivelle's obstinacy will lead to failure … It is fanciful to think that the second line will be crossed. With a carefully prepared attack and fair weather, it could be taken, but not easily. An offensive is required, but it should be limited to short-range well-defined attacks.'

Such a robust expression of doubt caused the French government to convene a summit meeting, chaired by President Poincaré himself, at Compiègne. Nivelle was of course present and was challenged by several generals, including Pétain. His response was typical: if the attacks were not seen to be immediately successful they would be called off after forty-eight hours, so there was no question of a battle remotely resembling the Somme; he had no intention of persevering if a costly impasse was on the cards. From soldier and politician alike the questions kept coming, however, and after an hour an incensed Nivelle saw red and offered his resignation. The politicians had gone too far, for should they accept it there would be egg on the faces of those who, only recently in the minds of the

nation, so strongly and publicly favoured Nivelle over Joffre – and schemed so deftly to make it happen. The General retained his position and the attacks began.

At 8.00 a.m. on 16 April, headquarters received the message that the infantry had made a 'good start' and that the 'the first line has been taken all over the front. At one point, south of Juvincourt, it is reported that our troops have reached the second line.' This may well have been true for the Juvincourt sector, but nowhere else. At 2.00 p.m. Jean de Pierrefeu released a communiqué which, given the day, the hour and the convulsions of expectation being felt by the entire *Entente*, was frighteningly bald: 'The artillery battle has become extremely violent during the night across the entire front between Soissons and Rheims'. No more; and no mention of the offensive. He later wrote of this day:

On April 16th hope was short lived. At eleven o'clock the Third Bureau had not yet sent in the accounts from the armies, although when operations had been in progress telegrams poured in hour after hour from the beginning of the attack. It was a bad sign. It was raining in torrents, a violent storm raged over Compiègne [location of French General Headquarters], and the barometer was at its lowest. I went to the Third Bureau to find an ominous silence reigning. No information had been received, they told me; but the first news was satisfactory. I knew that formula, and had no hope of discovering what was happening. At such times I merely asked whether I should draw up a victorious communiqué or strike a prudent note, and what line our troops could be described as having reached. But they told me I had better wait for the evening communiqué before announcing results, as those known up to the present were too vague. An excellent device, now used for the first time, but subsequently of great use. Meanwhile it was evident that the

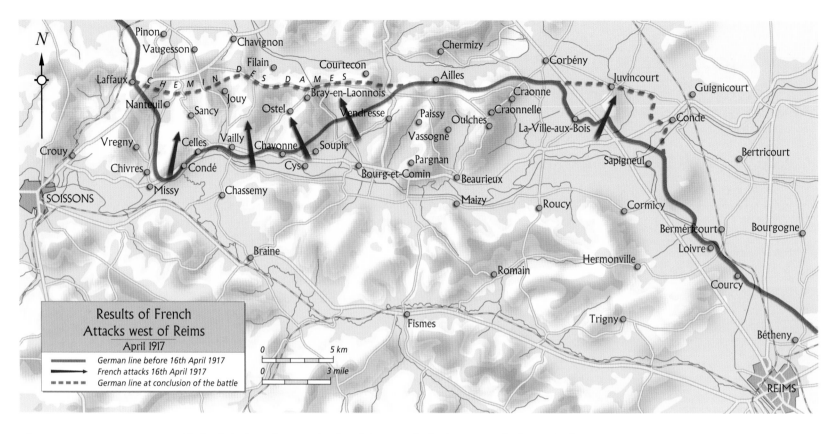

N

Pinon
Vaugesson
Chavignon
Chermizy
Corbény
Filain
Courtecon
Ailles
Juvincourt
Guignicourt
Laffaux   *CHEMIN   DES   DAMES*
Nanteuil   Jouy   Bray-en-Laonnois   Craonne
Ostel   Vendresse   Craonnelle   Condé
Sancy   Paissy   Oulches
Vregny   Celles   Vailly   Chavonne   Soupir   Vassogne   La-Ville-aux-Bois
Chivres   Cys   Bourg-et-Comin   Pargnan   Bertricourt
Condé   Beaurieux   Sapigneul
Crouy   Missy   Chassemy   Maizy   Cormicy   Bourgogne
SOISSONS   Roucy   Berméricourt
Braine   Hermonville   Loivre
Romain   Courcy
Trigny
Fismes   Béthény

REIMS

**Results of French
Attacks west of Reims**
April 1917

——— German line before 16th April 1917
——➤ French attacks 16th April 1917
- - - German line at conclusion of the battle

0   5 km
0   3 mile

advance was not commensurate with the desired results.

In the evening, in spite of the time that had elapsed, progress was no more marked. An attempt was made in the communiqué to emphasize the powerful resistance of the enemy, who had massed considerable forces. It was announced that we had occupied his front line between Soissons and Craonne, which was not strictly true, as in many places to the west of Craonne we had been driven back to our own trenches during the afternoon. But it was impossible to mention a single village as having been taken by us, although the district was thickly scattered with them. The attack upon Brimont had yielded no results; we had scarcely been able to maintain our position along the Aisne canal, but

in the plain towards Juvincourt we had contrived to reach the second line and to penetrate it slightly. The total of prisoners, happily fairly high, reassured Colonel d'Alenson, who found the communiqué not very brilliant, on the whole.

Ten thousand prisoners, that would hearten the public! It is true that the absence of captured guns spoiled the picture. It was true that our troops, not having reached the battery positions, were under fire, and that the next day would be a very difficult one. However, Colonel d'Alenson continued to hope obstinately. The Champagne attack was to begin on the 17th, at an early hour.
JEAN DE PIERREFEU, DRAFTSMAN OF DAILY PRESS
COMMUNIQUÉS AT FRENCH HEADQUARTERS

Above and opposite The results of Nivelle's endeavours astride Reims

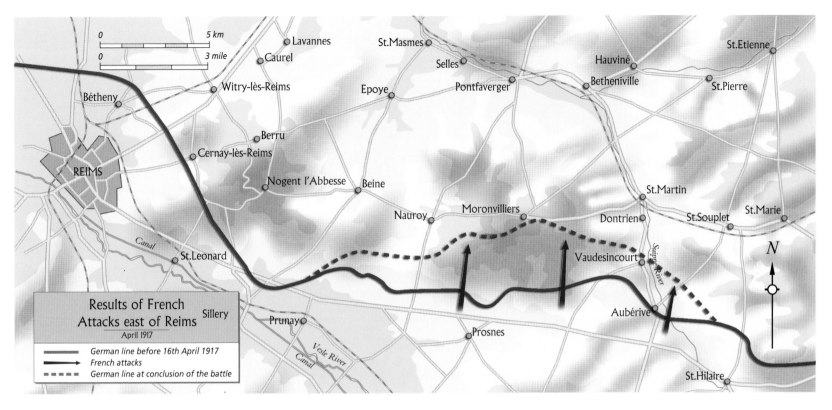

Results of French
Attacks east of Reims
April 1917

German line before 16th April 1917
French attacks
German line at conclusion of the battle

Ten thousand prisoners is almost exactly what the British had achieved at Arras. It heartened their military, their government and their public, and indeed the French. Having now lost the momentum, however, it was a question of maintaining the chimera of success for as long as it took to rekindle real impetus. None of the early French promise came to fruition. Several gains had to be relinquished on the first night – never a good sign – and then on the 17th the Fourth Army joined in east of Reims. Nivelle prayed for a reversal of fortune, and may have been momentarily hopeful as some advances of over 2 kilometres were made. Like Arras, they then hit an impenetrable wall of resistance. In the first week the French suffered 96,000 casualties with more than 15,500 dead, causing alarm in *Parlement* and growing indignation amongst the *poilus*. As the story unfolded the British looked on with concern.

16TH APRIL

The French have launched their long delayed attack this morning on a front of 25 miles on the River Aisne. Three Armies took part. The 5th Army on the right is said to have progressed well. The 6th Army next to it on its left only took the enemy's front trenches, but where the 3rd Army attacked on the left of the latter's attack, which was nearly at right-angles to the main attack, nothing at all seems to have been gained.

17TH APRIL

I could get no details from the French as to results of today's fighting, which is always a bad sign.

18TH APRIL

Wilson [General Sir Henry Wilson, head of the British Mission at French headquarters] states Enemy's position greatly strengthened in the two-and-a-half years since we left. [Sir Douglas Haig served in the sector during the Battle of the Aisne in autumn 1914.] So strong is this front now, that Wilson thinks that it ought not to have been attacked. GQG is disappointed, and they will look about for some excuse. One of them will be that the whole German Army is facing them and we have not succeeded in easing their load!

DIARY, SIR DOUGLAS HAIG

As early as 21 April, General Micheler, commander of the French Reserve Army Group, voiced the opinion that the offensive should be halted: the Germans either had or were in the process of falling back to the Siegfried Line; as a result of certain key failures French flanks were dangerously exposed; there was an entirely insufficient force of four divisions of reserves available; if the offensive was to continue stocks of ordnance were wholly inadequate. He concluded by saying:

The proposed exploitation north of the Aisne cannot be contemplated without a new general offensive over the whole front, given the need to cover the flanks. GAR does not have the means for this, which will no doubt demand supplementary forces, either to feed the attack or cover reliefs. One may furthermore wonder whether in the present circumstances the front of attack of GAR can possibly be exploited against a well-armed enemy who has had time to rally. Past experience should advise us against delusions in this respect.

Micheler could just as well have written the same paragraph to Sir Douglas Haig. But Haig was in a different position for he was supporting the French, and it was they who were in by far the deeper difficulty. Cooperation was more essential at this time than it ever had been. Nivelle chose to batter on, hastily forgetting the 'forty-eight hour' promise. In the British line in front of Arras, however, the strategy and tactics were lost on men whose sole interest for the moment was to be warm, dry – and to have a change of diet.

19.4.17

As usual

My dear old Basil I am writing this from the depths of an old German dug-out, about 40 feet below the earth and accordingly pretty bomb proof. We have gone up the line again and are now in reserve. Exactly what is coming off I can't say because I don't know. The weather is vile still, raining continually but not quite so cold. We have been living lately on iron rations more or less, in fact I haven't tasted bread since last Sunday week, 11 days ago. I have just heard that a loaf has arrived with rations tonight. So you can imagine my state of jubilation. Try living on bully beef and biscuits for a week and you will soon get enjoyment out of quite small things. I have had plenty of rum lately which has kept me going: you need a nerve-steadier pretty often on this game. I haven't seen a paper since last Monday, or to be more correct I have just seen last Monday's Daily Mail, so don't quite know who is winning the war. I have heard various rumours but know nothing definitely. Your letter of the 9th has just arrived, for which many thanks.

Best of luck,

Yours ever, James

LIEUTENANT JAMES BUTLIN, 6TH DORSETSHIRE REGIMENT

Right and overleaf Sections of British narrative maps showing British gains in mid-April. The thick grey line at left represents the original jumping-off positions on 9 April NA WO95-363

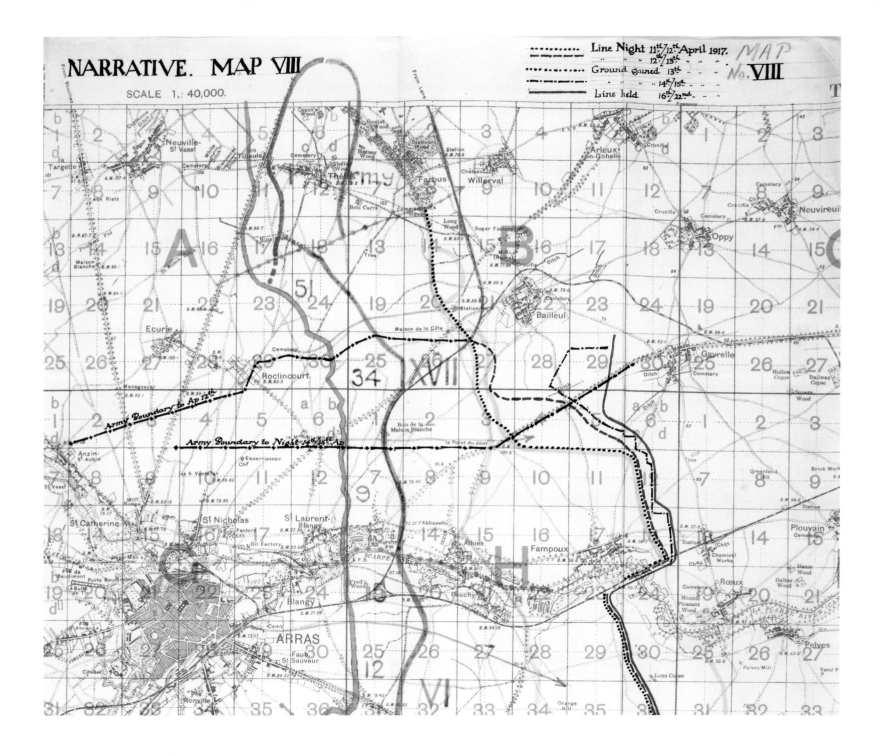

SCALE 1 : 40,000.

MAP No. VIII

Line Night 11th/12th April 1917.
—"— 12th/13th —"—
Ground gained 13th —"—
—"— 14th/15th —"—
Line held 16th/22nd —"—

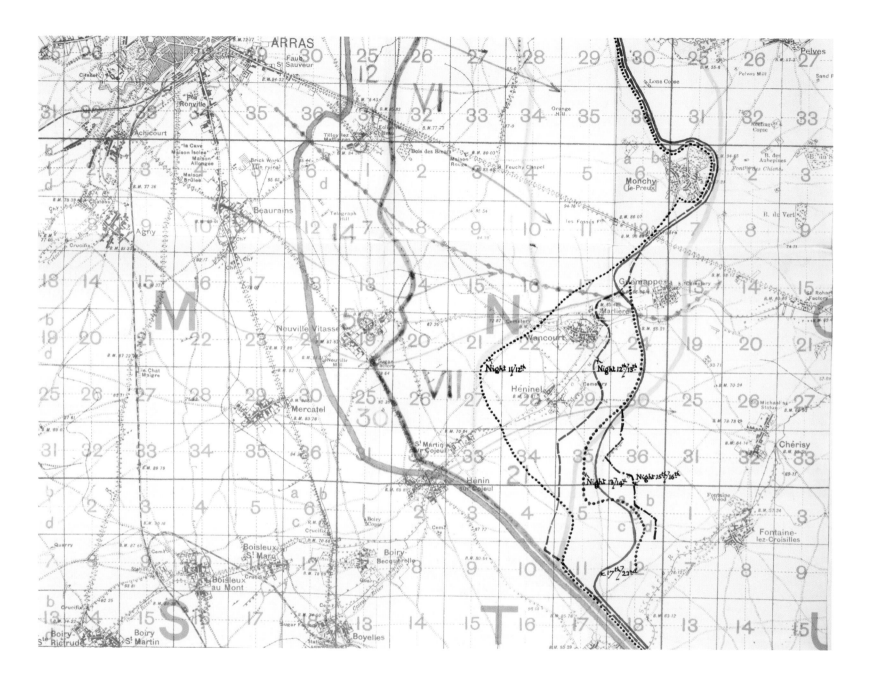

CHAPTER SIXTEEN
Tyde What May

It was just about this time that the French failure on the Chemin des Dames occurred, and that Sir Douglas Haig was used by the French GOG to tie down the Germans on our front by maintaining as a heavy presence on them as possible. Had we had unlimited resources in the way of reserves, this might have had some chance of success. As things were, however, we had nothing but tired divisions who had lost pretty heavily in the initial attacks of the 9th, 10th and 11th of April and it was quite evident, on the XVIIth Corps front at any rate, that we were up against fresh German divisions who had no intention of retreating. To hurl these depleted, and to some extent disorganised formations against good troops, who had had 3 or 4 days in which to place and dig in their machine guns, was to ask for failure. When further you realise that our communications were still elementary and that adequate supplies of gun ammunition could not be got up, and that the guns in their new positions had not really registered their targets properly, the chances of success were still further diminished.

The attacks we were ordered to deliver were hastily mounted and I am not surprised that they generally failed or only obtained partial success at an excessive cost in casualties to the infantry.

The policy of tying the enemy down and of preventing him from sending troops off elsewhere could equally well have been achieved by maintaining a strong and active force of artillery on our front. The Germans would never have dared to thin their troops out so long as the menace of our numerous guns remained. This policy could have "kept him guessing"; and, when the divisions who had taken part in the original victorious attack had had adequate rest, had absorbed their reinforcement and had had adequate time in which to stage a really well worked out attack, they could have embarked on a second stage of the Battle of Arras and I am sure could have achieved equally striking successes as they did on 9th April at a very much smaller cost in human life.

BRIGADIER GENERAL J.R. CHARLES, BGGS, XVII CORPS

---

*Tyde What May – Motto on Haig family coat of arms.

A private meeting was arranged with Nivelle so that Sir Douglas Haig might obtain an appreciation of events on the Aisne from the horse's mouth. The French had failed; that much was clear. What was most concerning was that the enemy were able both to repulse the colossal French offensive and stifle a seriously substantial British one. Continuing bad weather dictated that the St Pol resolution to attack again on 20 April must be modified. Haig listened and acted upon the fresh deliberations of his Army commanders. Although he had been at liberty to close down the Arras front on the 18th, the C-in-C finally elected to renew operations on 23 April, despite being unsure whether the French would still be in offensive mode on that date.

ST GEORGE'S DAY

B.E.F.
France
19.4.17
Dear Mother,
You will perhaps be anxious to know how I am faring during these stirring times, and I can assure you that we have been having a strenuous time of it. We have had four days of this new advance and I am glad to say I managed through without a scratch. I daresay had I been at home I would have been giving you quite a list of my fighting apparel for repairs, but unfortunately this is on too __prodigious__ a scale. We got on well in the attack, and from what I saw, we left very few dead on the field. On the whole we carried the advance forward about as far as the line at present appears, a distance of about five miles or so, so that was not a bad day's work, was it? Oh no, there's no holding of the Jocks once they get their blood up, but with bully beef and biscuits including a few days snow we soon came back to our normal again. There is only one fault in doing well in this war, and that

is the effects of an overdose. Sometimes in doing well, you do so well, that they think no other body can do so well, and in the end you finish with well, well, well and a long sigh. However, on the whole we make pretty light of matters – by far the best way when held in the clutches of despair.

PRIVATE WILLIAM JOLLY, 7TH CAMERON HIGHLANDERS

This was William Jolly's last letter home to his mother. Aged twenty-two, he was killed on 23 April near Monchy. He is one of the many 'missing' and is commemorated on Bay 9 of the Arras Memorial. Apart from its poignancy and somewhat awe-inspiring bravado, the letter is especially illustrative of the way 'successful' divisions such as his (15th Scottish) were used time and again. Before phase two more troops had been installed and shifted, the 51st (Highland) Division reappearing after an inadequate 48-hour break to relieve the battered 9th (Scottish) in the Roeux sector, whilst overnight on 20 April, the 37th Division took the place of the 4th north of the river, changing parentage to join XVII Corps.

At the beginning of the Second Battle of the Scarpe, Third Army were to attack as one, as they had done on the 9th, but in the same way as the latter stages of the Somme, with strictly limited objectives. The Germans were prepared. Having strengthened their wire and augmented artillery, which was now at least two-thirds stronger than on 9 April, the active defence was ready to be tested on a large scale.

Just eighteen tanks were in battleworthy condition to take the field on the misty Monday morning of 23 April. Eight were attached to VII Corps whose objective was to drive from the Héninel-Wancourt ridge down into and across the Sensée valley, whilst at the same time pushing south along the Hindenburg Line to forge a bridgehead across the river at Fontaine-les-Croisilles. 33rd Division's aspiration was to grab half a kilometre of enemy line south of the Sensée to prevent hostile fire against the main assault to the north. The 98th Brigade would bomb down and skirmish behind the German lines towards the river (with the assistance of tanks), roughly on an 800-metre front, whilst two battalions of the 100th Brigade made a traditional frontal attack to pierce the line in front of Croisilles,. In both sectors there was the added complication of the Hindenburg Tunnel, an extraordinary piece of German engineering that ran the full length of the Hindenburg trenches but 15 metres beneath them.

'Secret and Confidential' letters came up from the Brigade during the day. We were to capture about two miles of line by bombing down the front and support trenches as far as the village of Fontaine-les-Croisilles, there connecting with a battalion who were making a frontal attack on the village. This was not incidentally a healthy bit of line where you could stand up and have a good look round. It you could have done so you would not have been able to distinguish the village for it wasn't there any longer. So one's plans were made entirely from the map. Large quantities of bombs were sent up during the day and issued in their boxes to companies. Orders to companies were that the companies should proceed along the trench preceded by a bombing squad who would clear out the enemy. Here I first came up against the CO as Adjutant. I was a very new adjutant; he was a Boer War veteran. I had, however, learnt at a bombing course how one set about the sort of job that had to be done: he had never used bombs. The orders to companies had to go out under my signature and I felt they were all wrong. Why, I felt, should four companies walk down a trench under the enemy barrage – which would open at once – when only the few men at the head of the columns could actually do any effective work. A bombing squad needed a

thrower, carriers and a couple of bayonet men to rush round each traverse after the bomb had landed and burst. No one else could be effective except for replacing casualties and carrying bombs and looking out for a counter raid over the top by the enemy – a most unlikely proceeding. Therefore I said two companies at least should remain in reserve in the shelter of the tunnel – if only to preserve their strength and numbers to meet the almost inevitable counter attack. But I met as on other occasions with, 'Are you commanding this battalion or am I?' If I had had more experience of the 'Old Man' at that time I should have had a quiet word with Watson, the Brigade Major, on the phone or hopped back on the quiet to see the Brigadier but, alas, I did not commit this breach of military etiquette. How many lives it would have saved. How bitter I felt after as I looked at the torn bodies of those poor fellows hanging limp in the barbed wire through which they had tried to escape.

CAPTAIN CHARLES STORMONT GIBBS MC, 4TH SUFFOLK REGIMENT

The venture started well with the bombers making tremendous progress with the help of a tank, sweeping along both the first and second German trenches, engulfing score upon score of prisoners, and by 10.00 a.m. reaching a point just 250 metres from the Sensée.

The attack was only made along the trenches: there was no bombing along the tunnel. But as our men passed each tunnel entrance they had to chuck a bomb down and then go down and kill or capture. At least that was the idea – poor Suffolk peasants. Our artillery barrage was strong and accurate. It shattered the German positions sufficiently to make things easy and there was little resistance. In what I should guess to be some three hours the 4th Suffolks had taken all their objectives. The chief hero was a very small and young lance-corporal who descended to the tunnel at some point and returned with about seventy prisoners all following him like lambs. But

what a toll of casualties! Our companies had been in the open all the time and back to the aid post poured a continual stream of wounded along the tunnel. The doctor was working incessantly for three or four hours with only a five minute interval to slip into our den and eat a piece of bread and cheese with hands all over blood. I had helped him in intervals of dealing with messages, orders and telephone calls to Brigade. I remember a young corporal coming along with one arm hanging by a piece of flesh and skin. 'Turn your head round, lad,' said Gaston. Then he neatly cut off the arm and threw it under the bench. 'Off you go,' he said as the orderly quietly applied a dressing. And the man, like the rest, would have a mile or two to walk before getting to the Casualty Clearing Station. Then he would have found ambulances full of stretcher cases.

CAPTAIN CHARLES STORMONT GIBBS MC, 4TH SUFFOLK REGIMENT

As the parties dourly worked their bloody way towards the valley bottom, they were blocked by an equally fierce hostile bombing party. Through the most elementary of errors, they were unable to put up any resistance.

And soon came the news that we had no one left in the front trench – all were wounded or madly trying to escape with the wounded. Then came the report that our bombs which we kept hurling up to the front were duds. They were not exploding for they had not been detonated. A Mills bomb has a small detonator which is inserted at the ammunition dump under Brigade supervision before being sent up to the infantry. We had received a large number of bombs which had not received their detonators and so were useless – enough to cause a debacle, especially when the men were exposed to heavy artillery bombardment and had been reduced by casualties to a handful. When the enemy had driven us back for a considerable distance along our front line he was of course able to work down the communication trenches and get in behind our men who were holding their own in the support trench. When these were attacked in front and behind they tried to save themselves by bolting across the open. But they ran into barbed wire and were mopped up to a man by machine-guns.

The Brigade must be told the exact situation. I was in the signallers' den trying again at the telephone, with no effect. A runner must be sent. It would not take long and perhaps I could thus avoid what seemed certain death.

I rejoined the CO after sending back a full report to Brigade. He evidently felt the end of the war for us was approaching. He never showed fear but on an occasion of this sort he always changed and behaved in a human and cheerful manner instead of his usual rather fierce and surly way of carrying on. 'Well,' he said, 'they won't be here just yet but we had better get ready for them. We have got two men each; one of us must hold the front trench and the other the support.' Away down towards Fontaine, bombs were exploding intermittently as the enemy worked his way along against no resistance. I went back to have one more try on the phone. This time they had got it through; a sweating signaller was there who said he found the break nearly back as far as Brigade. I got through to Watson who had just got my report. His cheerful matter-of-fact voice was good to hear. 'So you've got to save the 33rd Division from disaster, have you? Well, you'll have a job but good luck!' And then he added, 'We are filling both trenches and the tunnel with barbed wire just in front of Brigade so that will probably stop them till we can get more troops up.' That was quite useful to know, though it did not affect us because we should be dead before the enemy reached that wire.

Preparations made, we waited. There was not much danger from shell-fire for the enemy gunners could not tell just how far their men had got and we were so close to the enemy that all the shelling was behind us. On the other hand since Brigade had got our report and knew the situation they had been able to put one gun to fire heavily on the advancing enemy. This was very fortunate because the explosion of shells concealed from the enemy the fact that they were meeting with no actual resistance by bombs. They probably expected to meet someone round each corner they went, though really no one was there. So I sat as the evening drew on. Slowly but surely the enemy came on. The bombs could be seen rising and heard falling, getting always nearer until at last perhaps they guessed they had re-taken all the ground they had lost. Would they come on?

I sat with revolver aimed at the next corner round which they would have to come. How long I don't know. Certainly till after dark. And there lamely the story ends in a complete memory fade-out.

We six were, of course, relieved during the night by another battalion – six hundred or so relieving six.

CAPTAIN CHARLES STORMONT GIBBS MC, 4TH SUFFOLK REGIMENT

Accounts of this action are understandably meagre. The advance to the rear protected by a creeping barrage, also developed well at first, with the 'inner' right-hand battalions tracking the Hindenburg Line alongside the bombers. On their left, despite more robust resistance, progress was also satisfactory for the 2nd Argyll and Sutherland Highlanders and 1st Middlesex, until a mistake by British gunners shattered all hopes. At a certain step in the creeping barrage line two artillery brigades had been assigned the identical coordinates; the result was a gap where no shells were falling. Before the error could be rectified, the Germans in the unmolested sector had taken advantage and choked the assault by machine-gun fire. Soon afterwards they counter-attacked, first isolating two British companies in the open, and then, by virtue of a clever dart down a communication trench into the Hindenburg Line, also cut off large numbers of British who had earlier bombed their way south past that point. In order to save their skins

these men were obliged to abandon the captured trenches and creep back using any cover they could find: their fate on the wire was described by Captain Stormont Gibbs.

It had been acknowledged before the attacks that any failure in the southernmost sector would place Major General J.M. Shea's 30th Division in great peril, whether or not his own endeavours proved successful. There was probably no more open and featureless a landscape on the Western Front as that which his troops were presented with: it was a gunner's dream, and much would depend upon how the British heavies had tamed German batteries. Here, as elsewhere indeed, it was shown that their efforts had failed, for the moment the British attacked a tremendous protective barrage descended. The first waves reached the German 'front line', but few enemy were found. When the advance moved deeper into the danger zone scores of machine guns cut it to shreds. The Germans, according to orders, had moved from where they were expected to be. The attacks withered; it was an object lesson in elastic defence.

It was at 2.25 p.m. that commanders each received a telegram from General Allenby. It simply said that the Blue Line – the first objective – must be taken at all costs. After a brief consultation Haldane settled upon 6.00 p.m.

We got a good tot and moved off. On the way we noticed a lot of dead men lying about. On arriving in the trench I reported to the Sergeant-Major. 'What about my pack?' I said. 'Leave it here,' he replied. 'I don't think you will need it again.' He must have known that we did not have much chance of coming out of this attack. The order to attack with the 19th Manchesters was ordered for 6 pm – zero. We went over in four waves, each of two lines. We had hardly left the trench when the enemy guns opened up from the front and both flanks. Despite casu-

alties the advance continued although at one point the whole line was temporarily held up on account of heavy machine-gun fire and also a lot of the officers had become casualties. The regiment was now led by two young officers – Sergeant Major C. Sedgwick was killed and the two young officers were hit. The regiment was reduced to about a hundred men and no officers. We got into the trench and hand-to-hand fighting took place. For about twenty minutes we were left in undisturbed occupation. Then the enemy launched a counter attack from the front and right flank with rifle-grenades. Strong parties of bombers advanced towards the trench and though the men put up a good fight using all their bombs with good effect, we were overwhelmed by weight of numbers and forced to retire. As we fell back, the enemy followed, showing great daring in bringing forward machine-guns. About 55 men got back to the old front line. Every officer who took part in the attack became a casualty and only a few managed to get back.
PRIVATE PADDY KENNEDY, 18TH MANCHESTER REGIMENT

Yet again, the British had been drawn into a trap. The 18th Manchesters suffered 361 casualties. Paddy Kennedy's experience mirrored that of his entire division, the 30th. The gains for the day were some old German practice trenches and a small section of front line. The chronicle of the 50th Division for 23 April was a slightly happier one, largely on account of the employment of classic attritional measures.

On April 23, St. George's Day, the 150th Infantry Brigade attacked from the top of Wancourt Tower Hill. A good number of prisoners were made, but Guémappe still held out and the Germans launched a heavy counter-attack along this part of the front. In the morning I went forward to some dugouts east of Telegraph Hill where the General, Brigade-Major, and Signalling Officer were stationed for this battle. Our Brigade of course was in reserve, except the 4th N.F. who were

The heavier guns are moved up. 60-pounders of the Royal Garrison Artillery firing from positions west of Monchy. IWM Q2018

attached to the 151st Infantry Brigade. From this place near Telegraph Hill I got a good view of the battle around Guémappe. About midday Brigadier-General Cameron of the 151st Infantry Brigade took over command of the 50th Divisional front, and at once made preparations to renew the attack in the afternoon. I was sent over to the Elm Trees dugouts to find out exactly what he proposed to do with the 4th N.F., and he was then busily engaged with the Artillery officers arranging the barrages. Before the attack was resumed, Guémappe was heavily shelled by our siege guns, a wonderful sight. The whole place seemed to disappear in dense clouds of dust and smoke. It had been a ding-dong battle all day, attack and counter-attack, and at this point neither side had gained much advantage. The Germans had not only repelled the attack on our right, but had attempted to push through into Heninel, in the Cojeul Valley. Fortunately, however, the 149th M.G. Company, commanded by Major Morris, stopped this movement by well-directed fire to our right flank. When, however, the attack was renewed in the afternoon things went better for us. The Germans were pushed down the hill from Wancourt Tower and Guémappe was taken. The 4th N.F. did well, getting to a place called Buck Trench. And the Divisional front was advanced to a point not far from the outskirts of Chérisy. It was unfortunate that we had no fresh troops at this juncture to press home the attack.

CAPTAIN FRANCIS BUCKLEY, 149TH INFANTRY BRIGADE STAFF, 50TH (NORTHUMBRIAN) DIVISION

As soon as the ridge was taken a hostile counter-attack began to cause no small degree of concern and even panic; in one sector it was acute enough to cause British field gunners to remove breach blocks. But fears were unfounded – the enemy appeared eager only to reoccupy ground lost on the day. But at least Guémappe and the ridge should be permanently eliminated from the equation, the former being evacuated after two hours, but for

some time remaining unoccupied by either side on account of shelling and the risk of counter-attack. When fighting subsided on the 24th the British line would lie a good 400 metres east of the crest of Wancourt Ridge.

At neighbouring Monchy, the unchanged shape and nature of the front meant that Haldane had some awkward decisions to make for his 15th (Scottish) on the right, 29th in the centre and 17th (Northern) Division hard up against the river. Within the sector the distance to the Blue Line varied from 800 metres to well over 2 kilometres. There was no time to carry out line-straightening, a seriously hazardous enterprise in any case, and none were sure of the enemy's dispositions, so the creeping barrage had to be designed to suit what was *believed* to be true. Given the history of the sector, the objectives – although not distant – appear ambitious: Pelves, the Bois du Sart and Bois du Vert, Infantry Hill (the closest target) and St Rohart Factory on the Cambrai road.

The 17th Division recorded scant profit – as a result of vicious artillery and machine-gun fire its line advancing a meagre 275 metres, at the close still bent stubbornly backwards. It was noted here that even in the midst of major action some enemy shellfire originated from the opposite side of the river, suggesting a disquietingly confident level of observation and control by German artillery – when they should have had their hands full with the 51st Division assaults. This was alarming, for if the high ground before Monchy was not taken but the divisions north of the Scarpe progressed, it would leave the British in a serious enfilade situation whereby the guns required to follow up the advance beyond Roeux would be open to lateral German observation; the valleys and folds in the ground which would otherwise hide

British 18-pounder batteries under hostile shellfire. IWM Q6292

and protect the guns would be in full view.

At noon on the 23rd the position about Monchy was not encouraging: it was taking longer than anticipated to clear the Wancourt Ridge and Guémappe, so both flanks were weak. Guns were nevertheless bravely brought forward early, and there was a thriving counter-attack in progress on VII Corps' centre. Because of the fractured nature of fighting in front of the village, more were expected, and they duly came – in force – at 4.00 p.m. It slowed everything down for the British.

Hostile counter-attacks, even failed or partly successful ones, had knock-on effects in that the considerable time required to fight them off and then resolve the subsequent confusion could have been employed to further one's own advance. This deliberate German tactic unsettled both the 15th and 29th Divisions, with the result that at nightfall there were once again troops spread all over the battlefield and no semblance of a line. Save for small elements, the Blue objective still could not be said to be in British hands.

Across the river Roeux, the Chemical Works, the station, Greenland Hill and the twin woods Hausa and Delbar that sat upon its northern extension faced Major General G.M. Harper's 51st (Highland) Division. On his left lay the 37th Division. Their objectives were divided into four lines. Since 10 April, at a cost of thousands of lives on both sides, hardly a consequential metre had been gained in the sector. XVII Corps commander, Lieutenant General Fergusson, was profoundly aware of the extraordinary contribution his troops had already made and the inadequate rest they had been allowed. So worried was he about their capabilities on 23 April, that he expressed his feelings directly to Allenby, adding by way of

extra persuasion that the proposed final objective lay at the extreme range of his field guns, weapons that were becoming less accurate through wear because of the hammering they had recently received. Could he therefore please restrict the objective in the first instance to the capture and consolidation of the environs of Roeux? The answer was negative, but as a pacifier two 34th Division battalions were loaned to the Corps. It would also have five tanks.

Above 37th Division, and taking the battleground to its northern boundary in a remarkably narrow sector, was 63rd (Royal Naval) Division. Entering the Arras scrimmage for the first time, their primary target was the village of Gavrelle; a leap of approximately a kilometre would deposit the land-locked sailors in the central *place*.

It was simply not possible to take a step beyond the ruins of Fampoux without drawing fire from Roeux, Greenland Hill or a selection of emplacements around Plouvain, all of which fell within the scope of Fergusson's troops when they jumped-off at 4.45 a.m. 154th Brigade's right-hand attack towards the village was instantly checked. One supposed protector, tank C7 commanded by Second Lieutenant Victor Smith, was not in place to assist, arriving late as a result of meeting a blockade of wounded on his approach route. The delay was only brief, and as Victor Smith's report outlines the contribution of his crew was great.

I soon caught up with the Infantry who were held up by machine gun fire in MOUNT PLEASANT WOOD. At their request I altered my course and made for the northern side of the wood running parallel with the trench which we held at the south of the wood and which the enemy held at the north. I was told that a bombing party would follow me up the trench. Having cleared this wood, I pushed on towards the village of ROEUX, where I again met the Infantry who had come round the other side of MOUNT PLEASANT WOOD, where they were again held up by machine gun fire which came from the buildings. Our barrage could only have been very slight to judge from the comparatively small amount of damage which was done to the buildings. Here I used 200 rounds of 6-pounder ammunition. It is difficult to estimate with any accuracy the number of machine guns actually "put out". One of my best targets was a party of thirty men whom we drove out of a house with 6-pounders and then sprayed with Lewis gun fire. I am sure that at least one shell dropped amongst these – this made a distinct impression. Another target that presented itself was a party of men coming towards us. I do not know whether they intended giving themselves up or whether they were a bombing party – I took them for the latter.

Parties were frequently seen coming up from the rear, through gaps in the buildings. Twice an enemy offi-cer rallied some dozen or so men and rushed a house that we had already cleared. Here again a 6-pdr. through the window disposed of any of the enemy remaining in the buildings. In regard to the machine guns in the wood, we could only locate them by little puffs of smoke at which we fired. We did not take our departure until these puffs had disappeared and there was in consequence reason-able grounds to suppose that the guns had been knocked out. Finally our infantry reached the village. Apparently there was no officer commanding our infantry in this part of the line.

The report also indicates the nature of the fighting in the village. A second machine, C22, went into action on time, following the partial shelter of the railway embankment towards the station. German 'K' ammunition was immedi-ately effective, however, wounding two inside including the OC, so the tank tracked back,

Segment of Third Army Panorama 560 showing the Roeux sector from a position near Hyderabad Redoubt, 11 May 1917. IWM

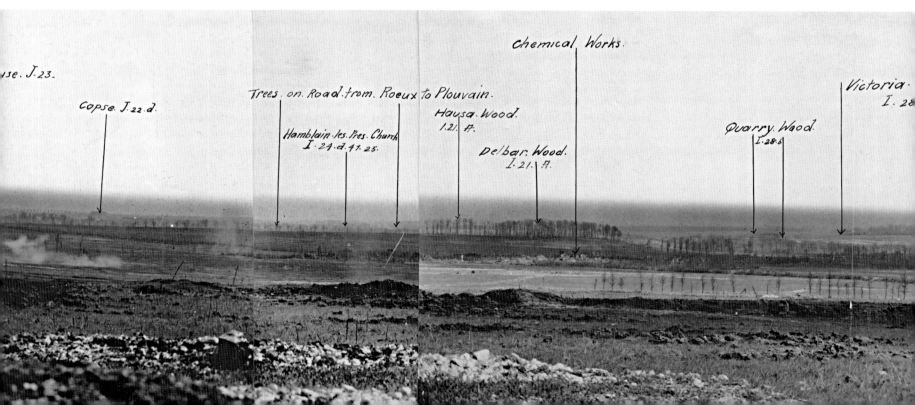

deposited its wounded, then set out again under the command of a Sergeant J. Noel. It too reached the buildings and took part in the desperate struggle to steal/maintain possession, the Germans fighting a furious battle in the knowledge that at any moment one of their own counter-attacks was likely to arrive and clean up the Scots. The counter-attack set out, but was caught by well-aimed British shrapnel, and machine guns firing from about the Hyderabad Redoubt.

153rd Brigade, north of the railway, had more space within which to work. They were ensnared by machine guns, H.E. and shrapnel, and forced to shell-hole hop down the slope towards the objective. Those who reached the railway worked their way methodically and grimly through the Chemical Works, joining tank C22 in clearing the surrounding build-

ings. The tanks were proving their worth. Amongst the buildings they were out of harm's way of artillery; the weaponry – Lewis guns and 6-pounders – was ideal for the task, slinging a shell though a window, or spraying attacking or fleeing Germans at short and medium range. But yet again little news was reaching headquarters, the mixture of dust and smoke obliterating direct view, whilst the German protective barrage cut telephone cables and blocked the routes of runners. Only in mid-morning was observation possible, just in time for British gunners to help annihilate the first of several counter-attacks from Greenland Hill.

The pressure remained intense throughout the day, with wild and confused fighting and tragic casualties. The result mocked the Highlanders. Having lost in the region of 2,000

dead, wounded and missing (as indeed had the Germans), but taken the village and the Chemical Works, a counter-attack in the gloaming of 23 April drove the Scots halfway back to their 4.45 a.m. positions.

Arras, and especially the Roeux sector, had been the ruination of the 51st Division; this fine unit could have done no more. 34th Division took over during the night and the Scots slogged wearily back to town.

That the enemy chose to invest so much effort in defending Roeux instead of taking up a flexible stance on Greenland Hill was perhaps testament to the strictness of their recent training. The garrisons had fought on and on as they had been instructed, always expecting the saviour counter-attack. Eventually one succeeded and the purpose was achieved. In the face of such grim determination, how could the necropolis be conquered? The solution surely had to be based upon the guns.

23RD APRIL

The 37th Division are using the smoke with H.E. barrage. The attack started at 4.45 a.m. It appeared to be very successful but, after many varied reports, we seem to have made good progress on our right but not on our left, partly owing to heavy casualties in officers and partly because the division on our left had not gone on. We have had numerous targets all day. Our losses are heavy especially in officers but the Hun must have lost far more; though the Hun seems to have more tactical instinct than our men – probably due to more training.

26TH APRIL

I reconnoitred the country beyond Fampoux looking for better gun positions but found that there were none available till the Division south of the River Scarpe on our right had taken the high ground that was now in front of them. But I did a sketch of the country showing

Greenland Hill and this, coupled with a captured German map, helped the Corps Commander, Sir Charles Fergusson, to decide about the next attack.
BRIGADIER GENERAL HENRY TUDOR, CRA 9TH (SCOTTISH) DIVISION

The British artillery were stumped. As long as Roeux, Greenland Hill and the Bois du Sart Ridge held out, German gunners astride the Scarpe retained a colossal advantage. The sheer continuing aggression of the enemy was the greatest shock, for they too had been in action for a fortnight. The 37th Division, whose first objective was the Roeux-Gavrelle road, also felt the full force of the 'new' German defence on the morning of 23 April.

When we got into the front line the platoon officer briefed us: Zero hour will be such-and-such a time then he would describe the objective in this case (brown and red lines), don't get too close to our barrage etc. etc. When zero hour arrived the officer would blow a whistle. If you didn't hear it you saw everybody mounting the parapet, so you did the same and on you went, with the best of luck and a spoonful of rum. Zero hour and over the top we went. Machine gun and artillery fire met us as we entered No Man's Land and took its toll. We had not gone far when two in our team were blown up by a shell which burst at their feet. We had gone about 50 yards when suddenly I was down and on my back. My leg felt as if it had been hit with an iron bar, my leg went numb – a bullet had passed through my thigh a few inches from my groin. George Brazewell picked up the gun, waved to me and went on. I rolled into a shell hole – it was already occupied by a chap who was moaning with pain. He was badly wounded in the foot and somewhere in his body. He was covered in blood. I was just going to see if I could help him when he sagged and stopped moaning. I realised he was dead. I was dressing my wound when two men who were wounded jumped

Left A family living in Roeux in 1916. BHK Abt.IV BS-N7/2 295

Below A shepherd in occupied Roeux. AJ

into the shell hole, then made a dash for our old front line. I am afraid I had made a poor job of bandaging my wound for it was still bleeding. I began to feel a bit sick. Then the Germans opened up a barrage in front of their line and it started to creep to our line. I peered over the edge of the shell hole, watching its progress. "This is it", I told myself, "no one can hope to live through this lot." My fear grew as it seemed the barrage tilled every inch of the ground around me. My stomach was in knots and my heart thumped alarmingly. The barrage inched nearer and I felt weak and although my leg was still numb I tried to crawl out of the shell hole to get back to our line. That was the last I remembered. I don't know how long I was out but when I came to and my wits returned I was being lifted onto a stretcher by stretcher bearers who took me to the first-aid station where they dressed my wound. From there I was transferred to the casualty clearing station.

PRIVATE JOHN MORTIMER MM, 10TH YORK AND LANCASTER REGIMENT

The York and Lancasters suffered more than others at the hands of the German defence. Elsewhere progress was better, even good, with tremendous localized success. The Division managed an advance of between 1.5 and 2 kilometres and could have gone further as outstanding gunnery fragmented large parties of advancing storm troops. Any escapees still moving forward were routed by machine guns. But because Roeux refused to fall, British efforts were in vain.

On First Army's left flank lay crumbling Gavrelle. The village was to be taken in three bounds: the twin trenches of *III Stellung* formed the first objective, Gavrelle centre the second and, 300 metres east of village, the *Gavrelle Riegel* was the final line.

During pegging out in preparation for laying tapes to guide troops in the attack just before dawn, it was found that the wire was poorly cut, the entanglements averaging 6 metres thick. It was for this very reason that no attacks had been planned at this time against the neighbouring Oppy sector. Aircraft reconnaissance confirmed the situation. Only on the left centre of Gavrelle in 189th Brigade territory were a few gaps evident. To the north facing 190th Brigade, the wire looked practically impenetrable. Postponement was requested but vetoed by divisional commander Major General C.E. Lawrie, so it was therefore decided to enter at the weakest points and bomb their way outwards in the same way as the 21st Division in the Hindenburg Line. A creeping barrage plan was laid, and batteries of Stokes mortars and Lewis-gun teams brought forward to help keep the enemy subdued whilst the initial penetration took place. A more general assault would follow. It was a fine morning, clear and dry, and the ground was not seriously damaged.

The men were to go into battle without their greatcoats or packs, but haversacks were to be carried on the back, with waterproof sheets on the top, under the flap. Each had three sandbags under the braces, across the back. Box respirators were worn in the 'alert' position. Ammunition consisted of not more than 120 rounds per man, with only 50 for bombers, signallers, scouts, runners, Lewis and machine gunners, Stokes mortar crews and carrying parties. Each bomber had 15 number 5 grenades, carried in buckets, waistcoats or sandbags. Rifle grenadiers were supplied with 15 number 23 grenades with rods and cartridges. All ranks had two number 5 grenades in each top pocket, with two aeroplane flares in the jacket side-pockets. Each company had 12 SOS rockets. The last two waves of each battalion carried picks and shovels, in the proportion of four shovels to one pick.

189 BRIGADE ORDER No. 88, APPENDIX IV

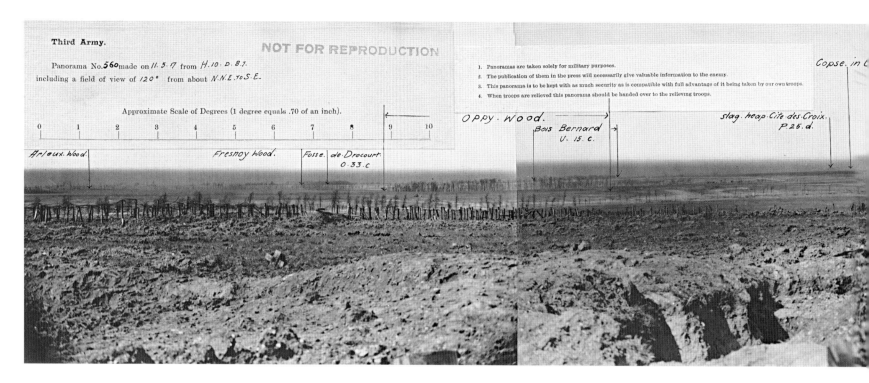

Third Army.

Panorama No.**560** made on *11.5.17* from *H.10.D.8.7.*
including a field of view of *120°* from about *N.N.E. To S.E.*

Approximate Scale of Degrees (1 degree equals .70 of an inch).

0 1 2 3 4 5 6 7 8 9 10

1. Panoramas are taken solely for military purposes.
2. The publication of them in the press will necessarily give valuable information to the enemy.
3. This panorama is to be kept with as much security as is compatible with full advantage of it being taken by our own troops.
4. When troops are relieved this panorama should be handed over to the relieving troops.

Arleux Wood.   *Fresnoy Wood.*   *Fosse. de Drocourt 0.33.c*   *Bois Bernard U. 15. c*   *OPPY. WOOD.*   *slag. heap. Cité des Croix. P.25.d.*   *Copse. in C*

Drake and Nelson battalions (the Royal Naval Division named its battalions after British maritime icons, their rank system also respecting the naval tradition) led and gained the first objective within ten minutes, as did the 4th Bedfords on their right flank. On the left there was no way through. It was known that the moment the attack began, a German protective barrage would fall on no man's land. To avoid this, Commander Arthur Asquith, commanding the supporting Hood Battalion, disobeyed orders and brought his troops forward early, following close behind the leading waves.

The instruction went that we were not to move until the barrage had lifted off the German front line, immediately in front of Gavrelle. Well any old campaigner knows that to wait until the barrage moves and have three or four hundred yards to walk is simply murder, because as soon as the barrage opens and they realize an attack is coming they start to shell the reserves. Asquith, instead of waiting until the barrage had lifted, took us forward – I think to within about 50 yards of the barrage. His judgement was perfect, and we were on their line before Jerry knew anything about it. I honestly think that we men of the Hood who survived the battle owe it to Asquith ignoring orders – and the orders were quite definite. Anyhow, we got mixed up: fighting in a village is different from fighting in the open. The ground in front of us and Gavrelle was not pockmarked with shellholes like the Somme; it was quite level and open. Ideal territory for tanks, but we didn't have any. We could go forward more or less in a line, whereas on the Somme you were in and out of shell holes that were all over the place. When we got into the village it was different. Jerries were in the cellars and we were in the open, and by then it was quite light, so we were perfect targets. In the village there were bricks flying about, rifle and machine-gun fire. You couldn't keep in any formation. Sometimes you got under a half blown-down house, and other times you got over the top. The wire in front was piled up in

Looking across the plain beyond the Point-du-Jour ridge towards the Oppy and Gavrelle sectors. IWM Third Army Panorama 560, 11.5.17.

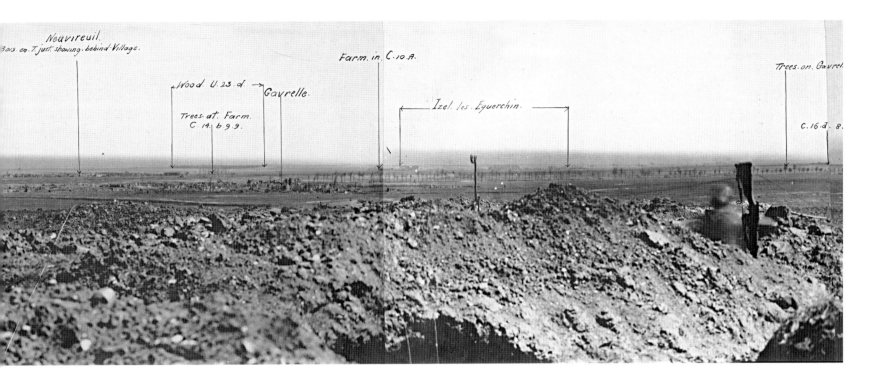

Neuvireuil.
Bois on 7 just showing behind Village.

Wood U.23.d →
Gavrelle.

Trees at Farm.
C.14.b.9.9.

Farm in C.10.A.

Izel les Eguerchin.

Trees on Gavrel

C.16.d. 8.

heaps, as it usually was by an artillery bombardment.

I remember as we got to the first objective it didn't seem too bad. We seemed to be organized, but when we got to the second objective [Yellow Line], a road that runs through the village, oh, dear me! There was no line and no sort of direction. You couldn't see any officers and you couldn't see any men. Sometimes there were three or four together, and sometimes you were on your own, wondering where everybody had got to. When I got into this trench, which was just in front of a road, about 10 to 15 yards from it, I came across an officer lying down. He was lying flat and I remember trying to undo some barbed wire on what was left of one of his legs. He was a sub-lieutenant. I also remember turning him over and there was a sort of a grin on his face, which was red because of the brick dust, as well as the blood. Because of the smoke and dust, you had to spit all the time – you just couldn't help it – and you also kept rubbing your eyes.
LEADING SEAMAN JOSEPH MURRAY, HOOD BATTALION, 63RD (ROYAL NAVAL) DIVISION

The creeping barrage marched across the village and out of the east side, leaving snipers and machine guns in hidden pockets. Asquith mentions being troubled by shorts from his own guns and although this was not an instantly soluble problem, the attack had to carry on regardless. Isolated parties of Germans were soon beginning to give themselves up, but as the attack reached the eastern edge of the village, in the distance they spotted the inevitable counter-attacks forming.

At 10 am I found Colonel Lewis, OC Nelson, at the west end of a ditch. Lines and driblets of enemy began to make their appearance, advancing over the plain from the east, north-east and south-east. About 10.30 am our barrage reopened, rather short of the oncoming enemy lines. Some ran back but most of them came on, and disappeared into a trench or hollow about 800 yards to our east front. Those north of the main Arras road could and did get to the high ground within about 200 yards of the north-east corner of the village.

At 10.53 am Colonel Lewis of the Nelsons received a signal, timed about 9 am, from brigade ordering him and the Hoods to advance at 10.30 am for about 300 yards. The 10.30 am barrage which was to cease at 11.15 am was to help us make this advance, not, as we had supposed, to impede the massing of the enemy opposite us. We decided that it was too late to attempt to do anything with this barrage. It was out of the question to organize any further attack in the remaining 22 minutes of barrage, even if the barrage had succeeded in quietening the snipers and machine guns on our front and north-east of us, which it had not. We sent back word to this effect.

OC Drake sent me a note about this time saying enemy were advancing in large numbers, could I send him a company. I sent Sub-Lieutenant Sennitt to tell him that they were also advancing on our front, and I did not wish to send a company by my only road to him, the exposed cemetery road. But I was close, and standing by to help him at any time. At this time we thought the enemy intended an immediate counter-attack. It was hot and cloudless. The troops were drowsy, tired and apathetic, it was difficult to stimulate them into any sort of energy or interest. The enemy had been shelling the western half of the village very heavily and were throwing some shells into our eastern part of it. Our own heavies dropped shell after shell into the buildings of the mayor's house which we held, forcing Sub-Lieutenant Grant Dalton, now commanding there in place of Sub-Lieutenant Cooke, to send away some of his garrison, and to put the rest in the cellars. I was anxious for our north and north-east flank, so I went north of the main Arras road to reconnoitre.

HOOD BATTALION WAR DIARY, ACCOUNT WRITTEN BY ARTHUR ASQUITH

Asquith found no one on his left flank. Unknown to him, the right had benefited through the remarkable action of a tank,

Second Lieutenant C. le Clair's C4 (No. 561), which reached the Roeux-Gavrelle road north of the inn and turned towards the village to destroy several machine guns. The guns were silenced, but not before they had wounded five, mainly through armour-piercing bullets. Le Clair turned his machine homewards to evacuate the wounded, rearm and find replacement crew members. He made it back, but the damage to the tank proved too severe and she was unable to return. At least Asquith's right flank was safe. Back in the village hostile sniping was causing serious problems, and counter-attacks were constantly forming to the north and east. Consolidation was frantic and by mid-afternoon it was becoming clear that no further offensive progress was likely.

At 4.30pm orders reached OC Nelson, OC Drake and me to name our own time for a barrage to enable us to push out 300-400 yards east and north-east. This order had taken about three hours to reach us. We all agreed that the situation did not admit to any further offensive action.

HOOD BATTALION WAR DIARY, ACCOUNT WRITTEN BY ARTHUR ASQUITH

The village had been cleared, but like Monchy it had become a perilous salient. Unable to fully repulse counter-attacks, the neighbouring 37th Division had ended up with a most peculiar shape to their line which did little to protect Gavrelle.

The right flank of the Drake Battalion was now in the air through the failure of the 111th Brigade, and we were in danger of being forced to yield the ground we had so gallantly fought for and won. All reserve machine guns were therefore rushed forward and a defensive flank was formed in time to meet the German counter-attacking troops. A hostile aeroplane flew over the front

Above German shell monument near Gavrelle. The inscription reads: *In Remembrance of the 1914/15 Campaign, 1st Reserve Field Artillery Regiment, 1st Battalion.* BHK Abt.IV BS-N 53/4A 46

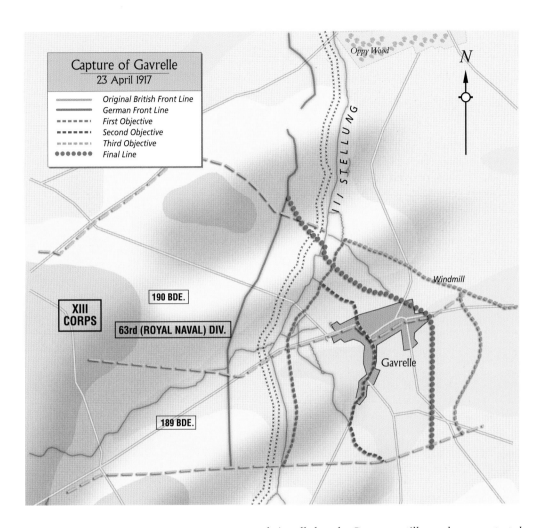

Capture of Gavrelle
23 April 1917

Original British Front Line
German Front Line
First Objective
Second Objective
Third Objective
Final Line

XIII CORPS

190 BDE.

63rd (ROYAL NAVAL) DIV.

189 BDE.

III STELLUNG

Oppy Wood

Windmill

Gavrelle

N

Above The action of the Royal Naval Division that captured Gavrelle on 23 April 1917

bombardments were repeated with such frequency that it seemed as if the enemy intended to blast us out of the village. When the fire lifted to our back areas, however, wave after wave of German infantry pressed forward, and counter-attack succeeded counter-attack. Our artillery were now functioning as never before. No sooner was each attack launched than they placed a heavy barrage behind the advancing columns, which crept towards our lines and met a protective barrage placed in front of our own positions. Through this inferno our men poured rifle and machine-gun fire. In all, seven organized attacks were met in this manner. Gavrelle was ours.
LEADING SEAMAN THOMAS MACMILLAN, CLERK TO THE 189TH BRIGADE

Although the Gavrelle *Riegel* and fortified Gavrelle Mill were still to fall, the work of the RND, who took 479 prisoners, was certainly the brightest note on another deeply dreary day north of the river. Thomas Macmillan was incorrect about 111th Brigade; considering the resistance faced, they had done every bit as well as the RND. However, having been presented with deeper advance, their final position left a sharp backward dog-leg in the line south of Gavrelle. Along the northern edge of the village a defensive flank of sorts existed, but because of 190th Brigade's failure to breach the wire, it was not as secure as had been hoped.

In the early evening as the fog of war slowly lifted, it became clear that British troops were on the Blue Line in only a handful of places.

No further progress was possible on the 23rd, so at 8.35 p.m. Allenby ordered all Corps commanders to prepare to gain the Red Line the following afternoon: the bull-at-a-gate attacks would continue. From dawn on 24 April intense shelling and violent counter-attacks were seen north of the Scarpe, all of which were beaten back. The troops were tiring now against

and signalled to the German artillery, who concentrated on the village with all the venom they possessed. When the fire cleared, the counter-attacking troops came on, but were caught in the open and decimated by our artillery and machine-gun fire. The hard fighting began to tell on the Hoods, and in response to an appeal for relief the Howe Battalion of the 188th Brigade was brought forward to replace them. At dawn on 24 April our positions were bombarded relentlessly, whilst throughout the day the

an enemy that was apparently ever strengthening. During the next few days positions remained static save for VII Corps securing most of the Blue Line overlooking the Sensée valley. At Monchy there were more attacks; gains could again be measured in tens of metres. Much as the British would have liked to occupy the Bois du Sart ridge, and the Germans reoccupy Monchy, neither was able to negotiate the valley slaughterhouse before Hill 100.

The tit-for-tat went on. Counter-attack pressure could now only grow, and although they were becoming less and less successful their permanent anticipation was debilitating in itself. As their amateur army, many entirely unacquainted with soldiering just a year before, battled on, the professionals – Haig, Allenby, Horne and their staffs – deliberated: resistance had *not* been as strong as heretofore, they decided, and the attack of 23/24 April had sufficiently weakened the enemy to make another phase that much easier. They knew the troops were drained, but the variation in performance by units who had seen the same number of days in action pointed to there being perhaps more localized reasons why some had profited to a degree whilst others had not.

The reason lay largely in how von Lossberg had examined and then chosen to defend particular localities. In places, such as the Hindenburg Line from Croisilles southwards, he was confident enough to let divisional commanders organize their own defence, but only having made certain they knew exactly when a position might best be abandoned. Troops must fall back and assume new positions and tactics at the optimum moment, having done maximum damage. Abandoning a trench line was no longer looked upon as dishonourable; indeed, if practised correctly it was supremely beneficial to

the Army *Gruppe* as a whole, for there now lay several deep zones of defence inside which a penetrating attack could be surgically dissected.

It left the secondary and tertiary lines of defence behind the original 9 April front, plus those which von Lossberg was in the process of installing, primarily for protection of the heavier artillery. Having accepted the fact that whatever defensive system they chose to employ, if the British were intent on pressing hard on a wide front German casualties were going to be numerous; von Lossberg was simply devising methods of not *permanently* losing territory: let the enemy have it, thin his ranks, then take it back again.

It was harsh but effective treatment, and repercussions were not long in appearing, especially in men who had 'seen a bit' and been unlucky enough to have missed out on their full quota of rest, such as it was.

Above Gavrelle – in British hands but under hostile shellfire. IWM Third Army Panorama 118. Undated.

Below British prisoners under guard in a farm building on the Arras-Cambrai road. AC

25 APRIL 1917

My dear Father,

I am deeply sorry to say I have had a nervous breakdown and am now in the VI Corps Rest Station (officers). I never thought this would happen to me but I cracked up all of a sudden and now I suppose all my prospects in the Army are gone. They have been damnably unfair to me just because I wasn't always grousing. I have had more service in the field than all the CO's in the Division, but just because I wasn't an original 29th Division officer I couldn't get the month's leave that they all got, but I suppose it is no good grousing.

I got finished up at Monchy after going through 4 days heavy bombardment in which we twice had to change dug outs and had two blown in on top of us. On top of the strain was the horror of walking out through the village on the bodies of dead men and horses. I know you will know that I have done my best.

With fondest love to you and Mother.

29 APRIL 1917

My dear Father,

I am out of bed now but still in the Corps officers Rest Station, this afternoon I am being sent to a Casualty Clearing Station and from there will be evacuated to England. The doctor says it will be three or four months before I shall be fit for France again. I feel so sick over the whole thing, if only I had been given leave after Sailly Sallisel for a short time to get right away from all the horrors here I should have been all right now and should have been fit to stand the horrors of Monchy le Preux. However it can't be helped now and at present I feel glad of a temporary relief from it all. As soon as the future takes shape I will write and let you know, at present I am quite in the dark.

Can't write any more.

Fondest love to both of you.

BREVET LIEUTENANT COLONEL GEORGE STEVENS DSO, 2ND ROYAL FUSILIERS

George Stevens recovered to re-enter the war and serve through to the end. For the time being he was out of the Arras fight, which was destined to continue until the French position became clearer.

Sir Douglas Haig's meeting with General Robert Nivelle on 24 April was a frank one. In private he outlined the various options open to the two Allies should the French choose to draw a line under their failing – indeed, already failed – offensive. Nivelle was typically ebullient, assuring Haig, whose eyes were now firmly fixed on Flanders, that not only would his offensive continue, but that he would arrange a Reserve Army for British use when the time came. The next day Haig directed Sir Henry Rawlinson (Fourth Army) and Sir Hubert Gough (Fifth Army) to prepare attacks to breach the Hindenburg Line south of Quéant to take place after Bullecourt had fallen, an endeavour which Gough was in the midst of planning.

Twenty-four hours later the Commander-in-Chief was in Paris where he found the French War Minister Paul Painlevé in grim mood, hinting more than strongly that Nivelle's days were numbered. Haig was well aware, and of the view that Nivelle's successor's days might be equally transitory unless something radical was made to happen. A few hours later, his opinion on the merits of replacing Nivelle with Pétain was solicited by the Prime Minister, Alexandre Ribot. The question was diplomatically evaded – he was not there to discuss anything but his own needs and plans. Haig knew Nivelle was finished, but could the French sack a commander-in-chief in the midst of a great battle? It was unheard of.

For three full days Haig sought assurances that should the British plan and carry out more attacks at Arras, they would be supported by continuation on the Aisne. He received them in full. Forty-eight hours later there was still no sign of German collapse, but the first indications of a French one, for on this day, 29 April, there were signs of mutiny in the French army.

Whilst Haig was away there were more attacks at Arras. The 12th Division (VI Corps) made another attempt to straighten the line between Monchy and the river. It was the same old story: the Germans knew where the sticking point was, and on the evening of 28 April plastered the British trenches in front of Pelves with heavies, then attacked. From 4.35 a.m. the following morning, on the same ground, the combination of shelling, bombing, and cross-valley enfilade, restricted several gritty attempts by Berkshires, Suffolks and Norfolks to take Bayonet Trench and a section of Rifle Trench, both part of the first objective. Resistance was simply too fierce and organized to make progress. Across the river, XVII Corps planned a more ambitious attack to bring their line up to the mark laid down on 23 April, including Greenland Hill. The task was handed to the severely depleted and traumatized 34th and 37th Divisions. Neither had a battalion that was up to strength, some being only 25 per cent of normal establishment. So serious had recent losses been that not a single company had a full complement of officers. All that could be gainfully said in advance of this venture was that many of those who did form up were at least experienced.

Zero at 4.25 – a heavy barrage on the Chemical Works, but the machine guns were in front of them. I went on top to see the show start; we had a wonderful overhead machine gun barrage, the noise of which heartened us immensely – it sounded like thousands of whips cracked in the best hunting style. We could only see by the glare of the barrage, but our men went well out of the quarry and seemed to get well and cosily under the barrage; and then the Bosch barrage came down; it wasn't at all nice coming back from the quarry to H.Q. The 27th were very funny: they came out in dribs and drabs and as the shells burst these small groups ran to one another and formed larger ones and they looked just like Irishmen at a Race Meeting. When daylight really came, we couldn't see a soul. The Chemical Works had been badly bent, but that was about all, and our men were apparently holding on about 50 yards short of the Works. Could get no answer by runners, so sent a lad up to find out. He came back with the comforting news that all the officers were casualties. The men in front of the Chemical Works would, of course, have to stick until dark, but I wanted to find out how A-B (companies) had got on. McAndrew, a gunner F.O.O., went with Downey, lugging a big roll of telephone wire. They got this across the road O.K – the sniping and M.G. was horrid down the road – and found our line strung out in shell-holes just east of the road, and then Downey got hit, sniped through the head, along the side of it. McAndrew had the telephone fixed up, so I went up myself – found stragglers of the 27th still in the trench, lying in cubby-holes in the side of the trench, poked them out with my revolver and chased them over the top. A sniper was very busy in the railway embankment and nearly got me several times, so I sent two of my stalwart escort to fix him up and they came back with his helmet, rifle, bandolier and bayonet. It was a very nasty do crossing the road and apparently no one had had the sense to dig it up, so I set some men on to dig both sides (I had already had two runners killed there), and by evening we had a sheltered crossing dug. Meanwhile we had to run the gauntlet of M.G. fire from the Chemical Works, and weren't so long in nipping across. I found things in a fearful schemozzle when I reached our men. They were in the Bosch front line, such as it was, just a line of shell-holes, joined up and of course blown to glory, however I found McAndrew and

German stormtroopers employing smoke to screen a counterattack. AJ

got hold of a sergeant. Poor Downey was badly hit, fracture of the skull, but we could not get him across the road – it was much too dangerous. He had a stretcher-bearer with him and was half unconscious and deadly sick. I meandered along with the Sergeant and found all the men asleep!! So I bustled them up; they'd done no consolidation and as there were no officers and precious few NCOs, they'd lost all initiative, so I put them on making strong points of shell-holes (there were plenty of choice of those and bags of sandbags). It was most unpleasant as the Bosch was in every shell-hole: he had been pinned by our barrage and when lifted out of his front line had gone doggo in the nearest shell-holes from whence he was sniping at anything he saw and we had to be jolly nippy dodging across the broken bits. We joined up with the 25th on our left, and I met one of their subalterns who said their line extended up the hill a bit, but ended in the air, as the division next to us hadn't been able to leave their trenches.

MAJOR BERTRAM BREWIN, TEMPORARILY COMMANDING 24TH NORTHUMBERLAND FUSILIERS

There had been a thick mist in the valley, blinding the FOOs to exactly where their shells were falling, and indeed the advance of enemy reserves. Some British parties got close to their objective before being forced back, others, such as along the riverbank, again got nowhere. In this latter area, it looked at one point as if a counter-attack might drive back the 101st Brigade (34th Division) beyond their original jumping-off positions, possibly even back to Fampoux. It was another demonstration of German capabilities.

As ever, the wounded were numerous and taken back by all manner of transport, including the recently introduced lighter system: barges towed by horse or mule along the now cleared Scarpe.

One tremendous advance by 37th Division troops took place on 28 April. Just south of Gavrelle substantial elements of 63rd Brigade routed the enemy, blasting through to the clutch of copses on the outskirts of Fresnes-les-Montauban, and breaking up counter-attacks with artillery, a skill that was fast developing. But there was not a single friendly face on either flank and they had punched their deep hole far north of the projected target area. Communication was as poor as the visibility and no one at Brigade or Division realized what had happened, nor where. There was therefore no possibility of support or protection by either infantry or artillery. In any case, no reserves had been put in place to meet such an eventuality. The party were on their own; eventually they were surrounded and captured. If it had been possible to plan the penetration properly and capitalize upon it, Gavrelle might have been made safe, Oppy pressurized further and Greenland Hill left open to lateral attack.

An attempt by 63rd (Royal Naval) Division to press forward further from Gavrelle also ended in failure, although the northern flank was extended a little, making the village slightly more secure. It had been another 'arrowhead' assault, wide open to hostile fire from the flanks. On the RND left, attacking Oppy Wood, the British 2nd Division were unable to assist, although the battalions on the left gained a small stretch of line to assist Arthur Currie's 1st Canadian Division to make the gain of the day: the village of Arleux. Its defences formed a salient in front of the *Wotan III* line; as a result, in this sector German commanders elected not to counter-attack but simply fall back to the stronger position: the village was dispensable. The Canadians completed the occupation of all three original objectives the following day. Albeit localized, as it was the only registerable

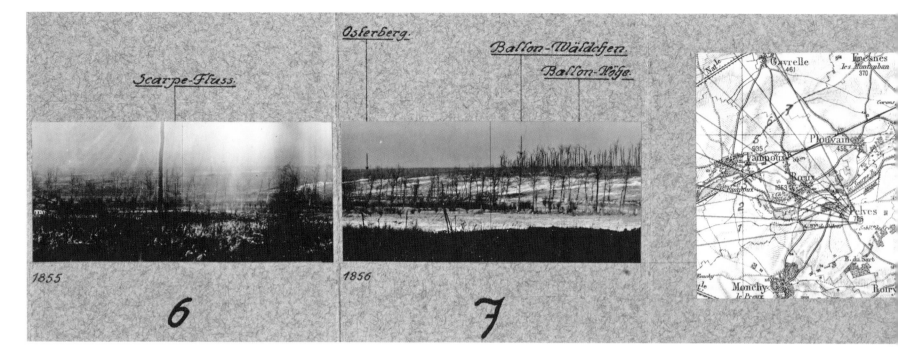

success for the period, so the actions of 28 and 29 April 1917 were accorded the title of the Battle of Arleux.

First Army had come back into the offensive fray with a welcome victory; for the Third Army it was another day to forget.

I then began to count the damage. It looked pretty rotten for a first effort – one officer left, Battalion H.Q. and goodness knows what else if anything. I had had a day full of adventure, and had taken for myself one big dent in tin helmet from High Explosive Shrapnel which knocked me endways but did no damage except a headache, one graze on forehead which bled like a pig, but was only superficial (due to my foolish and uneradicable habit of wearing my tin hat on the back of my head, and for the next few days I had to wear it on the back of my head!), a lump on the back of my hand from

a spent bit of shrapnel, and very sore ribs where a stone from a shell burst had taken me, one bullet through my collar, and one through the waist of my tunic, so I had something to remember the 28th April by.

Next day was a perfect spring day, not a cloud and quite warm, sitting in the big wide trenches in the sun out of the wind; saw numerous air-fights and three of our machines downed by a marvellously quick vermillion painted Boche scout, and nary a Boche down. Rather fed up! Had a perfect view of the battlefield which was perfectly peaceful, hardly a shell over and certainly no hate, and it looked ludicrously simple just to collect a mob and march on the Chemical Works. At 9 pm we marched out and were relieved by the 4th Division, who were the next on the list.

MAJOR BERTRAM BREWIN, TEMPORARILY COMMANDING 24TH NORTHUMBERLAND FUSILIERS

Above Segment of German panorama taken from Pelves looking across the Scarpe towards Greenland Hill (Ballon-Höhe). BHK Rundbild VII/9

Creeping Barrage Arleux
28th April

German Lines
Barbed Wire

118-130 S.O.S
115-118
112-115
116
108-111
107-108
104-106
101-103
96-100
91-95
86-90
10-85

Fresnoy

41-43
36-40
31-35
27-30
21-26
17-20
14-15
12-13
9-11
6-8
3-5
0-2

41-43
36-40
31-35
27-30
21-26
17-20
14-15
12-13
9-11
6-8
3-5
0-2

41-43
36-40
31-35
27-30
21-26
17-20
12-13
9-11
6-8
3-5
0-2

Arleux-
en-Gohelle

Crucifix

N

CHAPTER SEVENTEEN

The Void

From the 29th April till the night of the 2nd May was one long bombardment, and Hunland looked like a vast smoking inferno day after day. On the night of the 2nd the rate of fire was speeded up, and an incessant stream of gas shells and incendiary stuff was sent over. For once I found sleep rather difficult, as the whole earth shook like an animated jellyfish. The show kicked off at 3.45 a.m.

MAJOR NEIL FRASER-TYTLER DSO TD, 150TH (COUNTY PALATINE) BRIGADE, ROYAL FIELD ARTILLERY

Left British 9.2-inch howitzer firing from the ruins of Tilloy. IWM Q5221

Overleaf top Light and mobile German artillery – the bane of the tanks. AJ

Overleaf right Mobile German machine-gun teams employing shellholes for cover. AC

* Zero hour was actually 3.45 am

It might be thought that the disappointments of late April and the French situation could have caused the British to draw the line in Artois. They were in possession of the Wancourt-Héninel Ridge, Monchy and Guémappe, the Point du Jour, Gavrelle and the entire Vimy Ridge: all excellent defensive positions. In the Hindenburg Line sectors from Croisilles southwards, unless taunted, the Germans were settled and unlikely to wish to be belligerent. And the British guns were now 'up'. So why did Haig push on? There was an anthology of reasons.

On 18 April, two days after Nivelle's offensive opened, David Lloyd George had been told by the French Minister of Munitions that France had no intention of fighting a prolonged battle, and that the offensive would be truncated if substantial gains did not materialize. By 23 April, it was clear they had not, and very likely would not. With each passing day the situation grew more sombre, but there was no sign of truncation. When it came, the French mutiny was by no means general, but it was considerable and all too infectious. Most *poilus* were not refusing to serve, nor were they streaming from the battlegrounds in huge numbers: they would defend, but not attack. Two million casualties since August 1914 was enough. Ironically – and thankfully – for some time the German intelligence services did not become aware of the situation. In response Pétain chose to be both heavy and soft-handed at the same time. Whilst displaying traditional strong-arm military discipline in executing fifty-nine men as 'examples', he was well aware of the troops' need to rest, and for the High Command to 'reconnect' with the rank and file. In empathy, he suspended non-essential offensive action, granted widespread leave and upgraded the quality and quantity of food. None of this happened overnight, however, and Pétain did not become French C-in-C until 17 May. The process required time and the only people who could supply that commodity were the British – by patiently awaiting developments and pursuing their diversionary commitments at Arras.

But Sir Douglas Haig still believed the enemy could be broken there. This attitude was in no small part due to the influence of Brigadier General John Charteris, Chief of British Army Intelligence, a soldier perhaps best known for 'massaged' intelligence reports during the upcoming Third Ypres campaign, reports that misled many, especially the C-in-C himself, into making decisions that may have caused prolongation of the battle and the unnecessary loss of many lives. On Tuesday, 1 May, Charteris revealed that the Germans could draw upon only ten reserve divisions on the entire Western Front, at the same time producing documents that showed a forced decrease in battalion strength to around 750, and compulsory rationing of military foodstuffs. For Haig, the information was a powerful lever.

WEDNESDAY 2 MAY

Held conference at 11 am with Generals Gough and Allenby and fixed zero hour at 4.45 am* for tomorrow's operations. The difficulty is that on Gough's right the Australians must cross some open ground in the dark – while on First Army front opposite Oppy there is a wood that can only be passed conveniently by daylight. Allenby must conform to Horne. If Gough went in early, and the others attacked later, it is almost certain that Enemy would become alarmed and barrage our front line before the troops can get out of the trenches!

SIR DOUGLAS HAIG, DIARY

It was decided that – without excessive loss – the British must wear down the Germans at Arras for as long as was necessary to assist Pétain, on condition that the French play a similar offensive 'holding' role. Then Haig would deliver the decisive blow in Flanders – with French assistance of course. Added to this swirling strategic broth were other pungent ingredients: greater Russian involvement if revolutionary problems could be resolved; Italian offensive hopes; and of course the future arrival of the Americans, now certain. It was a pivotal period of the war, and one that demanded supreme collaboration between Allies. Even Lloyd George completed a u-turn, offering unequivocal support for *any* decision the General Staff might reach. Sir Douglas Haig had been handed a unique conjunction of circumstances that might allow him not only to illustrate how splendid were the British as

allies, but lead the vanguard of victory. He looked upon the prospects for summer success as 'reasonably possible'. At Arras, therefore, troops, materiel and time would require careful husbanding. May was going to be a busy month at GHQ. Rested troops came flooding back to Arras, amongst them great numbers of new and innocent faces.

The morning following our arrival in our old quarters in Arras our C.O. called a parade of all NCO, sergeants and corporals, and for about half an hour addressed them in one of the vaults adjoining ours. We men looked on from a distance and wondered what it was all about, but guessing that it boded no good! He told them not to impart any information to the men but we could see from their demeanour and gravity, apart from remarks passed between themselves on their return, that we were going up to another attack in the near future.

"You'd better write to mother and make your wills, you

Looking across the battlefield towards Monchy from Bullecourt. The wire of the Hindenburg Line crosses the image. March 1917. HS M706 M10 Nr. 397

blokes, 'cos you're for it!", said our cheerful Sergeant on returning.

"What's on, Sarge? Are we going over the top?" enquires one of the new draft, somewhat too eagerly. The Sergeant regards him for a moment as if 'weighing him up', then,

"Yes, but not to pick daisies but to shove 'em up."
PRIVATE PERCY CLARE, 7TH EAST SURREY REGIMENT

The Germans had given up precious little extra ground in the last week of April. Their tactics were still proving effective, in places costly perhaps, but given the Allied onslaught casualty figures were more than acceptable. Von Lossberg had now made his entire defence mobile, including some of the artillery. British observers had noted light guns sited in the open; when challenged they were hitched up, taken elsewhere and redeployed. It caused problems not only for tanks, but machine-gun crews and pockets of infantry. The problem was magnified by the fact that the British were largely occupying devastated ground with minimal cover, whilst the Germans lay in an arc of relatively undamaged terrain incorporating woods, copses, villages and sunken lanes.

THIRD SCARPE

The next round of attacks were going to be heavier than anything since 9 April, with all three armies working in unison along a front of 21 kilometres. The date was set: Thursday 3 May, but the hour turned into something of a debate. Horne's First Army objectives were Fresnoy and Oppy; Allenby's Third faced the usual targets in the Sensée valley, across the Cambrai road, Roeux and Greenland Hill through to Plouvain; whilst those for Gough's Fifth were Riencourt and Hendecourt – the Bullecourt sector. It is important to note that none of the divisions present for the later action had received any training in night attacks, but this is exactly what Gough's Anzacs now requested at Bullecourt. They knew the sector, had attacked there before,

Schornstein CHÉRISY   Itr FONTAINE - BULLECOURT   B. du VERT   B. du SART   Sabl't de Croisière
silos   Kirchturm CHÉRISY   Schornst. St ROHART   a Str ARRAS - CAMBRAI
Waldst auf Höhe 76   Waldshauf Höhe 76   Tiefpunkt 76
Waldstück 800 m. südöstl. v. d. Mühle (Südostl. Monchy)

enjoyed a curious propensity for not getting lost and had no qualms. They also refused point-blank to have anything to do with tanks. A 3.30 a.m. start was requested. Gough was happy with the proposal; Haig was not. The nature of Horne and Allenby's ground was generally unsuitable for night attack, and allowing Zero-Hour to be staggered could only result in the enemy being everywhere alerted by the earliest assault. The result would be violent defensive shellfire – a recipe for disaster, surely. Allenby did not agree: there was no reason the enemy should suspect that Gough's attack, the first, was not, like last time, an individual enterprise. The argument cut little ice and ultimately yielded a wicked compromise – three attacks all before dawn and all at the same time: 3.45 a.m. Sunrise was at 5.22, and daybreak just after 4.00. It instantly caused trouble, not least because earlier orders had already been received.

2ND MAY

We got orders for the next attack which was fixed for the next day. We pleaded for an attack at dawn so that the advance would be in daylight. But we were ordered to attack at 3.45 a.m. – i.e. in darkness. In our method of attack an advance in daylight is far better as the enemy would be blinded by smoke-shell whilst our men would be able to see their way. Unless the division on our right really attacks we cannot get on. I had a good look at the country in the afternoon and am worried about the enemy-machine-guns on the railway embankment away on our right.

BRIGADIER GENERAL HENRY TUDOR, CRA 9TH (SCOTTISH) DIVISION

How would the troops find the right attacking line? Could leapfrogging take place under such conditions? How would units know if they had reached the correct objective? How too, were FOOs to gauge the fall of shot for their guns? Queries – and objections – flooded in.

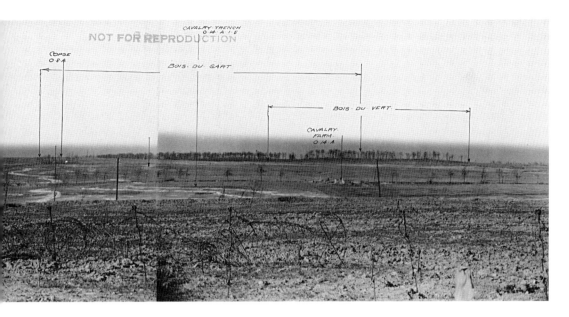

The scene of 3rd Division's suffering on 3 May: the the valleys and woods east of Monchy. IWM Third Army Panorama 556 taken on 6 May 1917

I regarded the change to a night attack at such short notice with dismay and anger and I did my utmost to get the decision changed. The ground over which the 3rd Division had to operate was particularly difficult in a night attack on a big scale, and was in an area in front of Monchy in which the hostile fire was intense. Monchy used to be subjected to sudden bursts of intense fire at varying times, and was one of the hottest places that I ever had to visit. There were good German concrete shelters but they faced the wrong way. A more unfortunate place for an unprepared night attack on a big scale could not have been found. So great was the confusion that it was reported to me that troops from a Division on our left "captured" the front line trench from which troops of the 3rd Division had started – it was started in confusion and the confusion grew. I told General Allenby what I thought about it when he came to see me when we came out of the line, and he was very "pious" and said that it was General Gough's fault that the change had been made to a night attack.

Major General C.J. Deverell, 3rd Division

Deverell's responsibility was a heavy one: the Monchy sector. His objections failed to achieve modification. Everywhere, the troops moved in and formed up.

At one o'clock on 3 May the Lewis gunners were ordered to overhaul their guns and inspect their ammunition, making sure that their panniers were full and that cartridges were clean and worked freely in the drums. At about 2 o'clock the platoon sergeant sent men to the dugout to draw two days rations for each man, and we then learned we were to go over the top to attack at 3.45 am. We knew it was coming. From the very first, even before it was launched, this attack was doomed to fail, and the feeling throughout the battalion was that it was hurriedly and badly planned. Our objectives were not known to us – no one mentioned it, the only order to reach us was to be ready to go over at 3.45 – and no one knew in what direction we were to go, where we were to stop, or what we were expected to do. No officer appeared in the trench, all orders being passed on through the medium of the NCOs who themselves were in sullen and resentful mood, and when asked questions expressed total ignorance of any plan or arrangement. At about 3 o'clock the orderly corporal brought up the battalion's mail, another evidence that the attack had suddenly been decided upon. To my dismay I received a large birthday parcel from home, which at any other time and place would have been most welcome, but now only proved an encumbrance. The men were irritable and grousing, being resentful at being thrust out as 'cannon-fodder', or sacrificed because some brass hat had committed himself. At 3.30 we clambered out of the trench more noisily than we should have done. There had been a great deal of bickering and discontent over the carrying of two day's rations. They should have divided them and made each man carry his own, but no responsible NCO was there to make any arrangement so at the last minute they detailed various men to carry the heavy bags. They very naturally didn't see why they should be burdened with other men's grub and were not slow to say so. Already we were ridiculously overweighted, and a ration bag full of bully beef is a serious addition to carry over No Man's Land in the dark during an attack. The NCOs met their objections by telling other men to relieve those who started with them after the first trench had been taken – for all the world as though we had been going on a picnic. Some had one, some two heavy bags, some others had 2-gallon petrol cans of water to carry in addition to their heavy load of personal equipment, extra bandoliers, bombs, spade or pick, and rifle. If we could appear and walk across the stage of London Music Hall loaded as we were, as "British troops going into action", what shrieks of laughter would greet our appearance. It was a positively ridiculous load and none but a British infantryman would have been ordered to advance to attack in such hopeless and helpless conditions, and none but British High Command would order storm troops to carry such impediments and expect them to be able to fight. The whole proceeding just shows what utter carelessness of lives there was.

PRIVATE PERCY CLARE, 7TH EAST SURREY REGIMENT

THE MUGGING

VII Corps were flayed on 3 May, von Lossberg's devices devouring the attacks. There is no better synopsis of what happened than that of the Official History:

The confusion caused by the darkness; the speed with which the German artillery opened fire; the manner in which it concentrated upon the British infantry, almost neglecting the artillery; the intensity of its fire, the heaviest that many an experienced soldier had ever witnessed, seemingly unchecked by British counter-battery fire and lasting almost without slackening for fifteen hours; the readiness with which the German infantry yielded to the first assault and the energy of its counter-attack; and, it must be added, the bewilderment of the British infantry

on finding itself in the open and its inability to withstand any resolute counter-attack.

CYRIL FALLS, *MILITARY OPERATIONS FRANCE AND BELGIUM, 1917*

Eyewitnesses sponsor Falls' words. To gain their objectives the troops were required to traverse between 1 and 2 kilometres of ground behind a fast-moving barrage: 100 metres every two minutes. Initially, there appeared to be a tremendous and rapid advance, but in fact the Germans were simply absorbing its energy.

Working in conjunction with one of the finest covering barrages that I have ever seen, the boys go over. There is soon some very good bayonet work and on our front we have a clean sweep, not so on the right, for the 12th Middlesex, 54th Brigade are soon in difficulties. Poor beggars make four attacks but are mown down like chaff, unable to get over the top of the trench. It is a terrible slaughter, and both reserve Battalions in company with every available man of Division are rushed into the line.

Above Troops coming out of the line near Monchy pass a battery of field guns and a tank. In the background the cavalry still await their chance. IWM Q5183

Right The 3 May plan south of the Arras-Cambrai road that incorporated attacks upon Chérisy, Fontaine and Bullecourt. NA WO95-1870

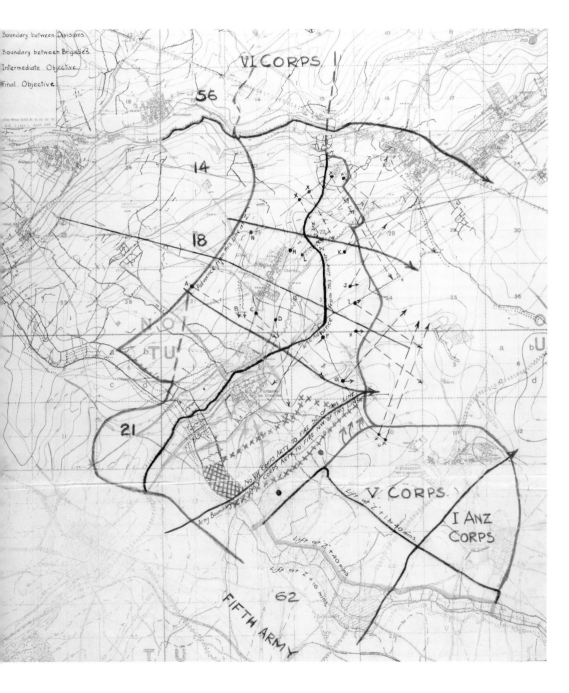

Boundary between Divisions.
Boundary between Brigades.
Intermediate Objective.
Final Objective.

VI CORPS

V CORPS

I ANZ CORPS

FIFTH ARMY

While this is being done, the position is this. On whole frontage of attack it is going well with exception of 1000 yards in centre and soon both flanks are 3000 yards advanced and being enfiladed. This is a capital move of Jerry looking at it from a purely strategical point of view. He had packed every available gun on this 1000 yards sector, and it is no fault of the troops engaged that they cannot get going. Very soon we see that Jerry is not letting his great chance slip, for soon through the gap in our front, thousands of fresh troops were pouring and extending both right and left. It is the first time I have seen Jerry firing from the hip. It is soon over, and very soon what was in promise a highly successful attack a few minutes before now developed into a rout. SOS for reserves are of no avail as we have no men behind us at all. Weight of numbers told and our chaps could not stave it off for long. In the conduct of this attack Jerry has shown that if his troops are not fighters, he has a staff that he can be justifiably proud of. The chaps retire back to our original front line and marvellous to relate, Jerry is quite content to let us stop. If only he knew, he could have taken Arras, for nothing could have stopped him. Another attack is timed for 6.45 pm. Remnants of all Battalions go over together, but now another unusual thing happens. Our artillery, which has kept up more or less a steady barrage all day, as time of attack drew near had almost exhausted all available stocks of shells.
PRIVATE ROBERT CUDE MM, 7TH EAST KENT REGIMENT (THE BUFFS)

The lines are telling and if Robert Cude had been a battalion officer with access to orders he may well have made additions to this account. It is probably just as well he was unable to see his Corps Commander's diary entry for 3 May.

Ding dong at it again. As far as I know all goes well up to now but one can never be certain as things change very quickly. We were up very early. Perfectly lovely weather, just like we had 2 years ago, the day we left

Potizje dug-out. I see in my diary that it is 2 years go today. The Hun hates being attacked like this and we do lump it in in the way of ammunition. I don't know whether D'Ewes is in today's fight as he left me. He's not far away however. I hear the cuckoo every day now. It and the wood pigeons seem quite undisturbed by the din. All seems to be going well. Fancy what a long day it must seem to men actually fighting since 3.45 a.m.
LIEUTENANT GENERAL SIR THOMAS D'OYLY SNOW,
VII CORPS

The retirement of Robert Cude's division, the 18th, was spotted by the leading waves of the 14th Division attacking south of Guémappe; they followed suit, pulling back to the start line. On their left the 56th Division were driving straight along the Arras-Cambrai road towards St Rohart Factory.

Zero hour 4 am, quite dark, wonderful intense creeping barrage started at 4.15am and over we went. The barrage though really marvellous was too slow, 3 miles an hour instead of 4 miles an hour, and some of our less experienced boys simply walked into it and so became casualties. A few yards this side of Fritz's line the barrage lifted like magic and started again just behind the enemy front line. We were into his first trench like winking and rapidly cleared it taking no prisoners, in fact I saw several groups arguing as to who should kill the prisoners, one saying he's mine and the other saying no he's mine. I left them to it and it didn't take long to finish off the bones of contention.

Arriving at Cavalry Farm we, being the first wave, passed quickly through it (obeying orders) and left it for the second wave to clear, an unheard of thing to do but 'orders are orders' and life and death the result. Obedience this time proved our undoing as no sooner had we passed through the farm than machine guns were switched on to us and they accounted for most of our casualties which were very heavy. In a matter of 20 min-

utes we had lost 7 officers and 200 other ranks. However some of our chaps got round the side of the farm and the machine gun party found they would eventually cop it so decided to show the white feather. This took the form of a white flag and one man who led out a party of 15. I beckoned the whole party towards me and they came a few yards when my Lewis gunner opened fire and cleared the lot.

With our usual luck the brigades on our left and right failed owing to heavy machine gun fire. The result was that we had got our flanks in the air.
SERGEANT HAROLD BISGOOD MM, 1/2ND LONDON
REGIMENT (ROYAL FUSILIERS)

Within moments of zero 167th Brigade on the left rose from cover into a deluge of shells – only possible if the Germans had been pre-warned. Survivors pushed on and were cut down by a torrential fusillade of fire from an unusually well-populated German trench (Tool Trench) just behind the crest of the ridge shielding the Bois du Vert. There was a knock-on effect in front of Monchy, now splintered and smashed after days of pummelling by German heavies. In the valley before the village the British troops received a brutal dose of gas and high explosive, as did their field artillery in the valleys behind the village. The two attacking brigades of 3rd Division, already enfeebled by losses after ten days in the line, were subjected to a rerun of the tactics deployed at Guillemont the previous year on the Somme: to avoid the British barrage the Germans moved *forward*, surprising the British and cutting them down wholesale. The advance crumbled as troops lost direction and order. Regiments mingled and command broke down. On the Division's far left, parties from the 9th Brigade doggedly gained their objective, driving on towards the Bois du Sart before counter-attacks

hurled them back, whilst to the rear, reserves were 'paralysed' by the ferocity of the hostile artillery; the Monchy attacks ground to a halt. The open left flank should have been occupied by the 37th Brigade (12th Division). A pre-dawn zero meant that for most of these men the battle was either chaos or simply nonexistent.

As we assembled outside the trench it was noticeable that our officers were the worse for drink, and certainly some of the NCOs were drunk. To make things worse, at this moment the Boche sent over gas, and the men put on their gas helmets. This created delay and confusion, for the night being pitch dark it was impossible to advance over such ground in gas helmets; we could not even see our own feet. Zero time was in a very few minutes and there was no time to lose. Our commanding officer passed down instructions to take off the helmets. The gas was not thick and we were ordered to get forward and through it as soon as possible. This we did and formed up along the top of the support trench, receiving the order to advance immediately. Even then contradictory orders were issued, and the men were exasperated and ready to skulk in shell-holes rather then be sacrificed for nothing, for it was obvious that we were doomed to be sacrificed and that attacking a powerful and entrenched foe in these conditions was simply farcical. At 3.45 am the massed British artillery crashed out a thunder of drumfire. The effects were very similar to the 9 April, but how different in other ways was this attack, and with what misgivings we went forward. SOS signals quickly arose from the German lines and the sky was alive with coloured stars, green, red, white, and orange. The Boche artillery very quickly responded, putting down a barrage on us and a curtain of fire behind us to cut off any retreat and prevent the advance of supports. Officers not responsible for their actions issued impossible or contra-dictory orders; men like a lot of silly sheep huddled together, appalled in the face of the barrage, the dark-ness, the absence of command, hesitating and bewildered.

I looked around to see them falling under enfilade machine-gun fire. Three minutes after we had crossed our own parapet there was no semblance of a line or wave, only the little groups of men bunching together, finally stopping, and those who were not shot down falling to seek cover in shellholes. The man who hesitates and goes to ground for cover will never leave it until the battle is over. Nothing will overcome his fear. Judge them not too harshly; judge them not at all, you who have not been similarly tried and passed the testing yourself. A great proportion of our number was composed of men who had never been over the top, indeed had not even been in trenches before. Not a single officer or NCO or man knew in which direction lay the enemy.
PRIVATE PERCY CLARE, 7TH EAST SURREY REGIMENT

Setting off into the blackness, troops used the sense of direction learned through experience: if they advanced along the same line as the shells howling overhead, they might eventually find some Germans.

Our little band seemed isolated in a fog: no friend, no enemy was visible. At last through a rift in the smoke our company commander Captain King came into view. He seemed distracted, utterly bereft, yelling and bawling for his lost battalion. He sighted us at the same moment and yelled to us to go half-right, but our sergeant said he was drunk (as he was) and told us to take no notice of his orders. A little while after this we saw opposite us a strip of German trench from which some dirty-looking, horri-bly ugly Huns were flinging bombs and firing rifle-grenades at us. They had seen us before we had noticed them. It was now nearly full daylight and we lay in shellholes to return their fire. I was glad to have a rifle; I had picked up the first dead man's I saw. Since starting I had not seen the Lewis gun team. Had this lit-tle lot been less eager and held their fire we should have been wiped out to a man. It was at this spot that we again saw Captain King. He had somehow got to a

Well-stocked German shell dump near Quéant. AJ

shellhole quite near us, and was standing up fully exposed to the Boche shouting to them under the impression in his befuddled state that they were his lost company. "Don't bomb, you bloody fools! I'm Captain King of the East Surreys". The response he received was two or three stick bombs, the first and second of which missed him. Someone with him in the shellhole appeared to drag him down, but a few seconds later he was up again shouting and swearing at the Huns, who probably thought he was defying them. Unquestionably he was drunk. The inevitable happened; a bomb at last hit him, exploding full on his chest killing him instantly as well as the people with him in the shellhole. So died a thoroughly competent, good-hearted and considerate officer, one worthy of a better end.

We made a rush at the Boche trench. A bomb struck my chest but did not explode until it had fallen to the ground and I had jumped over it. I saw another Hun who had thrown his last bomb snatch up his rifle to aim at me but I shot him in the act. Still another who had a stick bomb of which he had just pulled the string I bayoneted and toppled over into the trench on top of him as he fell, in a panic to escape the explosion of the bomb as it dropped on the ground on the parapet. A few seconds only and others of our chaps were leaping down into the trench and almost immediately all of the garrison who had not escaped by running back to the wood close behind were killed to a man. We were fourteen men in all, several desperately wounded and useless for defence holding a useless slit in the ground well within enemy reach. It was just in front of the Bois du Sart, a wood fortified and held by strong forces. The Bois du Vert was on the right hand. We were absolutely cut off from our on lines by the width of No Man's Land; in broad daylight no help could possibly reach us. We had no reserves of ammunition; no bombs, no food, no water, no hope. Quiet had settled over the battlefield and the battle – which was no battle – was now finished. The quiet of the enemy was all the more sinister. The sergeant-major walked up and down muttering "We must consolidate", but when a machine-gun opened up from the edge of the wood and a

stream of bullets came right into and along the trench he showed stark terror in his eyes. He said, "You blokes go on consolidating; I'll go back and bring out reinforcements". He preferred the risk of a journey in daylight while things were still unsettled, to the certainty of a painful death or imprisonment by remaining in the trench. He clambered out and we didn't see him again. He deliberately decided to abandon us to save his own skin. I saw it in his eye, and when he had gone I told the others so.
Private Percy Clare, 7th East Surrey Regiment

The party were slowly picked off by machine gun and then mortar fire until only Clare, Private Edward Gunnett and another seriously wounded man were left alive.

All the others were already killed, and the last mortar brought about a fall of trench wall which blocked us in effectually at the same time. We consulted on the chances of a dash over the top. It seemed certain death to try it, but we knew it was certain death to stay: better to die in the open trying to get away than like rats in a trap. The wounded man was the difficulty. A quick glance over the top showed us men gathering on the edge of the wood. I could see their bayonets glittering in the sunshine. I glimpsed some, running in crouching posture towards us, jumping from shellhole to shellhole. Before they could jump in on us, their own machine-guns must stop firing, and that seemed the one slender hope we had left of getting out over the top alive. The wounded man now begged in pathetic earnestness not to be left there to be bayoneted. He entreated us to shoot him before we left rather than desert him.
Private Percy Clare, 7th East Surrey Regiment

The man died as Clare and Gunnett were trying to lift him from the trench, struck in the abdomen by a bullet. On their own, and sitting ducks, the two men made a decision: they would not run but *roll* across no man's land.

Nowhere to hide. The bodies of two British soldiers in a shellhole, probably victims of German snipers. IWM HU95899

*Private Edward Richard Gunnett was killed on 20 November 1917 at Cambrai. His name appears on the Cambrai Memorial, Louverval.

Not with any uniformity of course. Sometimes we stayed a few seconds, sometimes a minute or two, sometimes we didn't stay at all so that the Boche marksmen could never anticipate where we would be. How far we rolled, I do not know, over most of France I thought. Bullets spattered the earth; quite a number cut through our clothes and equipment. I sobbed. I am not ashamed of it. I think my tears were tears of gratitude to God for my deliverance. Gunnett was a more phlegmatic soul and he sat muttering and swearing. We tested them once more by the old trick of raising our steel helmets on the end of an entrenching tool handle, and getting no response we decided to make a run for it.
PRIVATE PERCY CLARE, 7TH EAST SURREY REGIMENT

They dashed for the British line. Gunnett got in but Clare became entangled in his own wire, and was forced to stoop and bend back the barbs that gripped his trousers and puttees.

To have come so far safely it seemed I must perish. Bullets zipped and ricocheted on the wire; one pinged against the rim of my steel helmet barely grazing it but sounding like a hammer blow; another struck my bayonet scabbard and must have gone clean through between my legs. Whilst I was engaged in freeing myself I heard shouts and looking up saw two stretcher-bearers rushing out from our trench to help me. One was a man named Clegg, a Croydon tramdriver. It all happened in a flash; as they saw I was free, they turned to rush back for they knew the fearful peril they were in. Clegg got back safely; the other man in the act of turning was shot through the head. He spun and fell so that I had to leap over him. I found Gunnett already surrounded by a little group of onlookers who were congratulating him on his escape. They had watched our progress across, and had betted with each other against our safe arrival. Suddenly an idea shot into my mind and I asked, "What about you chaps. Where have you been all this while?" They began to disappear and lose interest suspiciously quickly. They had never been over. In the darkness and confusion they were of the lot who skulked in shellholes.*
PRIVATE PERCY CLARE, 7TH EAST SURREY REGIMENT

Without 12th Division success, progress on the north bank of the river was going to be doubly difficult, for the attacks were originally supposed to be mutually supporting and to take place at dawn. Having received the fresh orders just hours before assembly, there was confusion as the 4th Division lined up for yet another crack at the mass of ruins before them. Of all the sub-sectors along the 21-kilometre battle front, Roeux probably demanded the most careful of planning, troop education, preparation and execution.

The battalion returned to the front on 30th April, once again just to the north of the chemical works at Roeux. A renewal of the attack was already being planned. This attack was ordered for 3rd May just before dawn. The short notice was insufficient to enable all troops involved to study the ground and plan, both so essential to a night attack. Neither had any opportunity been given to practise the attack beforehand in the back areas. In view of this unpreparedness I protested to my Brigade Commander, Brigadier-General A. Carton de Wiart, V.C., that distinguished, gallant and much-wounded fighting soldier. (He had been nine times wounded in this and other campaigns and had lost an eye and an arm). General de Wiart passed on my protest to the divisional commander [Major-General W. Lambton]. The not unexpected reply was to the effect that the Essex attack was only a small part of a greater operation on a wide front and if Colonel Irwin did not wish to undertake it no doubt a successor to him in command could easily be found.
LIEUTENANT COLONEL NOEL IRWIN MC, 2ND ESSEX REGIMENT

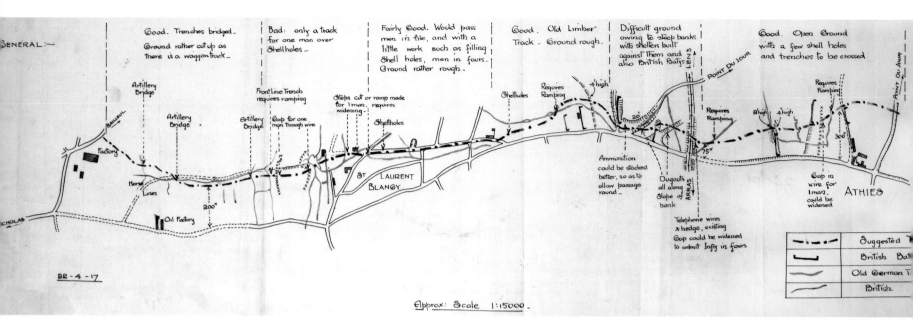

The map contains the following handwritten annotations:

GENERAL :—

Good. Trenches bridged. Ground rather cut up as there is a waggon track.

Bad: only a track for one man over Shellholes.

Fairly Good. Would pass men in file, and with a little work such as filling Shell holes, men in fours. Ground rather rough.

Good. Old Limber Track. Ground rough.

Difficult ground owing to steep banks with shelters built against them and also British Batys.

Good. Open Ground with a few shell holes and trenches to be crossed

Artillery Bridge
Artillery Bridge
Artillery Bridge
Gap for one man through wire
Front Line Trench requires ramping
Steps cut or ramp made for 1 man, requires widening.
Shellholes
Factory
Horse Lines
Oil Factory
200x
ST LAURENT BLANGY
Shellholes
Requires Ramping
4'high
Point Du Jour
Requires Ramping
8'high   4'high
Requires Ramping
300
Point Du Jour
20'
75'
ARRAS
Ammunition could be stacked better, so as to allow passage round.
Dugouts all along slope of bank
Telephone wires & hedge, existing Gap could be widened to admit Infy in fours
Gap in wire for 1 man, could be widened
ATHIES
22-4-17
Approx: Scale 1:15000.

Legend:
Suggested T...
British Bat...
Old German T...
British

To the men, especially those with experience, such posturing simply displayed lack of courage and contempt for the value of human life. The inflexibility and untouchability of the Higher Command engendered anger in the troops which could only be taken out upon those who had their best interests at heart – men like Irwin and his subordinates. The attacks went in – with the advancing Tommies silhouetted against a bright setting moon, a moon that had also revealed their assembly. The Germans were waiting.

The Battalion did magnificently; they went bang through together with some men of another Brigade and reached the second objective about 2000 yards away. There, all the surviving Officers were casualties, and the remnants of the Battalion fell back to the Black Line, about 1000yds ahead of our jumping off trench, and about 30 of them under a Company Sergeant-Major dug in there.

Meanwhile on the left the attack had failed completely. They even lost some of the front line trench, and though some men of the Brigade on the right had gone on they had never mopped the chateau and other buildings near it. I had detailed a very strong Company to mop up the Chemical Works and had warned every man personally that his job was not to go forward beyond there but to hold those buildings. The result was we held these all day, but the enemy had the houses on either side chock full of MGs and swept the gap. The men in the Chemical Works could only just hold on in shell holes etc. Two messengers from the Battalion got back and I tried all morning and early afternoon to get to them but not a single man got forward to them alive all day, after the attack had once started. I begged for reinforcements to take up and do a fresh attack on the chateau and the Brigadier tried hard to get them for me but they did not come till late that evening and meanwhile a heavy Bosch counter-attack had gone clean over the Black Line. The rest of that day I was holding a battalion front with my HQ party and one MG, and

Above Typically detailed improvements in infrastructure. RE plan of an infantry trackway designed for foot traffic through Blangy and Athies. NA WO153-1153, 13.4.17

about a third of the HQ party or more were knocked out. They had the worst barrage on us I ever saw and every time a man showed a hand about three MGs were on to him. Well, the reinforcements came up and took over the line. That night, exclusive of H.Q. Signallers, Runners etc the Battalion total was sixteen: we finally mustered 54 including 9 Brigade carriers who had not been over the top. The survivors were practically all moppers-up.
LIEUTENANT COLONEL ALFRED HORSFALL DSO, 2ND DUKE OF WELLINGTON'S (WEST RIDING) REGIMENT

On the left were the 9th Division. For two days tens of thousands of rounds of predominantly heavier calibre shells were dumped on the Roeux sector, the two small woods, Hausa and Delbar, and enemy positions on Greenland Hill, destroying trenches, keeping lanes in the wire open, and practising the various creepers for 3 May. Counter-battery work intensified, as did harassing fire on roads, junctions, railways and dumps. This was all very well for the guns, for they could fire from the map; the troops, however, were in the dark in every way. As so many had feared, when the attacks began there was instant confusion. Lieutenant Colonel W.D. Croft had spent three days in hospital; he returned to his unit on the day of the attack.

I walked up to rejoin near Gavrelle. Here I was collared by Frank Maxwell and kept at brigade headquarters for the battle of the 3rd May, a real bad day for the British Army. We were in reserve and got nothing much more than heavy shelling, but plenty of that. The Borderers, who were assaulting, had to make a left wheel and face to a flank – a pretty difficult operation at any time when under fire: a sheer impossibility, one would think, in darkness, and it was inky black when we started. A bad day for the British Army. The Borderers did their job, which was what one would have expected of them; but few, very few, out of those two companies who did their wheel and reached their objective ever got back. I think they were the only men who did reach their objective on the whole British front.
LIEUTENANT COLONEL W.D. CROFT CMG DSO, 11TH ROYAL SCOTS

Few parties reached the first objective, while a handful gained the second; both were then lost, the survivors creeping back after dark. In places units trying to take Roeux lost direction to such an extent that they ended up firing upon each other; casualties for the day came in at more than 2,000. Some battalions were practically destroyed. No advance was made between Roeux and Gavrelle.

Having relieved the 63rd (Royal Naval) Division, the 31st Division's task was to extend the line beyond Gavrelle, take Oppy Wood and village, and in conjunction with 2nd Division (who with only 1,800 men were only strong enough to attack on a narrow, single brigade front) keep contact with the 1st and 2nd Canadians in their advance out of Arleux upon Fresnoy and Acheville. All faced shrewd German tactics. In the hope of effecting surprise, the 93rd Brigade assembled in no man's land east of Gavrelle. They too had been spotted.

I remember how easy it was to get into the German trenches and how big a mistake we all made, because the Germans had emptied their trenches and put their artillery on them within a yard or two and those that were wounded on that occasion were left in the German trenches to be prisoners. You see, the Germans were too clever for us, I'll be quite truthful, their Generals were better than our fellows, and they let us get across and they had vacated their trenches and then when we got into them they blew them to hell. They blew us as well. Seven of us came back out of twenty-seven in my section.
PRIVATE ARTHUR DALBY, 15TH YORKSHIRE REGIMENT (LEEDS PALS)

Below New protective equipment issued to German troops immediately before the battle. AJ

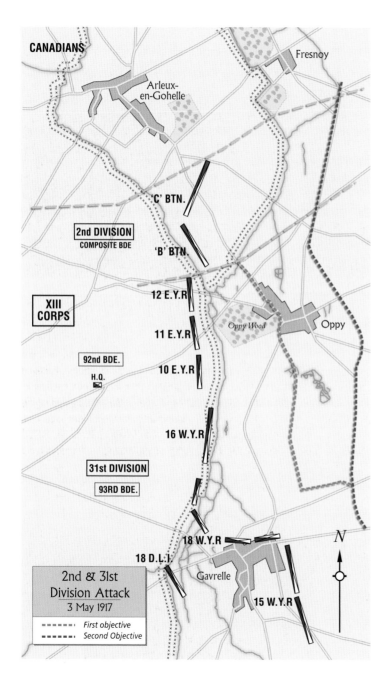

CANADIANS

Fresnoy

Arleux-
en-Gohelle

'C' BTN.

2nd DIVISION
COMPOSITE BDE

'B' BTN.

12 E.Y.R

XIII
CORPS

11 E.Y.R

Oppy Wood   Oppy

92nd BDE.

10 E.Y.R

H.Q.

16 W.Y.R

31st DIVISION

93RD BDE.

N

18 W.Y.R

18 D.L.I.

Gavrelle

2nd & 31st
Division Attack
3 May 1917

First objective
Second Objective

15 W.Y.R

Third Army.

Panorama No. 55/1 made on 4.5.17 from H 35 C 3.5.
including a field of view of 88° from about

NOT FOR REP...

Approximate Scale of Degrees (1 degree equals .70 of an inch).

· TREES · ON · RO...
70

On their left, the assembly 92nd Brigade was deluged with a hostile barrage so heavy they were unable to tell when their own creeper was lifting.

The wood was entered by small but tenacious parties of Yorkshiremen, only to be immediately swallowed amongst the tangled choirs of splintered timber. When the two Canadian brigades, rested, up to full strength and well-trained for the attack, made their move, they produced a final line similar in shape to that of Haldane's VI Corps at Monchy during the first week of battle – a vulnerable eastward bulge. On the right flank, the 2nd Division, although numbed by severe losses, managed to keep contact but on a sharply backward-angled line. Within the bulge lay

Third Army Panorama 118
April 1917   Sheet 51 B H 10 a 8.8
80 degrees NE - ESE   Bailleul

Oppy Wood

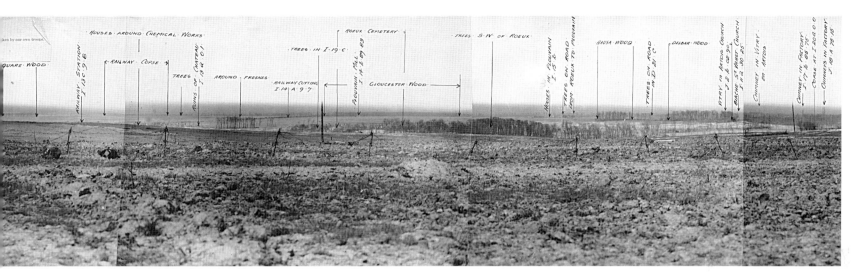

Above The view from the Point du Jour ridge on 5 May 1917, looking down upon Roeux and Greenland Hill – again the objectives. IWM Third Army Panorama 557.

Below Third Army Panorama 118 (IWM) shows the Oppy and Gavrelle sectors, with both British and German shells falling.

little Fresnoy – the only village conquest to buttress First and Third Army communiqués on the evening of 3 May. Chérisy may have joined Fresnoy, for elements of 55th Brigade (18th Division) had gained the ruins before being forced into surrender by the violent massed counter-attacks that rattled VII Corps on this day. Captain Thomas Price of 54th Brigade staff was later to tell Cyril Falls, 'It was a day we in the 18th Division always tried to forget.'

BACK TO BULLECOURT

In the south, 'Thruster' Gough entertained great hopes, as always, for his mixed Anzac and British (V Corps) force. He had more reason than usual to be elated with pride and anticipation, for three days earlier Sir Douglas Haig had offered him command of the main thrust in the Flanders campaign. With roads repaired and rail connections now in place in front of the

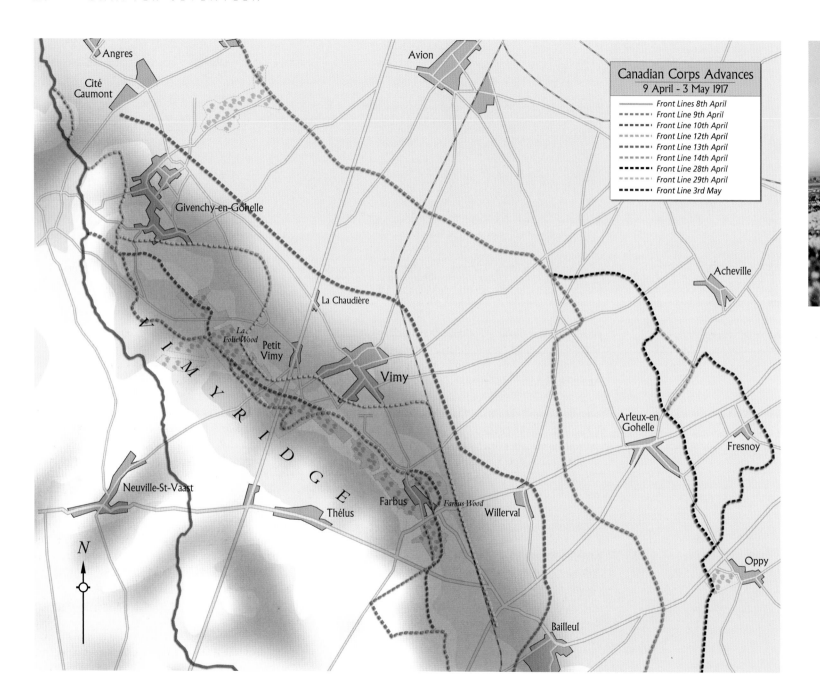

Angres

Cité
Caumont

Avion

Canadian Corps Advances
9 April - 3 May 1917

Front Lines 8th April
Front Line 9th April
Front Line 10th April
Front Line 12th April
Front Line 13th April
Front Line 14th April
Front Line 28th April
Front Line 29th April
Front Line 3rd May

HENDECOURT

Givenchy-en-Gohelle

La Chaudière

Acheville

V I M Y   R I D G E

*La
Folie Wood*

Petit
Vimy

Vimy

Arleux-en
Gohelle

Fresnoy

Neuville-St-Vaast

Farbus

Farbus Wood

Willerval

Thélus

N

Oppy

Bailleul

RIENCOURT LEZ CAGNICOURT   U. 16. C. 05.36   BULLECOURT   U. 21 A. 85.50

Above The ruined landscape of the southern battleground as seen on 26 May 1917. IWM Panorama 561 (no Army noted).

Left Canadian Corps gains east of Vimy Ridge from 9 April to 3 May.

Hindenburg Line, Gough's artillery presence was substantial, and supply assured. Most importantly, since the actions of 11 and 15 April, his men had enjoyed the luxury of time, to replenish ranks, train for night attack and prepare communication routes – cable trenches – for on this occasion, the General was determined to stay in touch. Failure here was not an option, for the demand to begin planning the Flanders campaign was already pressing. As ever, as soon as the massed guns spoke, spirits rose as the display of destructive might made everything seem so much more achievable.

MAY 2ND 1917

Relieved on early morning of 1st and came to tents near Bapaume. Going up again tonight, in reserve for the 5th and 6th Brigades. The stunt has been much spoken of, as if successful it means we have a pivot here of the so much prized Hindenburg Line, and once we get that, and therefore the natural defences, the enemy may retire to his own border. The fight he will put up will no doubt be stiff. About a dozen balloons up along the front yesterday. Weather splendid.
CORPORAL OSWALD BLOWS, 28TH BATTALION,
AUSTRALIAN IMPERIAL FORCE

Snow's VII Corps accomplishments had a direct bearing upon the prospects of Fifth Army, which was the only formation to engage in a 'traditional' frontal attack against firmly fixed lines. Originally, Third Army had expected a development of their triumphs by Gough's men; now they simply sought support to achieve a victory of their own, and a limited one.

As a result of three weeks of attention from augmented heavy batteries, Bullecourt resembled a wrecker's yard, which although making the British and Australians feel better about prospects, had actually done little damage to concrete and subterranean shelters, both ancient and modern. German casualties for the period between 15 April and 3 May stood at 133 in the village sector. Here, too, the

Hindenburg tunnel ran deep beneath the full length of the support line. By Zero-Hour, the trenches it served were blown to smithereens; wire too was substantially damaged, largely as a result of the widespread use of the 106 fuse, but the enemy had remained largely safe.

It was only the Australians that eschewed tanks on 3 May; in this nightmare sector British 62nd Division staff gratefully accepted the assistance of anything that might draw hostile fire, for they were deploying many unblooded troops. Just eight machines could be mustered, all of 12 Company, D Battalion, and their mission was not to lead as on 11 April, but simply to support.

With the moon setting brightly behind them, the V Corps troops advanced at 3.45 a.m. beneath an umbrella of massed long-range machine-gun fire, and before a creeper lifting 100 metres every three minutes. This time the wind favoured the enemy, a brisk north-easterly driving smoke and dust into the faces of the attacking troops.

Attacked at 4am. At that hour our artillery started firing, the idea being to follow up behind our own artillery barrage, but the enemy commenced at the same time, which proved that they knew all about the intended attack. The result was that there was considerable confusion, the shells falling so thickly that it was almost impossible to see where you were going through the smoke. I went about 30 yards and have a dim recollection of falling into a huge shell hole and was immediately wounded in face, right arm and chest. Lay stunned for a while until our chaps retreated, when I found that I could walk and struggled out.
CORPORAL ERNEST KING, 19TH BATTALION, AUSTRALIAN IMPERIAL FORCE

The 6th Australian Brigade managed to negotiate the protective barrage – again, uncannily prescient – to pierce the Hindenburg Line almost exactly where their 12th Brigade predecessors had done on 11 April, taking the same trenches on a length of about 600 metres. On the right in front of Riencourt 5th Australian Brigade were unable to emulate the achievement; although the wire was well cut the troops 'bunched' as they approached it, a great many falling victim to crossfire, the others going to ground or creeping through. Then an order to retire was heard and many stole back to the cover of a sunken lane. The attack had failed completely, but this was not what Brigade HQ understood: at 4.05 a.m. a signal rocket had been spotted and messages reported that both German lines had been captured. Two hours later the error was bloodily confirmed by the

Above The devastated main street of Bullecourt during the battle. HS 06/6/29

Right German wire entanglement designs in the Bullecourt sector. AC

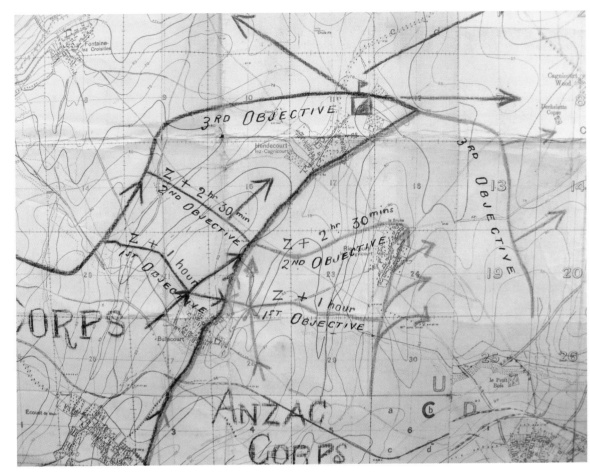

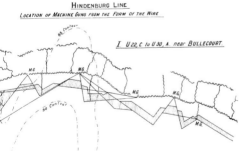

HINDENBURG LINE.
LOCATION OF MACHINE GUNS FROM THE FORM OF THE WIRE.

I. U 22, C to U 30, A. near BULLECOURT.

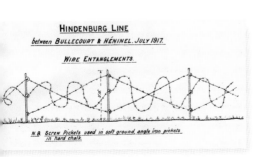

HINDENBURG LINE
between BULLECOURT & HÉNINEL. JULY 1917.

WIRE ENTANGLEMENTS.

N.B. Screw Pickets used in soft ground, angle iron pickets in hard chalk.

repulse of a second assault. There is, however, evidence that the rocket at least was authentic, for some 5th Brigade troops, a handful only, did indeed enter the enemy line.

In long lines we slowly but surely neared the German trenches. He sent up his usual flares and searchlights which made the scene all the more weird and also as bright as daylight and his guns and machine guns began to bark. The noise was terrific. The noise terrible, yet we reached his barbed wire and got through stumbling and slipping into numerous shellholes until we could go no further on account of our guns playing on his front trench so we got into shellholes for cover and to wait for our barrage to lift and for orders. Nothing came and we could not see our lads only those who were near us so we had to wait. Dawn broke and at midday and we were still in the holes, couldn't go forward or backwards and under very severe gun fire of all descriptions, expecting every minute something would happen. At last night came on and the officer told us to get rid of our weighty gear and make a dash for our own lines by crawling on our stomachs through the barbed wire, taking advantage of every hole we came to and risking the machine guns and rifles of Fritz. Well, we reached a small trench which was held by some of our lads and both sides of us were pleased to see the other. We were then told that a false order had been given and our boys obeyed. They said we were ordered back. But when they got back (those that did) they were ordered to charge again which they did. Where we were, we had been practically cut off between two fires and therefore had never had or heard the order. I lost a lot of my mates but some will come back again after getting over their wounds.

PRIVATE A.A.G. VOLLER, 19TH BATTALION, AUSTRALIAN IMPERIAL FORCE

On 6th Brigade's left flank the entire Bullecourt salient plus a further kilometre westward was all 62nd Division territory. Supported on both sides by tanks, two battalions of the West Yorkshire Regiment attacked the nose of the salient head on. Although three tanks breached the line, every infantry attack was repulsed with appalling loss, the troops being all too visible in the moonlight despite the smoke and dust. In the knowledge that Bullecourt was the prime target, the Germans had positioned static machine guns to cover the approaches; all the gunners needed to do was feed the weapons and let the British walk into the streams of lead. On the right, however, the 2/6th West Yorkshires got into the village and passed through to the far side, awaiting support. That support set off just after 7.00 a.m., met heavy gunfire, and was held up; seeing 186th Brigade troops on their left retiring, they followed suit. Yet some 185th Brigade men had also penetrated the German line and surged to the rear of the village and beyond. Those on the left 'face' of the salient drew close to the enemy line, were held up by uncut wire, and went to earth – within reach of German grenades. In the

meantime, troops who had fallen back were gathered up to attack again – unprofitably. On the far left, with the distraction of two tanks, elements of 2/4th and 2/5th York and Lancs forced a breach and reached the second line, the latter without noticing the first line, so devastated had it been by the guns! There were now several small parties of British troops and one large group of Australians within German territory, but without support annihilation was almost certain. Every attempt to reach the British failed, for the division had used all its battalions and had suffered almost 3,000 casualties.

Failure on both its flanks left 6th Australian Brigade in the same dreadful position as their comrades on 11 April: isolated in hostile territory. In the early afternoon supporting troops from 7th Australian Brigade managed to slip into the Hindenburg Line via a sunken road, however, and for the rest of the day tried to

Right Australian troops sheltering in the railway cutting near Bullecourt. IWM E2021

Below How the tanks fared on 3 May at Bullecourt.

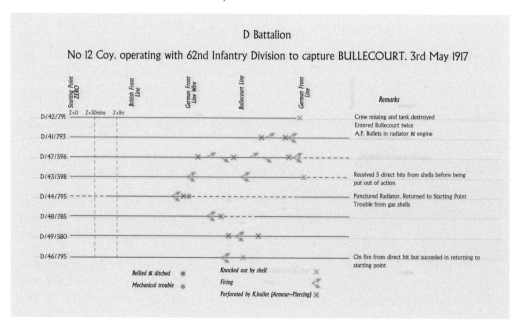

enormous pressure upon V Corps to redouble their effort to take Bullecourt and the trenches to the north of the village, for a decisive breach in the German defences here would at least be sufficient to keep the enemy occupied with attempted repossession. In the early afternoon Corps Commander, Lieutenant General Sir Edward Fanshawe, ordered the 7th Division to move up for an assault astride the eastern corner of the salient. Because of artillery readjustments the earliest it was able to attack was 10.30 p.m., another night-time venture. The first effort (by 22nd Brigade) pierced the line and was driven out by counter-attacks; at 4.00 a.m. the following morning the second received a perfect deluge of shelling whilst on the forming-up line.

One Battalion took their objective four times – each time being bombed out, at last they had to retire having run short of bombs. Whilst we were waiting our time to go over, the wounded were coming down in dozens, and we were under the severest bombardment I have ever known Fritz to send over. We knew it was certain death for all of us – orders are orders in the army and we had to obey them. Had we been lucky enough to take our objective we certainly could not have held it having no one behind us. At 4 am we advanced but owing to other battalions retiring (coming towards us we were hopeless and could not get through his barrage). All this time I stuck to Mr Gros, then we had to line up, dig ourselves in and prepare for his counter attack. I put my boss in a shell hole. He turned round and said to me – "Where's my faithful servant" – here Sir, then we made the hole big enough for two of us. Daylight was rapidly approaching so it was a case of having to get away whilst it was dark so we had orders to go back to the original trench we started off from. Oh we had terrible casualties – our Company went in 104 strong, came out 44.

PRIVATE ARTHUR BURKE, 20TH MANCHESTER REGIMENT

Below 1918 photograph showing German trenches captured, consolidated and renamed by the British and Australians in 1917, temporarily back in enemy hands during the spring offensive of the following year. AC

bomb their way eastward towards men of 5th Australian Brigade who might have reached enemy lines. The gain was meagre, the bombers being continually repulsed. As daylight faded, the Australians saw the remnants of 5th Brigade trickling back across no man's land having spent the day sheltering in shell holes in front of the German wire. An order to retire then reached 6th Brigade, still strongly holding their line against all comers. The order was based upon incorrect reports, but the Diggers elected to ignore it anyway – they were not going to give up these blood-soaked, hard-won trenches for a second time. They dug in and awaited relief. Reports (later proven premature) that Chérisy had fallen put

Fabriksschornst. nördl. V/5 en Artois u.d.Stw. BOIRY *VITRY-en-Artois* *HAUCOURT* *Stw. ARRAS-CAMBRAI* *Waldst. nördl. Hendecourt*
V/5 en Artois *S.hornst. u. Kirche V/5 en Artois* *Zurückliegend St. Servins F.*
BOIRY Notre-Dame *Weg v. Str. Arras südwest RIENCOURT n. FONTAINE*

No attack materialized. If 6th Australian Brigade could not somehow be supported, a rerun of 11 April was surely the only outcome. As pressure from hostile bombing from the west increased, so the Australian engineers came into their own. Between 2.00 p.m. and 9.00 p.m. the 2nd Pioneer Battalion managed to dig a communication trench a full kilometre long running alongside Central Road and connecting the railway embankment with the Hindenburg Line. Fresh troops passed into the line via this route, 'Pioneer Avenue' (see page 286), and so 6th Brigade was gradually relieved during the night of 3/4 May – whilst under counter-attack. By dawn the following morning the positions were consolidated, and about 1.00 p.m. the Australians began their own bombing campaign, pushing westward toward the village and gradually creating a gridiron defence with the interlinking German communication trenches. Soon they were bombing outwards in both directions, by 4.00 p.m. on 4 May extending the gain to almost 1,000 metres in breadth. Few prisoners were taken by either side – there was no one to deal with them.

No doubt we broke the German's heart yesterday and the fact that only a few prisoners were taken (which included two Majors) points to the bitterness of the struggle. How anyone can come back alive is past comprehension – can one wonder that so many are fatalities? What has to be will be. And how we all wish that this cruel war would end. If home people saw one tenth of the misery and the terrible sights I saw those suffering they would indeed cry and beg for what we have long fought for, and what at last we shall have. Perhaps it is a punishment for some of many sins we all possess – but what a punishment. We are moving further back sometime today and we are given to understand we are to have a spell. Our casualties on the 3rd were about 200 – a very big percentage of the strength of our very weak battalion. High proportion of wounded to killed – farewell Bullecourt!
CORPORAL OSWALD BLOWS, 28TH BATTALION, AUSTRALIAN IMPERIAL FORCE

Above German panorama segment from March 1917 showing the area attacked by the British 62nd and 7th Divisions in May. Part of the 'Red Zone' is visible at right in front of Bullecourt village. HS M706 M10 Nr. 397

Below A *Flammenwerfer* as used during the German counterattacks. IWM E802

Kirche BELONNE
Kirche GOUY sous Bellonne
Westrand HENDECOURT
Str. Station ECOUST u. BULLECOURT
BULLECOURT

It was by no means over yet. Now the Germans punished the interlopers, drenching the trenches on both sides of no man's land with shells. So heavy was the bombardment that troops destined to attack were too shaken to do so. The 5th of May passed with more shelling and a little more lateral Australian expansion in the Hindenburg Line to the west, but no major assaults. Small British patrols were sent into the village to gauge the strength of the German garrison. Bullecourt appeared deserted, but in fact the enemy was safe in cellars and caves, relying upon guards to warn of danger, a scene reminiscent of Thiepval.

On 6 May, hostile shelling reached a crescendo; as it eased there was a violent counter-attack against 3rd Brigade, followed by others from the north. They were beaten off with huge casualties, but then from the east came a blow that none were expecting: an assault led by flamethrowers. It drove the Australians back along the Hindenburg Line to the link with Pioneer Avenue. This critical junc-

tion could not be allowed to fall or the garrison to the west would be helpless. The surge was in large part halted by the action of Corporal George Howell of New South Wales who climbed out of the trench with a bag of bombs and attacked the Germans from above, flinging down grenade upon grenade until he was wounded. Howell was awarded the VC. With the flamethrowers neutralized, the Australians once more took up their eastward bombing campaign in a yet more vigorous style.

The set-back delayed a planned British attack on the village until 3.45 a.m. on 7th. In this the 2nd Gordon Highlanders and 9th Devons of 20th Brigade broke into the right corner of the village, snatched both the first and second German trenches and linked with Australians bombing westwards with consummate skill and determination. There was at last a precarious foothold in Bullecourt, and soon Mancunian pioneers had connected it to the railway embankment with a new communication trench that had actually been commenced on the night of 4/5 May: Bullecourt Avenue. The task now was not just to hold but extend this precarious gain to the entire village. Reliefs took place in the line and fresh troops were ordered up from Albert. The next key target was known as the Red Patch. The nomenclature was not a bloody one, simply that on artillery maps the uncaptured area of Bullecourt that required extra shelling was coloured red. As the Official History notes, however, it would live up to its name. For the next four days the British and Australians tried to add to their gains, each time nibbling ever further into and around the village, but not completing the conquest. By 12 May, the situation was bizarre. Still baulked on the front western half of the salient, the British had clawed their way around the back of the village, until the Germans were almost encircled in the Red Patch save for the thin umbilical cord of the Bullecourt-Hendecourt road. Elsewhere the Allies were static, with the enemy blocked on the right, but still within striking distance of Pioneer Avenue, whilst in front no more than the second line was in Digger hands. More hostile bombing had led to nothing and activity calmed; the Allies knew a different form of counter-attack should now be expected. On the night of the 12th/13th, the Australians were at last relieved, the entire line being taken over by Imperial units, except the small bulb of captured line east of Pioneer Avenue. The British continued to gnaw away at Bullecourt.

At 4.00 a.m. on 15 May, the expected blows fell as a sequence of heavy counter-attacks upon the whole of the captured ground. All were ultimately fought off with the loss of only a little ground in the village. On the 16th, the German first line on the front face of the Red Patch was captured as far as the Ecoust-Hendecourt road.

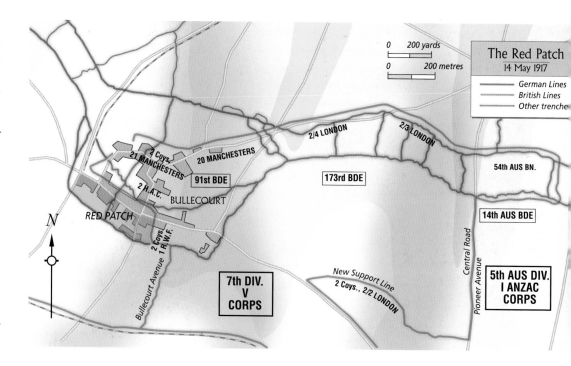

The situation here was now barely credible. Pressure was sustained, and eventually it paid off when from 2.00 a.m. on 17 May, the London Rifle Brigade and Post Office Rifles of 58th (London) Division overwhelmed the German garrison throughout the village. What had in fact happened was that the enemy were preparing to evacuate and were caught by surprise whilst in the process of planting demolition charges. To the British and Australians the nature of Bullecourt's fall was inconsequential; all they wanted was an end to the dreadful cycle of slaughter. Between them they had suffered 14,303 casualties for the gain of 1.5 kilometres of German line. The objectives – Riencourt and Hendecourt – were untouched, and would stay untouchable until the autumn of 1918.

Right The tortured remains of the Bullecourt sector after its mauling by the guns of both sides. AC

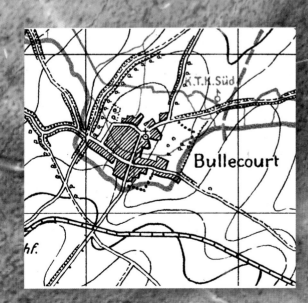

Bullecourt

CHAPTER EIGHTEEN

Final Steps

General Allenby (with map) enlightens the King of the Belgians. 17 April 1917. IWM Q2182

By the end of April our attack was nearly exhausted. The line was unstable. Bitter local attacks and counter-attacks were Infantry routine. Enemy artillery was again at full strength. Our bit of country had some attention; nothing to do with my intense loathing of the place. It was just the look of that cheerless slab of land which dispirited me – though far from being as bad as such slabs elsewhere. True, one saw a splash of colour in Monchy, a splash of terracotta and brick-red, when the sun shone, from the fragments of houses heaped there. It was the single brightness; unless one includes the flashes of a Hun 8-inch battery, plain to see from our H.Q. There was no green left on those slopes, only the dull sodden lifeless earth, pitted with shellholes, almost yard for yard. A few poor trees still fringed the Arras-Cambrai road. All others had gone, with the hedges, the ditches, the drains. Wrecked war-material littered the area. Unburied dead with swollen faces lay about. I set myself to bury them.

Except as a sanitary and aesthetic measure, this burying business was not my affair, yet I used to feel that if someone on the spot had time for the job, he should do it. The men had been left by another Division and no doubt because it had been out of the question to bury them. As a rule, I worked alone. Here Tomson joined me, sharing the thankless task of writing to relatives of men we buried. Brigade office dealt with identification discs and pay-books. Many letters came in answer to mine. Most asked how, when, where the men had died and were buried. All these men were unknown to me, so one could say practically nothing. I kept some of the replies. Many letters of the same kind must be hidden now. Most, perhaps, lost forever. Any record of the war years is impoverished a little by their absence. Women tended to write more briefly than men. From a widow:

Mrs A E Pickering
97b Tappesfield Road
Nimhead Green
SE15

9/5/17

Dear Sir,
I received your letter dated 26.4.17 last Thursday and for which I offer my sincere thanks. I have not heard yet from the War Office, but suppose will in due course. Could you enlighten me, as to whether my husband had a particular friend and if at any time he left a message for me, should like to know also the nature of his wounds, also where he is buried. I accept your sympathy and also thank you for your kindness in writing to me. It is a great shock for me to bear, as I am left with 6 little girls, the baby he has not seen is 1 year old. Please do your best in answering the above, as I should dearly like to know if there was any message for me at any time. Thanking you again, I remain yours very gratefully,

A.E. Pickering.

(WIFE OF LATE PTE W.T. PICKERING 3371, 2ND BATTALION, ROYAL FUSILIERS)

All I could tell her was roughly where he was buried. The difficulties, not to say risks of personal odium from one source or another, associated with the unofficial burying of abandoned and decomposing bodies were considerable. Secrecy forbade all mention of localities, nor could one say much about or expect a widow fully to understand circumstances in which a man's body had been left behind while his friends were withdrawn from the line and pushed off elsewhere. And one never knew a single thing about the men of whom one was writing. Very probably most of the men who were buried by me – on various parts of the front – were ultimately re-buried in military cemeteries.

CAPTAIN L. GAMESON, ROYAL ARMY MEDICAL CORPS, MEDICAL OFFICER TO 71ST BRIGADE, ROYAL FIELD ARTILLERY

Whilst the almost private action at Bullecourt ran its course, events elsewhere were proving equally arduous and equally brutal. The French military machine was in crisis and morale destructively low. The axe fell on Nivelle and a swathe of other commanders; Pétain became Commander-in-Chief, and General Ferdinand Foch took over as Chief of the General Staff. GQG sought out agitators, pacifists, communists and defeatists, but the reasons for unrest were many and far from straightforward.

In the first place, an unsatisfactory commander, whom the men rarely saw and who did not trouble himself about their comfort. In the second, a certain carelessness in the issue of rations and in the arrangement of the leave roster, of which the more cunning were always ready to take advantage. Then the feeling that the country was forgetting them, in spite of the nonsensical flattery which the newspapers heaped upon them; the letters which they received spoke of shirkers; the men who had been on leave reported that in rear of the armies nobody worried, and they were not far wrong.

On the other hand, they observed the great papers; those daily articles in which the offer of peace was described as a snare which must be avoided showed that there was only one way out for them, to beat the Boche. For this purpose a marvellous offensive was in preparation, advertised as being about to lead to a complete and decisive victory. The Boche retreat in March seemed to them a preliminary symptom of the coming end of their troubles. The troops were fired with unprecedented enthusiasm.

Then the offensive was launched. These brave men were stopped short everywhere, were massacred without being able to advance any further than on other occasions. The same machine-guns, the same barbed wire, stopped them. Not only was no progress made in the science of attack; but it even seemed that the dispositions were worse than ever. These were old soldiers, it must be remembered, who knew all about war and could not be imposed upon. If they had failed this time, then they would never succeed. The Boches would not break through, but no more should we. Why should we be expected to be more cunning than they? The Boche fought well. Who should know this better than soldiers who were always fighting him? All that was said about the demoralization of the enemy was rubbish.

Jean de Pierrefeu, draftsman of daily press communiqués at French headquarters

Whether exacerbated by defeatist elements or not, the Nivelle offensive had failed, and that failure was the catalyst for yet more action at Arras. On 5 May in Paris, a Franco-British conference came to the conclusion that limited attacks must continue, occupying German attentions until Sir Douglas Haig's summer plans for Flanders were ripe. Now the French took over a length of *British* line. But the great offensive was over; Arras would soon begin to lose artillery to Belgium, and many of its troops for refit and training. With almost immediate effect, the limitation of resources could only mean smaller operations in Artois. The majority of the original battlefront could be left as the lines now stood, but there still remained some priority objectives.

On the First Army front reliefs had taken place after the actions of 3 and 4 May, the task of incoming British units in the Oppy-Fresnoy sectors being to deal with the untidy wriggle in the line south of Fresnoy.

In the skies the British were now taking delivery of the new generation of scouts. The difference immediately began to tell, with day by day German aviators being engaged further and further behind the forward zone, allowing a more frequent and safe passage for RFC

reconnaissance aircraft. Losses to Richthofen's circus tumbled and there was a marked increase in the British 'kill' rate. This most welcome transformation had a noticeable effect on the ground, yet German resistance and aggression still appeared to be growing. Hostile shelling grew more intense than ever, gas became a permanent hazard in the gun lines and there never appeared to be a shortage of trained troops for counter-attack. By way of confirmation, on 8 May the Fresnoy salient was ruptured. Canadian and British troops were unable to withstand the force of 5th Bavarian Infantry Division, recently arrived in the area. On this sopping day they were thrown back to the 28 April line east of Arleux. The situation was perilous, for no defensive positions had yet been installed between Arleux and Vimy Ridge, and reserve companies were not readily to hand. Fortunately, the Bavarians were again content to recapture only recently lost ground. But the collapse of Fresnoy was heartbreaking, for it was the first setback of the battle that involved the loss of properly consolidated territory. Casualties were severe, and the shock palpable.

The sunken road and trench were lined, or rather crammed, with the wounded and the dead and many of the wounded were obviously dying.

All were lying in the mud at the bottom of the trench; a horrible scene of mud and blood. As well as the wounded were those on their feet. The remnants of the 12th Gloucesters, some Canadians, a few East Surreys and, for some reason or other, a few D.C.L.I. No officer could be found but there must have been one somewhere for as we entered the trenches we saw up above a small counter-attack starting, but five minutes afterwards the survivors, some wounded were back in the trench in confusion. As far as we knew the

Bavarians might appear at any moment firing down into the trench and finishing off the remainder with the bayonet. If this happened all the open ground, some two miles between Arleux and Vimy ridge would be lost, for there was no trench system or suitable defensive position with cover between the two. The immediate and essential action to be taken was to place posts on the top of the trench in positions from which they could bring fire to bear on attackers. The infernal trench, in which we were, although very useful for protection against shell fire, was useless as a position from which we could fight; one was quite blind in it owing to its great depth. So it was necessary to get someone to hoist me out over the parados where I was pleased to find a large number of shell craters. I could take cover in them and hop from one to another, thus getting cover from shell splinters. We had had no time, nor was it worthwhile, to try and organize the men of the various units we found unwounded in the trench. Their leaders were probably all casualties or captured in Fresnoy. Furthermore, they were to some extent demoralised by their experiences that morning. By the end of the morning they had disappeared. Where to? I have no idea.

The condition of the many wounded in the trench was deplorable with the rush of men up and down it, some of them were being trodden further into the mud. Many were shouting or groaning for water, requests usually not answered, though I remember giving water to a dying Canadian whose legs below the knee were more or less gone and his thigh bones sticking out. By the time the shelling ceased at about 12 noon I was relieved to see that he had died as had a number of the more desperately wounded and mangled, and I am afraid some of the less badly wounded who had bled to death through lack of medical attention; but such is war.

I met a young Lance Corporal of another platoon walking slowly down the trench towards me without equipment and without a rifle. His large brown, or almost black eyes, were wide open in an unwinking stare, looking, as it were, at nothing. He was like one walking

Above Part of the Arras battlefield as seen on 23 July 1917 showing (at bottom) Fresnoy, the only village to be gained and lost during the offensive. HS M706 M9 Nr.375

Left As the light fades British troops move up to the line once more. IWM Q2105

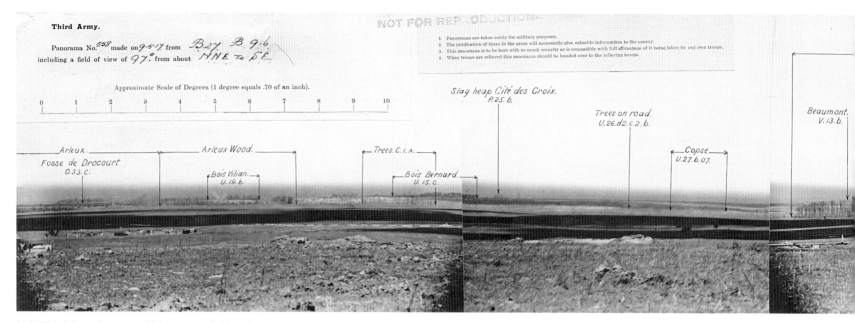

Third Army.

Panorama No.*558* made on 9·5·17 from *B.27 B.9.6* including a field of view of 97° from about *N.N.E. to S.E.*

1. Panoramas are taken solely for military purposes.
2. The publication of them in the press will necessarily give valuable information to the enemy.
3. This panorama is to be kept with as much security as is compatible with full advantage of it being taken by our own troops.
4. When troops are relieved this panorama should be handed over to the relieving troops.

Approximate Scale of Degrees (1 degree equals .70 of an inch).

0 1 2 3 4 5 6 7 8 9 10

Arleux. — *Arleux Wood.* — *Trees. C.1.A.* — *Slag heap Cité des Croix. P.25.b.* — *Trees on road. U.26.d2.c.2.b.* — *Copse U.27.b.07.* — *Beaumont. V.13.b.*

Fosse de Drocourt. O.33.C. — *Bois Vilian. U.19.b.* — *Bois Bernard. U.15.c.*

IWM Third Army Panorama 558 taken on 9 May 1917 showing the ground between Arleux and Roeux (Left half *above*, right half *below*)

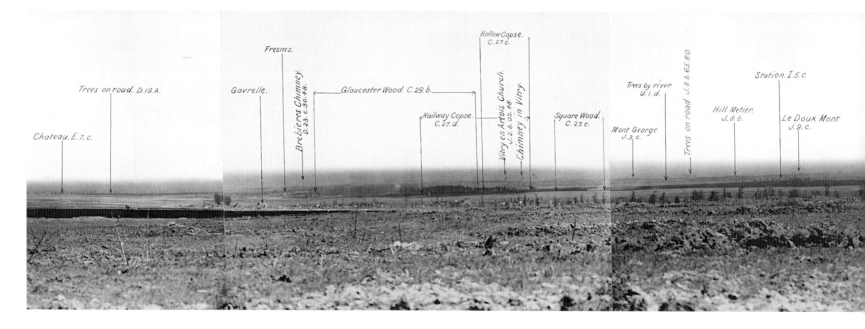

Trees on road. D.19.A. — *Fresnes.* — *Gloucester Wood. C.29.b.* — *Hollow Copse. C.27.c.* — *Trees by river. U.1.d.* — *Station. I.5.c.*

Gavrelle. — *Brebieres Chimney. D.23.c.30.48.* — *Railway Copse. C.27.d.* — *Vitry en Artois Church. J.2.b.02.88.* — *Chimney in Vitry.* — *Square Wood. C.27.c.* — *Trees on road. J.8.b.65.80.* — *Hill Metier. J.8.b.* — *Le Doux Mont. J.9.c.*

Chateau. E.7.c. — *Mont George. J.3.c.*

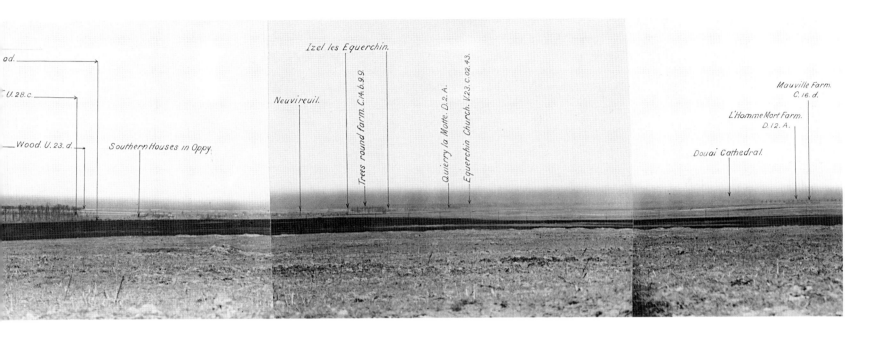

od.

U. 28. c.

Wood. U. 23. d.

Southern Houses in Oppy.

Neuvireuil.

Izel les Equerchin.

Trees round farm. C.14. b. 9. 9.

Quierry la Motte. D. 2. A.

Equerchin Church. V.23. c. 02. 43.

Douai Cathedral.

L'Homme Mort Farm. D. 12. A.

Mauville Farm. C. 16. d.

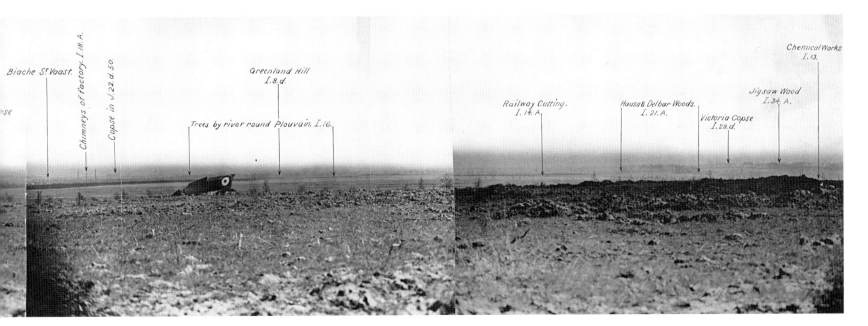

Biache St Vaast.

se

Chimneys of factory. I. 18. A.

Copse in J. 22. d. 50.

Trees by river round Plouvain. I. 16.

Greenland Hill I. 8. d.

Railway Cutting. I. 14. A.

Hausa & Delbar Woods. I. 21. A.

Victoria Copse I. 28. d.

Jigsaw Wood I. 34. A.

Chemical Works I. 13.

in his sleep. I shouted to make myself heard above the prevailing uproar, what was the matter? He made no reply except a sort of muttering or moaning. He appeared unwounded so I saw that he was completely unhinged by the shelling and the butcher's shop all around. What to do? He obviously could not be left to roam ghost-like down the trench; that would not be good for the morale of others. I decided to take him to the company headquarters dug out. So, I took hold of his hand and led him like a child to the entrance. It was a deep dug out so there was a long flight of stairs. I hoped he would follow me down. When I let go of his hand he did so. We arrived at the bottom and found a spacious room with wire frame beds or bunks one above the other in part whilst the other part was an office with tables and chairs obligingly left by the Germans. Lieutenant Wonnacott, who was acting as company commander, was busy trying to get through to Battalion H.Q. on the recently laid field telephone. As we could get no sense or answer out of the Lance Corporal we decided he would have to stay in the dug out until it was possible to evacuate him. The orderlies pushed him into a bunk. I did not see him again. I then noticed that there were two young officers who had joined the battalion of few days before this battle lying in bunks. They were groaning. I asked Wonnacott what was the matter with them. He said "One says he is gassed and the other that he is ill, but in my opinion the only thing the matter with them is that they have 'vertical wind-up'."

We went over to talk to them but got little in the way of acknowledgement except groans and the announcement by one of them that he felt as if he were going to die. This was too much for Wonnacott who gave him a good shaking and said "Die and be damned then".

LIEUTENANT L.H.M. WESTROPP, 1ST DEVONSHIRE REGIMENT

Counter-attack was obligatory. At 2.30 a.m. the following morning, the 5th Division and the 20th Canadian Battalion were expected to recapture the village. Once more it was as if the Germans knew, for the main point of assembly at Arleux

was shelled all night. Then the darkness beat the Canadians, who were unable to gather together the units to make the attack.

At about 1.50 a.m. Wonnacott re-appeared again and gave me a not very re-assuring piece of information. The Canadians had just told Captain Maton that they could not attack as their battalion had only just received orders to do so. In spite of this news it had been decided that we should still carry out the attack.

The whole line stood up and marched forward by the centre. We had not gone more than perhaps sixty yards when a man on my left in the front line bent his head down slowly on his chest and slowly, almost gently, sank to the ground. He had probably been killed instantaneously by a bullet through the heart. When this happens people usually subside quite quietly without any struggling. Soon after this there was a yellow flash from behind and a strong puff of air which pushed me on to my knees. I was unhurt; we had walked too close to our barrage. Some were not so lucky as I was. The whole line automatically knelt down and waited for the barrage to get further ahead. After, I suppose, three minutes we got up and walked forward slowly. Men were now beginning to fall fast from bullets or possibly fragments of German shell. I could now see vaguely through the smoke a line or slight mound perhaps some fifty yards away – the first enemy trench. I could see no flashes coming from it so the Germans, if any, must still have their heads well down. Some men came on guard [with rifle and fixed bayonet] which reminded me to pull out my revolver in case the Germans were in the first trench. I had just done so when my legs were swept away from under me and I went down like a shot rabbit. I hit the ground fairly hard which knocked the breath out of me. My right leg felt as if it had been hit by an eighteen-pounder shell at least! When I recovered my breath I looked sideways at my right leg which I saw had a very large hole on the outside with a bone sticking out and some boot with other things in it.

LIEUTENANT L.H.M. WESTROPP, 1ST DEVONSHIRE REGIMENT

German preparation had been prudent and the defence all too well organized between infantry and artillery; the only success fell to the 15th Royal Warwicks who alone got into Fresnoy; there they were either destroyed, surrounded and captured, or forced out. The prime source of the Allies' problems was hostile artillery. It seemed that no counter-battery fire could quell them. The unremitting German aggression was gradually breaking the British nerve.

Fresnoy would stay in German hands for the British had run out of fresh troops, and with Flanders looming GHQ dare not now draw upon other divisions. Only five days later First Army batteries began their move north. With much Third Army artillery requiring refurbishment Allenby was forced to shuttle guns between corps and divisions in order to continue his attacks. The areas it was now deemed essential to occupy were the Roeux sector (with Greenland Hill), Infantry Hill east of Monchy and the final section of the Hindenburg Line between Croisilles and Bullecourt. In finally conquering these key localities, the hope – no longer a belief – was that the enemy might still voluntarily fall back to the Drocourt-Quéant Line. There was little expectation of *driving* him back.

After a sequence of thundery days, Major General Lambton's 4th Division again received orders for Roeux. The village itself was not a target: if objectives beyond the Chemical Works were attained, the occupants would almost certainly be forced to evacuate. The Official History attributes the lack of success in the sector, 'partly to insufficient artillery preparation, partly to the distance of the objectives set, and partly to the absence of surprise in the attacks at dawn'. A stubborn enemy might have been added to the list. Apprehensive and considerably below establishment with only 2,444 rifles, a breathtaking array of artillery of

every calibre up to 15-inch was assembled to assist the assault, plus a mass of machine guns and Stokes mortars. The bombardment was to be a truly 'thick' affair, with 18-pounders lined up almost wheel-to-wheel (there were 6 metres between), each gun being allotted an astonishingly narrow 2-metre target corridor of ground. The creeper was to advance at 100 metres per four minutes, in conjunction with a second barrage delivered by 4.5-inch howitzers falling 100 metres beyond. Two 17th Division companies strengthened the left flank, and engineers were to go over with the machine-gunners to prepare positions from which the inevitable counter-attacks might be defied. The British were exhausted in mind and body, and were ever more aware of a general winding-down of the offensive.

The line has now been reorganised and all three Brigades are in the line. The last few days have been intensely hot and the smell of dead bodies all round Fampoux and the railway is simply awful – this will become a serious question soon. Went over to Savy to see the reinforcements. Have had two small drafts of twelve and thirteen. Went up and saw the Battalion this afternoon – they go into the trenches tonight and attack to-morrow evening at 7.30 p.m. against the station and buildings North of the railway; the East Lancs attack the Chemical Works on our right, and the Hants go for the Chateau. The 17th Division (6th Dorsets) attack on our left. This is our final effort against these hitherto impregnable positions which have cost us so many lives – we want to get beyond the whole collection of buildings and dig in on the far side by night, and then make another small advance on the morning of the 12th. Given a decent barrage and good artillery support, I don't anticipate any difficulty doing this, but it may be a nasty job hanging on as they are sure to shell the place to blazes. New assembly trenches have been dug and we have got a decent jumping-off position.

LIEUTENANT COLONEL R.T. FELLOWES, 1ST RIFLE BRIGADE

Fellowes was correct. The bloodshed could not continue *ad infinitum* in this sector. The men were wrecks. It would be the third attack that his division had thrown against the reviled neighbourhood; however, it was also true that preparations were more substantial than ever before. The tremendous artillery presence appended confidence even to the weariest of troops.

Timings were adjusted. The first attack was to begin at 7.30 p.m. on 11 May, a second being scheduled for the following day at 6.30 a.m. Then the guns played a practice overture, looking to tempt enemy batteries into revealing their presence, whilst in the air the new generation of scouts scudded well into German airspace, protecting the assembling Tommies from hostile eyes.

Thankfully, assembly remained a largely unmolested and clandestine affair. Zero-Hour probably witnessed the greatest concentration of organized gunfire of the war. And it was effective: the Chemical Works, station, chateau and surrounding buildings all fell, the enemy presence afterwards being marked only by a few isolated parties amongst the ruins. But could the position be held? At 6.30 a.m. on 12 May the second assault, again by elements of the same two divisions and supported by equally stupefying gunfire, surged in and through, establishing posts on the lower slopes of Greenland Hill. Despite accumulating extraordinarily large numbers of prisoners, in general these attacks were not especially profitable, but at least ground was being gained to straighten the existing line and consolidate the whole position. The hornet's nest was by no means cleared, but it was as much as the dead-beat 4th Division was able to achieve. They badly needed a break

and having made ground were immediately relieved by the 51st Division.

The changes of units after this second tour in the line opposite the Chemical Works was a nightmare. An unsuccessful attack had recently been launched through our position by another battalion and the remnants withdrawn, leaving my weakened battalion in charge of a very confused situation. The night was as black as pitch and the arrival of the relieving unit so delayed that dawn might break with the relief incomplete and arriving or departing troops caught in the open in full view of an alert enemy. Add to this the realisation that neither officers nor specially selected guides were sufficiently familiar with the geography of their sector or the disposition of their troops and you have all the ingredients of a truly disturbing situation, and a night of worry and anxiety for the commanders. Patiently as possible I sat in an insecure dug-out, awaiting in turn the arrival of the "relief completed" reports from the various companies. One after the other they came from three companies, each having added some depressing bit of news about casualties or misunderstandings or misadventures. Then followed a long and ever lengthening gap without sign or news of the fourth and last company. The hours passed. No rearward movement of troops could be heard or had been noted by sentries or headquarters personal. Orderlies sent to the front line to investigate returned to say that evidently the relief was complete as the new unit was in its trenches and that the last company must have gone out safely though for some inexplicable reason their report had not reached me. I then set off in search myself because I felt sure something was wrong, not merely a case of forgetfulness by the Company. The faint light of approaching dawn was beginning and served to emphasize the urgency of my position when an orderly of my headquarters stumbled on a body. It was the body of the commander of my fourth company, recognised in the dim light by a chain armour waistcoat he used to wear – so little had it availed him. He was himself the bearer of the news of the completion of his company's relief

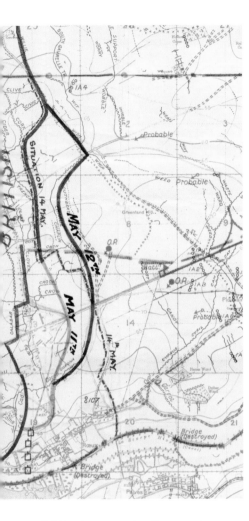

British advances against Roeux and Greenland Hill up to 14 May.
NA WO95-363

and travelling alone through the night had fallen silently to a chance bullet. A few yards away we had been waiting in rising anxiety for the news he had tried so hard to bring.
LIEUTENANT COLONEL NOEL IRWIN MC, 2ND ESSEX REGIMENT

Operations at Monchy were of a markedly different nature. Part of Tool Trench was taken in a surprise attack on 11 May, and the next day a three-battalion assault on Devil's Trench was repulsed; two days later another attempt gained no ground. And so it went on until the end of the month. The pattern was repeated against the remaining portion of the Hindenburg Line, where between 11 and 28 May there were linear gains west of Bullecourt through the interesting combination of bombing, frontal attack – and mining. The fact that the tunnellers had been called in is an eloquent testament to how fortunes had degenerated since 9 April. A return to siege warfare was the last thing anyone desired, yet here it was again, not in preparation for action but in its midst.

On May 20 we engineered a most successful underground operation, and very materially aided our infantry in capturing another 500 yards of the famous Hindenburg Line. About a week before... we were informed that two infantry assaults had come 'unstuck' and the parties composing them nearly all 'scuppered' by reason of the heavy and accurate machine-gun fire coming from a double machine-gun concrete emplacement some 200 feet in front of our most advanced barricade in the Hindenburg trench opposite the village of Fontaine-les-Croisilles. The artillery had endeavoured several times to destroy this position, but were not successful. It became necessary to remove it. The subsoil here was hard chalk, and the top-soil a sandy clay, the latter averaging seven to ten feet in thickness. It was essential to the success of our scheme that we confine our tunnel to the clay, it being possible to excavate in the clay almost without noise, while in the chalk below this could not be done.

Starting from an old dug-out entrance we constructed a tunnel approximately four by two feet for some distance, and from this point to or objective continued a 'rabbit-hole' three feet by two in size. As we had only an average of two feet of clay above our gallery we were considerably bothered by our own shells landing near, and on one occasion they destroyed it with an 18-pounder. At other times we broke through into shell-craters on our way over. One night after heavy rain I was on duty in the tunnel when we were pretty close to the German pill-box and their crew. The earth sloughed away from the top of the gallery and exposed the timber of our gallery sets [wooden frames used to support the earth of the tunnel walls and roof]. We blew out the candles at once and very carefully placed some muddy sand-bags over the exposed portion. Being so near the Boche sentries, we were fearful that they would have spotted our light, heard our low whispering, or even our heavy breathing.

The next night we struck the concrete of the emplacement, and very carefully excavating down to the bottom of the clay against the position, we placed a charge of some 500 pounds [227 kg] of high explosive, carefully inserted the usual detonators and electric leads back in the tunnel, and the next dawn at 'zero' hour fired the charge the instant the infantry went over the top. The resulting explosion very satisfactorily disposed of the troublesome 'Mebus' and largely enabled the 4th King's Liverpool Regiment to capture some 200 yards of the trenches.
CAPTAIN H.D. TROUNCE, 181 TUNNELLING COMPANY, ROYAL ENGINEERS

It was on 15 May that tension and apprehension began to escalate at Roeux as the German guns delivered a high-explosive prelude to onslaught. At its crescendo it was as heavy as anything the British had deployed throughout the entire battle, and at 3.45 on the morning of 16 May the expected blow fell. In the pre-dawn half-light counter-attacks swept across, punching holes and in places driving through almost 300 metres, but actually making only a limited impression upon the British gains of previous days. The defence was just as gritty and effective as the enemy had displayed elsewhere. Again following the German pattern, there were instant counter-measures, and as the day passed most of the early losses were regained, the enemy suffering far greater casualties than usual. With the darkness came time to consider the position. Roeux, the Chemical Works area and many forward posts and trenches were still firmly in British hands. There beneath the gaze of Greenland Hill the lines settled, and so they would remain for the rest of the year. In the meantime, even in this most blighted of regions, summer and all it entailed for the British was on the way.

17 MAY 1917

Dear Mother,

We have a great game of cricket which we play here. We use a tennis ball and a pick handle as a bat. The wicket is a box stood on end. The more shell holes about there are, the better. Yesterday the officers played a team out of the company at tip-and-run. The pitch was a path between shell holes. The men went in and made 34 and we just beat them when it began to rain. The shell holes make fielding great fun as when there is a catch if you watch the ball you probably fall into a shell hole and if the ball bounces it probably hits the side of a shell hole and goes off at right angles.

CAPTAIN WILLIAM VILLIERS, 9TH KING'S ROYAL RIFLE CORPS

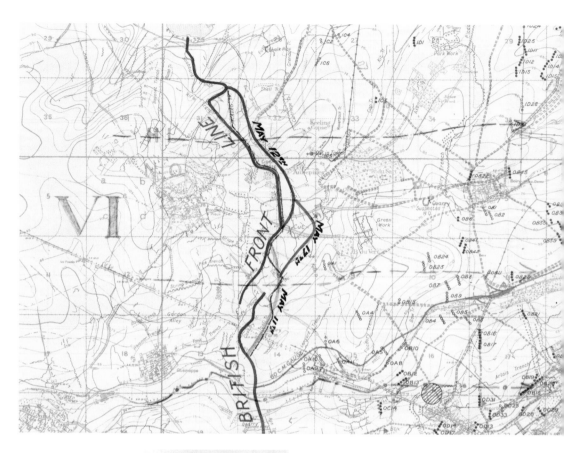

Above Results of the last push in the Roeux sector on 17 May. NA WO95-363

Left Observers watch the final bombardments. IWM Q3872

Right The final line after the battle

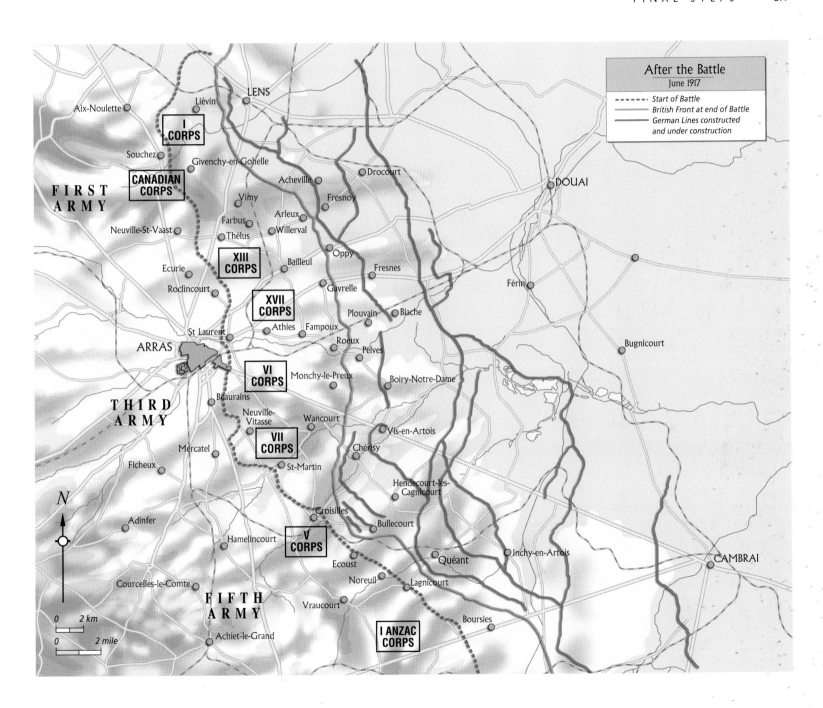

After the Battle
June 1917

- - - - - Start of Battle
——— British Front at end of Battle
——— German Lines constructed
and under construction

Aix-Noulette

Liévin

LENS

I CORPS

Souchez

Givenchy-en-Gohelle

FIRST ARMY

CANADIAN CORPS

Acheville

Drocourt

DOUAI

Vimy

Fresnoy

Farbus

Arleux

Neuville-St-Vaast

Thélus

Willerval

Oppy

Fresnes

Férin

XIII CORPS

Bailleul

Ecurie

Gavrelle

Bugnicourt

Roclincourt

XVII CORPS

Plouvain

Biache

St Laurent

Athies

Fampoux

ARRAS

Roeux

THIRD ARMY

Pelves

VI CORPS

Monchy-le-Preux

Boiry-Notre-Dame

Beaurains

Neuville-Vitasse

Wancourt

Mercatel

VII CORPS

Vis-en-Artois

St-Martin

Chérisy

Ficheux

Hendecourt-lès-Cagnicourt

N

Adinfer

Croisilles

Hamelincourt

V CORPS

Bullecourt

Ecoust

Quéant

Inchy-en-Artois

CAMBRAI

Courcelles-le-Comte

Noreuil

Lagnicourt

FIFTH ARMY

Vraucourt

0   2 km

I ANZAC CORPS

Boursies

0   2 mile

Achiet-le-Grand

Epilogue

ARRAS
JANUARY 25TH 1919

My own darling wife,

We arrived at 11.15 – a wonderfully quick journey. We went up to the old familiar ground of the trenches. On the way we went into a ruined church – there was rather a startling sight in it – the figure of Christ on the cross had lost both arms and the head, while that of his Virgin Mother had been moved on its pedestal so that it looked up, wonderingly at the mutilation. Further up the road we came upon that abomination of desolation – No Man's Land of 1916-17. It is much as I left it. Only the rank grass has overgrown the shell holes and barbed wire – but the holes and wire are still there. Here and there, small groups of Chinamen were at work, salvaging sheet iron and like stuff – but the debris of battle is still there. We found old bombs, trench mortars, rifles of all patterns, all sorts of rusted and decayed war material – and once we came upon the skull of a Fritz which still grinned up at the light of day from the long grass; while a jagged bone in the skull showed how quickly he had died. The war is over, but there is an awful mess to be cleaned up yet. I found the place where I fired my barrage on Easter Monday 1917, but night was falling and I did not have time to explore it thoroughly. We were tired and glad to get back on the road.

Tomorrow I hope to catch a car to Lens and then to walk backward over the ridge to Arras by nightfall. There is so much to see, and so little time to do it in. I wish you were here so that I could show it all to you, though it is a saddening experience. As we walked "home" the silence was oppressive; it was the silence of death and I almost longed to hear the dull thunder of the guns again and to see their red flashes and the white flare lights that used to float so continuously over No Man's Land. In those days, at least, there was action and work to be done; now all is desolation and loneliness.

CAPTAIN WALTER DARLING MC, 2ND CANADIAN MACHINE GUN COMPANY

The *Petite Place*, Arras. IWM

Officially, the Battle of Arras closed on 24 May 1917. In actuality, piecemeal assaults known as 'associated actions' continued throughout the summer and autumn until the Battle of Cambrai in November, each designed to attract German attention whilst first Messines and then the Third Battle of Ypres ran their contrasting courses. Under awkward prevailing circumstances the French played whatever part they were able to keep the enemy occupied.

The key aspect of the Anglo-British spring offensive of 1917 was that it gave the Germans every right to look upon the future with confidence – until the entry of the USA. At Arras and Vimy the majority of territorial loss had taken place during the first fifteen hours of battle, and it had come about largely as a result of attacks taking place sooner than expected. In no other clash did the events of a single day – 9 April – hold such promise to dramatically change the face of the wider conflict. The battles of 1915 were mere pinpricks by comparison, and the Somme a bloody training ground – for both sides. At Messines in early June 1917 victory was more complete, indeed almost 'perfect' if a battle can be described as such, but like the storming of Vimy Ridge just eight weeks earlier, it was designed as a limited attack with a strictly limited objective: to produce a stable platform for the Third Battle of Ypres. Towering success and brilliantly organized though it was, Messines can be discounted as representative of general capability, for it had the benefit of the nineteen great mines that shattered the morale and broke the spirit of the German defence – a unique benefit. And that subterranean enterprise only achieved its colossal scale as a result of British failure on the Somme, which in delaying Sir Douglas Haig's

Flanders plans added an unanticipated ten months for mine schemes to develop and multiply. Without the extra time only half as many charges would have been completed. There was also a deal of luck involved, for had the Germans taken heed of their own tunnelling chief, Colonel Otto Füsslein, who advocated that forward trenches should be evacuated, the mines would have exploded relatively harmlessly in no man's land. Nevertheless, in achieving everything that had been hoped for and considerably more, the battle was one of very few real triumphs of the war.

The dismal slog that followed Messines, the Third Battle of Ypres, was a drawn-out variation of Arras without the success of the first day. In mid-November when Cambrai was fought partly to sweeten the bitter pill of Passchendaele, the massing of 378 tanks revealed a key that half unlocked the door to victory, but although they temporarily laid bare the German defences, the infantry still had to complete the task. Only infantry *won* battles because only infantry could *occupy*, and without occupation battles are neither won nor lost. As on 10 April, through a mixture of indecision and disagreement in command, and sharp defensive practice by the enemy, they were again incapable of pressing a colossal advantage.

Arras claimed approximately 62,000 British and German lives. As one of the war's great offensives it stands alone as an example of missed opportunity, wasted lives, defective leadership and poor communication. The astonishing determination and doggedness of the troops of both sides is, as always, breathtaking, but long before the end of the battle those who took part could no longer find it within themselves to look back without murmuring, or forward without doubting. In defence the

Formation of the Front
October 1914

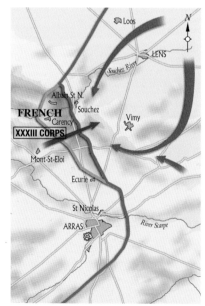

French break-through and German counter attack
May 1915

Franco-British Offensive
September 1915

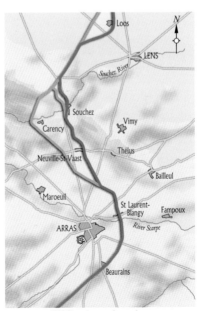

1916 Situation unchanged

British Army was as obstinate and gritty as its German counterpart, indeed as any army on earth, but throughout 1917 and despite the many improvements instigated since the Somme it remained a blunt instrument in offence, its efforts repeatedly deadened by the cruel mix of poor planning and command, and obsidian-sharp German tactical adaptation. But there was something unforgivably shambolic about Arras, and the blundering led to bitterness. Eyewitness testimonies contain more instances of exasperation about the way the battle was commanded than any other of the war. In the National Archives' CAB 45 papers one can find responses to enquiries made by the various authors of the British Official History. Although the Arras section was completed in the late 1930s, many respondents reveal a continuing resentment for the way the offensive was allowed to unfold.

There was however another reason for the failure … That was lack of cooperation between units, and lack of coordination from the higher command. In the operations from April 4th to May 3rd 1917, this lack of cooperation was most apparent – and there seemed to be no guiding hand from above to coordinate the attacks. Whether this was the fault of the Army command, or of G.H.Q., I am not prepared to say, but I suspect that it was the fault of both. As day after day went by, and one futile attack followed another with appalling waste of human life, the air of confidence which had been so evident at the start gave way to despondency. At no other time during the war did we experience such a feeling … How the Germans must have laughed at us! One futile attack succeeded another, with no cooperation, no guiding hand. It was no wonder that as casualties increased, so confidence disappeared.
R.A.C. WELLESLEY TO CYRIL FALLS, 1938. AT THE TIME OF ARRAS, BRIGADIER GENERAL WELLESLEY WAS CRA 21ST DIVISION.

GHQ selected Sir Edmund Allenby as the scapegoat. In London on 3 June 1917, the General was informed that he was no longer to be involved with the Western Front, nor even face the Germans as a foe: with immediate effect 'Bull' was despatched to command the Palestine force against the Ottomans. Byng took his place at Third Army, whilst Gough was already in Flanders preparing Fifth Army's onslaught against the ripple of ridges in front of Ypres. Hurtful and humiliating though Allenby's 're-appointment' may have been, he was to silence many a detractor by sweeping the Turks out of the war with victories at Jerusalem, Megiddo and Damascus, in so doing perhaps avoiding the ignominy that a European command might have led to. For these services he was later elevated to Viscount Allenby of Megiddo.

Sir Hubert Gough moved from one cruel battle to another, and then another. At Third Ypres his reputation for wantonly discarding the lives of his troops was further augmented, and in late March 1918 after suffering the wrath of the German spring offensive on the old Somme battleground, Fifth Army was taken from him. Gough never regained the confidence of his peers and spent much of his long life (he died in 1963) in attempting to re-apply gloss to his reputation. For his achievements against the ridge, General Sir Julian Byng became Viscount Byng of Vimy.

Throughout the writing of this book, the author has been drawn time and again to Sir Douglas Haig's obsession with Flanders. One can almost detect a sigh of relief when in late May he is able to turn his full attention towards Messines and Ypres. Haig's diary holds nothing to dispel the thought that Arras was merely a stepping stone, a duty, and that his heart was not really in the offensive. There is no immediacy, no urgency, no authentic exasperation or rage at the failure to make the most of what was achieved on 9 April. His papers are certainly fascinating, but at the same time they are slight, and so self-aware they may perhaps better be described as public rather than private; indeed they are believed by many to have been written with publication in mind. Ultimately, there is insufficient content to draw an adequate sketch map of the landscape of his mind. He will probably forever remain an enigma.

War is the state where man is at his most fallible, imperfect, brutal, and indeed sensitive. Arras was simply a tiny slice of the learning curve that began when man first took up arms against his fellow man. That curve arcs across the millennia and is extant and utterly undiminished today. Sadly, the human race has not travelled far along it. The only certain truth about the capabilities of British and French generals appears to be that they showed a greater propensity for not losing, than winning.

In 1918, the Arras sector fell under the massive cosh of the *Kaiserschlacht*, the colossal German effort to vanquish the *Entente* before American troops arrived in force. With offensive roles reversed, from 28 March exactly the same bloody fields were fought over once more. The results were a mirror-image of the events of spring 1917, with the British matching the Germans in stamina, resolution and skill in defence. Disputing every metre of ground they fractured Ludendorff's hopes of a sweeping victory, for to north and south great swathes of Allied line were deeply and bloodily bowed. But the city, the ridge and the Artois region held, again helping to bar the route to the Channel.

The vigour of the German thrust spent itself throughout the summer, breaking irreparably on 8 August 1918 to allow a flood-tide of Allied ferocity to sweep the invader from France and Belgium during the next twelve weeks. After the Armistice there followed an advance of another army: the army of displaced *Arrageois*, who for the next twenty years would replant the orchards, restore the tortured fields, and rebuild the grand and gracious city. And soon the first battlefield pilgrims arrived to search the pastures of memory, families seeking an intimacy with the place where until then their loss had been personified by a simple telegram or a letter from a chum or commanding officer. Old soldiers came to seek the remnants of 'their' personal battleground, the graves of comrades, and symbols of the profound but apparently irretrievable comradeship that it seems only war can produce.

[HARVEST TIME 1922]

Arras, close up, looks very stricken. She has suffered much through the centuries, but this time more than ever. The battering is not so obvious as in other and smaller towns, such as Béthune, simply because being bigger she has more houses still standing. She was always defiant; her inhabitants carried on their business with the same indomitable spirit throughout the War. Now, when the troops have departed, she has lost their particular brand of gaiety, but the hotels are crammed and she will, undoubtedly, with British help, be restored to new life. The Cathedral alone will, it is said, be left as a monument of German Kultur. Would that each town and village in Britain could adopt one of these ruined places – the villages outside the big towns, which are so soon forgotten. Arras is vastly changed – at first sight. The station is quite restored, and already its newness had toned down. The station square, however, still wears its old battered look, and on the crumbling walls of a former house there is a notice, Terrain à vendre. *Its*

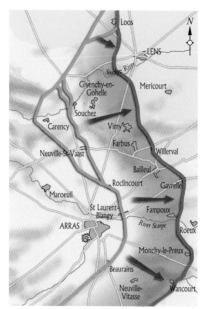

British Gains
April 1917

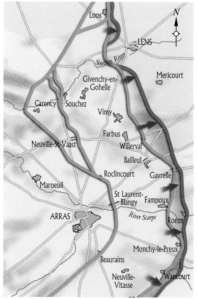

British Gains
April-May 1917

German Offensive
March 1918

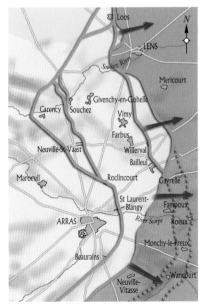

Victory Offensive
September 1918

previous occupant had no doubt decided to live in future at a more healthy distance from railway stations. The residents seem to prefer to live in houses which might just be deemed "structurally safe" to having them rebuilt or cleaned. The Hotel de Ville *is to be left as it stands. One could hardly do anything else to it except pull down the ruins. The management of the* Hotel du Commerce *appear to be of the same mind. To one used to dug-out life it is a comfortable enough spot to stay at, and to American tourists in search of thrills there could not be better, but as a modern hotel – No! The Officers' Club is no more, and the gardens where it once stood are now very trim and cool. They wear a peaceful look, as if nothing had ever disturbed their serenity. The Vimy of 1922 is a very different village. It is a dissipated spot now, for it boasts a cinema, and on a notice-board I read that the great Professeur –* "L'Homme le plus mysterieux du Monde" *– was appearing there for one night only. His programme was both "formidable" and "fantastique", and such strange things, I read, had never been seen in Vimy before.*

CAPTAIN H.U.S. NISBET, 1ST QUEEN'S OWN (ROYAL WEST KENT REGIMENT)

More than ninety years on, and with the last of the Arras veterans now passed, still the pilgrims come. Although perhaps not enjoying the same symbolism as Ypres or Verdun, Arras certainly belongs in the same notorious club, for it was a place that old soldiers would speak of with awe – and often a curious affection – for the rest of their lives.

It has been especially sobering to complete the writing of this book during July 2009, the month that the last two British veterans of the Great War, Henry Allingham and Harry Patch, both died. Only a few weeks before his death Harry had tapped his jacket pocket (wherein was secreted his passport), indicating a desire for another summer jaunt to Flanders. But it was not to be.

The era of the passing of his generation, a generation that holds a unique place in the consciousness of a score of nations, has been an extraordinarily long and strange one. For the first time in history, historians, filmmakers, journalists and newscasters have presented the world with an intimate and somewhat agonising chronicle of the demise of that unique generation – a 'slow drawing down of blinds' upon the Great War fraternity. Their vanishing leaves us with a chasm of unanswerable questions.

"SOUVENIRS" FROM WAR GRAVES.

Sir,—A number of letters have appeared in your columns on the subject of war graves in France and elsewhere, but not one that I have read has dealt with the matter of the desecration of the graves of unknown soldiers.

During a recent wandering across the battlefields of Europe I occasionally came across a wayside grave marked by a simple wooden cross, on which was written: "To an unknown English soldier." Sometimes the inscription was in French, which, together with a votive offering of gorgeous fresh-cut flowers, showed that humble French folk consider it an honour to spread their mantle of sympathy over the remains of a brave ally who has gone under in the mighty struggle.

I noticed that the crosses were invariably crowned by a shot-pierced or shell-shattered steel helmet that belonged to the sleeping warrior. Such crowns, one would think, are sacred. But one day I was walking along the white road that lifts itself over Vimy Ridge when, to my horror and intense disgust, I saw a smartly-dressed woman rapidly descend from a fat motor-car, snatch a helmet from a grave, and drive off with it. At Lille I met some Americans carrying battered helmets which, they informed me, they had just "collected" at Ypres and Armentières.

I suppose the battlefields of France, Belgium, and Flanders will soon be crowded with souvenir hunters. Cannot something be done to prevent human ghouls behaving in a manner that makes one ashamed to be alive?   HUNTLY CARTER.
Cercle Français de la Presse Etrangère, Paris.

BIBLIOGRAPHY

Official Histories:

Bean, C.E.W., *The Australian Imperial Force in France, 1917*, Sydney, 1933.

Falls, Cyril, *Military Operations France and Belgium 1917*, Macmillan, London, 1940.

Nicholson, G.W.L., *Canadian Expeditionary Force (Official History of the Canadian Army in the First World War, 1914-19)*, Ottawa, 1962.

Die Osterlacht Bie Arras 1917, Reichsarchiv, Berlin, 1929.

Les Armées Françaises dans la Grande Guerre, Service Historique, Paris, 1929.

Others:

'Aquila', *With the Cavalry in the West*, John Lane, The Bodley Head Ltd, London, 1922.

Baker-Carr, Brigadier General C.D., CMG DSO, *From Chauffeur to Brigadier*, Ernest Benn Limited, London, 1930.

Barton, Peter, *The Battlefields of the First World War*, Constable, London, 2008

Bishop, W.A., *Winged Warfare*, Penguin Books, London, 1938.

Blake, Robert (ed.), *The Private Papers of Douglas Haig 1914-1919*, Eyre and Spottiswoode, London, 1952.

Brown, Malcolm, *The Imperial War Museum Book of the Western Front*, Pan Books, London, 2001.

Buchan, John, *The History of the South African Forces in France*, Thomas Nelson & Sons Ltd., London, 1920.

Buckley, Francis, *Q6A and Other Places*, Spottiswoode, Ballantyne & Co. Ltd, London, 1920.

Buffetaut, Yves, *The 1917 Spring Offensives: Arras, Vimy, le Chemin des Dames*, Histoire et Collections, Paris, 1997

Charteris, Brigadier General John, *At G.H.Q.*, Cassell, London, 1931.

Coillot, André, *Guerre 1914-1918, Beaurains – Quatre Ans sous le Feu*, Documents d'Archéologie et d'Histoire du XX Siècle – No. 3, Le Cercle Archéologique Arrageois, Arras, 1996

Croft, Lieutenant Colonel W.D., CMG, DSO, *Three Years with the 9th (Scottish) Division*, John Murray, London, 1919.

Cuddeford, D.W.J., *And All For What?* Heath Cranton Limited, London, 1933

Davson, Lieutenant-Colonel H.M., CMG DSO, *Memoirs of the Great War*, Gale & Polden Ltd, Aldershot, 1964.

Desfossés, Yves, Jacques, Alain, Prilaux, Gilles, *Great War Archaeology*, INRAP, Editions OUEST-FRANCE, 2008

Devonald-Lewis, Richard (ed.), *From the Somme to the Armistice: The Memoirs of Captain Stormont Gibbs MC*, William Kimber, London, 1986.

Dolden, A. Stuart, *Cannon Fodder: An Infantryman's Life on the Western Front 1914-18*, Blandford Press Ltd, London, 1980.

Feldman, Gerald D., *Army, Industry and Labor in Germany 1914-1918*, Berg, Oxford 1992.

Fletcher, David (ed.), *Tanks and Trenches*, Alan Sutton, Stroud, 1994.

Fox, Colin, Cull, Ian, Chapman, John, McIntyre, Martin & Webb, Len, *Arras to Cambrai. The Kitchener Battalions of the Royal Berkshire Regiment, 1917*, University of Reading, 1997.

Fraser, David (ed.), *In Good Company: The First World War Letters and Diaries of The Hon.*

William Fraser, Gordon Highlanders, Michael Russell (Publishing) Ltd, Salisbury, 1990.

Fraser-Tytler, Lieutenant Colonel Neil, *Field Guns in France*, Hutchinson, London, 1922.

Fuller, Major General J.F.C., *The Conduct of War 1789-1961*, Eyre and Spottiswoode, London, 1962.

Fuller, Brevet Colonel J.F.C., *Tanks in the Great War 1914-1918*, Battery Press, Nashville, 2003.

Gilbert, Martin, *First World War Atlas*, Weidenfeld & Nicholson, London, 1970.

Girardet, Jean-Marie, *Guerre 1914-1918 Roclincourt-Ecurie, Un Verrou du Front d'Artois*, Documents d'Archéologie et d'Histoire du XX Siècle – No. 2, Le Cercle Archéologique Arrageois, Arras, 1995

Girardet, Jean-Marie, Jacques, Alain, Letho Duclos, Jean-Luc, *Somewhere on the Western Front*, Documents d'Archéologie et d'Histoire du XX Siècle – No. 8, Le Cercle Archéologique Arrageois, Arras, 2003

Girardet, Jean-Marie, Jacques, Alain, Letho Duclos, Jean-Luc, *Guerre 1914-1918 Tilloy-les-Moffaines et Monchy-le-Preux*, Documents d'Archéologie et d'Histoire du XX Siècle – No. 6, Le Cercle Archéologique Arrageois, Arras, 1999

Gleichen, Lord Edward (ed.), *Chronology of the Great War*, Greenhill Books, London, 2000.

Glubb, John, *Into Battle: A Soldier's Diary of the Great War*, Cassell, London, 1978.

Gough, Sir Hubert, *The Fifth Army*, Hodder & Stoughton, London, 1931.

Grant Grieve, Captain W. & Newman, Bernard, *Tunnellers*, Herbert Jenkins, London, 1936.

Greenwell, Graham H., *An Infant in Arms: War Letters of a Company Officer 1914-1918*, Lovat Dickson & Thompson Ltd, London, 1935

Groom, W.H.A., *Poor Bloody Infantry: The Truth Untold*, William Kimber, London, 1976.

Hart, Peter, *Bloody April: Slaughter in the Skies over Arras, 1917*, Cassell, London, 2006.

Heritage, T.R., *The Light Tracks from Arras (a descriptive account of the activities of the 19th & 31st Light Railway Companies, Royal Engineers during the World War)*, The Heathwood Press, 1931.

Home, Brigadier General Sir Archibald, KCVO CB CMG DSO CderLH, *The Diary of a World War I Cavalry Officer*, DJ Costello (Publishers) Ltd, Tunbridge Wells, 1985.

Irwin, Lieutenant General N.M.S., CB, DSO, MC, *Infantry Officer 1914-1918: The Record of Service as a Young Officer in the First World War*, Pearson & Lloyd Publishing, Southampton, 1995.

Jerrold, Douglas, *The Royal Naval Division*, Hutchinson, London, 1927.

Johnson, J.H., *Stalemate! Great Trench Warfare Battles*, Cassell, London, 1995.

Le Maner, Yves and Jacques, Alain, *Photographies de l'Enfer et du Chaos*, La Coupole, Centre d'Histoire et de Mémoire du Nord Pas du Calais. 2008

Letho Duclos, Jean-Luc, *Guerre 1914-1918 Saint-Laurent-Blangy dans la Grande Guerre*, Documents d'Archéologie et d'Histoire du XX Siècle – No. 7, Le Cercle Archéologique Arrageois, Arras, 1997

Letho Duclos, Jean-Luc, *Guerre 1914-1918 Saint-Laurent-Blangy: Trois Ans au Coeur des Combats*, Documents d'Archéologie et d'Histoire du XX Siècle – No. 1, Le Cercle Archéologique Arrageois, Arras, 1994

Liddell Hart, Basil, *The War in Outline*, Faber & Faber, London, 1936.

Lloyd George, David, *War Memoirs of David Lloyd George*, Ivor Nicholson and Watson, London, 1933-1936.

Ludendorff, Erich, *My War Memories 1914-18*, vol. II, Hutchinson, 1919.

Macleod, Lieutenant Colonel Norman, CMG, DSO, *War History of the 6th (Service) Battalion, Queen's Own Cameron Highlanders*, William Blackwood & Sons Ltd, Edinburgh & London, 1934.

Maze, Paul Lucien, *A Frenchman in Khaki*, Heinemann, London, 1934

McKee, Alexander, *Vimy Ridge*, Souvenir Press Ltd., 1966.

Milner, Laurie, *Leeds Pals: A History of the 15th (Service) Battalion (1st Leeds) The Prince of Wales's Own (West Yorkshire Regiment), 1914-1918*, Leo Cooper, London, 1991.

Mitchell, G.D., *Backs to the Wall*, Angus & Robertson, Sydney, 1937.

Neill, J.C., *The New Zealand Tunnelling Company 1915-1919*, Whitcombe and Tombs Ltd., Auckland 1922.

Neillands, Robin, *The Great War Generals on the Western Front, 1914-1918*, Robinson Publishing, London, 1999.

Nicholls, Jonathan, *Cheerful Sacrifice*, Leo Cooper, 1990.

Pierrefeu, Jean de, *French Headquarters, 1915-1918*, translated with notes by Major C.J.C. Street, Geoffrey Bles, London, 1924.

Ramsay, Roy, *Hell, Hope and Heroes: Life in the Field Ambulance in World War 1*, Rosenberg Publishing, Sydney, 2005.

Richards, John (ed.), *Wales on the Western Front*, University of Wales Press, Cardiff, 1994.

Richardson, Matthew, *The Tigers: 6th, 7th, 8th & 9th (Service) Battalions of the Leicestershire Regiment*, Pen & Sword, Barnsley, 2000.

Robertson, Field Marshal Sir William, *From Private to Field Marshal*, Constable and Company, London, 1921.

Rorie, Colonel David, DSO, MD, *A Medico's Luck in the War*, Milne and Hutchison, Aberdeen, 1929.

Russell, Arthur, *The Machine Gunner*, Roundwood Press, Kineton, Warwick, 1977.

Schneider, Alfons, *Dans la Tranchée devant Arras*, Documents d'Archéologie et d'Histoire du XX Siècle – No. 4, Le Cercle Archéologique Arrageois, Arras, 1997

Scott, Canon F.G., *The Great War As I Saw It*, F.D. Goodchild, Toronto, 1922.

Sellers, Leonard, *The Hood Battalion. Royal Naval Division: Antwerp, Gallipoli, France 1914-1918*, Leo Cooper, London, 1995.

Siepmann, Harry, *Echo of the Guns: Recollections of an Artillery Officer 1914-18*, Robert Hale Limited, London, 1987.

Smith, Aubrey, *Four Years on the Western Front*, Odhams Press, London, 1922.

Steel, Nigel & Hart, Peter, *Tumult in the Clouds, The British Experience of War in the Air 1914-1918*, Hodder and Stoughton, London, 1997.

Talbot-Kelly, Richard, *A Subaltern's Odyssey: Memoirs of the Great War 1915-1917*, William Kimber, London, 1980.

Thomas, Alan, *A Life Apart*, Victor Gollancz Ltd, London, 1968.

Trounce, Captain H.D., *Fighting the Boche Underground*, Scribner, New York, 1918.

Tucker, John F., *Johnny Get Your Gun: A Personal Narrative of the Somme, Ypres and Arras*, William Kimber, London, 1978.

Tyndale-Biscoe, Julian, *Gunner Subaltern 1914–1918*, Leo Cooper, London, 1971.

von Hindenburg, Field Marshal Paul, *Out of my Life*, Cassell, London, 1920.

Walker, Jonathan, *The Blood Tub: General Gough and the Battle of Bullecourt, 1917*, Spellmount, Staplehurst, 1998.

Warwick, George William, *We Band of Brothers: Reminiscences from the 1st S.A. Infantry Brigade in the 1914-18 War*, Howard Timmins, Cape Town, 1962.

Watson, W.H.L., *A Company of Tanks*, Blackwood, Edinburgh, 1920.

Wavell, Field Marshal Viscount, *Allenby: Soldier and Statesman*, White Lion Publishers, London, 1974.

Woodward, David R. (ed.), *The Military Correspondence of Field-Marshal Sir William Robertson, Chief Imperial General Staff December 1915–February 1918*, Bodley Head for ARS, 1989.

ACKNOWLEDGEMENTS AND SOURCES

Every effort has been made to trace the copyright holders of images and text excerpts; the author and the Imperial War Museum would be grateful for any information which might help to trace those whose identities or addresses are currently unknown.

My thanks are due to the following persons who have assisted in the production of this volume: Maggie Lindsay Roxburgh, Tom Barton, Clair Banning, Richard & Anna van Emden, the Clinch family, Mark Banning, Jon Nicholls, Nigel Steel, Les and Jane Dominey, Iain and Donna McHenry, Johan Vandewalle, Kristof Jacobs and Mick Forsyth, and Margaret Banning. To Stuart Arrowsmith for the generous use of his collection and the papers of Sergeant Harold Bisgood MM; Jonathan Walker for material from his book, *The Blood Tub;* Bob Mackay for Robert Lindsay Mackay's diary (http://lu.softxs.ch/ mackay/RLM_Diary.html); Alan Culpitt for George Culpitt's diary (www.culpitt-war-diary.org.uk); Ross Hearne for Corporal Ernest King's papers; Rod MacLean for Private AAG Voller's papers; Robert Macklin for George Mitchell's words; David Rosenberg for permission to quote from Roy Ramsay's book; Dr. Stephen Davies, Project Director of The Canadian Letters and Images Project (www.canadianletters.ca) for permission to use the following extracts: memoir of Raymond Ellsworth Ives, letter by Arthur Edward Southworth published in the Cobourg World newspaper, and Lieutenant Gerald Guiore's letter to the mother of Charles Douglas Richardson following his death on Vimy Ridge; Jonathan Wright for permission to quote from Julian Tyndale-Biscoe's *Gunner Subaltern 1914-1918;* the Trustees of the Liddell Hart Centre for Military Archives for General Edmund Allenby's letters to his wife; members of the Great War Forum who assisted Jeremy Banning in the research process: Andrew Pay, Ali Hollington, Jim Smithson, and to Jeremy Mitchell who alerted us to James Stout's letter; my thanks also to Margaret Stuart for permission to use this resource.

I am most grateful to the staff of the Department of Documents at the Imperial War Museum: Rod Suddaby, Tony Richards, Sabrina Rowlett and the ever-helpful Simon Offord. Thanks to the following people for permission to reproduce extracts from diaries, letters or memoirs written held in the department:

Julia Rush (papers of Corporal Oswald Blows); Andy Cope (Private Stanley Bradbury); Alexandra Ward (Private Percy Clare); Susan Ashton (Private Robert Cude MM); Barbara Cattle-Primeau (Gunner Edward Cullum); Mike Durham (Corporal GW Durham); Felix Gameson (Captain L Gameson); Mrs Peggy Edmonds (Major SR Greenfield MC); Jean Harris (F. E. Harris); W. D. Hubble (Rifleman Richard Harvey); Louisa Service OBE JP (Lieutenant Harold Hemming); Jeremy Woodhouse (Lieutenant Colonel Alfred Horsfall DSO); Joan Jolly (Private William Jolly); Rachel Littlewood (Major Martin Littlewood); Merle Blythe (Private John Poucher); Richard Snow (Lieutenant General Sir Thomas D'Oyly Snow); Audrey Kelly (Lieutenant Arthur Worman); Elizabeth Rowell (Captain Robin Rowell); Joy Cave and Patricia Edge (Major General Sir H. H. Tudor).

Images. The provenance of images is recorded in the captions as follows:
AC: Author's collection; AJ: Alain Jacques collection; IWM: Imperial War Museum; ING: Bayerisches Armeemuseum, Ingolstadt; BHK: Bayerisches Haupstaatsarchiv Kriegsarchiv (Munich); HS: Hauptstaatsarchiv Stuttgart; PC: Private collection; REL: Royal Engineers Library; NA: National Archives, Kew: SA: Stuart Arrowsmith; JB: Jeremy Banning

My thanks to all the staff of the photograph archive and dark rooms at the IWM.

Sources: Imperial War Museum – Department of Documents
Major A Anderson – 85/23/1
OS Blows – 81/19/1 & Con Shelf
S Bradbury – 81/35/1
AP Burke, Con Shelf
Lieutenant JH Butlin – 67/52/1
General Sir Philip Christison – GBE CB DSO MC DL, 82/15/1
P Clare – 06/48/1
R Cude MM – PP/MCR/C48
E Cullum – 05/54/1
Captain WD Darling MC – 95/37/2
GW Durham – 90/7/1
BF Eccles – 82/22/1
FJ Field – 85/39/1
Captain L Gameson – PP/MCR/C47 & P395-396 & Con Shelf
Major SR Greenfield MC – 05/8/1
FE Harris – 06/29/1
RT Harvey – 91/3/1
Lieutenant Colonel HH Hemming OBE MC – PP/MCR/155
Brigadier General Sir Archibald Home KCVC CB CMG DSO – 82/18/2
A Horsfall – 06/30/1
W Jolly – 05/71/1
PJ Kennedy – P321
Major CG Lawson – 98/15/1
Major MW Littlewood – 98/33/1
T Macmillan – PP/MCR/C56 & Con Shelf
M McIntyre Hood – 76/169/1
JG Mortimer MM – 75/21/1
F Mulliss – 98/33/1
Captain HUS Nisbet – 78/3/3 & Con Shelf
JM Poucher – 97/26/1
Sir Robin Rowell, CBE AFC – 85/28/1
Lieutenant General Sir Thomas D'Oyly Snow – 76/79/1
Brigadier General G A Stevens, CMG DSO – 06/5/2
Misc 175 (2658) – Major General Sir HH Tudor KCB CMG
Captain WE Villiers – Con Shelf
Colonel LHM Westropp – 75/25/1
RS Whiteman – 85/1/1
Lieutenant AS Worman – 01/60/1

IWM Sound Archive
Joseph Murray – 8201

The Royal Green Jackets Museum, Peninsula Barracks, Romsey Road, Winchester, Hampshire SO23 8TS. www.rgjmuseum.co.uk
With thanks to Mrs Christine Pullen.
Diary of Lt-Colonel RT Fellowes, 1st Rifle Brigade, Ref: 7A-0617

The Tank Museum, Bovington Camp, Bovington, Dorset BH20 6JG
www.tankmuseum.co.uk

Thanks to Janice Tait and David Fletcher.
Testimony of William Taylor Dawson – Ref: WW1/DAWSONWT

Australian War Memorial www.awm.gov.au
Sergeant William Groves, 14th Battalion, Australian Imperial Force – AWM 2DRL/0268 – Sergeant WC Groves, 14th Bn., AIF. "Experiences April 1917 (including Bullecourt 11/4/17). Capture and Experiences as a Prisoner of War"

Royal Engineers Museum, Prince Arthur Road, Gillingham, Kent, ME4 4UG
www.remuseum.org.uk Thanks to curator Rebecca Nash and her colleagues.
Major F. J. Mulqueen, 182 Tunnelling Company
Captain Stanley Bullock MC, 179 Tunnelling Company

National Archives, Kew, Richmond, Surrey, TW9 4DU
www.nationalarchives.gov.uk
Major Bertram Brewin's diary – WO95/2385
Lieutenant L.S. Chamberlen, 13th Rifle Brigade – WO95/2534
Second Lieutenant Charles F. Weber and Lieutenant Victor Smith reports – WO95/91
Brigadier General J.R. Charles, Major General C.J. Deverell, Brigadier General Wellesley, Lieutenant General Sir Charles Fergusson – all CAB45/116
Second Lieutenant Wilfred Cox – AIR 1/2391/228/11/149
Hood Battalion War Diary and 189 Brigade Order No. 88, Appendix IV – ADM137/3064

The following quotes come from *The Great War …. I Was There! – Undying Memories of 1914-1918*, edited by Sir John Hammerton and published by The Amalgamated Press, 1939 (material extracted from already published works).
Paul Maze, French Liaison Officer to General Sir Hubert Gough, Fifth Army
Maze, Paul Lucien, *A Frenchman in Khaki*, Heinemann, London, 1934
Captain Graham Greenwell MC, 1/4th Oxfordshire and Buckinghamshire Light Infantry
Greenwell, Graham H., *An Infant in Arms: War Letters of a Company Officer 1914-1918*, Lovat Dickson & Thompson Ltd, London, 1935
Lieutenant Colonel David Rorie DSO TD, 1/2nd (Highland) Field Ambulance, Royal Army Medical Corps
Rorie, Colonel David, DSO, MD, *A Medico's Luck in the War*, Milne & Hutchison, Aberdeen, 1929
Major W.H.L. Watson, D Battalion, Heavy Branch Machine Gun Corps
Watson, Major W.H.L., *A Company of Tanks*, William Blackwood & Sons, Edinburgh & London, 1920

In Germany.
My thanks to the staff of the **Bayerisches Armeemuseum** (BAM), Neues Schloss, Paradeplatz 4, 85409, Ingolstadt, www.bayerisches-armeemuseum.de; the **Bayerisches Hauptstaatsarchiv Kriegsarchiv** (BHK), Leonrodstrasse 57, 80636, München; and the **Hauptstaatsarchiv Stuttgart** (HS), Konrad-Adenauer-Strasse 4, 70173 Stuttgart, www.landesarchiv-bw.de/hstas

And a special thank you to Alain Jacques, head of the *Service Archéologue Municipale* in Arras, for the use of images, generous advice, splendid lunches at the *Grandes Arcades*, Arras, and a host of other kindnesses.

INDEX